The Record Shelf
Guide to the Classical Repertoire

Third Edition

How to Order:

Quantity discounts are available from Prima Publishing, P.O. Box 1260RECC, Rocklin, CA 95677; telephone (916) 786-0449. On your letterhead include information concerning the intended use of the books and the number of books you wish to purchase.

The Record Shelf
Guide to the Classical
Repertoire

Third Edition

Jim Svejda

Prima Publishing
P.O. Box 1260RECC
Rocklin, CA 95677
(916) 786-0426

Typography by A-R Editions, Inc.
Editing by Anne Montague
Production by Carol Dondrea, Bookman Productions
Interior design by Judith Levinson and Hal Lockwood
Cover design by The Dunlavey Studio

The radio version of "The Record Shelf" is produced by Public Radio Station KUSC, Los Angeles, a broadcast service of the University of Southern California and is distributed nationally via AMERICAN PUBLIC RADIO.

Prima Publishing
Rocklin, CA

Library of Congress Cataloging-in-Publication Data

Svejda, Jim.
The record shelf guide to classical repertoire / Jim Svejda.—
3rd ed., rev. & expanded.
p.   cm.
ISBN 1–55958–223–5
1. Sound recordings—Reviews.   2. Music—Discography.
I. Title.
ML156.9.S86 1992
016.78'026'6—dc20   92-25364
                                                              CIP

92 93 94 95 RRD 10 9 8 7 6 5 4 3 2 1
Printed in the United States of America

For Ben, who made me do it,
Kevin, who should have done it,
And Diane and Michael, for everything.

Foreword

I admit that I am not impartial when it comes to Jim Svejda. Long before I met him, I was an ardent fan of his radio program, *The Record Shelf*. His musical taste, his sardonic wit, his urbanity, and his unique connection with his listeners I find unequaled. And I am not alone. I have since learned—not from him—that of some three thousand letters received each month by KUSC, fifteen hundred are for Jim.

Some years ago, after conducting the Minnesota Orchestra, I had made dinner reservations with some musician friends. I couldn't budge them. They refused to go until they finished listening to that week's *Record Shelf*. To my surprise and ensuing delight, Jim began the program with a lusty Teutonic male choir, developed a comparison with my Sing A Longs, and concluded by featuring my oboe and English horn recordings from 1947 to 1951. Over the air, Jim anointed me his favorite oboe-English horn player of all time. The compliment was better than dessert.

When we finally did meet, my impressions were more than confirmed and we became instant friends. He truly loves music, being a former oboe player himself. The breadth of his knowledge is extraordinary. He thoroughly understands every kind of music, every conductor, composition, and nuance of performance, from early jazz through the entire classical repertoire. His taste is consummate; his integrity, unswayed by today's musical hype.

Sure, I am prejudiced, but so will you be after referring to this book for your recording needs. You may not always agree, but believe me, you'll *never be wrong* listening to Jim Svejda and *The Record Shelf Guide to the Classical Repertoire.*

MITCH MILLER

Acknowledgments

This book grew out of the comparative survey programs that are a regular feature of my weekly radio program, *The Record Shelf*, a production of KUSC, the radio station of the University of Southern California. I would like to thank Wally Smith and the staff of KUSC for their many kindnesses, especially Gene Parrish, who covered my tracks during a difficult time. To my closest musical friends, Kevin Mostyn, Robert Goldfarb, and Henry Fogel, no amount of thanks can adequately repay what I owe them. I also owe a special debt of gratitude to Dr. Christian Rutland, without whose encouragement this book might never have been begun, and to Dr. Karl-Heinrich Vogelbach, without whose timely intervention it might never have been completed. I was singularly lucky in having such a tolerant, music-loving publisher as Ben Dominitz, as well as the sharp eye (and even keener mind) of Anne Montague.

Introduction

When I first began collecting records several centuries ago, record collecting was a trivially easy hobby. I had what at the time seemed an infallible system: I bought records entirely on the basis of their covers. I would search, innocently mind you, through the bins of the Roxy Music Shop in La Porte, Indiana, after my weekly oboe lesson, and spend my hard-earned allowance on the most lurid, suggestive record jackets I could find. This was long before an adolescent could muster the courage to buy one of Mr. Hefner's forbidden magazines. Thus I had to content myself with the odd edition of *National Geographic*, and what must have been, at the time, the most complete collection of *Scheherazade* and *Belshazzar's Feast* recordings possessed by any thirteen-year-old in the world.

Eventually, after I passed out of my early "Record Collecting as an Excuse for Smuggling Home Soft-Core Pornography" phase, my requirements for records slowly began to change. I gradually became able to make distinctions between recordings I liked and recordings I didn't, and thus was well on my way to becoming the opinionated, elitist snob I am today. (Actually, all the arrogance is merely a pose, as is, the elitism, and I can prove it. The *one* thing a lifelong Detroit Lions football fan cannot be, by definition, is an elitist or snobbish *anything*.)

Now, as then, performances that offer nothing but all the notes neatly in place are crashing bores. Worse than bores, they are a disservice to the composer, the listener, and the very spirit that animates music itself: the desire for the human spirit to express its highest aspirations through that five-century tradition of serious music, which may well be the Western world's unique and most enduring contribution to the civilization of this planet. All of which is a rather grandiose way of saying that whatever else they may be, none of the recordings recommended in this book are boring.

Unlike other recording guides, this one does not pretend to be all-encompassing or objective. Following the pattern of the comparative survey programs that turn up regularly on my weekly radio program, *The Record Shelf*, I have tried to include something pointed, interesting, amusing, or enlightening about each work, and then suggest which of the many available recordings you should buy.

Although my enthusiasms will become obvious very quickly, it might be prudent and more fair to spell them out, just in case you happen to be one of those strange people who actually reads Introductions, and on that basis, actually decides whether or not to buy the book. (I in fact went to college with such a person, whom I believe is now living off the hospitality of the state of Michigan for ax-murdering some relative, or local politician. I've forgotten the details.)

In essence, this is clearly a book written by someone who was born fifty years too late. In general, I find that while the level of music-making today has reached a phenomenal state of technical perfection—made all the more so by the magic of editable recording tape—from an emotional point of view, recordings have had increasingly less and less to say.

My great musical heroes, from Wilhelm Furtwängler to throwbacks like Leonard Bernstein, all have one thing in common. Unfortunately, *that* commodity—an instantly recognizable musical personality—is becoming increasingly rare. This book is an attempt to separate the personal, the interesting, even the quirky and outrageous, from the dull, the routine, and the merely professional. It also attempts to do what probably can't be done, in selecting the *one* recording of a given work that is the most exciting, probing, and unique on the market today.

With the enthusiasms, even the casual reader will quickly discover a number of apparent prejudices that crop up throughout. As a matter of fact, I have no musical "prejudices" whatsoever. The contempt that incompetent bozos like Nikolaus Harnonourt have elicited, or even the hatred that beasts like Herbert von Karajan have evoked, has been earned honestly and over a period of many years. I even remain a great admirer of Karajan's early recordings, in spite of the numberless musical atrocities he perpetrated in the last twenty years of his career and his activities during the Second

World War. (Rumors have persisted through the years that he once conducted in an S.S. uniform.) In short, I find him thoroughly despicable on both musical and personal grounds.

On a few rare occasions, I have given two possible choices for a work, or have recommended other worthy contenders within the discussion of the piece. This is not because I have any trouble making up my mind, but because there are often several astonishing, though utterly different, interpretations, and each, in my opinion, belongs in every recording library.

Given the limitations of space, time, and my own endurance, the selection of works covered in this book is, of necessity, limited. Even so, the book is nearly twice as long as originally intended. Nevertheless, many items I would have liked to discuss have gone undiscussed, and much music that doesn't really interest me failed to make the final cut. For instance, with the exception of Bach and Handel, very little baroque music is included, and even less of the music of our time. I frankly admit that I don't understand very much modern music, although it's safe to say that 99 percent of it is either ephemera or trash. (This should not be read as an attack on modern music, since, as everyone knows, 99 percent of all the music produced during *any* given historical period was ephemera or trash.)

I hope you will find what follows more useful in putting your recording library together, or in enhancing your existing one, than buying merely on the basis of lurid record jackets, familiar, much touted artists and labels, or spurious record store sales. Aside from this, and earning a *lot* of money for the author, this book was written with no other purpose in mind.

A Note on the Second Edition

While preparing this Second Edition of the book, I was constantly reminded of what Samuel Johnson said about the process, something to the effect that revision was the last refuge of a scoundrel. But then again, Dr. Johnson—on principle—was less than keen on redoing anything once it had been done already. "To marry a second time," he ruefully suggested, "represents the triumph of hope over experience."

For the most part, the revisions contained herein were dictated by opportunity or necessity: the opportunity afforded by my indulgent publisher to add, rather substantially, to the book's original bulk, and the necessity of dropping certain listings because they were either discontinued or superseded by newer and better performances.

The most drastic revision, of course, is the virtual exclusion of long-playing records. In the two years since the *Guide* first appeared, the long-playing record has become all but extinct. While I have made an uneasy personal peace with the compact disc, I will miss those awkward, touchingly fragile artifacts which were such perfect metaphors for human frailty. To this day, there are certain pieces I can't hear in a concert hall without automatically bracing myself for especially loud scratches. Like scars, the clicks and pops that vinyl was heir to were nothing anyone wanted, especially; yet like scars, they were emblems of unpredictability, reminders of the exhilarating riskiness of life. I continue to recommend a handful of LPs in these pages—no more than a half dozen or so—but only because the extraordinary performances they contain cannot be found on CD or tape.

Along with broadening the range of the *Guide*—in addition to expanding the listings devoted to major composers, both older and newer music is far better represented than it was before—I have also taken the opportunity to correct some of the more grievous gaffes that managed to make their way into the first edition. None of these, I hasten to add, were the fault of my editors, but were attributable solely to my own indolence, ignorance, or inability to read.

A Note on the Third Edition

In addition to the fact that the Third Edition of this tome must now officially mourn the passing of the late and greatly lamented long-playing record *(Requiescat in pace)*, it is far more pleasant to report that in the two years since the publication of the Second Edition, the CD explosion has continued apace. Unfortunately, some of the inevitable by-products of that profligacy have begun to crop up as well, most notably in the proliferation of uninspired performances of *justly* neglected repertoire, and an even surer sign that CDs have come of age: the first CD cut-outs. Some of the recordings that were most enthusiastically recommended in the Second Edition of the *Guide* have been unceremoniously retired, which necessitated a hectic scramble to find alternate recommendations. As always, the same woefully subjective standards described in the Introduction apply to these revised choices. And again, all excesses and errors are wholly my own.

The Record Shelf
Guide to the Classical Repertoire

Adam, Adolphe-Charles
(1803–1856)

Giselle (complete ballet)

**Orchestra of the Royal Opera House, Covent Garden,
Bonynge. London 433007-2 [CD].**

The fame of the French composer Adolphe Adam continues
to hang on a dangerously slender thread. Apparently, though, the
thread is made of something with the tensile strength of piano wire,
since *Giselle*, the oldest Romantic ballet to retain a place in the
standard repertoire, shows no sign of losing any of its gooey appeal.
(I once saw a performance of this tenacious warhorse at the Bolshoi
in Moscow. The dancing, costumes, and scenery were beautiful, but
the auditorium was badly overheated, the audience fetid, and somewhere in the middle of the first act I managed to fall asleep.)

If this innocent, slightly oversweetened bonbon is to your
taste—although at well over two hours, "bonbon" is hardly the
appropriate metaphor—you can't possibly do better than Richard
Bonynge's sumptuous London recording. Over the years, Bonynge
has taken a good deal of undeserved heat from critics who have
suggested that he has gotten where he is *solely* because of his wife.
(Many still refer to him, churlishly, as "Mr. Joan Sutherland.") A
recording like this one should wring the neck of that honking ca-
nard. The performance is both warm and richly detailed, with superb playing from the Covent Garden orchestra. But even more to
the point, this is an engagingly *theatrical* interpretation: so much so
that for the first time ever, listening to old *Giselle*, I didn't nod off
once.

Adams, John (1947–)

The Chairman Dances; Two Fanfares, etc.

San Francisco Symphony, de Waart. Nonesuch 79144-2 [CD], 79144-4 [T].

For anyone who considers minimalism to be the dim-witted musical rip-off that it probably is, the music of John Adams presents a problem. Unlike Philip Glass, Steve Reich, Terry Riley, and the rest, Adams is a composer of demonstrable abilities and considerable charm, and this attractive recording will provide an excellent introduction to his humane and refreshingly *human* minimalist idiom.

While his most celebrated work to date, the controversial opera *Nixon in China* (Nonesuch 79177-2 [CD], 79177-4 [T]), may be too much of a not-so-good thing, the Chairman Dances from that work are pert, lively, and never wear out their welcome, and the five-minute "Short Ride in a Fast Machine" may be the most amusing and immediately appealing minimalist composition to date.

Edo de Waart and the San Franciscans are consistently alert and committed, and the recorded sound is close to ideal.

Albéniz, Isaac (1860–1909)

Iberia (Suite for Piano, 4 books)

De Larrocha, piano. London 417887-2 [CD].

Every so often a work becomes so completely identified with a specific performer that the interpreter and the thing being interpreted become all but indissoluble. A half century ago, Fritz Kreisler's version of the Brahms Violin Concerto, Wanda Landowska's *Goldberg Variations*, and the Furtwängler *Eroica* all existed on that remote, Olympian summit; so too, for more than three decades now, has Alicia de Larrocha's constantly growing version of that lexicon of modern Spanish music, Isaac Albéniz's *Iberia*.

In her latest and finest recording of the suite, de Larrocha probes more deeply, finds more color and drama, and somehow infuses *Iberia* with a rhythmic subtlety and life that even her earlier versions lacked. London's warmly detailed recorded sound is a worthy frame for a performance that will probably never lose its bloom and spontaneity.

The best available recording of the skillful orchestral suite arranged by the composer's friend Fernandez Arbós — Ravel was contemplating an arrangement of his own; when he learned of Arbós's project, he abandoned the idea and wrote *Bolero* instead — is the pleasantly erotic version by the London Symphony led by Enrique Bátiz on Angel (CDC-49405 [CD]).

Albinoni, Tomaso (1671–1750)

Adagio for Strings and Organ

I Musici. Philips 420718-2 [CD], 420959-4 [T].

It is one of the minor tragedies of musical history that Tomaso Albinoni had more money than he knew what to do with. The son of a wealthy Venetian paper merchant, Albinoni described himself proudly as a "dilettante Veneto." He was never forced to earn his living as a musician, and more's the pity. Had he been made to work a bit harder at the craft for which he was so perfectly suited, he may well have become one of the giants of the Italian Baroque, instead of the tantalizing "what if?" curiosity he remains today.

Although he composed numerous instrumental concertos and nearly fifty operas, Albinoni is known primarily through the arrangements of his music made by his German admirer Johann Sebastian Bach, and through the well-known Adagio for Strings and Organ, skillfully concocted by the modern Italian musicologist Remo Giazotto.

As Baroque confections go, the Albinoni Adagio is very nearly as popular as Pachelbel's equally high-cholesterol *Kanon* and has been recorded almost as frequently. I Musici gives the piece one of those typically aristocratic yet meltingly lyrical performances that neither cheapen the music nor rob it of emotional impact. The twenty-year-old recorded sound remains impressive on both the CD and the tape, and the Bach and Handel concertos (to say nothing of the Pachelbel *Kanon*) that fill out the collection make this one of the more attractive Baroque albums on the market.

Alfvén, Hugo (1872–1960)

*M*idsommarvaka; Symphony No. 2

Stockholm Philharmonic, Järvi. Bis CD-385 [CD].

Any investigation of the unaccountably unexplored riches of modern Swedish music should begin with the major works of Hugo Alfvén, whose *Midsommarvaka*—an utterly delectable Swedish meatball variously known as the "Midsummer Vigil" and the "Swedish Rhapsody No. 1"—made its composer an international celebrity in the years immediately after the First World War. Though Alfvén never managed to duplicate the popular success of this enchanting trifle, his five symphonies, written between 1896 and 1952, are all important and appealing works, especially the Second Symphony of 1899.

Predictably, Neeme Järvi proves to be an ideal advocate of this warm and instantly approachable music. The version of *Midsommarvaka* is easily the finest currently available, and the performance of the Symphony is more impressive still, sounding for much of the time like early Sibelius without the static basses or rough edges.

Superb performances and strikingly lifelike recorded sound.

Arnold, Malcolm (1921–   )

Four Cornish Dances; Four English Dances; Four Irish Dances; Four Scottish Dances

> **London Philharmonic, Arnold. Lyrita SRCD-201 [CD].**

With seven numbered symphonies to date, memorable scores for films like *The Bridge on the River Kwai*, and even a zany contribution or two to the Hoffnung Festivals, Malcolm Arnold has been one of the most prolific and versatile of all British composers. This Lyrita compilation of his four sets of British dances provides an ideal introduction to Arnold's eclectic, colorful, instantly digestible idiom, from the sassy Scottish Dances, with their vivid evocation of the skrill of highland pipes and the jaunty rhythms of the strathspey and reel, to the somber, often surprisingly substantial Irish Dances, written as recently as 1986. The interpretations, needless to say, are definitive, as is the swaggering playing of the London Philharmonic.

Bach, Carl Philipp Emanuel (1714–1788)

Symphonies (6): "Hamburg Sinfonias"

> **C. P. E. Bach Chamber Orchestra, Haenchen. Capriccio 10106 [CD].**

The most prolific and long-suffering of Johann Sebastian's sons—you'd suffer, too, if you had to spend twenty-seven years in the employ of Frederick the Great—C. P. E. Bach is finally beginning to be regarded with some of the awe with which his near-

5

contemporaries always viewed him. For Haydn, his influence was decisive—"For what I know I have to thank Philipp Emanuel Bach"—and for Mozart, a pupil of his brother Johann Christian, the "Berlin Bach" was an even more important figure. "He is the father," Mozart said, "and we the children."

While he is still best known for his keyboard music and the innumerable works he was forced to compose for his flute-loving employer (Frederick *was* a fair musician, but a complete musical reactionary), the so-called "Hamburg Symphonies," composed for the Baron von Swieten in 1773, are a superb showcase for his robust talent. Hartmut Haenchen and the C. P. E. Bach Chamber Orchestra, playing on modern instruments, offer alert and loving interpretations of these exhilarating works, and Capriccio's recorded sound is flawless.

Another unusually attractive Capriccio release (10101 [CD]) brings together a flock of the composer's flute sonatas in performances that are equally stirring.

Bach, Johann Sebastian

(1685–1750)

Brandenburg Concertos (6), S.1046/51

English Chamber Orchestra,Britten. London 425725/6-2 [CD].

English Concert, Pinnock. Deutsche Grammophon 410500/ 1-2 [CD]; 423317-4 [T].

Just as Johann Sebastian Bach was the final summation of all the Baroque era gave to music, the *Brandenburg* Concertos are the apotheosis of the concerto grosso, the most diverse and important of all Baroque instrumental forms.

For years, the standard recordings of the *Brandenburgs* were those wonderfully musical performances from the 1930s by the Adolf Busch Chamber Orchestra, an interpretation that can now be found along with Busch's equally memorable versions of the Orchestral Suites, on a brilliantly remastered set from EMI (64047-2 [CD]). While not for Baroque purists (the continuo is realized on a piano by a very young Rudolf Serkin), the playing is marvelously virile and delightfully old-fashioned: a memorable souvenir of the days when Bach was generally considered a stylistic contemporary of Robert Schumann.

Another persuasively romantic interpretation—and my favorite modern recording of the *Brandenburgs*—is that lush and stylish account turned in by the English Chamber Orchestra conducted by Benjamin Britten. The playing projects a wonderful aura of ease, freshness, and authority, together with that sense of instantly responsive give-and-take characteristic of chamber music making at its best.

If Baroque "authenticity" is an absolute necessity, the best choice is the version by the English Concert and Trevor Pinnock on Deutsche Grammophon. Although the recording has drawn extravagant praise from both the English and American press, I find much of it rather prissy and effete. Nevertheless, the English Concert version is an enterprise that deserves to be taken seriously, unlike the inept and embarrassing scandal perpetrated by Nikolaus Harnoncourt and his abysmal Concentus Musicus of Vienna.

Cantatas (212)

The 200-plus cantatas that he ground out like so many sacred sausages contain much of what is most ethereal and inspired, and a great deal of what is most gloomy and depressing, in Bach's music. Some seem literally to have been produced with the aid of divine intervention, while others find one of the giants of music dutifully and ponderously marking time. A generation ago, perhaps twenty or thirty of the most enduring of them were available to the record-buying public; today, all of them have been recorded, some more than once.

Although it is impossible to make specific recommendations for all of these works—I won't pretend I've heard each and every recording: life, as we know, is *much* too short for that—I can offer a few words of warning and encouragement to the prospective Bach Cantata Collector, beginning with the heartfelt injunction to avoid any of the Teldec recordings as though they were (to quote Baudelaire) the breeches of a man with the itch.

The Teldec series is divided up between Nikolaus Harnoncourt and Gustav Leonhardt, who gleefully take turns mauling the luckless pieces beyond recognition. The Harnoncourts are packed with the usual bellylaughs, and the Leonhardts aren't much better. It is almost as if these two clowns were engaged in some sort of bizarre contest as to who could conjure up the most screechy and etiolated instrumental sound and the most feeble choral outbursts. (I hate to sound like some sort of reverse sexist, but why give us a gaggle of struggling boys when a group of accomplished female singers would do so much better?)

On the other hand, virtually all the recordings made by John Eliot Gardiner, Helmuth Rilling, or Joshua Rifkin have lovely and important things to say, as does a handsome collection from Deutsche Grammophon (413646-2 [CD]) featuring Karl Richter and his spirited Munich Bach Orchestra and Choir.

Not only does the boxed set include many of the most popular cantatas—"Christ lag in Todesbanden," "Jauchzet Gott in allen Landen," "Ein feste Burg ist unser Gott," and "Gottes Zeit ist die allerbeste Zeit"—but the youthful devotion that characterized all of Richter's better recordings can also be felt throughout. The remastered recorded sound is warm, if a little fuzzy around the edges, and the soloists—from Edith Mathis and Peter Schreier to Keith Engen and Dietrich Fischer-Dieskau—are all superb.

*C*hristmas Oratorio, S. 248

> Argenta, von Otter, Blochwitz, Bär, Monteverdi Choir,
> English Baroque Soloists, Gardiner. Deutsche
> Grammophon 423232-2 [CD], 423232-4 [T].

The reason the *Christmas Oratorio* doesn't hang together as well in actual performance as that other seasonal staple, Handel's *Messiah*, is that its composer never intended it to be downed in one gulp. The six separate and discrete cantatas were meant to be heard over a half dozen days of the Christmas period, and taken in that dosage it constitutes one of the most rewarding and affecting of all Bach's works.

As in his festive recording of the Bach *Magnificat* (Philips 411458-2 [CD], 411458-4 [T]), which is also wholeheartedly recommended, John Eliot Gardiner here reaffirms his position as the foremost antiquarian of our time. From the exciting, brilliantly articulated opening with trumpets and timpani through the witty, briskly paced choruses, Gardiner infuses the music with an incomparable zest and vigor, without overlooking its gentle warmth and tenderness.

The soloists, the choir, and the always impeccable English Baroque Soloists are all at the top of their form, and if you're in the market for something to wash down the inevitable *Messiahs* and *Nutcrackers* during the holidays, search no further than this.

Clavier Concertos (7), S. 1052–1058

Kipnis, harpsichord; London Strings, Marriner. CBS Odyssey MB2K 45616 [CD], CBS MGT-39801/2 [T].

Most of Bach's seven surviving keyboard concertos—the first such works written by a major composer—are transcriptions of other concertos, primarily for the violin. As in all of the music that he so transformed, Bach exhibits the uncanny knack of making the music seem as though it couldn't possibly have been written for any other instrument: each of these glowing entertainments cries out "keyboard" as clearly as their original versions say "violin."

Igor Kipnis is one of those rare early-music specialists who are able to combine the often mutually exclusive qualities of scholarship and showmanship without compromising either: the interpretations are as thoughtful as they are impetuous, and he receives the usual imaginative help from Sir Neville and the gang.

Concerto in A minor for Violin, S. 1041; Concerto in E for Violin, S. 1042; Concerto in D minor for 2 Violins, S. 1043

Mutter, Accardo, violins; English Chamber Orchestra, Accardo. Angel CDC 47005 [CD].

It's hardly surprising that of all his innumerable instrumental concertos, these three works for the violin should remain among

Bach's most popular in the form. Lyrical, dramatic, and overflowing with rich and memorable melody, these concertos were often taken up as vehicles by Fritz Kreisler, Eugène Ysaÿe, and other important turn-of-the-century violinists, whose performances of any Baroque music tended to be as scarce as hockey players' teeth. Another sure sign of their enduring popular appeal was the enlistment of one of them for a key dramatic role in the hit film *Children of a Lesser God.*

For years, the most completely satisfying recording of all three concertos was that unabashedly Romantic account by David and Igor Oistrakh, which is still available on Deutsche Grammophon. Those achingly beautiful performances would have remained my first choice in a very crowded field had it not been for the release of an even more lush and lovely interpretation by the German violinist Anne-Sophie Mutter.

When Mutter first arrived on the scene, I must admit I took little if any notice. I simply assumed that as the latest of Herbert von Karajan's many protégés, she would inevitably develop along the same cold, impersonal lines. Fortunately—if this marvelous Angel recording is any indication—she has shed all vestiges of Karajan's reptilian influence to become one of the most magnetic young musicians before the public today.

Stylistically, her performances of the Bach concertos are throwbacks. Cast on a large scale and full of late-Romantic gestures—has anyone since Kreisler made the slow movement of the E Major concerto sound as languorously sexy as this?—the interpretations are a perfect complement to her immense tone and seamless technique. As usual, Salvatore Accardo, as conductor and second violinist in the Double Concerto, brings a wealth of warmth and experience to what I suspect may become *the* indispensable Bach concerto recording.

English Suites (6), S. 806–811

Schiff, piano. London 421640-2 [CD].

Even for those who, like Sir Thomas Beecham, are not especially enthralled by Bach's music—"Too much counterpoint," he breezily insisted, "and what is worse, *Protestant* counterpoint"—the English Suites are very hard to resist. With their catchy tunes, engaging rhythms, and transparent textures, they represent Bach at his most joyously unbuttoned: the light-footed secular flip side of the often turgid sacred composer.

The formidably accomplished András Schiff is a nearly perfect advocate of these alluring works. While admittedly not as individual as Glenn Gould in his revelatory CBS recording (M2K-42268 [CD]), he is neither as controversial nor as perverse. Like Gould, Schiff proves that the resources of the modern piano will do no serious injury to the composer's intentions, with playing that is as luxuriant as it is natural and unforced.

Kenneth Gilbert's excellent version for Harmonia Mundi (HMC-90.1074/75 [CD], HMC-40.1074 [T]) is the best alternative for those who automatically begin to hyperventilate whenever Bach's keyboard music isn't played on the harpsichord.

Goldberg Variations, S. 988

Gould, piano. CBS MYK-38479 [CD], MYT-38479 [T] (1955 version). CBS MK-37779 [CD], IMT-37779 [T] (1981 version).

Pinnock, harpsichord. Deutsche Grammophon 415130-2 [CD].

The most cogent observation anyone has ever made about that mystery wrapped in an enigma, Glenn Gould, was an offhand wisecrack dropped by the conductor George Szell shortly after he had performed with the Canadian pianist for the first time. "That nut is a genius," Szell was heard to mumble, and history should probably let it go at that. Willful, unpredictable, eccentric, reclusive, and maddeningly brilliant, Glenn Gould was easily the most provocative pianist of his generation and one of the great musical originals of modern times.

It was the 1955 recording of the *Goldberg Variations* that introduced Gould to an unsuspecting world and began an entirely new chapter in the history of Bach interpretation. Legend has it the *Goldberg Variations* were originally written as a soporific for a music-loving nobleman who was a chronic insomniac. Most recordings of the work support the legend. Gould changed all that with driving tempos, a bracing rhythmic vitality, and an ability to clarify and untangle the dense contrapuntal lines that was, and remains, amazing.

After twenty-five years of further study, Gould rerecorded the work in 1981, and the result was every bit as controversial as his original recording. While sacrificing none of the razor clarity of the earlier performance, the interpretation became more profound and reflective, with tempos that not only were dramatically slower but had been chosen—according to the pianist—to help each of the variations fit into a more homogeneous, integrated whole.

Since the release of the second version, I've been trying to choose between the two recordings, without very much success. But then, too, the choice boils down to either the youthful brashness of the original or the mature, studied brashness of the Revised Standard Version.

For those who insist on a harpsichord—though *I* am forced to agree with Sir Thomas Beecham, who said its sound reminded him of "two skeletons copulating on a corrugated tin roof"—try the alert, intelligent performance by Trevor Pinnock.

Mass in B minor, S. 232

> Monteverdi Choir, English Baroque Soloists, Gardiner.
> Deutsche Grammophon 415514-2 [CD],
> 415514-4 [T].

> Nelson, Baird, Dooley, Hoffmeister, Opalach, Schultze,
> Bach Ensemble, Rifkin. Nonesuch 79036-2 [CD],
> 79036-4 [T].

The Baroque revival of the 1960s was a very shrewd marketing ploy of the recording industry. Compared to operas or Mahler symphonies, Baroque music was far easier and, more important (at least from *their* point of view), far cheaper to record. Thus we were inundated by not only torrents of music by composers who for centuries had been little more than names in a book, but also well-intentioned and generally lamentable recordings by organizations like the Telemann Society, and such stellar European ensembles as the Pforzheim Chamber Orchestra of Heilbron.

Next, the Baroque Boom was further complicated by the emergence of the Baroque Authenticity Movement, whose exponents argued—at times persuasively—that for Baroque music to make the points the composer intended, it had to be presented on instruments of the period. Like all such upheavals, the period-instrument revolution spawned its fair share of frauds and fanatics: untalented, uninspired charlatans who forgot that making music *does not* consist entirely of making physically repellent noises and arcane musicological points.

The work of three English musicians, Christopher Hogwood, Trevor Pinnock, and, preeminently, John Eliot Gardiner, finally offers convincing evidence that the Authenticity Movement has at last grown up: Each of the three finest antiquarians before the public today is a musician first, a musicologist second. Gardiner's recording of the Bach Mass in B minor is as stirring and compassionate as his exhilarating recordings of the Handel oratorios. He mixes grace, finesse, and dramatic grandeur into an immensely satisfying amalgam, while managing to coax more physical beauty from those old instruments than any other conductor ever has before or since.

For an interesting companion piece to Gardiner, try Joshua Rifkin—a versatile and vastly gifted musician who did as much as anyone to make the musical establishment take the music of Scott Joplin seriously—and his controversial Nonesuch recording with the Bach Ensemble. Rifkin's recording of the Mass is a radical experiment that audaciously assigns only a single voice to each of the choral parts. From a musician of lesser stature, the project easily might have degenerated into yet another Baroque Authenticity gimmick. But Rifkin, in a brilliantly argued essay, and an even more convincingly argued performance, proves that "authenticity" has to do far less with editions and instrumentation than with the authentic gifts of the performers.

A Musical Offering, S. 1079

Stuttgart Chamber Orchestra, Münchinger. London 430266-2 [CD].

In addition to forging Prussia into a modern military state— with all the pleasant consequences for the world that that would have over the next two centuries—Frederick the Great was an accomplished amateur flutist and composer who early in his reign maintained one of the most musical courts in northern Europe. In 1747, he invited the aging father of his Kapellmeister, Carl Philipp Emanuel Bach, to Potsdam and was amazed when "old Bach" improvised a six-part fugue on a melody of the king's devising. Back in Leipzig, Bach expanded the idea into a work consisting of two ricercari, several canons, and a concluding trio, and dispatched *A Musical Offering* to Frederick as a bread-and-butter note.

Karl Münchinger's fine recording with the Stuttgart Chamber Orchestra is one of the few that manage to avoid making the *Offering* seem as irretrievably gloomy as it certainly can be. As a bonus, this medium-priced album comes with a vivid recording of the B minor Orchestral Suite, which features some splendid playing from flutist Jean-Pierre Rampal.

Organ Music

> Hurford, organ. London 421337-2; 421341-2; 421617-2; 421621-2; 425631-2; 425635-2 [CDs].

It is in his organ music that Bach is at his most personal and reactionary. That windy, glorious monstrosity was his favorite instrument, and the music he composed for it, largely during the Weimar period, all looked back into the past. In the forms he inherited from Buxtehude and Frescobaldi—from the brilliant, finger-twisting toccatas to those fantasias in which the finest keyboard composer of the Baroque era allowed his imagination free rein— Bach wove some of the most intricate and imposing of his inspirations. For many, the organ works represented not just his first great creative phase, but the summit of his art.

If you're one of those Bach lovers who can't seem to get enough of this stuff, Peter Hurford's six-volume, seventeen-CD set on London's medium-priced Jubilee label should very nearly satisfy you. The performances are invariably fresh, imaginative, and hugely accomplished, and the fact that the project was spread out over several years and numerous venues goes a long way to preventing any serious listener fatigue. Wisely, London has gathered together some of the best-known works on a "greatest hits" sampler (417711-2 [CD]), which is not only a revealing introduction to the series, but also one of the best single-CD collections on the market.

For the barbarians among us, London has also reissued Leopold Stokowski's Czech Philharmonic recordings of some of his gooey orchestral transcriptions (421639-2 [CD]). This breathtaking exercise in shameless self-indulgence easily ranks with the most enjoyable Bach recordings ever made.

St. Matthew Passion, S. 244

Schreier, Adam, Popp, Lipovsek, Dresden Children's Chorus, Leipzig Radio Chorus, Dresden State Orchestra, Schreier. Philips 412527-2 [CD].

There are several ways of viewing this towering masterpiece, the most common of which is to regard it as the greatest single sacred work—and quite possibly the greatest single *musical* work—yet devised by the human mind.

As a naive yet ridiculously hypercritical youth, I once took part in a performance of the *St. Matthew Passion* and the experience nearly killed me. Later, as a somewhat less demanding adult, I attended a production that Sir Georg Solti led early in his tenure as music director of the Chicago Symphony. Sir Georg presented his Eastertide version of the *Passion* Bayreuth-style, which is to say, it began early in the afternoon and—after a break for dinner—continued later that night. To my shame, I must admit that I and my wife (as she then was) availed ourselves of the opportunity to make a hasty getaway and take in a movie—which I still remember was the splashy, gory, well-intentioned *Waterloo*, with Rod Steiger and Christopher Plummer.

With its numberless arias, countless chorales, and interminable recitatives with the Savior speaking over an aureole of shimmering strings, the *St. Matthew Passion* has always been a severe test of concentration and patience that I have never been fully able to pass. And if that makes me a clod and a philistine, so be it.

For those who disagree—and they are certainly in the vast majority—Peter Schreier's Philips recording will demonstrate just how dead wrong I am. Not only is this most inappropriately named of all singers (*schreier*, in German, means "screamer" or "howler") a dazzling Evangelist, he also proves to be a vastly talented conductor who moves the music along with an uncommon lightness of touch without glossing over any of its obvious profundity. The soloists, who clearly respect Schreier the tenor, sing their hearts out for Schreier the conductor; the choruses and orchestra respond just as zealously, as do Philips's engineers.

For those who require a tape—though it's impossible to imagine *anyone* listening to the *St. Matthew* on a Walkman or while tooling down the freeway—the Harmonia Mundi recording (401155/7) led by Philippe Herreweghe is professional and intermittently inspired, but is no match for the triumphant Schreier set.

Sonatas (3) and Partitas (3) for Unaccompanied Violin, S. 1001–1006

Menuhin, violin. Angel CDHB-63035 [CD].
Perlman, violin. Angel CDCB-49483 [CD].
Heifetz, violin. RCA 7708-4 RC6 [T].

There is a compelling case to be made that Sir Yehudi Menuhin was the most accomplished teenage musician to have made commercial recordings. The San Francisco–born violinist's classic 1932 version of the Elgar Concerto made under the composer's direction (Angel CDH-69786 [CD]) remains one of the glories of the early electrical era, as do these soaring versions of the Bach sonatas and partitas, recorded between 1934 and 1936.

Listening to them more than a half century after they were made, one cannot help being amazed all over again at the young virtuoso's playing. Although the musicianship, like the technique, is utterly immaculate, it is the emotional content of the performances—now pristine, cool, and noble, now fiery, intense, and impetuous—that places them among the great violin recordings of the century. The CD transfer is so remarkably lifelike that after a few minutes you completely forget you're listening to an antique.

For those who insist on more up-to-date sound, Itzhak Perlman's flawless Angel set is obviously a first choice among the modern recordings; for a tape, the Heifetz offers plenty of whiz-bang technical fireworks, although the recorded sound—like the playing itself—tends to be uncomfortably chilly and harsh.

Suites (4) for Orchestra, S. 1066–1069

Academy of St. Martin-in-the-Fields, Marriner. London
430378-2 [CD], 414248-4 [T].

It was Nikolaus Harnoncourt's pioneering period-instrument recording of these works in the late 1960s that established his reputation as an interpreter of Bach's music. I remember buying it and being moderately enthusiastic at the time. Listening to it again, after nearly two decades, demonstrates what a woefully uncritical listener I was twenty years ago. It still seems to me the best of Harnoncourt's recordings, but that's a bit like trying to determine which of one's root-canal procedures bothered one the least. By no means should you waste your money buying this recording, but the next time you hear it on the radio, notice how crude and lifeless the playing is. In fact, in his driven, humorless approach to everything, Harnoncourt suggests nothing so much as a kind of technically inept Toscanini of the Baroque.

The first of Sir Neville Marriner's three separate recordings to date, the London version is a reissue of that dazzling Argo edition prepared with the help of the late English musicologist Thurston Dart. As in Marriner's interpretation of the *Brandenburg* Concertos, the playing is brisk and ingratiating, with memorable contributions by every solo voice.

Unaccountably, John Eliot Gardiner's wonderful period-instrument recording for Erato has been withdrawn, demonstrating once again that an alarming number of children who tear the wings off butterflies and push little old ladies into manure spreaders eventually grow up to become recording executives. Until those silly people come to their senses, the best of the "authentic" versions is a warm and bracing Trevor Pinnock recording for Deutsche Grammophon (423492-2 [CD]), which comes with equally satisfying period accounts of the *Brandenburg* Concertos.

Suites (6) for Solo Cello, S. 1007–1012

Starker, cello. Mercury 432756-2 [CD].

Ma, cello. CBS M2K-37867 [CD], IMT-39508/9 [T].

In the right hands, Bach's six Suites for Solo Cello can be an ennobling, thoroughly rewarding experience; in the wrong hands, they can be a crashing, unmitigated bore. There is certainly nothing boring about Pablo Casals's legendary recordings from the 1930s, still available on Angel. Professional musicians tend to admire them without reservation (Mitch Miller once told me that he developed his wonderful singing style on the oboe by trying to emulate the long lines that the cellist achieved on those famous old discs). My reaction to Casals's playing, however, has always been similar to Igor Stravinsky's: "Of course, he is a very great man. He is in favor of Peace, against General Franco, and plays Bach in the manner of Brahms."

My own introduction to the Cello Suites was that superb and now recently resuscitated Mercury recording by the always provocative János Starker. Like his great Galician predecessor Emanuel

Feuermann, Starker has always been a welcome foil to Casals's rough-and-tumble school of modern cello playing. His interpretations of the Bach Suites capture the essence of his unmannered, but always virile and distinctive, art with playing that mixes polish and control with fire and daring. As with all of the Mercury Living Presence recordings of the late '50s and early '60s, the sound on this one is astonishingly fresh and alive.

The eagerly anticipated account by Yo-Yo Ma, the most accomplished cellist of his generation, was a considerable disappointment. The playing itself is thrillingly beautiful, but there is a certain sameness in the performances that leaves one flat, as though we'd overheard a youthful run-through of what undoubtedly will be a great interpretation a few years down the road. Nevertheless, Ma's is still the preferred version in the tape format.

The Well-Tempered Clavier, S. 846–893

Gould, piano. CBS M3K-42266 [CD], M4T-42042 [T].

Gilbert, harpsichord. Deutsche Grammophon 413439-2 [CD].

In a charming little one-page essay called "Masters of Tone," the great American newspaperman, iconoclast, and linguistics scholar, H. L. Mencken, summed up the music of Johann Sebastian Bach as "Genesis I:1." Nowhere is Bach's seminal importance to the development of Western music more obvious than in that most significant of all Baroque keyboard collections, The Well-Tempered Clavier. Beginning with a disarmingly simple C Major prelude that makes Beethoven's Für Elise seem like the Third Rachmaninoff Concerto, The Well-Tempered Clavier moves triumphantly through all the major and minor keys with forty-eight masterworks that not only encapsulate the entire scope of Baroque contrapuntal thinking, but also epitomize the essential greatness of Bach's mature keyboard style.

Like The Art of Fugue, The Well-Tempered Clavier was probably never intended for public performance and is in fact dedicated to the "musical youth, desirous of learning." Be that as it may, some of the major keyboard artists of the twentieth century, beginning with Wanda Landowska and Edwin Fischer, have left immensely personal visions of this towering monument which continues to exert an irresistible fascination for performers today.

As a *performance*, the most staggering modern interpretation could be heard on a Melodiya/Angel recording by Sviatoslav Richter, now long out of print. Like Serge Koussevitzky's Beethoven, Richter's conception of *The Well-Tempered Clavier* may have had very little to do with the music of the composer, but as a lesson in the art of piano playing given by the most fabulously complete pianist of the last forty years, it has never been approached.

As in his recording of the *Goldberg Variations*, Glenn Gould's performance remains a model of imaginative musical brinkmanship. In spite of all the eccentricities—which include some of the fastest and slowest performances the individual preludes have ever received—the playing is a triumph of Gouldian textural clarity and pizzazz: the way he manages to make the most complicated fugues sound so trivially easy will leave the jaws of the ten-fingered dragging on the floor.

For a less personal, though by no means anonymous, vision supplied by one of today's preeminent harpsichordists, the Deutsche Grammophon recording by Kenneth Gilbert offers many quiet and unexpected revelations. With playing that is alternately relaxed and pointed, Gilbert—without ever letting us forget that we are in the presence of a major artist—allows us to focus our entire attention where it properly belongs: on the music itself.

Balakirev, Mily (1837–1910)

Symphony No. 1 in C; *Tamara*

Royal Philharmonic, Beecham. Angel CDM-63375 [CD].

After César Cui, whose music has slipped into an oblivion from which it seems unlikely ever to emerge, Mily Balakirev (accent on the second syllable) remains the most obscure member of that group of Russian composers the critic Vladimir Stasov dubbed "The Mighty Five." As a conductor, composer, teacher, and propagandist

Balakirev probably did more for the cause of a Russian national music than anyone, including his more celebrated colleagues Borodin, Mussorgsky, and Rimsky-Korsakov.

With the glistening Oriental fantasy *Islamey*—which, while it currently lacks a first-rate recording in its impossibly difficult piano version, is handsomely represented on a Philips collection led by Esa-Pekka Salonen (412552-2 [CD])— the Symphony in C Major is the most enjoyable and representative of Balakirev's works, especially in Sir Thomas Beecham's classic 1955 recording. The effortless sweep of this zestful, sparkling work completely belies its extraordinary thirty-two-year gestation, and the performance, one of Beecham's best, only serves to underscore its stature as one of the great Russian symphonies. The version of *Tamara*, a mono-only recording made the year before, is no less sensational.

Barber, Samuel (1910–1981)

Adagio for Strings (from String Quartet, Op. 11)

Los Angeles Philharmonic, Bernstein. Deutsche
Grammophon 427806-2 [CD], 423169-4 [T].

Even before achieving celebrity as "The Love Theme from *Platoon*," Barber's moltenly beautiful Adagio for Strings had acquired many powerful nonmusical associations. In fact, the case can be made that it was the moving use to which the work was put during Franklin Delano Roosevelt's funeral that established Samuel Barber's popular reputation.

Of all the many recordings the Adagio has been given so far, none can come within hailing distance of the live performance—preserved superbly by Deutsche Grammophon—that the late Leonard Bernstein gave a few years ago with the Los Angeles Philharmonic. Adopting a tempo so measured that the music is almost guaranteed to fall apart, Bernstein, with vast dignity and deliberation, wrenches the last ounce of pain and pathos from the

Adagio, while building one of the most devastating climaxes any piece has received in recent memory. While the Barber is clearly the principal selling point, there are also equally thrilling interpretations of Bernstein's *Candide* Overture, William Schuman's *American Festival Overture*, and Aaron Copland's *Appalachian Spring* (*see page 104*), thus making this one of the most exciting recordings of American music released in a decade.

For those interested in the ravishing string quartet from which the Adagio was taken, a searing performance by the Concord Quartet is available on a Nonesuch cassette (78017-4).

Overture to *The School for Scandal;* Essays for Orchestra Nos. 1–3; *Medea's Meditation and Dance of Vengeance*

> New York Philharmonic, Schippers. Odyssey YT-33230 [T].
>
> St. Louis Symphony, Slatkin. Angel CDC-49463 [CD], 4DS-49463 [T].

Except for the powerful and powerfully original Symphony No. 1 (which has never had a completely satisfying recording since Bruno Walter—of all people!—left his blazing account during the 78 era), these two treasurable releases contain most of the works on which Samuel Barber's reputation as a composer of orchestral music will probably rest.

Thomas Schippers's credentials as a Barber conductor were unassailable. An intimate friend of the composer, Schippers was responsible for perhaps the finest of all Barber recordings: an ineffably tender account of the composer's masterpiece, *Knoxville: Summer of 1915.* Shamefully, RCA has allowed that luminescent recording with Leontyne Price to slip out of print, and the Nonesuch release with the usually splendid Dawn Upshaw (79187-2 [CD], 79187-4 [T]), while gorgeously sung, is dramatically uninvolved and uninvolving.

On the Odyssey tape, the New York Philharmonic is on its best behavior, and Schippers was never better in the recording studio. The Adagio for Strings is also included; Schippers's is the only one that compares favorably with Bernstein's. The Overture crackles with gaiety and wit—Harold Gomberg's oboe solo is dumbfoundingly beautiful—and *Medea's Meditation and Dance of*

Vengeance is unleashed with such horrifying fury that it almost persuades you that Mother's Day ought to be canceled. The gem of the collection, however, is the Second Essay for Orchestra (the First and Third aren't included on the Schippers set), in which lyricism, passion, and architectural integrity are kept in nearly perfect equilibrium by one of the most strangely underrated conductors of his time.

Like his electrifying version of the Barber Violin Concerto with Elmar Oliveira (Angel CDC-47850 [CD]), Leonard Slatkin's Angel recording of the same repertoire confirms *his* position as the foremost Barber conductor in the world today. The St. Louis Symphony—which is now second to no orchestra in the country—romps through the music as though it were part of the standard repertoire, and Slatkin's interpretations are both refreshing and insightful. Especially valuable are the performances of the two "unknown" Essays: the First, for a change, sounds neither as monotonous nor as grim as it frequently can, and the Third—Barber's last major work—is imbued with all the richness and dignity of a genuine valedictory. The recorded sound, like the playing, is state-of-the-art.

Vanessa

Steber, Elias, Resnik, Gedda, Tozzi, Metropolitan Opera Chorus and Orchestra, Mitropoulos. RCA 7899-2-RG [CD], 78994-4-RG [T].

If ever there was a contemporary opera for people who think they hate contemporary operas, it is Samuel Barber's *Vanessa*. The reason, of course, is obvious: *Vanessa* is a full-fledged nineteenth-century grand opera, even though it may have had its world premiere in 1958.

From the mid-1930s until his death, Barber was something of an anomaly among the major twentieth-century American composers. Recognition came early, his first musical champions included figures as diverse and powerful as Arturo Toscanini, Serge Koussevitzky, and Bruno Walter, and for the next half century he enjoyed the kind of popular and critical acclaim that might have ruined the career of a lesser man.

To the very end, his expressive idiom remained stubbornly and unashamedly Romantic, though it was a Romanticism guided by a commanding modern intellect, coupled with extraordinary elegance and finesse. After George Gershwin, he was also the most gifted melodist of his generation, the American composer whose art was most firmly grounded in the natural grace of song.

While *Vanessa* may not be universally regarded as a *great* opera—though I, for one, am inclined to think that it is—there has been little argument that it is a haunted and haunting work, with moments of rare and voluptuous beauty. For instance, Erika's tiny throwaway "aria," "Why must the winter come so soon?" is in itself nearly worth the price of admission.

It was extremely decent of RCA to reissue this historic recording, made with the original cast in 1958. Eleanor Steber, for whom the *Hermit Songs* and *Knoxville: Summer of 1915* were written, more than lives up to the legend in the title role. The supporting cast is uniformly excellent (Rosalind Elias and Nicolai Gedda especially so), and that largely unsung hero of modern music, Dimitri Mitropoulos, leads a performance in which the unearthly lyricism and dramatic tension of the piece are given free and equal rein.

For lovers of Barber, opera (modern or otherwise), glorious melody, and lovely singing, this one cannot be passed up.

Bartók, Béla (1881–1945)

*B*luebeard's Castle

Martón, Ramey, Hungarian State Opera Orchestra, Fischer.
CBS MK-44523 [CD], MT-44523 [T].

Bartók's greatest stage work is certainly not something for children or sissies. And this has nothing to do with the gruesome violence of the piece, since there is none. What makes *Bluebeard's Castle* so taxing for most people is that it has only two extremely talkative characters and practically no action. But because it is a work about a man who values his privacy, the pathologically private composer threw his entire being into the project, producing a score of unsurpassed richness, subtlety, and depth. Besides being prime early Bartók, it's also—since so little actually takes place on stage—an ideal opera for home listening. While the brilliant London recording (414167-2 [CD]) has much to recommend it, especially the conducting of István Kertész, who turns in the most powerful realization of the orchestral part, it is the singing on the more recent CBS version that sets it apart and will probably keep it ahead of the competition for decades. With its inky, resonant lower register and brilliant baritonal top end, the voice of Samuel Ramey is perfect for the hero. Eva Mártón, vocally phenomenal as always, here seems capable of shattering flowerpots, much less wineglasses. Adam Fischer is an able accomplice, keeping the tension at an almost uncomfortably high level from beginning to end.

Concerto for Orchestra

Chicago Symphony, Reiner. RCA 60175-2 RG [CD], 60175-4 RG [T].

New York Philharmonic, Boulez. CBS MK-37259 [CD], MYT-37259 [T].

Like his near-contemporary George Szell, Fritz Reiner was one of the consummate orchestral technicians of the twentieth century. There was nothing that his minuscule, but infinitely various, beat could not express, and even less that escaped his hooded, hawklike eye. He was also a humorless despot who terrorized orchestras for more than fifty years. Once, a jovial bass player whipped out a huge brass telescope at a Reiner rehearsal and shouted, "I'm looking for the beat." The man was fired on the spot.

Like Szell—of whom one frequently hears the same nonsense —Reiner was often accused of being rather chilly and aloof in his performances, a kind of radioactive ice cube who sacrificed depth and emotion in favor of brilliantly polished surface details. Dozens of Reiner recordings ably refute that preposterous contention, none more convincingly than his stupendous version of Bartók's *Concerto for Orchestra.*

Reiner's association with the *Concerto* in fact began *before* the piece was written. Without Bartók's consent or knowledge, it was Reiner and his friend the Hungarian violinist Joseph Szigeti who persuaded Serge Koussevitzky to commission the work from the destitute, dying composer in 1942. Reiner made the first commercial recording of the *Concerto* with the Pittsburgh Symphony, and the very first stereo recording with the Chicago Symphony in 1955.

In its new compact disc format, this ageless performance sounds as though it might have been recorded a few years ago, instead of at the very dawn of the stereo era. Reiner's characteristic combination of complete flexibility and cast-iron control can be heard in every bar of the interpretation, from the dark melancholy of the opening movement to the giddy reaffirmation of life in the finale.

If Sir Georg Solti's more recent Chicago Symphony performance on a London compact disc offers clearer sound and slightly better orchestral execution, the brusque and intermittently vulgar reading is no match for Reiner's. In fact, the only serious competition comes from Pierre Boulez, who, in one of his finest New York Philharmonic recordings, offers a brilliantly analytical yet glowing performance, marred only by the occasionally slipshod playing of the Philharmonic brass. But since the Reiner compact disc offers, as a bonus, the most hair-raising of all recordings of the Music for Strings, Percussion, and Celesta, it constitutes—at something over sixty-five minutes—one of the few authentic bargains on the market today.

Concertos for Piano and Orchestra (3)

> Ashkenazy, piano; Chicago Symphony, Solti. London 425573-2 [CD].
>
> Bishop-Kovacevich, piano; London Symphony, BBC Symphony, Davis. Philips 426660-2 [CD].

The three Concertos, which Bartók composed primarily for his own use, are so central to the language of twentieth-century piano music that one wonders why they aren't performed and recorded more frequently. While the percussive First Concerto is still a fairly difficult pill for most people to swallow, and the fiendish Second is all but unplayable, the lyrical, sweet-spirited Third should have entered the standard repertoire years ago. A deceptively simple, often childish piece, it should pose no problem for anyone who enjoys Rachmaninoff or Tchaikovsky and, further, becomes an ideal invitation to explore the more complex pleasures of the two masterworks that precede it.

On a generously packed pair of CDs—which also feature a distinguished performance of the Sonata for Two Pianos and Percussion—Vladimir Ashkenazy, Georg Solti, and the Chicago Symphony dance their way through this demanding music with just the right blend of ardor, sarcasm, poetry, and rhythmic bite. Solti, always an imaginative and sympathetic accompanist, is especially telling in the First and Third Concertos, where the vivid backdrop he supplies is almost operatic in its theatricality. Ashkenazy, too, has some of his finest moments on records, especially in the meditative slow movements to which he brings an uncommon eloquence and restraint.

The medium-priced Philips recording of all three Concertos on a single CD is obviously a major bargain. The performances by Stephen Bishop-Kovacevich and Colin Davis, recorded between 1968 and 1975, while considerably less pointed and dramatic than Ashkenazy's, are nonetheless exceptionally fine. Lyrical, thoughtful, though peppered with moments of reckless abandon, they are a perfect foil to the more intense versions on London, especially for listeners who want to acquire them for substantially less than half the price.

Concerto No. 2 in B minor for Violin and Orchestra

Chung, violin; Chicago Symphony, Solti. London 411804-2 [CD].

Perlman, violin; London Symphony, Previn. Angel 4AM-34718 [T].

Like the life-affirming *Concerto for Orchestra,* which was written while the composer was dying of leukemia, the exuberant B minor Violin Concerto was produced during an unusually harrowing period of Bartók's life. Begun during the dark months of 1938, when the composer was fearing the spread of Nazism throughout Central Europe and worrying, correctly, about "the imminent danger that Hungary, too, will surrender to this system of robbers and murderers," the Second Violin Concerto is one of his most optimistic and proudly nationalistic statements. Folklike melodies permeate the entire fabric of the score, as does a giddy virtuosity that makes it one of the more challenging and rewarding works in the violinist's repertoire.

Kyung-Wha Chung brings a towering technique to the music and a sharp objectivity that many might find distant or cold. The approach works exceptionally well in the often uncompromising outer movements of the Concerto, and Solti's equally cool yet idiomatic accompaniment clearly places the piece in the mainstream of twentieth-century violin concertos. The recording also offers a brilliant performance of the Berg Violin Concerto as a filler, thus making an already desirable recording even more so.

Itzhak Perlman and André Previn take a far more old-fashioned yet equally valid tack, with ripe, affectionately caressed playing that is closer to the spirit of Brahms than Bartók.

The Miraculous Mandarin (complete ballet)

Ambrosian Singers, London Symphony, Abbado. Deutsche Grammophon 410598-2 [CD].

A close friend of mine had an extremely effective method of getting rid of visitors who overstayed their welcome. Rather than yawn ostentatiously, or consult his watch every five minutes, he would put on a recording of *The Miraculous Mandarin* and within minutes would find himself alone.

Although written as long ago as 1919, Bartók's savage, sensational, frequently sickening ballet remains a startlingly modern work. Emotionally, if not necessarily musically, it often seems more advanced than Stravinsky's *Rite of Spring*; at the very least, it is one of the first important musical works that seem to have completely digested the horrific implications of the recently concluded First World War.

Early in his unhappy stay in Chicago, Jean Martinon made a recording of the *Miraculous Mandarin* Suite for RCA that may always be the last word in orchestral ferocity; coupled with an equally memorable version of Hindemith's ballet on the life of St. Francis of Assisi, *Nobilissima visione*, it was one of the best of RCA's Chicago Symphony recordings and certainly deserves a CD reissue.

Among available recordings, none is finer than Claudio Abbado's interpretation of the complete ballet for Deutsche Grammophon. One of the more gripping of the Italian conductor's London outings, it is a barbaric rampage from beginning to end, which still takes ample note of the score's considerable subtleties. The finale—made all the more gruesome by a grunting, wordless chorus—is as mindlessly cruel and ferocious as anyone could wish, and the playing of the LSO and the recorded sound are both of demonstration quality.

Bartók's vastly different fairy-tale ballet, the warm and cuddly *Wooden Prince*, is now best represented by a sumptuous Chandos recording (CHAN-8895 [CD], MC-1506 [T]) by the Philharmonia Orchestra under the ubiquitous Neeme Järvi. In addition to being the only note-complete version now available, it is also one of the most vividly graphic recordings of *any* ballet. Järvi's gifts as a musical storyteller are such that one can easily follow the dramatic argument without the slightest hint of what's going on. The performance of the *Hungarian Sketches* that comes as a filler is no less splendid.

String Quartets (6)

Emerson Quartet. Deutsche Grammophon 423657-2 [CD].

Chilingirian String Quartet. Chandos ABTD-1280; 1323; 1346 [T].

With the possible exceptions of the quartets of Dmitri Shostakovich, Arnold Schoenberg, and Leoš Janáček, those of Béla Bartók are the most significant contribution a twentieth-century composer has yet made to the form. Each of these adventurous masterworks is an important signpost in the evolution of Bartók's stylistic development: from the folklike elements that pervade the early works, to the astringent flirtation with atonality in the middle two, to a more direct and simple mode of communication in the last two works of the series.

For more than three decades, the cycle has very nearly been the private property of the Juilliard String Quartet. When their most recent recording was withdrawn (possibly to be reissued as a CBS compact disc), many of us despaired of ever hearing its like again —at least until the arrival of the new Deutsche Grammophon recording by the Emerson Quartet.

There are many who insist that the Emerson is the finest young American string quartet now before the public. I would agree with that assessment, if one were to drop the modifiers "young" and "American." Judging from the series of "Great Romantic Quartets" they recorded for the Book-of-the-Month Club and this hair-raising version of the Bartók Quartets, there seems to be nothing that the Emersons cannot do. They play with the all the fire and polish of the old Juilliard, yet still produce a sinuous beauty of tone reminiscent of the Guarneri Quartet in their prime. It is also the only quartet in living memory that literally has no second fiddle: the two violinists change roles from concert to concert and often from piece to piece.

This is easily one of the finest Bartók cycles yet recorded, with interpretations that are large, audacious, brooding, risky, colorful, and richly histrionic, in the best possible sense of the word. The hell-bent performance of Second Quartet may be the most frighteningly exciting ever, and the Fifth has never seemed more amusing or profound. While no currently available tape can begin to equal the Emerson's achievement, the Chandos cassettes by the fine Chilingirian Quartet are as presentable as any.

Bax, Sir Arnold (1883–1953)

The Garden of Fand; The Happy Forest; November Woods; Summer Music

Ulster Orchestra, Thomson. Chandos CHAN-8307 [CD], ABTD-1066 [T].

After Ralph Vaughan Williams, Sir Arnold Bax, late the Master of the King's Musick and composer of the score for David Lean's immortal movie version of *Oliver Twist*, was the major English symphonist of the twentieth century. While his gentlemanly yet deeply Romantic music contains occasional echoes of Vaughan Williams and Sibelius, there is a strong, highly individual personality that informs the best of it, especially the four masterly tone poems with which Bryden Thomson and the Ulster Orchestra began their complete cycle of Bax's music for Chandos. In all of them, the composer's obsession with Celtic legend and his fascination with French impressionism are clearly evident: these are darkly chromatic, vividly evocative scores, which become all the more fascinating on repeated hearings.

For those who find themselves drawn to Bax—and I treasure him almost as much as Walton and Tippett—the next logical step is to explore the seven symphonies, all of which have been recorded by Thomson and the London Philharmonic. The quality tends to vary, but at least four of them rank with the finest symphonies ever written by an Englishman. The Second, composed for Serge Koussevitzky, is a sweeping, deeply spiritual work, with an almost Baroque opulence of ornamental detail (CHAN-8493 [CD]). The mystical Third—first recorded in 1943 by Sir John Barbirolli—is perhaps the most accomplished and original of the cycle (CHAN-8454 [CD]), while the Fifth (CHAN-8669 [CD], ABTD-1356 [T]) and Sixth (CHAN-8586 [CD]) are clearly the works of an independent master who owes nothing to anyone or to any school.

Thomson and the orchestra cannot be praised too vigorously for their meticulous execution and their ability to immerse themselves so completely in the composer's unique idiom. As with that other great nature poet, Frederick Delius, Bax is decidedly an acquired taste; yet like many acquired tastes, he can quickly turn into an acquired passion.

Beach, Mrs. H. H. A. (Amy Marcy Cheney)

(1867–1944)

Symphony in E minor, *Gaelic*

Detroit Symphony, Järvi. Chandos CHAN-8958 [CD],
ABTD-1550 [T].

Mrs. H. H. A. Beach, to use the designation that this hugely
proper and very gifted Bostonian preferred, wrote what has the distinction of being only the second symphony ever published by an
American composer, the *Gaelic* Symphony of 1896. As with virtually all serious American music written at the time, the spirit of
Dvořák hangs heavily over Mrs. Beach's major orchestral score, as
do the shades of Schubert, Brahms, and Liszt. Still, the *Gaelic* is a
skillful manipulation of a series of familiar Irish folk tunes and a
work of considerable power and charm.

The new Chandos recording—the first since the game but not
especially inspired outing released by the long-defunct Society for
the Preservation of the American Musical Heritage—features the
resurgent Detroit Symphony sounding better that it has in years,
with Neeme Järvi providing his predictable blend of insight and
enthusiasm. The versions of Barber's First Symphony and Overture
to *The School for Scandal*, if not the first choice for either piece,
make for an attractive and generous filler.

Beethoven, Ludwig van

(1770–1827)

Choral Fantasy (Fantasia in C minor for Piano, Chorus, and Orchestra)

> R. Serkin, piano; Westminster Choir, New York
> Philharmonic, Bernstein. CBS MYK-38526 [CD], MYT-
> 38526 [T].

This odd, hybrid piece (no one would again write for this combination of forces until Ferruccio Busoni unveiled his mammoth Piano Concerto, albeit for Piano, Orchestra, and *Male* Chorus, more
than a century later) owes much of its popularity to the fact that
it is usually viewed as a kind of dry run for the finale of the Ninth
Symphony. It isn't, really, but its choral theme *is* a close cousin of
the "Ode to Joy," and in the right hands, it can be intriguing and
uplifting.

In my experience, only one recording has ever made this peculiar hodgepodge come off, and that is the version taped in the
early 1960s by Rudolf Serkin and Leonard Bernstein. As usual, Serkin's seriousness of purpose imbues the music with a dignity and
significance that no other interpretation does, while Bernstein's enthusiasm proves a perfect foil to the high-mindedness (though never
high-handedness) of his partner. A vintage Serkin interpretation of
the Third Piano Concerto fills out both the compact disc and tape.

Concertos (5) for Piano and Orchestra

> Fleisher, piano; Cleveland Orchestra, Szell. CBS M3K-
> 42445 [CD].
>
> Schnabel, piano; London Symphony, Sargent. Arabesque
> Z-6549/50/51 [CD], 9103-4 [T].

Since the extravagantly gifted William Kapell died in a plane
crash near San Francisco in 1953, the careers of America's finest
pianists have been the cause of great sadness, consternation, and
alarm. The mercurial, high-strung Byron Janis began canceling appearances on such a regular basis that his brilliant career was over
almost before it began; similarly, the unjustly maligned Van

Cliburn, after years of abuse from the critics, lapsed into a stony silence from which he has yet to emerge. Gary Graffman has been plagued in the last decade by a crippling neurological disorder, as has the most accomplished American pianist since William Kapell, Leon Fleisher.

The CBS compact disc reissue of Fleisher's classic account of the Beethoven Concertos with George Szell and the Cleveland Orchestra is a major cause for rejoicing. Rarely, if ever, have a pianist and conductor shown more unanimity of purpose and execution in this music. The rhythms are consistently crisp and vibrant. The phrasing is meticulous almost to a fault, and the hair-trigger reflexes of the Cleveland Orchestra are a perfect complement to Fleisher's then fabulous technique. Although some listeners might find the approach uncomfortably patrician, Fleisher and Szell manage to scrape off so many layers of accumulated interpretative treacle that we are able, in effect, to hear these familiar and frequently hackneyed works as if for the first time.

If state-of-the-art recorded sound and mechanical perfection are not absolute necessities, the recordings made in the 1930s by Fleisher's great teacher, Arthur Schnabel, are still the standard by which all other recordings must be judged. Never a pianist's pianist, Schnabel exhibited technical imperfections that were the butt of countless jokes among his colleagues. When told that Schnabel had been exempted from military service for physical reasons during the First World War, that mordant turn-of-the-century virtuoso Moriz Rosenthal quipped, "Naturally, the man has no fingers." Nevertheless, it was the force of Schnabel's personality that virtually rediscovered Beethoven's piano music in the 1920s and '30s, and in Arabesque's immaculate transfers, these impetuous, headstrong, and always deeply personal interpretations emerge as touchstones of twentieth-century keyboard art.

Concerto for Violin and Orchestra in D

Menuhin, violin; Philharmonia Orchestra, Furtwängler. Angel CDH-69799 [CD].

Perlman, violin; Philharmonia Orchestra, Giulini. Angel CDC-47002 [CD], 4XS-37471 [T].

It has been argued—and argued persuasively—that Yehudi Menuhin has yet to make a finer recording than the 1932 version of the Elgar Violin Concerto, made when that extraordinary child prodigy was only sixteen years old. But in the last couple of decades, Menuhin's Olympian technique has eroded alarmingly. Although the warmth and musicianship are still there in ample supply, the digital dexterity is now a mere shadow of its former self.

With the Elgar, this famous recording of the Beethoven Concerto ranks with the violinist's greatest achievements. In it, the high-minded nobility and melting tenderness of this unique musician are conspicuously on display. Add to that the surging yet impeccably disciplined accompaniment Wilhelm Furtwängler provided in one of his final commercial recordings, and we are left with something very close to a Beethoven Violin Concerto for the ages.

For those who require more up-to-date sound—although in Angel's compact disc transfer of the Menuhin recording the 1954 acoustics sound remarkably detailed and warm—the best modern version comes from Itzhak Perlman and Carlo Maria Giulini. The violinist offers his usual blend of exuberance and arching lyricism, while the conductor's elegant yet probing support confirms his reputation as one of the great modern accompanists.

Concerto for Violin, Cello, Piano, and Orchestra in C (Triple Concerto)

Beaux Arts Trio, London Philharmonic, Haitink. Philips 420231-2 [CD].

Although it doesn't exactly bear the same relationship to Beethoven's other concertos that *Wellington's Victory* does to the symphonies, the Triple Concerto can be a lame, long-winded thing, even when given the most committed kind of performance. For the already converted—I myself will remain a nay-saying heretic to the end—the Beaux Arts Trio, Bernard Haitink, and the London Philharmonic give the piece every opportunity to sound important and interesting. Everyone—including Philips's engineers—works together beautifully. Only the Concerto itself refuses to cooperate.

Fidelio

Ludwig, Vickers, Frick, Berry, Philharmonia Orchestra and Chorus, Klemperer. Angel CDMB-69324 [CD], 4AV-34003 [T] (excerpts).

Nearly two hundred years after *Fidelio*'s first successful production—and none of the composer's works would ever cost him as much time, pain, and back-breaking labor—Beethoven's one and only opera still provokes heated debates. Is the rickety rescue melodrama worthy of the magnificent music that fleshes it out? Is *Fidelio* a successful *opera* at all, or simply a breathtaking collection of musical essays in the composer's mature middle-period style?

No one ever made a stronger case for *Fidelio* both as music and as musical theater than Otto Klemperer, whose legendary recording from the early 1960s features some of the noblest conducting ever captured on records. With a monumentality and scope that dwarf the competition, the Klemperer *Fidelio* is also a gripping dramatic experience. Leonore's "Abscheulicher!" Florestan's second-act aria, the dungeon scene, and the exultant finale all crackle and pop with an immediate and vivid realism, beside which all other recorded performances seem flaccid and pale.

Obviously, Klemperer was aided and abetted by an exemplary cast of singers: the ink-black Pizarro of Gottlob Frick, the intensely moving and musical Leonore of Christa Ludwig, and the incomparable Florestan of Jon Vickers, who throughout sounds like what he has been so clearly for more than thirty years—the greatest dramatic tenor of his time.

Mass in C

Ameling, Baker, Altmeyer, Rintzler, New Philharmonia Orchestra and Chorus, Giulini. Angel CDZB-62693 [CD].

The standard reaction among people hearing this stirring work for the first time is to wonder why they had never heard it before. The Mass in C Major is prime middle-period Beethoven: grand, heroic, and sublime, and Carlo Maria Giulini's recording is the one that makes its comparative neglect seem most perplexing. In both its sweep and meticulous attention to detail, this is one of the conductor's finest recordings. All the participants are inspired to give their absolute best—Dame Janet Baker's performance is predictably moving—and the original sound has been freshened considerably. The only problem is that EMI has coupled the Mass with Giulini's far less memorable performance of the *Missa solemnis*, which, aside from some genuinely perverse tempos (especially in the

Gloria), has little to recommend it. Thus what should have been a major bargain turns out to be more expense than a single full-price CD. Fie!

Missa solemnis in D

Moser, Schwarz, Kollo, Moll, Hilversum Radio Choir, Concertgebouw Orchestra of Amsterdam, Bernstein. Deutsche Grammophon 413780-2 [CD].

During his tenure with the New York Philharmonic, Leonard Bernstein made a splendidly dramatic recording of this greatest of Beethoven's choral works, a performance superseded—as is every other recording in the catalog—by this sublime interpretation, pieced together from two live performances he led in the Netherlands.

There are still people for whom Bernstein's name instantly conjures up images of glitz and glitter. For three decades, his public persona certainly encouraged many to take him less than seriously, and the publication of a shallow and vulgar biography a few years ago certainly didn't help. Yet beneath it all, Bernstein was always a profoundly serious musician, and a recording like this one only confirms what I have suspected for many years: Leonard Bernstein was, at the very least, the most consistently interesting and, in all probability, the greatest conductor the world has seen since Wilhelm Furtwängler.

Like Furtwängler, Bernstein frequently turned the act of music-making into a deeply spiritual, often mystical experience, an experience we feel from first note to last in this transcendent *Missa solemnis*. The performance itself is by no means perfect: The soprano soloist is barely adequate to her brutally demanding part, and even the normally flawless Concertgebouw Orchestra has the occasional—if barely noticeable—slip. Of course, such minor quibbles hardly matter: No recorded version of the work has ever come close to the depth and ethereal beauty of this one, and it's extremely unlikely that one ever will.

Overtures

Bavarian Radio Symphony, Davis. CBS MDK-44790 [CD], MDT-44790 [T].

Philharmonia Orchestra, Klemperer. Angel CDM-63611
[CD], 4AE-34441 [T].

Vienna Philharmonic, Abbado. Deutsche Grammophon
429762-2 [CD].

Sir Colin Davis's superbly played and flawlessly recorded collection of Beethoven's most popular overtures very nearly takes the
sting out of CBS's senseless decision to withdraw its brilliant set
with the Cleveland Orchestra and George Szell. (A few of the Szell
recordings have returned as filler for his Beethoven cycle on Sony.)
The Davis interpretations are taut and dramatic when the music
demands (*Coriolan, Egmont, Leonore* Nos. 1 and 3), yet are easygoing and flexible in the more lightweight fare (*Ruins of Athens,
Creatures of Prometheus*).

The classic Klemperer recordings are now finally available on
compact disc, and the collection is worth the price of admission for
the incomparable *Consecration of the House* alone. Klemperer invests this Handelian nod to Beethoven's favorite composer with an
incomparable grandeur, and the closing bars erupt in a suitably joyous flurry.

Although Claudio Abbado's recording of the complete overtures offers spirited playing from Vienna Philharmonic and up-to-
date recorded sound, the interpretations lack the character of some
of the best from Abbado's rivals—most notably, those other DG
Vienna Philharmonic recordings by Leonard Bernstein, which, alas,
have yet to be gathered onto one convenient disc.

Piano Sonatas (32)

Schnabel, piano. Angel CDHH-63765 [CD].

Kempff, piano. Deutsche Grammophon 429306-2 [CD].

Even more than in his pioneering recordings of the five
Beethoven piano concertos, it was Arthur Schnabel's great recorded
cycle of the Piano Sonatas that sparked the modern revival of interest in Beethoven's keyboard music and ensured (as much as mere
recordings ever can) this extraordinary pianist's immortality. Originally recorded by the Beethoven Piano Sonata Society on a subscription basis between 1932 and 1935 (the idea of recording so
many completely unknown works commercially was unthinkable),
the Schnabel interpretations have lost none of their originality or

wisdom over the years. Even the technical flaws, with time, have acquired an aura of quaintness, like the dings on a beloved jalopy or the chips in your grandmother's china. This is one of the supreme accomplishments in the history of recording, and still the place where any journey into the heart of this music must begin.

The modern cycle that most closely rivals Schnabel's in terms of depth of insight is Wilhelm Kempff's second complete recording from the mid-1960s. Although markedly less individual than Schnabel, Kempff is also less willful. The interpretations have a distinct, intellectually probing personality all their own and a stature that consistently dwarfs all the cycles by Kempff's younger contemporaries. Moreover, the bargain price makes the set all but irresistible.

Piano Sonatas: No. 8 in C minor, Op. 13 *Pathétique*; No. 14 in C-sharp minor, Op. 27 no. 2 *Moonlight*; No. 23 in F minor, Op. 57 *Appassionata*

R. Serkin, piano. CBS MYK-37219 [CD], MYT-37219 [T].

Rudolf Serkin often told an amusing story about his Berlin debut in the 1920s, when he performed Bach's fifth *Brandenburg* Concerto with the man who would eventually become his father-in-law, Adolf Busch. Following the audience's warm reception, Busch invited the young pianist to favor them with an encore. Serkin responded with the whole of Bach's *Goldberg Variations*. As Serkin later recalled the scene, "At the end of the evening there were only four people left in the hall: Adolf Busch, Arthur Schnabel, [the musicologist] Alfred Einstein, and me." Throughout his career, there was an endearing, almost boyish earnestness in Serkin's playing, and to the music of Beethoven, Mozart, Schubert, and Brahms he has always brought a special authority and integrity none of his contemporaries could match.

In this attractive collection of three of the most popular Beethoven piano sonatas, Serkin's lofty, thoroughly committed approach serves this familiar music extremely well. The performances are vastly intelligent without ever becoming pedantic, selfless though never self-effacing, impassioned yet never overblown. Until some recording company is canny enough to reissue Ivan Moravec's impossibly beautiful, though now deleted, Connoisseur Society recording of the *Moonlight* Sonata, Serkin's will remain the standard performances of all three.

Piano Sonatas: No. 21 in C, Op. 53 *Waldstein*; No. 23 in F minor, Op. 57 *Appassionata*; No. 26 in E-flat, Op. 81a *Les Adieux*

Gilels, piano. Deutsche Grammophon 419162-2 [CD].

The popular *Waldstein* and *Les Adieux* sonatas have never been given more distinguished performances than in these recordings made in the mid-1970s by Emil Gilels. Toward the end of his life, Gilels—always a searching and dynamic Beethoven interpreter—began to find a subtlety and depth in the composer's music that were unique even for him. The *Waldstein* has a mechanical perfection that few recordings can begin to match, while the wistful poignancy of *Les Adieux* recalls the historic version made by Arthur Schnabel in the 1930s. With a two-fisted, heaven-storming *Appassionata* to fill it out, this is one of the most desirable Beethoven sonata recordings now in the catalog.

Piano Sonatas: No. 28 in A, Op. 101; No. 29 in B-flat, Op. 106 *Hammerklavier*; No. 30 in E, Op. 109; No. 31 in A-flat, Op. 110; No. 32 in C minor, Op. 111

Pollini, piano. Deutsche Grammophon 419199-2 [CD].

There are many—and for years, I had to include myself among them—who never fully recovered from the Beethoven Bicentennial of 1970. Virtually everything was so overplayed, overbroadcast, overrecorded, and overpackaged that more than one sensitive sensibility snapped. It's only been in the last five years that I have again been able to sit through the Fifth Symphony or the *Egmont* Overture without feeling an urge to run amok with a meat cleaver, and my best friend—who knows every note of the man's music—has flatly refused to listen to Beethoven for the rest of his natural life, except as penance or on salary.

Fortunately, a handful of works remained unsullied in that shameless marketing orgy, primarily the last handful of piano sonatas, which will *never* be transformed into popular commodities. Except for the *Hammerklavier*, to which only the bravest musicians sometimes turn during their most masochistic moments, these sublimely imponderable creations remain as mysterious and unfathomable to us as they must have been to audiences of the early nineteenth century. They represent Beethoven at his most private, withdrawn, and mystical: a voice that hardly seems to be speaking to anyone at all, except, perhaps, to himself or to God.

While more impressive individual performances of some of these pieces can certainly be found—Emil Gilels, for instance, turns in a *Hammerklavier* of titanic strength and unmeasurable scale (Deutsche Grammophon 410527-2 [CD]), and Rudolf Serkin, in the slow movements of the last three sonatas, finds a shattering stillness no other pianist can seem to hear (Deutsche Grammophon 427498-2 [CD], 427498-4 [T])—Maurizio Pollini's integral set from the late 1970s is one of the great modern Beethoven recordings and probably this gifted pianist's finest outing to date. Like Gilels, Pollini brings ample amounts of power and poetry to the music: each of the interpretations is full of character and individuality, yet each seems utterly natural, devoid of any pointless originality or excess. The restored recorded sound is for the most part warm and spacious, if a touch muddy when the going gets rough.

Sonatas (5) for Cello and Piano

Rostropovich, cello; Richter, piano. Philips 412256-2 [CD].

These five alluring works have never achieved the popularity of the composer's violin or piano sonatas for reasons that are not so easy to explain. While the first two are ingratiating early pieces that contain echoes of both Haydn and Mozart, the Op. 69 is from the heart of Beethoven's heaven-storming middle period, and the pair of Op. 102 sonatas are among the forward-looking of his final works.

Although several recent releases offer some stiff competition (preeminently those by Lynn Harrell and Vladimir Ashkenazy for London and Yo-Yo Ma and Emanuel Ax for CBS—and why, oh why, can't those last two artists get together with that well-known German violinist to form the Lizzie Borden, or Ax-Ma-Mutter, Trio?), this Philips recording with Mstislav Rostropovich and Sviatoslav Richter from the early 1960s still mops the field. Richter is as gracious and powerful as ever, and Rostropovich has never been more probing or refined. Listening to the work of that once peerless cellist, one can only wonder why he has devoted so much of his time in the last twenty years to becoming the World's Greatest Amateur Conductor.

Sonatas (10) for Violin and Piano

Oistrakh, violin; Oborin, piano. Philips 412570-2 [CD].

During the iciest years of the Cold War, David Oistrakh was a warm reminder that the Soviet Union was a nation not only of dour commissars and sinister KGB hoods but also of magnificent artists who had much to say to their not-so-very-different neighbors in the West. In many ways, this rumpled, pugnacious-looking fiddler was the best-loved of Russia's cultural ambassadors: a violinist of inestimable accomplishment, and a human being whose rare powers of communication probably touched more hearts more deeply than any other Soviet musician of his time.

With his famous Dresden recordings of the Brahms and Tchaikovsky concertos reissued by Deutsche Grammophon (423399-2 [CD]), these superlative versions of the Beethoven Violin Sonatas may prove to be Oistrakh's most enduring memorial. Recorded in the early 1960s with the always polished, sensitive Lev Oborin, Oistrakh's interpretations are textbook examples of that high art which conceals high art. Beneath the unmannered and apparently straightforward surfaces of the performances lies a wealth of character and finesse. While not as technically dazzling as the London recordings by Itzhak Perlman and Vladimir Ashkenazy, this version exhibits a knowing sense of give-and-take between the performers that creates the feeling of a real and fascinating conversation, and the warmth of the playing practically makes the speakers glow. The recorded sound, though perfectly adequate, is a little mushy around the upper edges; aside from that, this is a moving souvenir of a great musician and an even greater man.

Sonata No. 9 in A for Violin and Piano, Op. 47 *Kreutzer*

Huberman, violin; Friedman, piano. Angel CDH-63194 [CD].

Perlman, violin; Ashkenazy, piano. London 410554-2 [CD].

I have had countless heated arguments with violinist friends over the years whenever I made so bold as to suggest that Jascha Heifetz was not the great violinist of the twentieth century. Granted, his was probably the most phenomenal technique since Paganini's, but with a couple of recorded exceptions—the Second Prokofiev

Concerto and the D Major Concerto of Erich Wolfgang Korngold—I have always found his playing heartless, distant, and cold. When challenged to name a finer violinist, I typically supply a list of at least a half dozen possibilities—a list that invariably begins with the name of Bronislaw Huberman.

Like Fritz Kreisler, Jacques Thibaud, Joseph Szigeti, and the other giants of the era, Huberman was never a note-perfect player. Nor was he a paragon of consistency: more often than not, his performances were flawed by the most elementary kind of mistakes, even though his technical finish could be nearly as impressive as Heifetz's whenever the occasion arose. For Huberman was of that generation of violinists for whom technique was never an end in itself: always a great musician who only *happened* to play the violin, he was far more deeply concerned with what lay between and beneath the notes.

Compare this justly celebrated 1930 recording of the *Kreutzer* Sonata with any of the several versions Heifetz left, and you'll begin to understand the difference between flesh-and-blood music-making and mere superhuman facility. In spite of some minor slips and the errant sour note, Huberman invests every bar of the piece with passion, profundity, and an instantly recognizable musical personality. It is an interpretation riddled with rubato, portamenti, and other Romantic liberties, yet a performance of such conviction that everything sounds utterly natural, inevitable, and right. The playing of pianist Ignaz Friedman more than lives up to its almost mythic proportions. In addition, this priceless collection preserves virtually all the commercial recordings the legendary Polish pianist ever made.

The most completely satisfying modern version of the *Kreutzer* is the London compact disc by Itzhak Perlman and Vladimir Ashkenazy, who also turn in a delectably verdant account of the composer's *Spring* Sonata.

String Quartets (16)

Alban Berg Quartet. Angel CDC-47126 [CD] (Op. 18); CDC-47130 [CD] (Opp. 59, 74, 95); CDC-47134 [CD] (Opp. 127, 130, 131, 132, 135, *Grosse Fuge*).

Talich Quartet. Calliope 4631/40 [T].

If it is in the nine symphonies that Beethoven became the composer who had the most seismic impact on the development of nineteenth-century music, then it is with the astonishing series of sixteen string quartets that we are introduced—more revealingly than anywhere else—to the man inside the public figure. Beethoven reserved the most personal and intimate of his musical thoughts for his chamber works, and in them, the most restlessly original composer in the history of music became his most consistently adventurous.

Since the days of those pioneering, and still magically effective, recordings made by the Lener Quartet during the 78 era, virtually every important ensemble has come to terms with the cycle, and none more successfully in recent years than Vienna's Alban Berg Quartet, named after the great Viennese composer and probably without equal in the world today. They play with a finesse and finish that only the Guarneri Quartet, at the height of their fame, could begin to match. The Berg Quartet's technical prowess is reminiscent of the young Juilliard's, and the engaging warmth and mellowness of their physical sound have probably not been heard since the disbandment of the great—and greatly lamented—Quartetto Italiano.

For the audiophile or the novice listener, the Berg Quartet's complete recording of the Beethoven quartets is a nearly perfect introduction to the cycle, and even the most jaded collector will find much here that seems startlingly fresh, original, and new. The Op. 18 collection sparkles with a suitably Haydnesque wit and charm; the middle-period quartets are appropriately tempestuous and heroic. If in those final mysterious masterworks the Berg Quartet are unable to probe quite so deeply as the Busch Quartet did a half century ago, their performance is still more than adequate to leave most of the current competition far behind.

For the tape collector, the performances by the brilliant Talich Quartet, while not quite so polished as the Berg Quartet's, are full of character, bite, and youthful enthusiasm. Their recording also has the distinction of being one of the few not available solely on compact discs.

Symphony No. 1 in C

English Chamber Orchestra, Thomas. CBS MDK-44905 [CD], MDT-44905 [T].

Philharmonia Orchestra, Klemperer. Angel 4AE-34423 [T].

Here is a pair of superlative recordings that will go a long way toward demolishing the preconceptions many listeners have about the two conductors involved: the adroit but essentially lightweight Michael Tilson Thomas, and the stodgy, ponderous Otto Klemperer, who near the end of his life made recordings that bore an uncanny resemblance to Easter Island monoliths.

Using an ensemble whose reduced forces are those of the standard Mozart orchestra, Thomas turns in a beautifully proportioned, refreshingly vigorous interpretation of the work, and Klemperer, far from being lethargic—which he most assuredly *never* was—responds with the same light and delicate touch that characterized all of his admirable Haydn recordings. Until Philips sees fit to reissue that spontaneous wonder Sir Neville Marriner and the Academy of St. Martin-in-the-Fields unleashed a decade and a half ago, these are the recordings that will probably dominate the catalogs for years.

Symphonies: No. 2 in D; No. 8 in F

London Classical Players, Norrington. Angel CDC-47698 [CD].

The thought of a group of musicians actually going out of their way to wrestle with those treacherous and invariably vile-sounding antiques known as period instruments has always reminded me of my quasi-hippie, back-to-the-basics friends of the 1960s, who took such inexplicable pride in outdoor plumbing, home-ground grain, and miserably inefficient (to say nothing of vastly malodorous) wood-burning stoves. Thank goodness, times have changed. It's now possible to dismiss such nonsense for what it was without people suspecting you of having been a secret supporter of the Vietnam War.

Imagine, then, my dumbfounded amazement at being so thoroughly swept away by this electrifying period-instrument recording, further heartening proof that the Authenticity Movement has finally moved out of the finger-painting stage. The London Classical Players are obviously crackerjack musicians one and all, as opposed to the hacks and second-raters that the phrase "period instrument" always seemed to imply. They play with genuine polish and fire and, urged on by Roger Norrington, deliver two of the most ferociously exciting Beethoven symphony recordings released in years. Had such recordings been available when the period-instrument revival began, I might have given up eating Wonder Bread years ago.

Symphony No. 3 in E-flat, Eroica

Vienna Philharmonic, Furtwängler. Angel CDH-63033 [CD].

Cleveland Orchestra, Szell. CBS MYK-37222 [CD], MYT-37222 [T].

From 1922, the year he succeeded Arthur Nikisch as music director of both the Berlin Philharmonic and Leipzig Gewandhaus Orchestra, to his death in 1954, Wilhelm Furtwängler was the most potent and eloquent spokesman for a style of interpretation that could trace its roots to the work of Richard Wagner, the major conducting force of nineteenth-century music. In Furtwängler, Wagner's radical theories about phrasing, tempo modification, and the idealized image of the interpreter as an artist on equal footing with the composer were given—depending on one's point of view— their final grotesque or glorious expression.

For those who grew up under the spell of Arturo Toscanini's new objectivism, Furtwängler was an anachronism: an unpleasant reminder of a time when Romantic excesses practically made a composer's intentions unintelligible. For those who were unpersuaded by the Italian conductor's manic, though essentially simpleminded, approach, Furtwängler was one of the last of the heroically subjective individualists, a man whose mystic, almost messianic faith in his own ideas transfigured all he touched with the sheer force of his personality alone.

If any other recording of Beethoven's Eroica does more to justify the symphony's subtitle, I have yet to hear it. Only Otto Klemperer found a comparable grandeur in this music; however, along with the titanic scale of Furtwängler's performance come a dramatic power and animal magnetism that remain unique. No one has ever transformed the funeral march into the stuff of such inconsolable tragedy, nor has any conductor perceived such individuality in each of the final movement's variations, or galvanized that movement into such a unified, indissoluble whole. In short, one of the great recordings of the century.

For a more brilliant modern version of this popular work, George Szell's recording with the Cleveland Orchestra—like all the performances from his memorable Beethoven cycle—has stood the test of time magnificently. The sound in both formats, especially the compact disc, simply refuses to show its age.

Symphony No. 4 in B-flat

Bavarian State Orchestra, Carlos Kleiber. Orfeo 100841 [CD].

Columbia Symphony, Walter. CBS MYK-37773 [CD], MYT-37773 [T].

It was Robert Schumann who inadvertently invited posterity to think of the Fourth as something of a weak sister among the Beethoven symphonies when, in one of his poetic moments, he described it as a Greek maiden standing between two Norse gods. If so, Orfeo's volcanic souvenir of a live performance given in Munich suggests that the maiden is one hell of an interesting girl.

With his customary flair, Carlos Kleiber virtually rethinks this essentially light and graceful symphony. The outer movements—especially the finale—rush by at a breakneck clip, while the slow movement and Scherzo are invested with an uncommon significance and weight. Given the extraordinary demands he makes on them, the courageous Bavarian State Orchestra's playing is exemplary. Listen especially to the principal clarinet and bassoon, who, in their cruelly difficult solos in the finale, sound like men who were born with the tongues of snakes.

For cost-conscious collectors who can't quite bring themselves to spend their hard-earned money on any recording, however spectacular, that offers barely a half hour of music, the best alternative is Bruno Walter's gentle yet potent 1959 interpretation with the Columbia Symphony, in which the Eighth Symphony is also included.

Symphony No. 5 in C minor

Vienna Philharmonic, Carlos Kleiber. Deutsche Grammophon 415861-2 [CD], 415861-4 [T].

Dozens of recorded versions of this popular symphony have come and gone since the mid-1970s, when this withering recording introduced many of us to one of the most electric musical personalities of the our time. For nearly twenty years, only one other version, that majestic and tremendously adult interpretation by Carlo Maria Giulini and the Los Angeles Philharmonic, also on Deutsche Grammophon (410028-2 [CD]), has seriously challenged what may well be the single most exciting Beethoven recording of the stereo era.

The first movement is a triumph of cataclysmic energy and hushed mystery, while the ensuing *Andante con moto* has never seemed more poetic and refined. Yet in the Symphony's final movements, Kleiber leaves the competition panting in the dust. The Scherzo is transformed into a diabolically grotesque witches' sabbath, and the finale, with the incomparable Vienna Philharmonic in full cry, sweeps all before it in a flood of C Major sunshine.

As in his recording of the Fourth Symphony, Kleiber's Fifth offers fewer than thirty-four minutes of actual playing time. Still, considering the quality of this historic issue, either the tape or the compact disc (to coin a cliché) would be a bargain at twice the price.

Symphony No. 6 in F, *Pastorale*

Columbia Symphony, Walter. CBS MYK-36720 [CD], MYT-36720 [T].

Symphony No. 7 in A

Columbia Symphony, Walter. CBS MK-42013 [CD].

Like dogcatchers, truant officers, old-time sideshow geeks, and syndicate hit men, recording company executives have always had a rather unsavory reputation: cost-conscious bureaucrats whose artistic standards—such as they are—have always taken a distant backseat to the pursuit of the almighty bottom line. In fact, with a slight change of gender, their behavior has reminded many musicians and music lovers of Dr. Samuel Johnson's pronouncement on Lady Diana Beauclerk: "The woman's a whore, and there's an end on't."

And yet the recording executive at Columbia Records—now CBS/Sony—who in the late 1950s turned the octogenarian Bruno Walter loose on the heart of his repertoire deserves some sort of medal or, at the very least, our undying gratitude and admiration. For like the Homeric series of recordings Otto Klemperer made in London during the final years of his career, Walter's protracted recording swan song is an enduring monument to one of the greatest twentieth-century conductors.

For more than six decades—and Walter had been conducting professionally for three years *before* the death of Johannes Brahms —the *Pastorale* was one of his most famous house specialties, and this beautiful recording, so full of freshness, wide-eyed innocence, and vivid nature painting, has never been approached.

Similarly, a finer recording of the A Major Symphony does not exist. If the tempos in the first three movements tend to be on the leisurely side—and on records, only George Szell conducted the second movement as a true *allegretto*—the rhythms are so firm and infectious that we scarcely notice, much less mind. The finale, on the other hand, dashes off in such a good-natured jumble of barely controllable exuberance that we are reminded why Wagner called this swirling masterpiece "The Apotheosis of the Dance."

Among recordings with more up-to-date sound, Carlos Kleiber's Vienna Philharmonic performance (Deutsche Grammophon 415862-2 [CD]) is nearly as incisive as his famous recording of the Fifth; of the available tapes, a scrappy yet endearing and virile performance Pablo Casals conducted at one of the Marlboro Festivals in the 1960s is still immensely satisfying (CBS MYT-37233 [T]).

Symphony No. 9 in D minor, *Choral*

Curtin, Kopleff, McCollum, Gramm, Chicago Symphony Orchestra and Chorus, Reiner. RCA 6532-2-RG [CD].

Shortly after the beginning of his final season as music director of the Chicago Symphony, Fritz Reiner became so seriously ill that many feared he would never lead the orchestra again. (My father and I had tickets for the concert where Erich Leinsdorf stepped in at the last moment to officiate at Sviatoslav Richter's American debut.) Reiner recovered sufficiently to return for the final subscription concerts of the season, programs that were devoted to Beethoven's First and Ninth symphonies, both of which he recorded in the following week.

Perhaps it is simply my vivid memory of those concerts (and for the first five years of my career as a concertgoer, Fritz Reiner's Chicago Symphony was the only professional orchestra I ever heard), but this recording has always seemed to me something breathlessly close to the ideal realization of Beethoven's Ninth. Brilliantly played and beautifully sung, it is a suave, rugged, polished, explosive, and inspiring performance that captures Reiner's special gifts at, or very near, their peak. In its original 1963 incarnation, the sound—like that of most of the recordings made in pre-renovation Orchestra Hall—was a wonder of clarity, warmth, and detail. In RCA's elegant compact disc transfer, the sound still rivals all but the very best on the market today.

On tape, George Szell's electrifying interpretation from about the same period (CBS YT-34625) is nearly as convincing as Reiner's. There are some wonderful eccentricities in the performance (including some brass outbursts in the finale that will lift you out of your chair), but essentially the recording is vintage Szell—equal parts polish, precision, passion, and fire.

Trio No. 4 for Piano, Violin, and Cello in D, Op. 70 no. 1 *Ghost*; Trio No. 6 in B-flat, Op. 97 *Archduke*

Beaux Arts Trio. Philips 412891-2 [CD].

More than any other ensemble of the last quarter century, the Beaux Arts Trio have been almost as much fun to *watch* as to hear. Much of the fun came from the contrast between the group's rather stoic-looking former cellist, Bernard Greenhouse, and the trio's nervous, restless, hyperkinetic Ewok of a pianist. On stage, Menahem Pressler is alert to the point of distraction. Hunched over the keyboard like a watchmaker over a priceless heirloom, fingers flashing, eyes darting everywhere at once, he *is* quite a sight. Watching him, one is reminded of what the Pittsburgh Pirate great Willie Stargell once said of the twitchy mannerisms of the pitcher Luis Tiant: "That guy would make a cup of coffee nervous."

The recordings of Beethoven's two most popular trios are vintage Beaux Arts performances, full of energy, wit, pith, and vinegar.

While the Suk Trio on Denon (CO-1586 [CD]) give them a run for their money in the *Archduke,* the diaphanous playing in the *Ghost* is unapproachable, and the two trios offered together on a single CD represents a major bargain.

Wellington's Victory

Cincinnati Symphony, Kunzel. Telarc CD-80079 [CD].

As if it weren't bad enough losing most of his army to the Russian winter and then getting mauled at Waterloo, poor Napoleon—and what else could actually make one feel *sorry* for that miserable little cretin?—also had to have his nose rubbed in it by two of history's supreme masterpieces of musical schlock: Tchaikovsky's refined and tasteful *1812 Overture* and this embarrassing garbage by Beethoven. Until the historic recording led by Antal Dorati is reissued (remember the miniature French and English flags you could put on your speakers so as to tell who was shooting at whom?), this generally impressive effort from Telarc should keep most people happy. The performance itself is excellent, though the musketry sounds a trifle anemic, almost as though no one was really all that angry.

Bellini, Vincenzo (1801–1835)

Norma

Callas, Stignani, Filippeschi, Rossi-Lemeni, La Scala Chorus and Orchestra, Serafin. Angel CDC-47303 [CD].

There are few words that get the true opera lover's juices flowing more effusively than the title of Vincenzo Bellini's masterpiece, *Norma.* In one of his rare bouts of genuine humility, an opera lover named Richard Wagner said that he hoped *Tristan und Isolde* would some day be seen as the German equivalent of the opera he loved more than any other. The celebrated Wagnerian soprano Lilli Lehmann insisted that a half dozen Isoldes were far less physically and emotionally exhausting than one encounter with Bellini's Druid priestess.

In this century, the great exponents of what is widely regarded as the most brutally demanding of all soprano roles can be counted on one hand. In the 1920s, the matchless American soprano Rosa Ponselle began the modern *Norma* revival with an interpretation whose sheer vocal splendor has never been equaled. In more recent times, the Norma of Dame Joan Sutherland was a technical wonder, if something of a dramatic joke. And then of course, for a few brief seasons in the 1950s, there was the Norma of Maria Callas, which both as a vocal and theatrical experience ranks with Lotte Lehmann's Marschallin and the Boris Godunov of Feodor Chaliapin as one of the supreme operatic experiences of the twentieth century.

Angel was extremely wise to choose this 1954 recording for reissue as a compact disc. Unlike her much less successful, but still overwhelming, stereo remake, in the 1954 *Norma* Callas's voice had yet to acquire many of the hooty, wobbling eccentricities for which her admirers are always needlessly apologizing and to which her detractors fasten like barnacles to a once majestic ship. Here the voice is heard at its youthful best, from the velvety grace of the "Casta Diva" to the spine-tingling fireworks of "Mira, o Norma." The Pollione and Oroveso might just as well have phoned their performances in, but the choice of the indestructible Ebe Stignani as Adalgisa was an inspired one. Although well past her prime at the time the recording was made, this greatest Italian mezzo of the 1930s and '40s was still a worthy foil for perhaps the finest Norma history has so far known.

Run, don't walk, to buy this one.

I Puritani

Sutherland, Pavarotti, Ghiaurov, Cappuccilli, Luccardi,
Orchestra and Chorus of the Royal Opera House,
Covent Garden, Bonynge. London 417588-2 [CD].

There are at least two overwhelming pieces of evidence that unlike Ponchielli, Leoncavallo, and Mascagni, Vincenzo Bellini was more than a one-opera composer. The first is the delightfully coquettish *La Sonnambula*—best represented by the 1957 Angel recording featuring Maria Callas and the usual suspects (CDCB-47377 [CD]); the second is his final stage work, *I Puritani*.

While the wooden, intermittently goofy story about English Roundheads and Cavaliers lacks the weight and dramatic thrust of *Norma* (although the same might be said of virtually any bel canto opera), there are some glorious things in this hugely underrated score. The aria "Qui la voce" is cut from the same radiant cloth as *Norma*'s great hit tune, "Casta Diva"; for once in a Bellini opera, the tenor has as much important music to sing as the half-mad heroine, and the hectoring duet "Suoni la tromba" which closes Act II is as fine a bit of martial drum-thumping as exists in Italian opera.

The London recording achieved something close to legendary stature on the day it was first released and has only improved with age. Whatever one might think of Joan Sutherland, she can't really be touched in a role like this one, perhaps because all—all!—Elvira really needs to do is sing magnificently without paying any special attention to the words or the dramatic context in which they appear. Dame Joan has not fluttered and warbled more thrillingly since her first recording of *Lucia di Lammermoor,* made in the late 1950s.

Yet the real stars of the show are Richard Bonynge, who tightens the often flaccid action into something as lean and mean as middle-period Verdi, and Luciano Pavarotti, who here gives the performance of his life. The singing has a suppleness and taste that recall the feats of Fernando de Lucia, Alessandro Bonci, and other late-nineteenth-century giants, and the high F-sharp above high C that he uncorks in the final scene will curl the hair on a steel brush. The supporting cast is uniformly excellent—in fact, the Cappuccilli-Ghiaurov delivery of "Suoni la tromba" very nearly hijacks the show.

Berg, Alban (1885–1935)

Concerto for Violin and Orchestra

Krasner, violin; BBC Symphony, Webern. Symposium SBT-1004 [CD].

Grumiaux, violin; Concertgebouw Orchestra, Markevitch. Philips 422136-2 [CD].

If there is a single work that establishes Alban Berg's credentials as one of the giants of twentieth-century music, it is his moving and powerful Violin Concerto, finished only a few weeks before his death. Written to "the memory of an Angel"—the young Manon Gropius, daughter of Alma Mahler—the Concerto was obviously Berg's own requiem as well. According to Louis Krasner, the American violinist who commissioned the work (and for whom Berg's teacher, Arnold Schoenberg, would also write *his* Violin Concerto), Berg was fully aware that the Concerto would be his final work. "It was not written with ink," Krasner would later insist, "but with his own blood."

Although it might be difficult to find, the imported Symposium CD of a 1936 recording is a document of incalculable historic interest. It not only captures the authoritative interpretation of Louis Krasner, it offers the unique insights of Berg's friend Anton Webern, who was to have conducted the world premiere at the ISCM Festival in Barcelona but became so unhinged at the rehearsals that he had to be replaced by Hermann Scherchen.

Among modern recordings, none has ever superseded the profound and profoundly moving interpretation Arthur Grumiaux recorded a quarter of a century ago. The Belgian violinist's grasp of both the Concerto's structure and its spiritual underpinnings remains amazing, while the playing itself has an ease and naturalness that make the work almost as accessible as the concertos of Mendelssohn and Brahms.

Lyric Suite for String Quartet

LaSalle Quartet. Deutsche Grammophon 419994-2 [CD].

This great work was already clearly established as one of the cornerstones of modern chamber music when a series of sensational discoveries proved what many listeners had long suspected: There was a bit more to the *Lyric Suite* than met the eye. The composer himself offered a key to the *Lyric Suite*'s mystery, with that cryptic and, until recently, inexplicable quotation of the "Love Potion" motif from Wagner's *Tristan und Isolde* embedded in the work's final movement.

It was the brilliant American composer and Berg authority George Perle who finally discovered what the piece was really *about*. A score, annotated by Berg himself, came into Perle's possession which contained the startling revelation that the *Lyric Suite* had in fact been written to a secret program. Called by the composer "A small monument to a Great Love," the work traces the events of a lengthy and passionate love affair the composer conducted with a lady who was not his wife. The final movement is in fact a wordless setting of "De Profundis Clamavi," a tortured poem about doomed, impossible love from Charles Baudelaire's *Fleurs du mal.*

Needless to say, though the fact that the cat, after a half century, is finally out of the bag does add to our understanding of Berg's motives and emotional state when he composed the *Lyric Suite,* nothing could seriously add or detract to what has been, in all that time, one of the most profound and profoundly moving of all twentieth-century chamber works.

The famous recording by the LaSalle Quartet is available only as part of a larger release that includes most of the major chamber works of Berg, Webern, and their teacher, Arnold Schoenberg. Although a considerable investment, the set is more than worth the expense. The performance of the *Lyric Suite* is especially warm and, appropriately, lyrical. And unlike so many performances, which make the music seem far more complex and forbidding than it needs to be, their fluent, natural grasp of its language and vocabulary makes it as lucid and approachable as one of the middle-period Beethoven quartets.

Altenberg Lieder; Lulu: Suite for Soprano and Orchestra; Three Pieces for Orchestra

> M. Price, soprano; London Symphony, Abbado. Deutsche Grammophon 423238-2 [CD].

Peter Altenberg, the flamboyant Viennese coffeehouse poet whose verses jotted down on picture postcards served as the basis for Alban Berg's great orchestral song cycle, was one of the most colorful figures in an era known for its colorful figures. He used to brag, regularly, that he slept with all the windows open on the coldest night of the year. Calling his bluff one winter evening, a group of his friends—including Berg and Schoenberg's son-in-law, Felix Greissle—went over to check up. All the windows were tightly shut and they began berating Altenberg from the street. When reminded of his boast, the undaunted poet said, "But it isn't the *coldest* night."

The sensuous *Altenberg Lieder* are served up with a provocative sexiness by Margaret Price, Claudio Abbado, and the London Symphony, as is the *Lulu* Suite—a perfect introduction for those who are not quite willing to take the plunge into the whole of Berg's repulsive, alluring, hypnotic masterpiece. For those who become hooked, or are already converted, the complete *Lulu*—with the unfinished final act put into performing shape by Friedrich Cerha—is currently available in the staggering Paris Opéra production led by Pierre Boulez (Deutsche Grammophon 415489-2 [CD]).

One of the most appealing Berg recordings now on the market is rounded out by a taut, poetic version of the Three Pieces for Orchestra, a work which, with Schoenberg's Five Pieces and the Op. 31 Variations, has a fair claim to being the quintessential orchestral work of the Second Viennese School.

Wozzeck

Silja, Wächter, Jahn, Laubenthal, Zednik, Vienna
Philharmonic, Christoph von Dohnányi. London
417348-2 [CD].

With Puccini's *Turandot,* which had its world premiere only four months later, *Wozzeck* was the last great opera to enter the standard repertoire. From the perspective of three quarters of a century, it is now obvious that these two wildly disparate works have far more in common than was once supposed. In spite of its once radical, atonal musical language—to say nothing of its lurid subject matter—*Wozzeck,* like *Turandot,* is an old-fashioned, intensely Romantic opera that creates a darkly lyrical universe all its own. Should anyone tell you that the opera has no singable arias or memorable tunes, invite that person over to hear this lovely London recording; if it isn't *precisely* late Puccini, then it is certainly something not too far removed.

Much of the credit for the success of the recording must go to Christoph von Dohnányi, whose approach to *Wozzeck* might be loosely described as treating it as though it were a Mahler symphony with words. His eye for the larger structures is as keenly developed as his ear for the minor details: the music unfolds with all the sweep and power anyone could wish, yet in its textures and inner voices, it has the character of fine chamber music. In short, by the time Marie's orphaned child delivers his final "hop-hop" at the end of the performance, we feel as annihilated as we always should; yet it is a subtle, enthralling feeling of annihilation, as at the end of Debussy's *Pelléas et Mélisande*.

While Dohnányi and—in this music—the incomparable Vienna Philharmonic are the principal selling points of the recording, the cast is also excellent. Vocally, the title role is something of a struggle for Eberhard Wächter, although the rough-and-ready raggedness somehow suits the character very well. Anja Silja is superb as Marie, as she is in the blistering performance of Schoenberg's monodrama *Erwartung* which comes as a generous bonus.

Berlioz, Hector (1803–1869)

The Damnation of Faust (complete oratorio)

Veasey, Gedda, Bastin, Ambrosian Singers, London Symphony Orchestra and Chorus, Davis. Philips 416395-2 [CD].

Hector Berlioz could never quite make up his mind about *The Damnation of Faust*, so it's hardly surprising posterity hasn't either. He hedged his bets by calling it "A Dramatic Legend," and while it can be—and has been—staged as both an opera and an oratorio, for most people the piece consists of that trio of familiar excerpts,

Minuet of the Will-o'-the-Wisps, Dance of the Sylphs, and the Rákóczy March, based on a Hungarian tune the composer learned from his friend Franz Liszt.

While there is a good deal more to *The Damnation of Faust* than that, the piece can be unbearably tedious, as any of a half dozen previous recordings clearly prove. Sir Colin Davis's recording from the mid-1970s earns high marks for Nicolai Gedda's singing, the crispness of the orchestral execution, and the generally sensitive attention to detail. For those who might not need the full catastrophe, the London album (410181-2 [CD]) of excerpts from Sir Georg Solti's rivetingly dramatic recording should more than fill the bill.

Harold in Italy, for Viola and Orchestra

Imai, viola; London Symphony, Davis. Philips 416431-2 [CD].

Ironically, the foremost champions of the music of France's major nineteenth-century composer have tended to be British. It was Sir Hamilton Harty—an Ulsterman by birth, and proud of it, thank you—who began the modern Berlioz revival through his revelatory performances with the Hallé Orchestra of Manchester in the 1920s, and Sir Thomas Beecham whose zany, scintillating interpretations in the middle decades of the century finally helped make the music of this strange and original composer a bona fide box office draw. From the mid-1960s onward, this long and fruitful tradition has been ably continued by Sir Colin Davis—in the opinion of many, the finest Berlioz conductor the century has so far produced.

A comparison of his two recorded versions of *Harold in Italy* provides a fascinating glimpse into Sir Colin's growth as a Berlioz conductor. In the first, made with Yehudi Menuhin, Davis was much too deferential to a far more famous colleague. It was as if both the soloist and the conductor had forgotten that whatever else *Harold in Italy* may be, it is certainly *not* a viola concerto. (After all, Niccolò Paganini, who commissioned the work to show off his new Stradivarius viola, actually refused to play it in public, complaining that it gave him far too little to do.)

On the other hand, Sir Colin's second recording is clearly the conductor's show. As in all his Berlioz performances, the image of the composer Davis tries to project is that of an arch-Romantic whose roots were firmly planted in the classical past. While the interpretation has an appealing sweep and impulsiveness, it is also meticulously controlled. The Japanese violist Nobuko Imai plays her pivotal role with great zest and distinction, offering an unusually urbane and sensitive approach to phrasing and a physical sound whose size and beauty will make you want to check the record jacket to make certain she really *does* play a viola, not a cello.

Les nuits d'été (song cycle)

Crespin, soprano; L'Orchestre de la Suisse Romande, Ansermet. London 417813-2 [CD].

Even though he never actually composed any chamber music—and what could you expect from a man whose ideal ensemble included a total of 465 musicians, playing everything from 120 violins and five saxophones to an ophicleide in C *and* an ophicleide in B?—the delicate song cycle *Les nuits d'été* has a hushed intimacy that almost suggests what a Berlioz string quartet might have been.

Although many celebrated singers have recorded the cycle in recent years—and the dreadfully dull versions by Jessye Norman and Dame Kiri (or is that *Dreary?*) Te Kanawa are to be avoided at all costs—Régine Crespin's famous thirty-year-old recording hasn't lost a speck of its magic. With a voice more supple, luxurious, and feminine than that of any of her colleagues, she weaves her way around and through this fragile music with a sirenlike seductiveness. "The Spectre of the Rose" is particularly adroit and heartbreaking, proving that Crespin was one of the few singers of her generation who was equally comfortable with opera and song.

While several volumes could be written about the variety of color that Ernest Ansermet coaxes out of the orchestral accompaniment—to say nothing about the equally memorable version of Ravel's *Shéhérazade* that fills out the disc—three words will do it: Buy this *now*.

Overtures

London Philharmonic, Hallé Orchestra, Harty. Pearl 9485 [CD].
London Symphony, Davis. Philips 416430-2 [CD].

There are many who insist that the Ulster composer and conductor Sir Hamilton Harty was the finest Berlioz conductor of the twentieth century, and these electrifying recordings from the 1930s tend to bear that out. Not only are they among the most highly charged recordings ever made of this composer's music (the speeds generated in the *Roman Carnival Overture* will nearly cause you to do a double take), they are also among the most refined and sophisticated. Even through the occasionally furry sound, the subtle finish and physical presence of the performances come through to a remarkable degree.

Among more recent Berlioz conductors, Sir Colin Davis has been as admired and influential in our time as Harty was in his. Davis's overture collection is the most consistently satisfying modern one available, combining carefully judged tempos and textures with a sophisticated feeling for detail and genuine panache.

Requiem (*Grande Messe des Morts*)

Dowd, tenor; London Symphony Orchestra and Chorus,
Davis. Philips 416283-2 [CD].

Of all his major compositions, including the sprawling *Damnation of Faust,* the Requiem is probably Hector Berlioz's most problematic work. For just as that other great Requiem by Giuseppe Verdi is an opera thinly disguised as a sacred service, the *Grande Messe des Morts* is a dramatic symphony which, almost incidentally, takes as its point of departure one of the most moving texts of the Roman Catholic liturgy.

To date, it is Sir Colin Davis's 1970 recording that best reconciles the Requiem's not completely resolvable sacred and secular conflicts: the *Tuba mirum,* for once, sounds more like worship than the usual sonic sideshow, and throughout the performance Davis consistently maintains an appropriate sense of decorum, without ever allowing the music to become ponderous or dull.

As an eye- and ear-opening bonus, the compact disc reissue comes with an unbelievably civilized and serious reading (and how did Davis keep a straight face?) of what is surely the most embarrassing half hour of unregenerate schlock ever perpetrated by a major composer: the brazen *Symphonie funèbre et triomphale,* an utterly mindless twenty-odd minutes of musical trash which, I blush to confess, I love without reservation.

Roméo et Juliette

Quivar, Cupido, Krause, Montreal Tudor Singers, Montreal
Symphony Orchestra and Chorus, Dutoit. London
417302-2 [CD].

In the last decade, Charles Dutoit has worked a minor miracle in Montreal, transforming a fine regional ensemble into an orchestra of international importance. On a good day—and to hear their recordings or broadcast concerts, they seem to have nothing but *very* good days—the Montreal Symphony must now be considered one of the great orchestras of the world. Beginning with their intoxicating version of Ravel's *Daphnis and Chloë*, they have had such an unbroken string of recording triumphs that their gifted music director has become the first superstar conductor of the digital age.

Dutoit's recording of Berlioz's *Roméo et Juliette*—the most far-reaching and startlingly modern of all that composer's scores— has much in common with Sir Colin Davis's famous London Symphony recording for Philips, which has recently resurfaced on compact discs (416962-2). All of the famous set pieces have tremendous character and individuality, while the connecting episodes refuse to sound (as they so often do, alas) like patchwork filler in which both the composer and the performers are merely marking time. The Dutoit performance benefits from a chorus that sings with marvelously idiomatic French inflection and feeling, to say nothing of state-of-the-art recorded sound, but the real surprise is the ease with which the orchestra outplays even the great London Symphony, which on records is an all but impossible feat.

Four stars to all concerned.

Symphonie fantastique

Concertgebouw Orchestra of Amsterdam, Davis. Philips
411425-2 [CD].

Boston Symphony, Munch. RCA 7735-2-RV [CD], 7735-4-
RV3 [T].

In many ways, this odd and perplexing masterpiece remains the most daringly original large-scale orchestral work produced during the entire Romantic era. Completed barely eight years after the premiere of Beethoven's Ninth, the *Symphonie fantastique* helped to define an entirely new compositional aesthetic that would have an incalculable effect on the subsequent development of nineteenth-century orchestral music. For unlike the modest nature painting Beethoven had employed in his *Pastorale* symphony, the *Symphonie fantastique* was one of the first important orchestral works that attempted to tell a distinct and detailed story. Thus it became one of the seminal works in the development of program music, which would be further expanded in the tone poems of composers from Liszt and Smetana to Richard Strauss. And in his use of the *idée fixe,* a recurrent melody associated in the composer's mind with the heartthrob of the symphony's hero, Berlioz anticipated the use of leitmotif technique, the structural glue that would bind the gargantuan music dramas of Richard Wagner.

Since the invention of electrical recording in the mid-1920s, Berlioz's bizarre, colorful, and outrageously flamboyant score has been handsomely served on records. Bruno Walter and Felix Weingartner made famous early recordings, though perhaps the greatest single recording ever made—a 1929 version by Pierre Monteux and a Parisian pickup orchestra, long treasured by 78 collectors—has never, to the best of my knowledge, surfaced as an LP.

Sir Colin Davis has so far recorded the *Symphonie* three times, initially with the London Symphony—a taut, dramatic performance now available on Philips's medium-priced Silver Line series (422253-2 [CD], 422253-4 [T])—and then as the first work he chose to record with Amsterdam's great Concertgebouw Orchestra. It is Davis's second recording that continues to offer the most balanced and exciting view of the *Symphonie fantastique* presented in the last half century. It goes without saying that the playing of the Concertgebouw Orchestra is a model of modern orchestral execution, and the conception, while beautifully organized, is also wonderfully detailed. Except for Jean Martinon, whose Angel recording is only a hairsbreadth less effective, Davis is the only conductor on records to make use of the haunting cornet part in the Scene at the Ball. Similarly, he is the only conductor who sees fit to observe the all-important repeat in the opening section of the March to the Scaffold. The first three movements are superbly disciplined and the final two are as exciting as those of any Berlioz recording on the market today.

For a delightfully scatterbrained and thoroughly exhausting second opinion, consult Charles Munch's first Boston Symphony recording, reissued, with his equally madcap performance of the

Requiem, on a pair of RCA compact discs. Never one of the century's great disciplinarians—at his very first session with the orchestra, Munch cut the rehearsal short and invited such members of the orchestra who were so inclined to join him for a round of golf—he, like Beecham before him, believed that *under*rehearsal was the key to excitement and spontaneity. If the menacing, insanely driven performance of the Witches' Sabbath is any indication, he certainly had a point.

Les Troyens

> Lindholm, Veasey, Vickers, Glossop, Soyer, Orchestra and
> Chorus of the Royal Opera House, Covent Garden,
> Davis. Philips 416432-2 [CD].

Even though it has had its fair share of enthusiastic advocates—Sir Thomas Beecham was preparing a new production of it at the time of his death—Berlioz's elephantine opera in two parts, *The Trojans,* has always seemed to me to suffer from one of two possible flaws: it is either an hour too long or two hours too short. Part I is simply too brief to do justice to an event as fraught with possibilities as the Trojan War. The role of Cassandra, one of the most rewarding in the show, could stand to be twice again as long, as could the scenes involving Troy's royal family, who are given very short shrift. Perhaps Berlioz simply couldn't wait to get to Carthage and on with the *real* business of the opera, the romance of Dido and Aeneas, which did indeed yield some of the most inspired passages the composer would ever produce.

This quibble aside, the triumphant Philips recording ranks among the dozen or so supreme achievements in the history of the gramophone. With his uncanny, instinctive grasp of Berlioz's intentions, Sir Colin Davis tightens and clarifies the sprawling action to the point where we are almost persuaded we are listening to something as succinct and economical as *Salome* or *La Bohème.*

The cast, which could have included the incomparable Dido of Dame Janet Baker but didn't, is more than equal to the opera's formidable challenges, except, perhaps, for the Cassandra of Berit Lindholm, who sounds hard-pressed and uncomfortable much of the time. Josephine Veasey is a warm and winning Dido, and Jon Vickers's Aeneas is the stuff of legend, a worthy addition to his already storied Otello, Tristan, and Peter Grimes.

Originally released in the early 1970s, the recording was widely regarded as the outstanding entry in that flood of releases which accompanied the hundredth anniversary of the composer's death in 1969. Two decades later, it seems even more clearly the most significant Berlioz recording yet made.

Bernstein, Leonard

(1918–1990)

Chichester Psalms; Songfest

Vienna Youth Choir, Israel Philharmonic; Soloists, National Symphony, Bernstein. Deutsche Grammophon 415965-2 [CD].

Leonard Bernstein made no secret of the fact that he was rather embittered over the reception most of his music received. Apart from the apparently imperishable *Candide* Overture, none of his pieces established a serious foothold in the concert hall, and aside from the composer himself and a few of his friends, conductors have seemed reluctant to program Bernstein's music, however fine that music might be.

The *Chichester Psalms* and *Songfest,* written in 1965 and 1977 respectively, are among the most instantly affecting of Bernstein's compositions. The *Psalms*—jazzy, colorful, unpretentious, and devout—may well be the most important choral work yet written by an American; *Songfest* is a feverishly inventive orchestral song cycle which by all rights should *not* add up to more than the sum of its wantonly eclectic parts, but somehow, magically, does. The performances, it goes without saying, are definitive.

West Side Story

Te Kanawa, Carreras, Troyanos, Ollmann, Horne, Chorus and Orchestra, Bernstein. Deutsche Grammophon 415253-2 [CD], 415253-4 [T].

If there are any lingering doubts that *West Side Story* ranks with Gershwin's *Porgy and Bess* as one of the two greatest works of the American musical theater, this indispensable Deutsche Grammophon recording should go a long way toward dispelling them. While Bernstein may have written more important or more obviously "serious" works—the endlessly inventive Serenade for Violin, Strings, and Percussion and the deeply moving *Chichester Psalms* —it is this inspired transformation of Shakespeare's *Romeo and Juliet* that will probably outlast anything any American composer, except for Gershwin, has written before or since.

The controversial choice of José Carreras as Tony—and one quickly gets used to the dramatic incongruity of a Jet singing with a heavy Spanish accent—is far less problematic than the Maria of Dame Kiri Te Kanawa. As always, listening to that gorgeous instrument is an unalloyed pleasure, and, as always, she does little with it other than make an admittedly beautiful collection of sounds. (Compare her performance to that of the brilliant Marni Nixon—Natalie Wood's voice in the Robert Wise film—and you'll begin to hear just how emotionally and theatrically deficient Te Kanawa's interpretation is.)

The rest of the performances, especially the sly, earthy Anita of Tatiana Troyanos, are uniformly excellent, yet it is the composer's conducting that is the real revelation. Each of the numbers is infused with the last degree of depth, tenderness, and animal excitement, from the inspired poetry of the love music to the jazzy bravado of "Cool" and the great Quintet.

Even if you don't normally respond to Broadway musicals, don't worry: *West Side Story* is no more a mere Broadway musical than the Grand Canyon is a mere hole in the ground.

Berwald, Franz (1796–1868)

Symphony No. 1 in G minor, *Sérieuse;* Symphony No. 2 in D, *Capricieuse;* Symphony No. 3 in C, *Singulière;* Symphony No. 4 in E-flat, *Naïve*

Gothenburg Symphony, Järvi. Deutsche Grammophon 415502-2 [CD].

The next time you're in the mood for a Romantic symphony, but can't bear the thought of yet another dose of the Sibelius Second, Tchaikovsky's *Pathétique,* or anything else too well known or serious, the pleasant, unassuming symphonies of Franz Berwald might just do the trick. The first Scandinavian symphonist of any consequence, Berwald was a fine craftsman whose music owed much to that of his hero, Felix Mendelssohn. And though echoes of other voices—primarily those of Beethoven and Weber—can also be heard throughout his work, Berwald could often be modestly original, in a limited but altogether charming way.

Though the four Berwald symphonies have been recorded before, Neeme Järvi and the Gothenburg Symphony make the strongest case that has ever been made for them. Järvi takes a fresh, no-nonsense approach to the music, and the Gothenburgers, with their usual combination of flair and rigid discipline, waltz through these unfamiliar works as though they were cornerstones of the standard repertoire.

As a gift for the music lover who has practically everything, you can't go wrong with this—even if the gift is for yourself.

Bizet, Georges (1838–1875)

L'Arlésienne (incidental music); Symphony in C

Royal Philharmonic; French National Radio Orchestra, Beecham. Angel CDC-47794 [CD], 4AE-34476 [T].

After *Carmen* and the sadly neglected *Pearl Fishers* (one of the most hauntingly lovely of all French operas, but, alas, hamstrung by its relentlessly vapid and dippy text), the incidental music that Georges Bizet wrote for Alphonse Daudet's play *L'Arlésienne* is the most attractive and justly popular of all his theatrical scores.

No recording has ever made the *L'Arlésienne* music seem as colorful, original, or utterly fresh as that luminous miracle Sir Thomas Beecham taped with the Royal Philharmonic in the 1950s. As in his celebrated versions of Grieg's *Peer Gynt* and Rimsky-Korsakov's *Scheherazade*, Beecham's ability to rejuvenate and revitalize a warhorse remains uncanny. Each of the individual sections of the two *L'Arlésienne* suites emerges like a freshly restored painting: the rhythms are consistently infectious, the phrasing is pointed and always original, and as is so often the case in a Beecham recording, the solo winds are given a degree of interpretative freedom that no other major conductor would ever dare allow.

The same qualities dominate Beecham's performance of the composer's youthful C Major Symphony. While the playing of the French National Radio Orchestra is not quite up to the standard of the Royal Philharmonic, the octogenarian conductor's obvious affection and boyish enthusiasm easily make this the preferred recording of the piece.

Carmen

Stevens, Albanese, Peerce, Merrill, Robert Shaw Chorale, RCA Victor Orchestra, Reiner. RCA 7981-2-RG [CD].

Troyanos, Te Kanawa, Domingo, Van Dam, John Alldis Choir, London Philharmonic, Solti. London 414489-2 [CD], 414489-4 [T].

The Micaela is badly miscast, the Don José is stiff and uncomfortable, and the Escamillo, though he makes an impressive physical sound, is dramatically and emotionally flat. All of which begs the inevitable question, Why is the RCA *Carmen,* taped in the mid-1950s, one of the most thrilling operatic recordings ever made? The answer can be summed up in four words: Risë Stevens, Fritz Reiner.

The Metropolitan Opera's leading Carmen throughout the 1940s and for much of the 1950s—and in the opinion of many, the finest Carmen of the last half century—Stevens brought not only an unbelievably sexy voice to the role but a cunning sense of characterization that made Bizet's amoral cigarette maker a fascinating amalgam of grande dame, girl next door, and vicious, man-eating animal. Glimpses of the interpretation steamed up that otherwise wholesome family film classic *Going My Way,* and it still all but explodes from this historic recording.

If Stevens doesn't get much help from the other principals (the usually wonderful Licia Albanese is shockingly sour and whiny, and the always reliable Jan Peerce for once disappoints), then Fritz Reiner unleashes a flood of smoldering passion to match her own. Rumor has it that one opera lover actually managed to sit still through their whirlwind version of the Gypsy Dance; it was later discovered that he had succumbed during a performance of *Faust* on the previous evening.

Although the recorded sound has held up extremely well—especially in its CD resurrection—it might be too brittle and constricted for audiophiles. For them, the brilliant Solti recording remains the one to have. The highly publicized Jessye Norman recording for Philips is pretty grisly. Though the soprano sings well enough, her Carmen is slow, fussy, and overdone. In fact, for most of the time she sounds like one of the finalists for the Barbra Streisand Overenunciation Prize.

Carmen Suites

> **Montreal Symphony, Dutoit. London 417839-2 [CD],**
> **417839-4 [T].**

For those who prefer *Carmen*'s greatest hits without the singing—and someone did define opera as "that thing fat foreigners do until you get a headache"—Dutoit's suave and slinky performances of the Suites are easily the best around, with a very honorable mention going to the overripe but completely winning CBS recording Leopold Stokowski made while in his nineties (MYK-37260 [CD], MYT-37260 [T]). Both recordings also include the *L'Arlésienne* music; Dutoit's superlative account is possibly the best since Beecham's.

Les pêcheurs de perles

Hendricks, Aler, Quilico, Toulouse Capitole Orchestra and Chorus, Plasson. Angel CDCB-49837 [CD].

Except for the ravishing duet "Au fond du temple saint," which many of the greatest tenor-baritone combos of the century recorded in every language except Esperanto, neither history nor the recording studio has been very kind to *The Pearl Fishers*. In 1916 the Metropolitan mounted it with a dream cast headed by Frieda Hempel, Giuseppe de Luca, and Enrico Caruso. The production was a resounding failure and, with a couple of exceptions, International Big-Time Opera has ignored it ever since.

A decade ago, the New York City Opera unveiled a new production which proved beyond question that given half a chance, *The Pearl Fishers* will not only work but can make for a very rewarding evening. The performances featured City Opera's characteristically earnest but bargain-basement vocal talent, and some conducting from the late and greatly lamented Calvin Simmons that ranks with the finest I have ever heard in an opera house.

If this Angel recording won't convince everyone that *The Pearl Fishers* is a neglected masterpiece, then at very least it will win it some surprised and delighted friends. The best things in the production are the Leïla of Barbara Hendricks and the conducting of Michel Plasson. The soprano makes more than almost anyone could out of what may be the dizziest role since Pamina in Mozart's *Magic Flute,* and Plasson contributes an interpretation that is full of quiet insight while maintaining the long, uninterrupted line. If John Aler and Louis Quilico don't exactly efface the memory of Caruso and de Luca, Björling and Merrill, Domingo and Milnes, and the countless others who have recorded *the* duet, both sing admirably throughout.

Carmen lovers and/or the only slightly adventurous really should give this lovely little ball of fluff a try.

Bloch, Ernest (1880–1959)

Schelomo (Hebraic Rhapsody for Cello and Orchestra)

Harrell, cello; Concertgebouw Orchestra of Amsterdam, Haitink. London 414162-2 [CD].

Though Ernest Bloch's creative life spanned more than six decades, it is for the music the Swiss-born composer produced from about 1915 through the mid-1920s that he is best remembered, and rightly so. For the major works of Bloch's so-called Jewish Period—when he made a conscious attempt to give musical expression to "the complex, glowing, agitated Jewish soul"—contain some of the most expressive and individual music written by a twentieth-century composer.

Schelomo (Solomon), the Hebraic Rhapsody for Cello and Orchestra, has long remained Bloch's most popular and frequently recorded work. Gregor Piatigorsky left an impassioned account of this brooding, exotic piece in the 1950s, a recording that was joined by equally distinguished interpretations by János Starker and Mstislav Rostropovich.

On balance, this London recording by one of the best known of Piatigorsky's pupils, Lynn Harrell, comes closer to capturing the elusive essence of the exquisite Rhapsody than any performance has in years. Harrell, a player with vast technical resources, has had a habit of being needlessly restrained in his commercial recordings. In *Schelomo,* he follows the *un*restrained lead of his famous teacher with an interpretation in which passion and discipline are joined in almost perfect balance. As always, Bernard Haitink is an adroit and sympathetic accompanist and, as always, the Concertgebouw Orchestra sounds like what it may very well be: the greatest orchestra in the world.

Fortunately, Arabesque has begun releasing the Portland String Quartet's versions of the five quartets Bloch composed between 1916 and 1956. The recording of the somewhat Brahmsian First Quartet (Z-6543 [CD]) is a good introduction to a group of works that not only follows the composer's development over a forty-year period but also constitutes one of the undiscovered silver mines of twentieth-century chamber music.

Boccherini, Luigi (1743–1805)

Quintets (3) for Guitar and Strings, Op. 50

Pepe Romero, guitar; Academy Chamber Ensemble. Philips
420385-2 [CD].

The Italian cellist and composer Luigi Boccherini, who spent
his most productive years as court composer to the Infante Luis and
later King Carlos III of Spain, was in many ways the classical era's
answer to Georg Philipp Telemann: a greatly respected, fabulously
prolific composer—he wrote 102 quartets alone—whose civilized,
well-made music all sounds pretty much the same.

There are a few exceptions. His wildly popular "Ritirata notturna di Madrid"—a series of variations on the nightly retreat that
the city's military bands would play to call the soldiers back to the
barracks—was the eighteenth-century equivalent of "Stardust,"
and the minuet from his E Major String Quintet contains one of the
most famous tunes in musical history. (This is the music Alec Guinness and his band of desperadoes "played" in Mrs. Wilberforce's
upstairs room throughout the imperishable Ealing comedy *The Lady-
killers*.) Rather unbelievably, Boccherini's one lasting contribution
to Western civilization is now represented by only two recordings.

Among the more attractive and individual of Boccherini's
works are those several quintets he wrote for guitar and strings. In
them, the local color that the traditional Spanish instrument evokes
is handled with enormous skill and tact—don't expect any flamenco
fireworks or shouts of *Olé!*—and the three (Nos. 4, 5, and 6) that
Pepe Romero and members of the Academy Chamber Ensemble
present are among the composer's most appealing pieces.

The performances are flawless, as is the recorded sound.

Boito, Arrigo (1842–1918)

Mefistofele

Treigle, Caballé, Domingo, Ambrosian Opera Chorus,
London Symphony, Rudel. Angel CDCB-49522 [CD].

It is rare that a single performer, through the force of his or
her personality, will provoke a drastic reevaluation of a work that
had always been dismissed as unimportant or uninteresting. *Boris
Godunov* never made much of an impression outside Russia until
a lunatic named Chaliapin began terrifying audiences with it shortly
after the turn of the century; by the same token, most people were
probably persuaded that Boito's *Mefistofele* was little more than
souped-up, cut-rate Verdi until they saw and heard Norman Treigle
in the title role. And it was something to hear *and* to see: the lithe,
slight, almost painfully emaciated body of a consummate actor from
which that unimaginably cavernous, ink-black instrument would
rumble forth. On stage, the Treigle Mefistofele was one of the great
operatic experiences since the end of the war; on record, this indispensable Angel recording captures much of the Treigle miracle
intact.

This is also, by several light-years, the most persuasive recorded performance the opera has ever received. Another New York
City Opera alumnus, Placido Domingo, is nearly perfect as Faust,
and Montserrat Caballé is both alluring and dignified, keeping the
scooping and drooping to a bare minimum. Julius Rudel's contribution is only slightly less distinguished than Treigle's. The action
flows more easily than it ever has, giving the lie to the nonsense that
Mefistofele is a fatally episodic work, and in the thrilling choral
passages—the celebrated "Prologue in Heaven" and in the opera's
finale—Rudel musters a collection of sounds that Verdi would have
been proud to have included in his Requiem.

Borodin, Alexander

(1833–1887)

Prince Igor: Overture, *Polovtsian Dances*

London Symphony, Solti. London 417689-2 [CD].

Boston Pops, Fiedler. Victrola 7813-4-RV [T].

The most ecstatic of all recordings of the familiar *Prince Igor* overture and *Polovtsian Dances,* an Angel recording from the early 1960s by the Philharmonia Orchestra conducted by Lovro von Matačič (available for a time on the Quintessence label), is, alas, no longer in print. Should the performance ever surface again, or should you come across it in the LP cutout bins, buy at least a half dozen copies: three for yourself, and three to lend out to friends. (If your friends are like mine, you'll never see the records again.)

Nearly as arresting as the Matačič were those versions Sir Georg Solti recorded with the London Symphony, out now on one of those hypercheap London Weekend Classics CDs. With a hell-for-leather dash through Glinka's *Russlan and Ludmilla* Overture and a bone-chilling reading of Mussorgsky's *Night on Bald Mountain,* this is one of the finest of all Solti recordings and a rather melancholy reminder of a what a dull, housebroken musician he has since become.

Among available tapes, the performances by Arthur Fiedler and the Boston Pops, in a handsome package of Russian orchestral showpieces, are more than competitive with the best on the market today.

String Quartets No. 1 in A; No. 2 in D

Borodin Quartet. Angel CDC-47795 [CD].

Alexander Borodin was without question the greatest composer in history who was also a chemist. After his dipsomaniacal, atrabilious friend Modest Mussorgsky, he was the most original of that group of Russian composers who came to be known as "The

Mighty Five," and like Mussorgsky, he left much important music unfinished at the time of his death. A true weekend composer, Borodin spent decades putzing around with his masterpiece, *Prince Igor,* which had to be wrestled into performing shape by Rimsky-Korsakov. (Borodin never bothered to write the Overture down; fortunately, Rimsky's pupil Alexander Glazunov had heard him play it so often that he was able to reconstruct it from memory.)

Among the works that Borodin *did* manage to complete, the String Quartets rank very high in his canon; the lesser-known A Major Quartet is full of energy and invention, and the familiar D Major Quartet is one of the most justly popular of all Russian chamber works—made all the more so by the famous Nocturne, which has enjoyed a life of its own as a freestanding concert piece and by a couple of tunes that eventually found their way into the Broadway musical *Kismet.*

In their most recent recording, the Borodin Quartet give both works unusually thoughtful, natural-sounding interpretations, as though their eponym had actually written the music specifically for them. The playing is relaxed and efficient, with results that are deeply Romantic without ever becoming self-indulgent.

A tape of the two quartets together cannot currently be had for love or money, but an equally fine performance of the D Major by the Emerson Quartet is available from Book-of-the-Month Club Records (21-7526 [CD], 11-7525 [T]). The good news is that the recording is every bit the equal of the Borodins'. The bad news is that it can only be had as part of a four-CD or three-tape set called "The Great Romantic Quartets." The *best* news is that their versions of the popular quartets of Ravel, Debussy, Dvořák, Smetana, Schumann, Tchaikovsky, and Brahms are among the finest ever recorded.

Symphony No. 2 in B minor

L'Orchestre de la Suisse Romande, Ansermet. London
430219-2 [CD], 430219-4 [T].

Why a completely memorable performance in up-to-date sound of one of the most justly popular of all Russian symphonies cannot be had remains a frustrating mystery. Each of the nine readily available recordings of the marvelous work is plagued with problems, from the ponderous but beautifully recorded version by Valéry Gergiev for Philips to the fairly ridiculous effort by the Ljubljana (!) Symphony for Stradivari.

As an *interpretation,* the most satisfying of all is Ernest Ansermet's recording for London. Dating from the early days of stereo, the sound is now uncomfortably brittle and tubby. And while the conductor always managed to do wonders with his plucky radio orchestra, the strings were thin and edgy, the horns crooned like saxophones, and the woodwinds often resembled a plate of overcooked string beans. Still, the performance itself surges with life and romance, and for six bucks, what do you expect?

Boyce, William (1710–1779)

Symphonies (8)

English Concert, Pinnock. Deutsche Grammophone 419631-2 [CD].

William Boyce found himself in the unenviable position of being a native-born English composer at a time when the English musical scene was completely dominated by a Saxon immigrant named George Frideric Handel. Like his near-contemporary Thomas Augustine Arne, the composer of a masque named *Alfred* which contained a fairly memorable ditty called "Rule, Britannia," Boyce spent his career in Handel's immense shadow, apparently without bitterness or regret. A friend said of him, "A more modest man than Dr. Boyce I have never known. I never heard him speak a vain or ill-natured word, either to exalt himself or to deprecate another."

Thanks to the '60s Baroque Boom, the eight tiny "symphonies" Boyce composed have enjoyed a considerable vogue on records. All are gems in their way, full of wit, emotion, and imagination, and—if nothing else—they prove that *something* was happening in homegrown English music between Purcell and Elgar apart from *The Beggar's Opera* and Gilbert and Sullivan.

The period-instrument recording by Trevor Pinnock and the English Concert is an undiluted joy. The Symphonies emerge as the work of not only an important talent, but of an uncommonly healthy, intensely likable man. The best are as full of life as Handel's better concerti grossi, and if you have yet to make the acquaintance of the good Dr. Boyce, here is an ideal opportunity.

Brahms, Johannes (1833–1897)

Alto Rhapsody; *Begräbnisgesang; Nänie; Gesang der Parzen*

> **Hodgson, mezzo-soprano; Bavarian Radio Orchestra and Chorus, Haitink. Orfeo C-025821 [CD].**

The Alto Rhapsody, the best loved of Brahms's choral works after *A German Requiem*, was easily the most peculiar wedding present ever given to anyone. The composer bestowed this fretful, stygian work on Julie Schumann, the daughter of Robert and Clara, a girl he himself had hoped to marry, but of course never would. (Brahms was never able to maintain anything approaching a normal romantic relationship. From his youth, spent playing the piano in the bordellos of Hamburg's red-light district, he developed a life-long dependence on prostitutes that made love with "ordinary" women impossible.)

This handsome Orfeo recording combines an eloquent version of the Rhapsody with three beautifully sung performances of other Brahms choral pieces, including the rarely heard *Gesang der Parzen* (Song of the Fates) and *Begräbnisgesang* (Funeral Ode). The British mezzo Alfreda Hodgson has a voice whose sable resonance frequently recalls that of her great compatriot Kathleen Ferrier. Bernard Haitink, for years a superlative Brahmsian, brings his usual virtues to all the performances: The emotions are carefully controlled but never bullied; there is passion aplenty but nothing is overstated or overdone. Now that he has been succeeded as music director of the Concertgebouw Orchestra of Amsterdam by Riccardo Chailly, who is as accomplished as the average truck driver, except for the fact that he can't drive a truck, let's hope Haitink will assume the post of Permanent Guest Conductor of the World.

Concerto No. 1 in D minor for Piano and Orchestra

R. Serkin, piano; Cleveland Orchestra, Szell. CBS MYK-37803 [CD], MYT-37803 [T].

To many, Brahms's early D minor Piano Concerto has always seemed less a concerto than a large, turbulent orchestral work with a very significant piano obbligato appended almost as an afterthought. The feeling is more than understandable, for the Concerto actually grew out of discarded materials for a projected D minor symphony that the composer could not bring himself to complete. (For more than half his creative life, Brahms was constantly on the lookout for ways of making symphonic noises without actually having to produce that dreaded First Symphony. Sadly, his morbid fear of the inevitable comparison with Beethoven delayed its composition until he was well past forty.)

For more than twenty years no recording has fought more ferociously for the Concerto's identity *as* a concerto than the explosive and poetic performance of Rudolf Serkin and George Szell. Serkin's playing in this famous recording is magisterial, delicate, and shatteringly powerful—qualities that made him as effective in the music of Mozart as he was in the works of Liszt.

George Szell, in one of the best of his Cleveland recordings, provides a muscular and exciting backdrop for his old friend. The playing of the Cleveland Orchestra is above criticism, and the digitally remastered sound is superb.

Concerto No. 2 in B-flat for Piano and Orchestra

Gilels, piano; Chicago Symphony, Reiner. RCA 60536-2 [CD], 60536-4 [T].

For most of his distinguished and rewarding career, Emil Gilels was known unfairly as "The Other Russian," a man condemned to live out his entire professional life under the enormous shadow cast by his great contemporary Sviatoslav Richter. While Gilels may have lacked his friend's charisma—a short, stocky, unpretentious man, he was the very image of a third assistant secretary in the Ministry of Textiles—he was a formidable musician whose playing matched Richter's in its depth and intensity, even if it lacked the last fraction of a percentage point of that unapproachable technique.

Gilels's final recording of the Brahms B-flat Concerto made with Eugen Jochum and the Berlin Philharmonic in the 1970s is in every way exceptional, but it is the Chicago recording, made a decade before, that captures his immense talents at their absolute best. As in all of his finest and most characteristic performances, Gilels's interpretation, while completely unmannered, is also possessed of a unique power and panache. No recorded performance of the Scherzo communicates half of this one's driven assurance or feverish pain, and the finale is played with such a natural and unaffected charm that for once it is not the anticlimax it can frequently be.

Fritz Reiner proved to be an ideal partner in this music: generous, sensitive, and deferential, yet never afraid of showing off a little power and panache of his own. And even if in its sonic face-lift the recorded sound remains a trifle thin and shrill, this is a trivial flaw in one of the most flawless concerto recordings ever made.

Concerto in D for Violin and Orchestra

> Kreisler, violin; Berlin State Opera Orchestra, Blech. Music and Arts CD-290 [CD].

> Perlman, violin; Chicago Symphony, Giulini. Angel CDC-47166 [CD], 4XS-37286 [T].

When I am packing up the trunk of recordings to haul off to that mythic desert island—though since my mother didn't raise a fool, the island I'll probably pack myself off to is Maui—Fritz Kreisler's 1929 version of the Brahms Concerto will probably be put close to the top of the stack. While not the most perfect recording the Concerto has ever received, this is far and away the noblest and most inspiring. In the sweep of its patrician phrasing, melting lyricism, and hell-for-leather audacity, this is as close as we will ever come to a Brahms Violin Concerto from the horse's mouth. (It should be remembered that for a time in the 1880s, one of Kreisler's Viennese neighbors was the composer himself.)

Among modern recordings of the Concerto, none is more completely engaging than Itzhak Perlman's with Carlo Maria Giulini and the Chicago Symphony. Perlman is a spiritual descendant of Kreisler: a wonderful exponent of Kreisler's own music, he also plays with that indescribable, untranslatable quality the Viennese call, in its closest, but very approximate, English equivalent, "beautiful dirt." This is a dark, luxurious Brahms Concerto cut from the same cloth as Kreisler's, but one in which the modern preoccupation with technical perfection also makes itself felt. In short, it sounds very much like the kind of performance one would give almost anything to hear: one in which Heifetz's iron fingers were guided by Kreisler's golden heart.

Concerto in A minor for Violin, Cello, and Orchestra

> Francescatti, violin; Fournier, cello; Columbia Symphony, Walter. CBS MK-42024 [CD].

With the classic Angel recording by David Oistrakh, Mstislav Rostropovich, George Szell, and the Cleveland Orchestra now inexplicably out of print, the pickings among available recordings of the Double Concerto are surprisingly slim. Until that very special performance returns to the catalog (it was one of the final commercial recordings Szell would ever make), the Francescatti-Fournier-Walter version will have to do. Apart from some occasionally wayward contributions from the violinist, the performance is actually a very strong one: the splendid Pierre Fournier is as polished and virile as always, and Bruno Walter, whose attention seems to wander from time to time, nevertheless inspires some rich and spirited playing, especially from the Columbia Symphony strings.

A fine tape of an earlier Oistrakh recording with Fournier, the Philharmonia Orchestra, and Alceo Galliera is now available from Angel (4LZ-62854).

Ein deutsches Requiem

> Schwarzkopf, soprano; Fischer-Dieskau, baritone; Philharmonia Orchestra and Chorus, Klemperer. Angel CDC-47238 [CD].

In one of the first of his incontestable masterworks, Brahms produced what remains the most gently consoling of all the great Requiems: a work which seems to tell us, with the utmost civility and compassion, that dying is neither the most frightening nor the most terrible thing a human being can do.

Since it was first released in the 1960s, Otto Klemperer's otherworldly recording has cast all others in the shade. Along with the characteristic breadth and depth he brings to the interpretation, the frail but indomitable conductor also projects such a moving degree of fragile tenderness that the performance will quietly, but firmly, tear your heart out by the roots. Neither of the soloists ever made a more beautiful recording, and the singing of the Wilhelm Pitz–trained Philharmonia Chorus remains an enduring monument to the greatest choral director of his time.

Hungarian Dances (21)

Leipzig Gewandhaus Orchestra, Masur. Philips 411426-2 [CD].

Katia and Marielle Labèque, pianos. Philips 416459-2 [CD].

After Brahms settled permanently in Vienna in 1862, his life was completely uneventful. Aside from several concert tours and summer holidays to the Austrian lakes and to Italy, his daily routine consisted of composition and those twice-daily trips to the Red Hedgehog, a coffeehouse where he caroused with his artistic cronies and from which he would set off for his regular assignations with the city's ladies of the night. He had no hobbies, and his idea of relaxation consisted of making arrangements of German folk songs for various combinations of voices and turning out trifles like the popular Hungarian Dances.

A serious and, on occasion, somewhat stolid conductor, Kurt Masur leads the Leipzig Gewandhaus Orchestra through a sparkling tour of these magical works. Here, the Leipzig winds play with as much character as those of any orchestra in Europe, and the strings gush with an authentic gypsy flair.

For the Dances as originally written for piano four-hands, the version by the Labècque sisters is without equal. The Labècques are so glamorous and have been hyped so mercilessly that we tend to forget what absolutely thrilling musicians they are.

A London CD (417696-2) features the surprisingly schmaltzy performances of eight of the Dances that Fritz Reiner recorded with the Vienna Philharmonic in the early 1960s, together with some equally affectionate versions of a handful of the Slavonic Dances by Dvořák.

Liebeslieder Waltzes

Los Angeles Vocal Arts Ensemble; Guzelimian, Herrera, pianos. Nonesuch 79008-2 [CD], 79008-4 [T].

One of the few musical issues about which Brahms and Wagner were in perfect agreement was their admiration for the music of Johann Strauss. The irresistible lilt of the Waltz King's music may have actually influenced Wagner in the seductive Flower Maidens scene from *Parsifal*, and it can certainly be felt in the two sets of *Liebeslieder* Waltzes that Brahms composed under the spell of his famous Viennese neighbor.

No recording of these irresistible but formidably difficult works has ever captured more of their freshness or sheer inventiveness than this one by the Los Angeles Vocal Arts Ensemble. Musically and vocally, the performances are all but flawless, with the singers missing none of the music's sheer joy or romance (and few of its nuances) and the pianists offering some exceedingly deft support.

Piano Music: Two Rhapsodies, Op. 79; Three Intermezzi, Op. 117; Six Pieces, Op. 118; Four Pieces, Op. 119

Lupu, piano. London 417599-2 [CD].

When the Romanian pianist Radu Lupu first arrived on the scene in the late 1960s, I must admit I heaved an enormous yawn at the prospect of yet *another* oppressed victim of Communism seeking artistic freedom—to say nothing of a few bucks here and there—in the West. These were the days when overzealous press agents were hailing that ham-fisted oaf Lazar Berman as the "new Horowitz"—a process which has continued even into the age of *glasnost* with the storm of nonsense generated over the very modestly equipped Vladimir Feltsman.

Lupu, as everyone quickly discovered, was something quite different: an inquisitive, deeply spiritual pianist whose playing reminded many of that other incomparable Romanian, Dinu Lipatti. Although over the last two decades Lupu has made comparatively few commercial recordings, each of them has been something of a milestone: witness this extraordinary series of late Brahms piano works, originally recorded in 1971.

No living pianist—and only a handful from the past—can rival either the depth or the intensity of Lupu's performances. When he is at his best, as he clearly is here, there is also a wonderfully paradoxical quality in the playing which suggests that every detail has been worked out ahead of time *and* that he is making it all up as he goes along: a kind of "interpretation" which frequently crosses that thin dividing line into active creation, without doing any disservice to the composer or his work.

No one who loves Brahms or great piano playing will fail to be moved.

Piano Quartets: in G minor, Op. 25; in A, Op. 26; in C minor, Op. 60

Domus. Virgin Classics VC-790709-2 [CD], VC-790709-4 [T] (Opp. 25 and 60); VC-790739-2 [CD] (Op. 26).

It was with his first two Piano Quartets that the twenty-eight-year-old Brahms introduced himself to Viennese musical society in 1861. The debut was auspicious and, for the composer, rather unnerving: On the strength of these pieces, one of the city's leading critics dubbed him "Beethoven's heir," an honor and curse that would haunt him the rest of his life. The early Piano Quartets were Brahms's first important chamber works and, with the stormy C minor String Quartet that followed three years later, they remain pillars of Romantic chamber music.

The group calling itself Domus is one of many young ensembles adding fuel to the argument that as far as chamber music performance is concerned, we may be passing through a new Golden Age. Technically, they are completely seamless, as we have automatically come to expect; musically, they show as much poise and savvy as any of the finest chamber groups in the world today. In the tempestuous finale of Op. 25, for instance, they play with a wild, fearless abandon, yet in the more somber moments of Op. 60, they probe the rueful depths of the composer's heart in a way that would make a thoracic surgeon gasp.

The Op. 26 is coupled with the very Brahmsian Piano Quartet Movement that the teenage Gustav Mahler composed during his Vienna Conservatory days; these two generously packed CDs set a standard in this music that's going to be very difficult to match.

Piano Quartet in G minor, Op. 25 (orchestrated by Arnold Schoenberg)

City of Birmingham Symphony, Rattle. Angel CDCB-47300 [CD].

Suddenly and for no apparent reason—other than the obvious explanation that conductors and recording companies are belatedly discovering what a tremendously entertaining and marketable work it is—there are now *five* excellent modern versions of Arnold Schoenberg's inspired orchestration of Brahms's G minor Piano Quartet. Arguing that in all the performances he had ever heard the piano part always overbalanced the strings, Schoenberg produced what has been called with some justification "The Brahms Fifth": an imaginative and for the most part utterly faithful adaptation of one of Brahms's most colorful chamber works.

While the recent recordings by Sergiu Comissiona and the Baltimore Symphony and the London Philharmonic led by Gennady Rozhdestvensky are exceptionally fine, it is Simon Rattle's gleaming Angel performance that is the most polished and effervescent of all.

For the most convincing reading of the Quartet as it was actually composed, the Virgin Classics recording by Domus (see above) continues to lead the field. (I blush to confess that because I first learned the Quartet through Robert Craft's old Chicago Symphony recording of the Schoenberg orchestration, the original version has always seemed slightly pale. In fact, the finale never sounds completely right without that wildly incongruous xylophone.)

Piano Sonatas (3)

Zimerman, piano. Deutsche Grammophon 423401-2 [CD].

At the time Brahms composed his youthful Piano Sonatas, he was already demonstrating what an unusual Romantic he was. Few composers of his generation concerned themselves with anything so cumbersome and outmoded as the sonata: for the young Romantics, the short, lyrical "musical moment" was the favored form of communication. It was Schumann who first recognized the yearning for symphonic expression inherent in these turbulent works, calling them "veiled symphonies," and it was the composer's performance of one of them that led to the famous entry in Schumann's diary, "Brahms to see me, a genius."

Krystian Zimerman is an ideal champion of these often problematic works. He brings a commanding intelligence to bear on their structural challenges—they seem more coherent and closely argued than they ever have before—together with a winning amalgam of exuberant power and melting warmth. The same qualities can be heard in his performance of the four *Ballades*, Op. 10, which make for a very attractive bonus.

Quintet in B minor for Clarinet and Strings

Shifrin, clarinet; Chamber Music Northwest. Delos DE-3066 [CD].

Zukovsky, clarinet; Sequoia Quartet. Nonesuch 79105-4 [T].

Although the two clarinet sonatas and the *Four Serious Songs* were Brahms's actual valedictory, no composer ever wrote a more breathtakingly beautiful farewell than the slow movement of the Clarinet Quintet. In it, Brahms's celebrated mood of "autumnal melancholy" can be heard at its most burnished and wistful.

Either of these haunting recordings has a fair claim to being the best currently available. In the opinion of many, David Shifrin might well be the finest clarinetist alive. His fingers are as nimble as anyone's and he plays with a tone the size of a four-bedroom house. His musical personality is a combination of heroic swagger and melting sensitivity, both of which are heard to special advantage in this great work.

Michele Zukovsky, the sterling principal clarinetist of the Los Angeles Philharmonic, turns in a performance that is perhaps a shade less exciting, but every bit as lovely. The Nonesuch tape is also a bittersweet reminder of the art of the now-disbanded Sequoia Quartet.

Serenades: No. 1 in D; No. 2 in A

London Symphony, Kertész. London 412628-2 [CD].

Brahms at his most relaxed, joyous, and lyrical in performances that will wash over you like the first spring rain. Superlatives fail me. *Buy* this one.

String Quartets (3)

Melos Quartet. Deutsche Grammophon 423670-2 [CD].

As with the symphonies, the relative dearth of Brahms string quartets was the direct result of his festering Beethovenphobia, that debilitating fear of following his god and hero into any form the master had made his own. Brahms did not complete the C minor Quartet—cast, significantly, in the same key as his First Symphony—until sixteen years after he first sketched it. As with the Second Symphony, the A minor Quartet followed almost immediately, and the series ended abruptly a few years later with the B-flat Major Quartet, Op. 67. Like the symphonies, each of the Quartets is the work of a mature and confident master, and no two are even remotely alike: No. 1 somber and turbulent, No. 2 tender, graceful, elegiac, and No. 3 whimsical and good-natured.

Although finer individual interpretations of each of the three do exist—the Emerson Quartet's tumultuous recording of the C minor (Book-of-the-Month Club Records 21-7526 [CD], 11-7525 [T]) and a glowing version of the A minor by the Gabrieli Quartet (Chandos CHAN-8562 [CD])—the cycle by the Melos Quartet of Stuttgart is as rewarding as it is convenient. Further, it comes with the added bonus of all the Schumann quartets in performances that are equally crisp, dramatic, and sympathetic, if a bit tight-lipped and literal. While not an ideal choice, this is probably the *best* choice in repertoire that is shockingly underrecorded.

String Sextets (2)

Raphael Ensemble. Hyperion CDA-66276 [CD], KA-66276 [T].

Given their scope, charm, and elegance, it has always been a little surprising that Brahms's two wonderful String Sextets have not been more popular. They are among the most ingratiating and symphonic of all his chamber works and inspired a largely self-taught twenty-six-year-old composer named Arnold Schoenberg to write a string sextet of his own called *Verklärte Nacht*.

The Sextets have probably never been served more handsomely than by this beautiful recording by the Raphael Ensemble. While no subtlety of surface detail or inner voicing escapes their attention, it is their response to the Romantic sweep of the music that ultimately carries the listener away.

Would that the Raphaels would now turn their attention to the ravishing String Quintets, which are ably—if not unforgettably—represented by a sturdy Nonesuch recording (79068-2 [CD], 79068-4 [T]), featuring the Boston Symphony Chamber Players.

Symphony No. 1 in C minor

Columbia Symphony, Walter. Odyssey MBK-44827 [CD], YT-30311 [T].

Berlin Philharmonic, Furtwängler. Deutsche Grammophon 427402-2 [CD].

Even though Otto Klemperer's titanic recording from the early 1960s has returned on an Angel compact disc (CDM-69651), Klemperer still faces some formidable competition from his old friend Bruno Walter, whose final recording of the Brahms First Symphony was made at about the same time.

Walter's 1936 Vienna Philharmonic recording was one of the great glories of the 78 era: lithe, sinewy, and intensely passionate, it was every bit the dramatic equal of Arturo Toscanini's famous interpretation, while investing the music with an expressive freedom of which the Italian maestro scarcely could have dreamed.

Although Walter was well past eighty when the Columbia Symphony recording was made, there is no hint of diminished concentration in the performance; if anything, the first movement unfolds with such searing intensity that we are almost forced to wonder what the elderly conductor had for breakfast that day. Although, as usual, Walter is without peer in the Symphony's gentler passages, the great theme of the final movement rolls out with an unparalleled sweetness and dignity, and the performance concludes in a blaze of triumph.

While Wilhelm Furtwängler's live 1952 Berlin Philharmonic performance may not be the ideal Brahms First for day-to-day use—the sound is both boxy and uncomfortably tubby—the energy, willfulness, and withering power of the performance have never been surpassed.

Symphony No. 2 in D

Vienna Philharmonic, Bernstein. Deutsche Grammophon 410082-2 [CD].

Recorded live in Vienna in 1983 as part of a larger Brahms cycle, Leonard Bernstein's performance of the composer's sunniest symphony is the most invigorating since Sir Thomas Beecham's. The general mood is one of relaxed expansiveness, and while tempos tend to be on the leisurely side, the phrasing and rhythms never even threaten to become lethargic or slack. Which is not to say that the familiar Bernstein fire is not available at the flick of a baton: the finale crackles with electricity and ends with a deafening roar of the incomparable Vienna Philharmonic trombones.

As a bonus, the recording includes a performance of the *Academic Festival Overture* whose sly humor and rambunctious good spirits are all but impossible to resist. Among the current crop of tapes, George Szell's hyperkinetic CBS recording (MYT-37776) is a clear first choice.

Symphony No. 3 in F

Columbia Symphony, Walter. CBS MK-42022 [CD], Odyssey YT-32225 [T].

Cleveland Orchestra, Szell. CBS MYK-37777 [CD], MYT-37777 [T].

All the qualities that make Walter's recording of the First so special can be heard in even greater abundance in his version of Brahms's most concise and original symphony. If you have the chance to audition the recording before you buy it, listen to the last three minutes. For in this daring coda—which marked the first time an important symphony ended on a quiet note—Walter is so ineffably gentle that those three magical minutes should be more than sufficient to make the sale. An equally warmhearted account of the *Variations on a Theme by Haydn* fills out this unusually generous and irresistibly attractive compact disc.

George Szell's stunning Cleveland Orchestra recording runs Walter a very close second. The recorded sound and playing are both superior, and the performances shine with the typical Szell gloss. An even more impassioned Szell interpretation with the Concertgebouw Orchestra of Amsterdam (in perfectly acceptable 1951 mono sound) is now available on London (425994-2 [CD]), coupled with their legendary recording of the Dvořák Eighth.

Symphony No. 4 in E minor

Royal Philharmonic, Reiner. Chesky CD-6 [CD].

Vienna Philharmonic, C. Kleiber. Deutsche Grammophon 400037-2 [CD].

In spite of formidable competition from Bernstein, Walter, Klemperer, and the always provocative Carlos Kleiber—whose stunning Deutsche Grammophon recording is perhaps the most impressive of those that are relatively easy to find—the recent release of this Reiner version from the small Chesky Records label preserves one of the loveliest Brahms symphony recordings ever made. Available for a time on Quintessence, the performance was originally recorded for—are you ready for this?—one of those omnibus, great-music-for-us-just-plain-folks collections produced by the *Reader's Digest.*

At the playback that followed the recording sessions, Reiner was quoted as saying, "This is the most beautiful recording I have ever made," and many have been tempted to agree. Wisely, Reiner chose to capitalize on the particular strengths of the Royal Philharmonic, without trying to turn them into a British carbon copy of his own Chicago Symphony. From a string section that produced a sound at once darker and less perfectly homogenized than what he was used to in Chicago, Reiner coaxed the aural equivalent of a carpet made of Russian sable. While their playing in the second movement is especially memorable, the contributions of the woodwinds and brass are equally outstanding. (At the time the recording was made, the orchestra was still, in essence, Sir Thomas Beecham's Royal Philharmonic, which is to say as fine a collection of individual soloists as any orchestra in Europe could boast.)

As an interpretation, this Brahms Fourth is vintage Reiner: tautly disciplined yet paradoxically Romantic. The outer movements are brisk and wonderfully detailed, and the recording of the energetic third movement is probably the most viscerally exciting yet made.

On tape, Angel is offering a generous pairing of the Fourth and Second Symphonies in those heroic Philharmonia Orchestra performances led by Otto Klemperer (4AE-34413).

Trio in E-flat for Horn, Violin, and Piano

> Tuckwell, horn; Perlman, violin; Ashkenazy, piano. London 414128-2 [CD].
>
> Boston Symphony Chamber Players. Nonesuch 79076-4 [T].

Like Aubrey Brain and his brilliant but tragically short-lived son, who was killed in his favorite sports car while rushing home from a concert at the 1957 Edinburgh Festival, Barry Tuckwell, for more than a quarter of a century, has been living proof of the unwritten law that says the world's foremost horn player must be an Englishman. As the longtime principal horn of the London Symphony, and throughout an equally distinguished solo career, Tuckwell has proved to be the only horn player of the last thirty years whose artistry has been compared favorably with that of the legendary Dennis Brain.

Tuckwell's impeccable recording of the Brahms Horn Trio dates from 1969, or from roughly that period when he began his ascendancy as the preeminent horn player of his time. From a purely technical standpoint, the playing is as flawless as horn playing can possibly be. Add to that a rich, singing tone, a musical personality which is a winning blend of sensitivity and swagger, and the immaculate performances of his two famous colleagues, and we're left with a recording of the Brahms Horn Trio that will probably not be bettered for a generation.

The fine performance on Nonesuch by members of the Boston Symphony Chamber Players can be considered competitive *only* if you have failed to acquire a compact disc player.

Trios (3) for Piano, Violin, and Cello

> Golub, piano; Kaplan, violin; Carr, cello. Arabesque Z-6607/8 [CD].

When Clara Schumann heard Brahms's B Major Trio for the first time, she found fault with everything, especially the opening movement. Bursting with confidence as usual, the composer withdrew the piece, revising it entirely thirty-seven years later. If Brahms—or anyone else—ever wrote a more beautifully poignant theme than the one that begins the Trio, it has yet to be heard. All three of the Trios, for that matter, are full of extravagantly lovely moments, in which a youthful enthusiasm vies with a mature resignation in that mood of ineffable sadness which was this composer's alone.

The Trios have enjoyed some superb recordings over the years, by the Beaux Arts and Borodin Trios, and by an ad hoc dream ensemble made up of the American pianist and Brahms specialist Julius Katchen, cellist János Starker, and violinist Josef Suk, whose London recordings (421152-2 [CD], 425423-2 [CD]) remain singularly moving. And yet for all the wonders contained in those and other famous interpretations—Rubinstein-Szeryng-Fournier; Fischer-Schneiderhan-Mainardi; Istomin-Menuhin-Casals—the Arabesque recording by three young American kids shoots to the very top of the list.

Individually, pianist David Golub, violinist Mark Kaplan, and cellist Colin Carr are all world-class virtuosos poised on what will undoubtedly be major solo careers; as a trio, they have few—if any—equals. As in their superlative recording of the Schubert trios (see page 367), they demonstrate that they have already learned the secret of great chamber-music playing: the ability to function as a single well-oiled unit without losing any of their individual identities. The performances are fresh, warmhearted, audacious, lyrical, and dramatic, depending on the demands of the piece, but above all they are supremely musical, without so much as a single false or unnatural-sounding step.

Not to be missed.

Triumphlied for Chorus and Orchestra

Prague Philharmonic Chorus, Czech Philharmonic
Orchestra, Sinopoli. Deutsche Grammophon 435066-2
[CD].

There is a variety of party record that I have never been able to resist. (A "party record" is precisely what the phrase suggests:

something you whip out at a party to amuse, amaze, or completely befuddle your musical friends.) While a friend of mine in San Francisco is an enthusiastic devotee of the game in which a recording is played backward and to win, you must name not just the work but the specific *performance,* my own, far more plebeian tastes run to the time-honored Guess Who Wrote *This* quiz.

Brahms's occasional work *Triumphlied* (Song of Triumph)— the only positive thing to have emerged from the Franco-Prussian War—is my current favorite: Arnold Schoenberg's early D Major Quartet, with its echoes of Schubert and Dvořák, is simply becoming too well known. Not only would you never guess that this buoyant, joyous, unbuttoned piece had actually been written by Johannes Brahms, but also—when it's lost its party shock value— you're left with an important and engaging twenty-five minutes, for this virtually unknown choral work is a masterpiece of its kind. Giuseppe Sinopoli and his forces, in *Triumphlied*'s world premiere recording, give the work a terrific send-off, but I have the feeling that this is only the first of many fine recordings to come.

Variations on a Theme by Haydn

Columbia Symphony, Walter. CBS MK-42022 [CD], Odyssey YT-30851 [T].

If I've managed to talk you into buying Bruno Walter's stellar recording of the Brahms Third Symphony, you have this richly various version of the *Haydn Variations* already (if you bought the CD, not the tape). Wasn't that easy?

Bridge, Frank (1879–1941)

The Sea

Ulster Orchestra, Handley. Chandos CHAN-8473 [CD].

To the present day, this gifted English composer is principally known as the teacher of Benjamin Britten. In fact, for decades after his death his name was largely kept alive by that famous pupil's act of homage, the *Variations on a Theme of Frank Bridge*. As the world has belatedly begun to recognize, Bridge was one of the most individual English composers of his generation, a nature poet whose finest inspirations rank with those of Frederick Delius. His voice, if not always unique, is utterly distinctive: clearheaded, manly, subtle, with few obvious echoes of any music other than his own.

His most celebrated orchestral score, *The Sea*, is not only one of the most vividly colorful ever produced by an Englishman, it is one that can be favorably compared with *La Mer* by Debussy. Vernon Handley and the Ulster Orchestra give it a thrilling and sumptuous send-off, and the recording is rounded out by two other splendid British seascapes: Britten's *Four Sea Interludes* from *Peter Grimes* and *On the Sea Shore* by Sir Arnold Bax.

Britten, Benjamin
(Lord Britten of Aldeburgh) (1913–1976)

Billy Budd

Pears, Glossop, Shirley-Quirk, Luxon, Langdon, Brannigan,
Ambrosian Opera Chorus, London Symphony, Britten.
London 417428-2 [CD].

Even counting *Death in Venice,* with its explicitly homoerotic
theme, *Billy Budd* is in many ways the most daring of Benjamin
Britten's operas. For one thing, Herman Melville's parable of good
and evil on the high seas would seem far too top-heavy with sym-
bolism to make for successful dramatic—to say nothing of
operatic—treatment; for another, since it *is* set on a British man-
o'-war, the cast is confined entirely to men. Asking an audience to
sit through what might have been a waterlogged, black-and-white
morality play is one thing; asking them to sit for more than two
hours without hearing a single female voice is quite another.

In spite or perhaps because of these limitations, what Britten
delivers with *Billy Budd* might just be his most important opera
after *Peter Grimes:* a kind of all-male English *Otello* with the mood
and scent of Wagner's *Flying Dutchman.* Among Britten's other
stage works, only *A Midsummer Night's Dream* can rival *Budd*'s
musical inventiveness and imagination, and in Captain Vere, the
essentially good and decent man trapped in an impossible moral
dilemma, Britten may have created his single most memorable
character.

As Vere, Sir Peter Pears gives one of the great performances
of his career in this not-to-be-missed recording. But then again, under the composer's sharply disciplined yet sympathetic leadership,
virtually everyone in the cast is ideal, from Peter Glossop's naive,
heroic Billy to the Iago-like darkness of Michael Langdon's Clag-
gart. The last opera project the legendary English record producer
John Culshaw was to undertake, the recording is a model of clarity,
vividness, and realism. The CD transfer could not have been more
effective, especially in the barely audible closing lines of Captain
Vere's final monologue.

And as if all this—a major modern opera, brilliantly performed and produced—weren't enough, there's more. The first CD begins with two of Britten's finest song cycles, featuring the composer accompanying the singers for whom they were written: Pears's last and most moving recording of *The Holy Sonnets of John Donne* and Dietrich Fischer-Dieskau's version, in almost impeccable English, of the witty, hard-edged, frequently bitter *Songs and Proverbs of William Blake*.

A Ceremony of Carols; Hymn to St. Cecilia; Jubilate Deo; Missa brevis; Rejoice in the Lamb; Te Deum

Choir of King's College, Cambridge, Willcocks, Ledger. Angel CDC-47709 [CD].

For some, it wouldn't be Christmas without *Miracle on 34th Street* and Nat King Cole singing "The Christmas Song"; for others, it wouldn't be Christmas without throbbing headaches, swollen credit card balances, and those obnoxious relatives they've spent the entire year successfully managing to avoid. If Britten's *Ceremony of Carols* hasn't yet taken its place beside plum pudding, Alastair Sim's Scrooge, *The Nutcracker,* and the other seasonal favorites, it certainly should.

The sweet-voiced King's College Choir are nearly ideal in this most appealing confection, as well as giving first-rate performances of a generous selection of Britten's other soft-sell sacred works.

God bless them, every one.

Folk Song Arrangements

Pears, tenor; Britten, piano. London 430063-2 [CD].

Like virtually every other important English composer of this century, Britten was an enthusiastic arranger of English folk songs, primarily for use as encores in his many recitals with Peter Pears. This famous recording, first released on LP in the early '60s, brings together many of very best, from the exuberant version of "The Minstrel Boy" to a grimly disjunctive setting of "The Miller of Dee" that recalls some of Schubert's penny-dreadful ballads. Neither Pears nor Britten ever made a more enjoyable recording.

A Midsummer Night's Dream

Harwood, Veasey, Watts, Pears, Deller, Shirley-Quirk,
London Symphony Orchestra and Chorus, Britten.
London 425663-2 [CD].

After Verdi's *Otello* and *Falstaff,* Britten's *Midsummer Night's Dream* may very well be the most completely successful Shakespeare setting in all of opera. Using a skillful digest of the play which loses little of its essence, Britten responded to the challenge with one of his most brilliantly imagined scores. The scenes with the four befuddled lovers have genuine romance and urgency, the fairy music is on a par with Mendelssohn's, and the play within the play, wherein the rustics put on their botched version of *Pyramus and Thisbe,* is a wickedly funny parody of the conventions of bel canto opera. While not overloaded with memorable tunes—pregnant lines like "The course of true love never did run smooth" are frequently tossed off like afterthoughts—*A Midsummer Night's Dream* can be an authentic crowd-pleaser, as recent productions by Glyndebourne and the Los Angeles Music Center Opera clearly prove.

The composer's own recording is a wondrous one, with the ethereal Oberon of countertenor Alfred Deller and the coarsely amusing Bottom of Owen Brannigan among the standouts of the large and accomplished cast. The London Symphony is in spectacular form, and the recording, which features many examples of John Culshaw's sonic wizardry, is one of London's very best.

*P*eter Grimes

Pears, Watson, Brannigan, Evans, Orchestra and Chorus of
the Royal Opera House, Covent Garden, Britten.
London 414577-2 [CD].

Along with *Classics Illustrated*—a vivid collection of comic book versions of *Robinson Crusoe, Frankenstein,* and *Moby Dick* that got me through many a high school book report—and the not-to-be-missed and invariably memorized latest issue of *Mad Magazine,* one of my most cherished bits of boyhood reading matter was a book called *A Pictorial History of Music.* I still own the book and leaf through it from time to time.

The pictures are as entertaining as ever and the text, which I never bothered to read as a boy, becomes increasingly fascinating. In all seriousness, the author—Paul Henry Lang—blithely informs us that not one of Gustav Mahler's works achieves "true symphonic greatness." (I wonder whether Solti, Haitink, Tennstedt, and others realize they've been wasting their time all these years.) Lang further explains that the symphonies of Anton Bruckner are not really symphonies at all. Instead, they are massive "organ fantasies" (liver? pancreas?), all of which are indistinguishable from one another. (At least that puts Bruckner in fairly good company: Except for that "organ" business, Igor Stravinsky said almost the same thing about every concerto Antonio Vivaldi ever wrote.) About Benjamin Britten, Dr. Lang is even less flattering. While duly noting his native facility, he eventually dismisses him as a pleasant but shallow and irretrievably minor composer, a kind of late-twentieth-century English version of Camille Saint-Saëns.

These days, of course, we tend to take a decidedly different view of Lord Britten of Aldeburgh, not only as the foremost English composer of his generation but as the man who, virtually single-handedly, roused English opera from a three-century sleep. The most significant English opera since Purcell's *Dido and Aeneas*, *Peter Grimes*—which the man who commissioned it, that inveterate mauler of the English language Serge Koussevitzky, called "Peter und Grimes" until the end of his life—is one of the handful of twentieth-century operas that have found a substantial audience. And with good reason. For *Peter Grimes* is not only gripping theater, it is a powerful and consistently rewarding musical work.

In terms of authority and understanding, the composer's own recording from the late 1950s cannot, almost by definition, be approached. It features many of the singers who had created these parts, chief among them Peter Pears, for whom the demanding and complex title role was written. In its compact disc reissue, this famous recording becomes more vivid and atmospheric than ever. The well-known *Sea Interludes* have an especially wonderful color and mystery, and the stature of the individual performances only grows with the passage of time.

Serenade for Tenor, Horn, and Strings

Pears, tenor; Tuckwell, horn; London Symphony, Britten. London 417153-2 [CD].

With the possible exception of the marriage of Robert and Clara Schumann, the longtime relationship of Benjamin Britten and Peter Pears was the most productive love affair in the history of music. It was for Pears's plaintive and eccentric voice, which Britten heard in his mind whenever he composed, and for the great artist who possessed it that some of the most important vocal music of the twentieth century was written.

Nowhere is Pears's intimate understanding and complete mastery of the idiom heard to greater effect than in this last of his three recordings of the Serenade for Tenor, Horn, and Strings, a work that in the fullness of time may very well prove to be Britten's masterpiece. There is no subtle inflection, no nuance, no hidden meaning in either the words or the music that escapes Pears's attention. The composer's conducting is as warm and witty as can possibly be imagined, and the almost insolent grace with which Barry Tuckwell negotiates the formidable horn part must be heard to be believed. With equally impressive performances of two other magnificent Britten song cycles, *Les Illuminations* and the *Nocturne*, this generously packed compact disc is not to be missed.

Sinfonia da requiem; Symphony for Cello and Orchestra; *Cantata misericordium*

> Rostropovich, cello; Pears, tenor; Fischer-Dieskau, baritone; English Chamber Orchestra; New Philharmonia Orchestra; London Symphony Orchestra and Chorus, Britten. London 425100-2 [CD].

There was a certain inevitability in bringing these three wondrous performances together on a single CD. The *Sinfonia da requiem*, written in memory of his parents, was one of the young Benjamin Britten's first important orchestral works; the Cello Symphony, composed for his friend Mstislav Rostropovich, was his last. The little-known *Cantata misericordium*, though it came more than two decades after the *Sinfonia*, shares much of its sound and mood: the final *Dormi nunc* contains many echoes of the *Sinfonia*'s haunting final bars.

In his 1964 recording—which shows no sign of sonic crow's feet or liver spots—Rostropovich gives an overwhelming performance. Even those who have not always admired his earthy, frequently vulgar approach to his instrument (to say nothing of being put off by his lamentable conductorial shenanigans) cannot fail to be bowled over by the passionate conviction of his playing. If someone were to suggest that this is the one recording on which Rostropovich's reputation will ultimately rest, I wouldn't disagree.

The interpretations of the *Sinfonia* and the *Cantata* are equally valuable, especially of the latter, which, although an unquestioned masterpiece, remains all but unknown. Cut from the same basic cloth as the *War Requiem*, it is a far simpler and gentler piece, but one that—bar for bar—is every bit as involving.

Spring Symphony

Vyvyan, Procter, Pears, Chorus and Orchestra of the Royal Opera House, Covent Garden, Britten. London 425153-2 [CD].

What a completely enchanting, endlessly inventive work the *Spring Symphony* is! And like the incidental music Sir Edward Elgar composed for the 1915 play *The Starlight Express*—an orchestral song cycle that concludes with a richly Edwardian peroration on the familiar Christmas carol "The First Noël"—the *Spring Symphony* ends with one of the most cleverly sprung and completely appropriate surprises in English music. For as the tenor soloist is busy trying to conclude a magnificent setting of Rafe's address to London from Beaumont and Fletcher's play *The Knight of the Burning Pestle*, the chorus and orchestra come crashing in with a lusty quotation of the bawdy medieval lyric "Sumer is icumen in."

Like most of us who love this great work, I was introduced to the *Spring Symphony* by the superb London recording made by the composer in the mid-1960s. If not quite as fine as André Previn's deleted Angel recording, the composer's own still has much to recommend it. It is, to its credit, one of the least *polite* of all Britten's recordings. There is an urgent immediacy in the performance, a sense of expectancy that never flags, even in the more reflective moments. Pears is in exceptionally fine form—his delivery of the final declamation is thrilling—and the rest of the huge company respond with equal measures of gusto and finesse.

War Requiem

Vishnevskaya, Pears, Fischer-Dieskau, Melos Ensemble, Bach Choir, Highgate School Choir, London Symphony Orchestra and Chorus, Britten. London 414383-2 [CD].

With Elgar's *The Dream of Gerontius* and Sir Michael Tippett's *A Child of Our Time*, Britten's *War Requiem* is one of the three most important large-scale choral works written by an English composer since the time of Handel. A poignant, dramatic, and ultimately shattering experience, the *War Requiem* is an inspired fusion of the traditional Latin Mass for the dead and the poems of Wilfred Owen, those starkly horrifying visions from the trenches of the Western Front which are now universally regarded as the greatest poems on the subject of war yet produced in the English language. (Owen was killed at the age of twenty-five a week before the Armistice.)

In retrospect, it's hardly surprising that the *War Requiem*, like *The Dream of Gerontius*, was a failure at its world premiere. Its interpretative problems are so daunting, the performing forces so enormous and complex, that it was only with the release of this path-breaking recording that the *War Requiem*'s deeply universal appeal properly can be said to have begun.

As a performance, it remains one of Benjamin Britten's most outstanding achievements. The playing and singing are consistently urgent, vivid, and immediate, and the composer controls the work's quickly shifting textures, from the chamber episodes to the most aggressive mass eruptions, like the undeniably great conductor he eventually trained himself to be.

The only serious flaw remains the contribution of soprano Galina Vishnevskaya. Though she is undeniably impressive in the more declamatory moments, with repeated hearings the straining and bellowing become increasingly grating—like trying to sit still in the presence of a wobbly air raid siren.

On the other hand, the interpretations of the composer's other close friends, Peter Pears and Dietrich Fischer-Dieskau, will probably never be bettered. Their performance of "Strange Meeting" is all the more moving when we remember not only who but also *what* the singers were: a lifelong British pacifist, and a former foot soldier of the Wehrmacht who actually spent time in an Allied prisoner-of-war camp.

Musically, emotionally, and historically, this is a milestone in the history of recording. No tape is currently available.

The Young Person's Guide to the Orchestra (Variations and Fugue on a Theme of Purcell)

Royal Philharmonic, Previn. Telarc CD-80126 [CD].

From almost the moment it was first heard in the British documentary film *The Instruments of the Orchestra* in 1945, Britten's *Young Person's Guide* has remained his most popular and frequently recorded work. Over the last forty years, there has been no dearth of first-rate recordings of the *Guide*, including the one I grew up with: a long-vanished but thoroughly electrifying performance made for one of those small music appreciation–type labels featuring an anonymous pickup orchestra conducted by George Szell. (As with my youth, I have been searching for a copy of that recording for years. To anyone who can locate it for me, I'm willing to trade any ten Herbert von Karajan recordings and what's left of my once-complete collection of 1957 Topps baseball cards.)

A narrated recording is probably redundant at this late date, unless of course you have an impressionable kid you'd like to hook as I once was. Among the recordings in which the *Guide* is allowed to speak for itself, which it does with great eloquence, André Previn's Royal Philharmonic performance is to be preferred above all others, including, rather incredibly, the composer's own. While Benjamin Britten brought a keen wit and insight to his famous London recording (425659-2 [CD]), Previn brings even more. The personalities of the various instruments are painted in broad yet wonderfully subtle strokes. Rarely, for instance, have the bassoons sounded quite so buffoonish, nor has anyone ever made the percussion cadenza seem so ingenious or so musical. The Royal Philharmonic, especially in the Fugue, plays with a hair-trigger virtuosity, and the recorded sound could not have been bettered.

Bruch, Max (1838–1920)

Concerto No. 1 in G minor for Violin and Orchestra

Perlman, London Symphony, Previn. Angel 4XS-36963 [T].

Chung, Royal Philharmonic, Kempe. London 417707-2 [CD].

In 1906, toward the end of his long career, the Hungarian violinist Joseph Joachim, for whom Brahms and Dvořák had written their violin concertos, left what still remains a fair assessment of the Central European history of the form:

> The Germans have four violin concertos. The greatest, the one that makes the least concessions, is Beethoven's. The one by Brahms comes closest to Beethoven's in its seriousness. Max Bruch wrote the richest and most enchanting of the four. But the dearest of them all, the heart's jewel, is Mendelssohn's.

To date, the richest and most enchanting recording of Bruch's G minor Violin Concerto is the first of the two Itzhak Perlman has made for Angel Records. Unlike Perlman's digital remake with Bernard Haitink and the Concertgebouw Orchestra of Amsterdam—a strangely inert and calculated performance from two such warmhearted musicians—the Previn recording finds Perlman at his most irresistibly boyish and romantic. There is an appealing improvisatory feeling in the playing, and the rhapsodic support André Previn supplies could not have enhanced the interpretation more.

Kyung-Wha Chung is also very fresh and spontaneous-sounding in this music. And since Perlman's earlier version is unlikely to be remastered any time soon, the brilliant young Korean's London recording should be considered the first choice among currently available compact discs. Anne-Sophie Mutter plays astonishingly well in her Deutsche Grammophon recording (400031-2 [CD]), but Herbert von Karajan's cloying, manipulative, utterly sterile accompaniment drowns an otherwise lovely performance in a vat of rancid strawberry jam.

Although not quite on a par with his masterpiece, Bruch's Second Violin Concerto is more than worth investigating, especially when paired with the popular *Scottish Fantasy* and given swaggering, lyrical performances by Itzhak Perlman at the top of his form (Angel CDC-49071 [CD]).

Bruckner, Anton (1824–1896)

Symphony No. 4 in E-flat, *Romantic*

Vienna Philharmonic, Furtwängler. Deutsche Grammophon
427403-2 [CD].

Symphony No. 5 in B-flat

Berlin Philharmonic, Furtwängler. Deutsche Grammophon
427774-2 [CD].

Symphony No. 8 in C minor

Berlin Philharmonic, Furtwängler. Music and Arts CD-624
[CD].

More than those of any other major composer—and be assured that this squat, homely, diffident man ranks with the greatest
composers of the Romantic era—the symphonies of Anton Bruckner need all the help they can get. Unlike the virtually foolproof
music of Beethoven, Tchaikovsky, or Brahms, which can resist all
but the most rankly incompetent mauling, for the Bruckner symphonies to emerge as the great works they so obviously are nothing
less than *great* performances will do. While they contain much that
is immediately appealing, including some of the most heroic brass
writing in all of music, their finest moments tend to be private and
internal: the deeply spiritual utterances of an essentially medieval
spirit who was completely out of step with his time.

For the interpreter, the single most pressing problem in performing Bruckner is trying to maintain the level of concentration
that these often mammoth outbursts require. If the intensity relaxes
for a moment, the vast but terribly fragile structures will almost
inevitably fall apart. In short, it's altogether possible that many who
are persuaded they dislike Bruckner are confusing the composer
with the *performances* of his music they've heard. Indifferent, good,
or even *very* good interpretations, which in recent years is about the
best the composer can expect, simply will not do.

Wilhelm Furtwängler was unquestionably the greatest Bruckner interpreter of whom we have an accurate record. All that is best

and most characteristic in the composer's music—its drama, grandeur, mysticism—is revealed more powerfully and clearly in Furtwängler's recordings than in those of any other conductor. Although the recorded sound in these performances from the 1940s and early '50s ranges only between barely adequate and good, several books could easily be written on each of the individual interpretations—from the apocalyptic holocaust Furtwängler conjures up in the last movement of the Eighth Symphony to his unutterably beautiful performance of the Adagio from the Fifth, in which we become a party to one of the most moving spiritual journeys ever undertaken by a nineteenth-century composer. While the point could be labored indefinitely, suffice it to say that if you have yet to experience these astounding recordings, it's unlikely you've ever really *heard* the Bruckner symphonies at all.

For collectors who are unable (or unwilling) to come to terms with Furtwängler's intensely personal conceptions, or for those who grow impatient with less than state-of-the-art recorded sound, a handful of recent recordings can be recommended as reasonable, if not completely satisfying, alternatives. In the *Romantic* Symphony, Eliahu Inbal's recording of the original 1874 version with the Frankfurt Radio Symphony (Teldec 42921 [CD]) is as persuasive as it is fascinating, including, as it does, a Scherzo entirely different from the one that is usually heard. Of all modern recordings of the Fifth and the Eighth, none has yet surpassed either the warmth or virtuosity of Bernard Haitink's Philips recordings with the Vienna Philharmonic (422342-2 [CD]) and Amsterdam Concertgebouw Orchestra (412465-2 [CD]). And for the closest thing we have to a Furtwängler Ninth in up-to-date sound, Bruno Walter's handsomely remastered recording from the early 1960s with the Columbia Symphony comes surprisingly close to filling the bill (Odyssey MBK-44825 [CD], YT-44825 [T]).

Anyone looking for recordings of all the symphonies who also wants the convenience of a boxed set will find Eugen Jochum's admirable cycle for Deutsche Grammophon (429079-2 [CD]) an authentic bargain. The performances, by the Berlin Philharmonic (1, 4, 7, 8, and 9) and the Bavarian Radio Symphony (2, 3, 5, and 6), are for the most part admirably direct and intensely noble, while the recorded sound rivals all but today's best. Similarly, another medium-priced Deutsche Grammophon collection of virtually all of the composer's choral music (423127-2 [CD]) finds Jochum in equally persuasive form. No finer versions of the three Masses are currently available; the Motets emerge with far more individuality than most interpreters find. The team of vocal soloists is excellent, the choruses sing with devotion and finesse, and the recorded sound, although no longer of demonstration quality, is still exceptionally fine.

Busoni, Ferruccio (1866–1924)

Concerto in C for Piano and Orchestra (with Male Chorus)

Donahoe, piano; BBC Symphony and Singers, Elder. EMI CDC-49996 [CD], EL-49996-4 [T].

Unlike his friend Gustav Mahler, Ferruccio Busoni is a composer whose time has not yet come. Best remembered for his arrangements of the music of Bach, as an inspired and influential teacher, and as one of history's consummate keyboard virtuosos (those who heard them both insisted that his playing was superior even to Liszt's), Busoni was an odd combination of Italian Romantic composer and North German philosopher-mystic who was one of the major musical heroes of his age and *could* be one of ours. Perhaps the best introduction to this absorbing and endlessly complex personality is the titanic Piano Concerto he composed between 1902 and 1904, one of the most involved and entertaining concertos ever written for the instrument and—at seventy minutes—the longest.

John Ogdon's historic first recording of the work, which will undoubtedly be the English pianist's most enduring memorial, has temporarily been withdrawn, presumably to make way for the newer and exceedingly impressive recording by Peter Donohoe. While Donohoe's alternately thunderous and mercurial reading makes a splendid case for the piece, there was no excuse for deleting one of the great recordings of the last thirty years.

Busoni admirers—or simply anyone who would like to know this captivating musician a good deal better—should waste no time acquiring Deutsche Grammophon's CD reissue (427413-2) of the composer's final opera, *Doktor Faust*. The 1969 recording, with a cast headed by Dietrich Fischer-Dieskau, confirmed what many Busoni fanciers had been claiming for years: that his last, unfinished work was not only his ultimate masterpiece but also one of the most disturbingly original operas of modern times.

Butterworth, George
(1885–1916)

The Banks of Green Willow; Two English Idylls; A Shropshire Lad

English String Orchestra, Boughton. Nimbus NI-5068 [CD].

Like the poets Edward Thomas, Isaac Rosenberg, and Wilfred Owen, George Butterworth was of that tragic English generation decimated in the trenches of the Western Front. He enlisted during the week World War I began and was killed at the battle of the Somme two years later. During his brief career he was an inveterate collector of English folk songs, helped Vaughan Williams arrange material for *A London Symphony*, and wrote a handful of inspired miniatures that suggest he might have become one of the most significant English composers of his time.

The four bewitching works found on this gorgeous Nimbus CD represent Butterworth at his most beguiling. If you are touched by the folk-inspired music of Delius, Holst, and Vaughan Williams, you will find Butterworth irresistible. And once you find yourself in his gentle but viselike grip, don't fail to investigate a Chandos recording of his Housman song cycles—*Bredon Hill and Other Songs* and *Six Songs from "A Shropshire Lad"*—in the eloquent readings by baritone Benjamin Luxon (CHAN-8831M [CD]).

Canteloube, Joseph
(1879–1957)

Songs of the Auvergne

Te Kanawa, soprano; English Chamber Orchestra, Tate.
London 410004-2 [CD] (volume 1); 411730-2 [CD],
411730-4 [T] (volume 2).
Von Stade, mezzo-soprano; Royal Philharmonic, Almeida.
CBS MK-37299 [CD], IMT-37299 [T] (volume 1);
IMT-37837 [T] (volume 2).

For much of his life, the indefatigable French composer Joseph
Canteloube devoted himself to collecting and arranging the charming, haunting, and frequently scintillating folk songs of the Auvergne region of central France. Although none of his original
works ever succeeded in making much of an impression, the four-
volume *Songs of the Auvergne* are well on their way to becoming
modern classics. Beginning with the pioneering recordings of
Natania Davrath (Vanguard OVC-8001/2 [CD]) and Victoria de los
Angeles (Angel CDM-63178 [CD]) in the late 1950s and early '60s,
famous singers have been drawn almost irresistibly to these minor
masterworks, not only because they are so vocally and musically
rewarding, but also because any album with *"Songs of the Auvergne"* on its cover is almost guaranteed to sell.

Dame Kiri Te Kanawa, in some of her finest work in the studio
to date, has so far recorded two excellent collections, and her ravishing, peaches-and-cream instrument serves the music very well.

Frederica von Stade, if not as completely attuned to this music
as she is to Mozart and Massenet, turns in a pair of recordings that
will disappoint no one; vocally, they are delectable; musically, they
are beyond reproach.

Carter, Elliott (1908–)

Piano Sonata

Lawson, piano. Virgin Classics VC-7-91163-2 [CD].

During the last four decades, Elliott Carter has become the most uncompromising and, for many, one of the most forbidding of modern American composers. Igor Stravinsky was quoted as saying that Carter's Double Concerto of 1961 was the first true American masterpiece, and in the increasingly complex music he has written since then—from the astonishing *Concerto for Orchestra* to the mysterious *Enchanted Preludes* for flute and cello—he has proven to be, with Milton Babbitt, the most consistently challenging composer of his generation.

The Piano Sonata, finished in 1946 and revised substantially in 1982, is probably the greatest piano sonata yet written by an American. Composed toward the middle of Carter's neoclassical phase, it is a rich, serious, elegantly made work which includes, among its many wonders, one of the finest fugues since Beethoven. Peter Lawson's electrifying Virgin Classics disc will allow you to judge whether it really *is* the Great American Piano Sonata, since, with the exception of the magnificent piano sonata of Charles Tomlinson Griffes, it includes the only other possible contenders: those of Samuel Barber and Aaron Copland, in equally authoritative performances.

This is easily one of the most important recordings of American piano music yet released.

Chabrier, Emmanuel

(1841–1894)

España; Marche joyeuse; Gwendoline Overture; *Bourrée fantasque; Danse slave; Suite pastorale*

Detroit Symphony, Paray. Mercury 434303-2 [CD].

Gustav Mahler once shocked the members of the New York Philharmonic by calling Emmanuel Chabrier's *España* "the foundation of modern music." Precisely what Mahler meant by that we'll probably never know, but he certainly put his baton where his mouth was: During his two-year stay in America he programmed it half a dozen times, always in performances in which he took the liberty of quadrupling all the wind parts.

Although we now tend to think of *España* as not much more than the foundation of many a pops concert, there was a time when the reputation of its abrupt, lively, immensely likable composer was far more imposing than it is today. No less a figure than the American musicologist Gilbert Chase once wrote, "He was the direct precursor of Debussy and Ravel, whose most daring effects he anticipated"; for their part, Debussy and Ravel always admitted their fondness for the music of this late-blooming composer and celebrated salon wit. (Chabrier's caustic sense of humor was legendary. He once said, "There are three kinds of music: the good, the bad, and that of Ambroise Thomas.")

Paul Paray's wonderful Chabrier recordings from the late 1950s cannot be welcomed back into the catalog too warmly. In this repertoire—in French music in general—Paray had few rivals among the major conductors of his generation, and he invests each of the pieces with an abundance of life and a character uniquely its own. The Detroit Symphony has rarely sounded so sensuous or alert, and the original Mercury Living Presence recording has been revived with astonishing vividness.

Chausson, Ernest (1855–1899)

Poème for Violin and Orchestra

**Chung, violin; Royal Philharmonic, Dutoit. London
417118-2 [CD].**

One of the most provocative of all "what if?" musical speculations concerns the effect on the subsequent development of French music had Ernest Chausson been as accomplished a bicyclist as he was a composer. His premature death, from injuries sustained when he rode into a brick wall in 1899, robbed French music of the most distinctive and original voice it had produced between Hector Berlioz and Claude Debussy.

With the Symphony in B-flat, the best German symphony ever written by a Frenchman—Charles Munch's glorious Boston Symphony recording has recently returned on a Victor CD (60683-2)—and the sumptuous orchestral song cycle *Poème de l'amour et de la mer*—best represented these days by Linda Finnie's haunting Chandos recording (CHAN-8952 [CD], ABTD-1546 [T])—the *Poème* for Violin and Orchestra is one of the finest and most justly popular of all Chausson's works: a finished masterpiece by an already established master, and a tantalizing, heartbreaking suggestion of what might have been.

The greatest performance the *Poème* has ever received on, or probably off, records was that rich and passionate recording the tragically short-lived French violinist Ginette Neveu made in the late 1940s. Kyung-Wha Chung's London recording resembles Neveu's in its emotional depth and technical facility. As usual, the support Charles Dutoit gives Ms. Chung is as imaginative as it is sensitive, not only in the *Poème* but also in Saint-Saëns's *Havanaise* and *Introduction and Rondo capriccioso,* and Ravel's *Tzigane,* the other popular violin showpieces that round out this extremely appealing release.

Chopin, Frédéric (1810–1849)

Concertos for Piano and Orchestra: No. 1 in E minor;
No. 2 in F minor

> Zimerman, piano; Los Angeles Philharmonic, Giulini.
> Deutsche Grammophon 415970-2 [CD].

In addition to being central works in the concerto literature for the instrument, the Chopin Piano Concertos go a long way toward dispelling several myths that continue to cling to one of history's most popular composers. There are those who still insist that Chopin was essentially an incomparable miniaturist who was uncomfortable with—and, indeed, incapable of sustaining—larger-scale forms. These are the same people, no doubt, who are convinced that this first important composer of piano music constructed entirely in *pianistic* terms was thoroughly incapable of writing gracefully and idiomatically for other instruments—which is to say, for the nineteenth-century orchestra. Hogwash. Both as larger forms and as concerted works for piano and orchestra, these two Concertos are as masterly as those any composer of the Romantic era produced.

It was one or the other of these two exceptional performances on Deutsche Grammophon that probably introduced most of the world to the great young Polish pianist Krystian Zimerman. As a general rule, I am extremely suspicious of the phrase "great young" when applied to anyone, but in Zimerman's case, it most assuredly *does* apply. He has instinct, technique, and temperament to burn, together with a maturity and insight that many pianists twice his age would be hard-pressed to match. (Compare his playing with that of his highly touted near-contemporary Ivo Pogorelich. The difference is one between a precocious yet very nearly finished artist and a precocious but unruly and self-indulgent child.)

Zimerman's performances of the Chopin concertos are as nearly perfect as any that have been heard in a generation. In them, poetry and youthful impetuosity are combined with a highly disciplined musical intelligence, and the results are an unalloyed delight for both the heart and the mind. The backdrops provided by Giulini and the Los Angeles Philharmonic could not be more suave or sympathetic, and the recorded sound has a warm and natural bloom.

Vigorously recommended.

Piano Sonatas: No. 2 in B-flat minor, Op. 35; No. 3 in B minor, Op. 58

Kapell, piano. RCA 5998-2-RC [CD].

Here is some very persuasive evidence in the case for William Kapell as the finest pianist America has ever produced. Only thirty-one at the time of his death in a plane crash in 1953, he was already a performer of epic abilities. His technique was the most formidable of his generation, and his powers of communication were broadening and deepening to the very end. With the Romantics he was dashing and fearless, with Bach he was dignified and self-effacing, and his Mozart impressed the dreaded Claudia Cassidy, the virtually unimpressible critic of the *Chicago Tribune*, as the purest, most effortless music-making she had ever heard.

Kapell's versions of the two popular Chopin sonatas—one recorded in the studio, one taken from a concert given in the last months of his life—make for an exhilarating, exhausting, ennobling experience. The playing is that of one of the century's towering instrumentalists: powerful, confident, poetic, and introspective, with just the right combination of an immediately recognizable personality and absolute fidelity to the spirit of the text. One of the acid tests of any performance of this music is the ability to listen to the well-known Funeral March from the B-flat minor Sonata with a perfectly straight face. Kapell invests it with such heartrending pathos that we are left in pieces on the floor.

Rounded off with Kapell's brilliant recordings of ten of the Mazurkas, this may be the single most valuable Chopin disc on the market.

Solo Piano Works

Ballades (4); Scherzos (4). Rubinstein, piano. RCA RCD1-7156 [CD], CRK2-5460 [T].

Mazurkas (35). Rubinstein, piano. RCA 5614-2-RC [CD], CRK2-5171 [T].

Nocturnes (21). Rubinstein, piano. RCA 5613-2-RC [CD], CRK2-5018 [T].

Polonaises (7). Rubinstein, piano. RCA 5615-2-RC [CD], CRK2-7036 [T].

Waltzes (14). Rubinstein, piano. RCA RCD1-5492 [CD], CRK2-5018 [T].

Although this phenomenally popular body of music has attracted almost every important pianist of the last 150 years, it's unlikely that Frédéric Chopin ever found, or will ever find, a more ideal interpreter than Artur Rubinstein. To be sure, pianists like Josef Hoffman, Leopold Godowsky, and Vladimir Horowitz gave infinitely more brilliant performances of the music. Even some of the brighter lights of the younger generation, Dinu Lipatti in the 1950s and Maurizio Pollini in our time, managed to find an intellectual and spiritual depth in Chopin that Rubinstein, for much of his career, never did. Yet on balance, these remain the definitive recordings of Chopin's piano music, as authoritative and unapproachable in their way as Furtwängler's recordings of the Bruckner symphonies, or the music of Frederick Delius led by Sir Thomas Beecham.

The key to Rubinstein's greatness as a Chopin interpreter was the combination of his utter naturalness as a performer and his enormously sophisticated musical mind. Nothing ever seems forced or premeditated; there are no sharp edges or sudden flashes of insight. In fact, the illusion the performances create is one of the music flowing, without benefit of a human intermediary, directly from Chopin's heart to the listener's. Of course, only the most accomplished artists are able to create such illusions, and then only after a lifetime of study, experience, self-examination, and back-breaking work.

At almost every moment in these classic recordings, Rubinstein discovers some wonder of color or phrasing, brings out a beautiful inner voice it seems we've never heard before, and in general creates the impression of a man for whom playing this often fiendishly difficult music is no more difficult than making love. In short, Rubinstein's great and completely unaffected humanity breathes such life into these performances that they will continue to move, enlighten, and inspire for as long as people require such things from recorded music.

With the Rubinsteins as the backbone of any Chopin collection, there are some superb second opinions that really should be consulted too. Most important of all are the recordings of the Czech pianist Ivan Moravec, who is probably to the present generation of Chopin interpreters what Rubinstein was to his. With playing of an almost otherworldly refinement and purity, Moravec's Nonesuch recording of the Nocturnes (79233-2 [CD]) may well be the loveliest Chopin recording ever made. His 1976 Supraphon recording of the Preludes (11-0630-2 [CD]) is both more technically impressive than Rubinstein's and probes even deeper beneath the surface; his recent Dorian recording of the Scherzos (DOR-90140 [CD]) offers insight and excitement in virtually equal amounts.

Krystian Zimerman's Deutsche Grammophon recording of the Ballades (423090-2 [CD], 423090-4 [T]) features playing as fresh as it is powerfully dramatic, and Maurizio Pollini on another DG recording (431221-2 [CD]) demonstrates that he is still the undisputed master at solving the formidable technical and musical problems of the Études. (The set of three bargain CDs also includes his impeccable versions of the Preludes and Polonaises.)

Finally, Dinu Lipatti's unutterably moving recording of the Waltzes, made in the last year of his tragically abbreviated life, can be found on an imported EMI CD (CDH7-69802-2) and on an Odyssey tape (YT-60058E). At almost no time since they were first issued in the early 1950s have these miraculous performances been out of print, and with good reason. In their unfailing eloquence and deceptive simplicity, they are not only touchstones in the history of recording, they stand among the enduring triumphs of human communication.

Coates, Eric (1886–1957)

Orchestral Music

London Symphony, Mackerras; Royal Liverpool
Philharmonic, Groves; City of Birmingham Symphony,
Kilbey. Classics for Pleasure CFPD-4456 [CD].

Admittedly, there are people who cannot abide the music of
the English composer Eric Coates. But then, too, there are people
who dislike champagne, caviar, and other acquired tastes.

With his near-contemporary the longtime Boston Pops arranger Leroy Anderson, Coates was one of the indisputable masters
of "light music." In his familiar suites and bracing marches, Coates
was a man who not only knew the value of a good tune but was
also singularly successful in producing them over the years, from the
unforgettable "Knightsbridge March" from the *London Suite* to
that equally memorable inspiration from *The Three Elizabeths*
which served as the signature tune of public television's *Forsyth
Saga*. It is music that never tries the patience, overstays its welcome,
or fails to amuse, entertain, and delight.

On these two generously packed, reasonably priced, and very
aptly named Classics for Pleasure CDs, two of the all-time great
Coatesians, Sir Charles Mackerras and Sir Charles Groves, bring the
music so vividly to life that you suspect it will last an eternity; the
contributions of the City of Birmingham Symphony under Reginald
Kilbey—what a perfect name for a Coates conductor!—are hardly
less enjoyable.

If you have the willpower, or simply the cussedness, to resist
this collection, you have my admiration and sympathy.

Copland, Aaron (1900–1990)

Appalachian Spring

Los Angeles Philharmonic, Bernstein. Deutsche
Grammophon 413324-2 [CD], 423168-4 [T].

St. Paul Chamber Orchestra, Davies. Pro Arte CDD-140
[CD], PCD-140 [T].

Aaron Copland was, in many ways, the most dramatic musical manifestation of the "melting pot" genesis of American culture. For the composer who, in his most popular works, seemed to capture the very essence of Middle America and the Western frontier was in fact born in a working-class Jewish neighborhood of Brooklyn, and received his principal musical training with Nadia Boulanger in Paris.

Appalachian Spring, a ballet composed for the celebrated American dancer Martha Graham, is probably Copland's masterpiece. All the hallmarks of his "Enlightened Populist" style are heard to their best advantage. Bracing, wide-open harmonies and folksy, unforgettable melodies are bound together with Copland's expressive idiom, which mixes tenderness, exuberance, sentimentality, and sophistication, in roughly equal amounts.

Like the exhilarating recording Leonard Bernstein made with the New York Philharmonic in the 1960s, this version with the Los Angeles Philharmonic is an unqualified triumph. The orchestra plays with great delicacy and conviction, and the special excitement all Bernstein's live performances generated can be felt throughout.

For a somewhat less compelling but thoroughly satisfying look at the ballet in its original version for chamber orchestra, the performance led by Dennis Russell Davies handily defeats all other contenders, including the recording by the composer himself.

Billy the Kid; Rodeo

St. Louis Symphony, Slatkin. Angel CDC-47382 [CD], 4DS-37357 [T].

For more years than anyone could remember, Leonard Bernstein, one of Copland's oldest and closest friends, virtually owned this music. His CBS recordings of these immensely appealing cowboy ballets (both of which quote more actual frontier tunes than a typical Zane Grey novel) have been all but unapproachable in their dramatic flair and authority. That is, at least, until now.

Leonard Slatkin, who in the last decade has galvanized the St. Louis Symphony into one of America's finest orchestras, leads a pair of performances that are even more successful than Bernstein's. The rhythms are tighter and more infectious, the phrasing is consistently more alert and imaginative, and the playing of this great young ensemble sounds every bit the equal of that of any orchestra in the world. Along with demonstration-quality sound, the recording has the further advantage of presenting both ballets note-complete. While this represents only a few extra minutes of actual music, it makes what is already an immensely attractive recording virtually irresistible.

Fanfare for the Common Man; Danzón Cubano; El salón México; Appalachian Spring

> New York Philharmonic, Bernstein. CBS MYK-37257 [CD], MYT-37257 [T].

The advantage of this particular lineup—and CBS is repackaging Bernstein's hugely marketable Copland recordings in a variety of combinations—is that it brings together definitive performances of three of the composer's shorter works and a version of *Appalachian Spring* which is second only to the conductor's Los Angeles Philharmonic recording for Deutsche Grammophon.

If the *Fanfare* is slightly compromised by the wobble of the Philharmonic's principal trumpet, the performance as a whole is gloriously gutsy. (Be warned, though: This is not the original version of the score, but instead an extract from its memorable appearance in Copland's Third Symphony.) On the other hand, the two Latin items are unapproachable, especially *El salón México*, which here becomes a triumph of salsa and swank.

Symphony No. 3; Quiet City

> New York Philharmonic, Bernstein. Deutsche Grammophon 419170-2 [CD].

Among the candidates for the musical equivalent of the Great American Novel, the Copland Third has always ranked high on most people's lists. I have never been persuaded that this is, in fact, the Great American Symphony—my own nominee is the Roy Harris Third—nor am I usually inclined to think of it as a great American *anything*. The gritty, affably belligerent Scherzo is prime Copland, the incorporation of the *Fanfare for the Common Man* is clever, exciting, and all of that, but for the most part the Symphony has always seemed to me a melancholy victory of manner over matter: one of the major *shallow* masterpieces of American music. Except when conducted by Leonard Bernstein.

His final version, taken from a live New York Philharmonic performance, proves once again that Copland never had a more eloquent advocate. No other recording of the work, including the two the composer made himself, can begin to match this one in nervous tension and sustained energy. Moreover, what can seem merely rhetorical in other hands is miraculously transformed in Bernstein's into deeply felt emotion; no one, for instance, has ever made the *Fanfare*'s final apotheosis seem more inevitable or just.

With one of the loveliest of all versions of *Quiet City* as the welcome filler, this would seem to be a recording no Copland lover could afford to pass up.

Corelli, Arcangelo (1653–1713)

Concerti Grossi (12), Op. 6

English Concert, Pinnock. Deutsche Grammophon 423626-2 [CD].

Along with being one of the finest violinists of the Baroque era and a man who did as much as anyone to codify the form and substance of the sonata and concerto grosso, the penurious Arcangelo Corelli was far and away the tightest-fisted cheapskate in the history of music. He refused to buy new clothes until the old ones literally disintegrated on his back, and although he was an avid collector of paintings and sculpture, he never went to public galleries on days when admission was charged.

Yet for all his personal idiosyncrasies, Corelli was as admired by his contemporaries as he is largely unappreciated today. The richly inventive Op. 6 Concerti Grossi were among the most influential works of the High Baroque. In addition to the well-known "Christmas" Concerto—which is about as Christmasy as a Fourth of July parade—the eleven other works in the set contain one felicitous idea after another. In addition to the innovative melodic and harmonic thinking, the craftsmanship is of an order that would not be surpassed until Handel's own Op. 6 collection, which owes Corelli's an incalculable debt.

Trevor Pinnock's enthusiastic period-instrument performances make an exceptionally strong case for these works. The interpretations are as bracing and articulate as the music itself, and the recorded sound is wonderfully lifelike and clear.

Debussy, Claude (1862–1918)

Children's Corner Suite; *Images* for Piano, Books I and II

Michelangeli, piano. Deutsche Grammophon 415372-2 [CD].

Without much question, Arturo Benedetti Michelangeli is the most exasperating musician of his generation. A monstrously gifted pianist and a wholly unique musical personality, Michelangeli could have become a household word long ago had he only been a little more interested in playing the piano. The public appearances of this cult figure, who has a small but fanatical following, have been likened to the sightings of a rare and exotic bird. Michelangeli plays whenever he feels like it (which isn't often), and records even less.

This Debussy collection, taped in the early 1970s, reveals just what kind of spellbinder this fabulous oddball was in his prime. The playing itself is largely unbelievable, and the interpretations have an almost Promethean originality. Only Ivan Moravec could find such wondrous charm in the familiar *Children's Corner* Suite, and even the great Walter Gieseking would have been hard-pressed to wring more color or individuality from the bewitching *Images*.

What a pity that one of the most accomplished musicians of modern times should have been such a thoroughgoing spook.

Images for Orchestra; *Prelude to the Afternoon of a Faun*

London Symphony, Previn. Angel CDC-47001 [CD], 4DS-37674 [T].

Boston Symphony, Thomas. Deutsche Grammophon 419473-2 [CD], 415916-4 [T].

Claude Debussy despised the term *impressionism* whenever it was applied to his own music, largely because he did not want anyone to think that he had merely created a slavish aural imitation of the paintings of Monet and the poetry of Stéphane Mallarmé. Of course, the composer was absolutely right. For his music represents one of the great turning points in the history of music: a rethinking of musical color and texture so complete that its influence would rival that of Wagner's harmonic upheaval, or the rhythmic revolution begun in Stravinsky's *Rite of Spring*.

This spectacularly fine-sounding Angel recording (the very first digital recording the company released) conveniently brings together two of the composer's most important scores: the *Prelude to the Afternoon of a Faun*, with which Debussy launched his gentle revolution in 1892, and the *Images* for Orchestra, one of his final and most ambitious orchestral works.

While there have been more vivid interpretations of *Images*, and recordings of the *Prelude* that capture more of its tenderness and mystery, no Debussy recording on the market today is more brilliant or revealing than this one. The recorded sound captures every nuance of these tremendously adroit and poetic performances. In the final few minutes of *Ibéria*, for instance, we seem able to hear more notes (and even more instruments) than we have ever heard before. If you have just bitten the bullet and bought a compact disc player, this is an ideal vehicle for showing what your new toy will do.

For an interpretation with just a bit more pizzazz and character, the Deutsche Grammophon recording by Michael Tilson

Thomas and the Boston Symphony is also unusually attractive. Recorded at the very beginning of Thomas's career, the performance projects a youthful enthusiasm, coupled with an interpretative maturity and brilliance of execution that continue to make it unique.

La Mer

Chicago Symphony, Reiner. RCA 60875-2 [CD].

New Philharmonia Orchestra, Boulez. CBS MYK-37261 [CD], MYT-37261 [T].

When Pierre Boulez's recording of Debussy's most evocative work was first released two decades ago, it was widely hailed as a major revelation, and, to be fair, no other recording has ever succeeded in presenting this stunning, magically atmospheric work with greater precision and clarity. Still, the final test of any performance of *La Mer* is the extent to which it makes you see, taste, and smell the sea.

The wonderful recording Fritz Reiner made with the Chicago Symphony in the late 1950s still does that more effectively than any other. In the compact disc reissue, the range of color in this virtuoso performance is as incredibly rich and varied as ever, and the drama that Boulez's otherwise fine interpretation lacks, Reiner finds in abundance. Listen, for instance, to the electrifying playing in the final bars, where the conductor whips up such visceral excitement that you might almost suspect you're listening to the finale of a Tchaikovsky symphony.

Originally, and rather incongruously, coupled with Reiner's final and finest recording of Strauss's *Don Juan*, the digitally remastered compact disc now brings you the sexiest of all commercial recordings of Rimsky-Korsakov's *Scheherazade* (see page 335).

Nocturnes for Orchestra; *Jeux*

Concertgebouw Orchestra of Amsterdam, Haitink. Philips 400023-2 [CD].

Boston Symphony, Munch. RCA 6719-4 [T].

I blush to confess that it took me far too long to see the light on the subject of Bernard Haitink. As an ardent admirer of his great predecessor in Amsterdam, Eduard van Beinum, and an absolute fanatic on the subject of van Beinum's predecessor, Willem Mengelberg, for years I regarded Haitink as merely a competent journeyman, a talented but rather anonymous figure who could be relied on for polite and handsomely organized performances, little more. For the last decade, with the release of every new Haitink recording I have eaten Brobdingnagian helpings of crow. In almost every recording he has made, recordings that cover an unusually broad range of repertoire, he combines intelligence, passion, craftsmanship, and utter professionalism more thoroughly than any other conductor before the public today. If Haitink, like Felix Weingartner and Pierre Monteux before him, may not be the most glamorous conductor of his generation, he is probably the most consistently satisfying.

Naturally, he faces formidable competition in one of the most popular of Debussy's major works, yet no other modern recording of the *Nocturnes* can begin to match the effortless perfection of this one. The interpretation of "Nuages" is a masterpiece of mood and texture, "Fêtes" crackles with electric excitement, and "Sirènes" is so seductively alluring that you begin to understand why countless ancient mariners were more than willing to crack up on these dangerous ladies' reefs.

And Haitink's interpretation of *Jeux* is nothing less than a revelation. Whereas other conductors have made this strange tennis court ballet seem an interesting work at best, Haitink dares to suggest that it may actually be an unjustly neglected masterpiece.

Charles Munch's Boston Symphony recording is one of his very best, an engaging mixture of color, brilliance, and panache that makes it the first choice among currently available tapes, though it lacks "Sirènes" and *Jeux*.

*P*elléas et Mélisande

Alliot-Lugaz, Golfier, Henry, Carlson, Cachemaille, Thau, Montreal Symphony and Chorus, Dutoit. London 430502-2 [CD].

From its disastrous premiere in 1902 to the present day, *Pelléas et Mélisande* has never been a popular opera. Although the

first-night disturbances were organized by friends of the playwright
Maurice Maeterlinck, who disowned the project when he was told
that his mistress Georgette Leblanc would not be cast as the heroine,
there is more than enough in *Pelléas* to irritate the more conservative opera-lover, beginning with a virtual absence of memorable
arias. Moreover, it has no big scenes, no dramatic outbursts—the
entire score boasts only four *fortissimos*—and the work can seem
to move in a hazy, ill-defined half light.

It is also an opera that overflows with the most subtle musical
invention, offers ample dramatic challenges (it was *Pelléas* that
made Mary Garden a star), and creates an expressive universe
wholly and unmistakably its own. Its adherents insist it is the one
indisputably great French opera after *Carmen*, a claim its finest recording to date would seem to substantiate.

With this triumphant new recording, Charles Dutoit proves
yet again that he is the most resourceful and sensitive conductor of
French music before the public today. Although almost without exception the cast of superb singers do everything that is asked of them
and more—Colette Alliot-Lugaz and Didier Henry are both radiant
and utterly believable as the lovers, while Gilles Cachemaille is
probably the most three-dimensional villain since the legendary
Martial Singher—it is ultimately Dutoit's wondrous conducting
that will make this a *Pelléas* to dominate the catalog for years.

Preludes for Piano, Books I and II

Jacobs, piano. Nonesuch 73031-2 [CD], N6-3031 [T].

The American pianist Paul Jacobs has the tragic distinction of
being the first well-known musician to die of AIDS. A versatile performer who brought a special fire and poetry to the music of the
twentieth century, he was one of the most persuasive advocates of
modern American piano music, and his recordings of the works of
Arnold Schoenberg (Nonesuch 71309-4 [T]) are among the few that
can be mentioned in the same breath with those of the composer's
friend and pupil Eduard Steuermann.

Even though he faces formidable competition in this popular
repertoire, Jacobs's recordings of the Debussy Preludes are second
to none. His humanely analytical approach and meticulous attention to detail serve all of the music—especially the better-known
pieces—extremely well. Like the restorers of the Sistine Chapel, he

scrapes the decades of accumulated interpretative treacle off favorites like "The Girl with the Flaxen Hair," yet manages to do so without robbing them of any of their essential tenderness and charm. There are also healthy helpings of passion and fireworks whenever they are required, together with a sly and knowing wit.

In all, this is one of the most satisfying of all Debussy albums and a suitable memorial to a fine and talented man.

Sonatas (3) for Various Instruments

Athena Ensemble. Chandos CHAN-8385 [CD].

Debussy was already in the final agonizing stages of rectal cancer when he began writing that curiously anachronistic series of works with which he would conclude his career: three instrumental sonatas modeled on eighteenth-century forms. Though occasionally they might suggest a diminished concentration—especially in the Violin Sonata, his final piece—the sonatas contain an abundance of intriguing ideas and ripe invention: the Cello Sonata seems, for the most part, to be deliberately written *against* the instrument's principal strengths, while the Sonata for Flute, Viola, and Harp is so ethereal it seems the work of the inhabitant of another world.

All the performances by the Athena Ensemble are highly distinguished, and as a bonus the disc includes the *Petite pièce* and *Première rapsodie* for Clarinet and Piano, together with the haunting *Syrinx* for solo flute. If the absolute last word on the Violin or Cello Sonata is necessary, the listener can hear it spoken by David Oistrakh on a superb violin recital from Philips (420777-2 [CD]) or by Mstislav Rostropovich accompanied by Benjamin Britten on a justly famous London recording (417833-2 [CD]).

String Quartet in G minor

Guarneri Quartet. RCA 60909-2 [CD], 60909-4 [T].

A relatively early work (even though it was the last piece Debussy would compose in an identified key and to which he assigned an opus number), the String Quartet is nonetheless the finest of the composer's chamber works and a cornerstone of the modern quartet literature.

For years, the most meltingly beautiful of all its many recordings was a version by the Guarneri Quartet for RCA, now reissued on a dirt-cheap, no-frills (such as program notes) CD. Though the Guarneri have been perhaps the most maddeningly inconsistent of the world's great quartets, they are at their absolute best in both the Debussy and its inevitable companion piece, the String Quartet of Maurice Ravel. The playing has such a natural ease, sensitivity, and unanimity of frankly Romantic purpose that the recording easily sweeps a very crowded field.

Suite bergamasque; Estampes; Images oubliées; Pour le piano

Kocsis, piano. Philips 412118-2 [CD].

Given the fact that Debussy was responsible for some of the most original and popular piano music produced after Chopin, there is a surprising (one is tempted to say *scandalous*) dearth of first-rate recordings now in print. Perhaps we are simply going through one of those predictable droughts, during which the major recording companies are gearing up to reissue the Debussy piano treasures in their vaults as compact discs. Whatever the explanation, virtually none of the definitive recordings made by that arch-poet Walter Gieseking are readily available, and Debussy's greatest living interpreter, the Czech pianist Ivan Moravec, is currently represented by only a few tantalizing bits and pieces.

This generous and brilliantly played collection by the young Hungarian pianist Zoltán Kocsis is one of the few genuine treasures in a shockingly barren field. Kocsis, who obviously possesses an important technique, plays with great subtlety and refinement. The *Suite bergamasque* is particularly successful, offering considerable wit, admirable control, and an attractively understated account of the famous *Clair de lune* (which the incomparable Victor Borge, before all of his inimitable performances, invariably introduced by saying, "English translation: Clear the saloon"). The recorded sound offers one of the most realistic re-creations of piano timbre that has yet been heard.

Delius, Frederick (1862–1934)

*On Hearing the First Cuckoo in Spring, Brigg Fair—An
English Rhapsody; Sleigh Ride; A Song Before Sunrise;
Intermezzo from Fennimore and Gerda; Prelude to
Irmelin; Songs of Sunset; Over the Hills and Far Away;
Marche caprice; Florida Suite; Dance Rhapsody No. 2;
Summer Evening; Summer Night on the River*

> Forrester, contralto; Cameron, baritone; Beecham Choral
> Society, Royal Philharmonic Orchestra, Beecham. Angel
> CDCB-47509 [CD].

With the possible exception of the amoral, egomaniacal, virulently anti-Semitic, and treacherous Richard Wagner, who repaid the unswerving loyalty of at least two of his most ardent supporters by sleeping with their wives, Frederick Delius, of all the great composers, was probably the most unpleasant human being. Cruel, ruthless, pathologically selfish, and a self-styled incarnation of Nietzsche's idealized Nordic superman, Delius fought his long, lonely struggle for recognition while making the lives of everyone around him (especially that of his devoted, long-suffering wife Jelka) miserable. As much as his apologists, his amanuensis Eric Fenby and the Australian composer Percy Grainger, have tried to pardon his unpardonable behavior, Delius, to the day he died (a blind and paralyzed victim of tertiary neurosyphilis), was a complete and thoroughgoing beast.

And yet contained within this difficult, often despicable man was one of the most original and rarefied talents in musical history. At its best, Delius's music is among the most delicate and ineffably gentle ever produced by an English composer, and as one of the last of the late-Romantic nature poets, he remains unique.

For those of us who are hopelessly addicted to his admittedly limited but irresistibly appealing art, or for those perfectly sensible, though sadly misguided, souls who gag at the very mention of his name, this comprehensive Angel recording is the most valuable single release since the introduction of the compact disc. For contained on these two tightly packed and handsomely remastered CDs are all the stereo recordings of Delius's music that his greatest champion, Sir Thomas Beecham, ever made.

In Beecham's hands (though, alas, in few others' since the conductor's death) the music of Delius clearly emerges as that of a major composer. Almost every bar of these famous performances is shot through with Beecham's special interpretative wizardry. *On Hearing the First Cuckoo in Spring* very nearly says as much as the whole of Beethoven's *Pastorale* symphony, and the legendary version of *Brigg Fair* sounds not only like the finest Delius recording ever made, but also preciously close to the most magical fifteen minutes in recording history.

For dyed-in-the-wool Delians, this is an invaluable release; for the unconverted, an ideal invitation to join us.

A Song of Summer; Prelude to *Irmelin*; Fantastic Dance; *Idyll; A Late Lark; Songs of Farewell; Two Aquarelles; Caprice and Elegy;* "La Calinda" from *Koanga; Cynara*

Soloists, Ambrosian Opera Chorus, Royal Philharmonic, Fenby. Unicorn-Kanchana DKPCD-9008/9 [CD].

These recordings by Eric Fenby, who took dictation and abuse from Delius during the composer's final years, would be remarkable for their historic value alone. To hear the molten *Song of Summer* led by the man who actually wrote it down, note by note, makes for a slightly eerie experience. For that matter, Delius's ghost hangs almost palpably over all these proceedings, as well it should, since they are overseen by someone who knew him—both as man and musician—as intimately as anyone.

Beyond their documentary interest, these are absolutely marvelous performances, as loving and individual as Beecham's, which they complement but in no way supplant. While the versions of *A Song of Summer,* the *Irmelin* Prelude (which Fenby arranged), and the little-known *Fantastic Dance* (a piece Delius dedicated to Fenby) are understandably authoritative, it is the conductor's handling of the larger works that makes the recording so priceless. The extended love scene called *Idyll* (for soprano, baritone, and orchestra) has a Puccini-like redolence, and the *Songs of Farewell,* in Fenby's hands, emerges as one of the composer's most singular and unforgettable works.

The sensitive, devoted contributions of the soloists, the Ambrosian Singers, and the great Royal Philharmonic only help to prove that for this composer, there *is* life after Beecham.

A Village Romeo and Juliet

Field, Davies, Hampson, Mora, Dean, Schoenberg Chorus, Austrian Radio Symphony, Mackerras. Argo 430275-2 [CD].

A Village Romeo and Juliet, the fifth of Delius's six operas, is easily his most successful work for the stage. The familiar, matzo-thin plot, centered around a feud between a pair of Swiss families and the two children tragically caught in between, drew from the composer some of his most ravishing music, including the unspeakably touching "Walk to the Paradise Garden."

The gap left by the withdrawal of Sir Charles Groves's sumptuous recording from the 1970s has been brilliantly filled by Sir Charles Mackerras's new version, which is far and away the finest recording of a Delius opera yet made. All of the singers—especially Helen Field and Arthur Davies as the kids and the heartthrob baritone Thomas Hampson as the Dark Fiddler—are excellent, and Sir Charles's conducting has a warmth and felicity that recall Beecham at his best.

One only hopes this is the first in a series.

Diamond, David (1915–)

Symphony No. 2; Symphony No. 4; Concerto for Small Orchestra

Seattle Symphony, New York Chamber Symphony, Schwarz. Delos DE-3093 [CD].

It is in the work of David Diamond that a particular species of American symphony may have reached its most polished and exuberant form of expression. During the late 1940s and early '50s, Diamond became one of the principal purveyors of the neoclassical American symphony, a composer whose finest works in the form rival the best brought forth upon this continent.

The three works presented in what will presumably be the first volume in Delos's Diamond series show the composer at his most characteristic and attractive. If Gerard Schwarz's performance of the wonderful Symphony No. 4 doesn't completely efface the memory of Leonard Bernstein's pioneering recording from 1958, it is still a superb reading, with warmth, energy, and individuality to burn. Here, as in the other pieces, Schwarz continues to reveal himself as the most sympathetic and significant champion American music has had since the death of Howard Hanson.

Anyone responding to Diamond's fresh and bracing idiom will certainly want to investigate the music of two of his near-contemporaries. The sparkling *Symphony for Classical Orchestra* by Harold Shapero, together with the snappy *Nine-Minute Overture*, are brilliantly served by André Previn and the Los Angeles Philharmonic (New World NW-373-2 [CD]).

The extent of what American music lost when the gifted Irving Fine died in 1962 at the age of forty-seven may be guessed from his stunningly effective Symphony, written in the last year of his life. Captured in a live performance by the Boston Symphony under the composer's direction, it is now available from Phoenix (PHCD-106 [CD]). Fine's Partita of 1948, which has a fair claim to being the best woodwind quintet yet written by an American, can be found on a superlative album of his chamber music from Nonesuch (79175-2 [CD], 79175-4 [T]).

Dohnányi, Ernst von

(1877–1960)

Variations on a Nursery Song

Wild, piano; New Philharmonia, Christoph von Dohnányi.
Chesky CD-13 [CD].

Until relatively recent times, the smart money insisted that
Ernst von Dohnányi was the greatest Hungarian composer of the
twentieth century. A late Romantic whose painstaking craftsmanship earned him the sobriquet "the Hungarian Brahms," Dohnányi
would eventually be overtaken and almost completely overshadowed by his younger, more radical contemporaries Béla Bartók and
Zoltán Kodály. In fact, the extent to which Dohnányi's reputation
is now in eclipse may be gathered from the fact that only a handful
of recordings of his most popular piece, the witty and ingratiating
Variations on a Nursery Song, are available.

Why the American pianist Earl Wild is not better known has
always been something of a mystery. Technically, he is one of the
most formidably equipped pianists of his generation. And although
a musician of considerable taste and refinement, he is also among
the more viscerally exciting musicians of our time. As in his superb
set of the Rachmaninoff concertos (see page 320), this recording
from 1967 finds him at the peak of his form. The interpretation is
as fiery as it is playful, featuring a combination of a thunderous
pianism that recalls the legends of the old barnstorming days and
an ability to spin out the music's delicate filigree that is almost unheard of today.

Christoph von Dohnányi is a predictably sympathetic advocate of his grandfather's music, in both his best-known piece and
the virtually unknown *Capriccio* in F minor that accompanies it.
Another Wild performance—in both senses of the phrase—rounds
out this bargain release: the old *Reader's Digest* recording of the
Tchaikovsky First Concerto that could stand a cue ball's hair on
end.

Donizetti, Gaetano

(1797–1848)

L'elisir d'amore

Sutherland, Pavarotti, Malas, Cossa, Ambrosian Opera
Chorus, English Chamber Orchestra, Bonynge. London
414461-2 [CD].

Even as one who has never been carried away by Dame Joan
"The Woman Without a Tongue" Sutherland, and who cordially
(well, actually, *virulently*) despises what the self-indulgent, self-
congratulatory Luciano Pavarotti has become—even *I* can recognize one of the great Donizetti recordings when I hear it. As a
comedienne, Sutherland is deliciously effective: coy, girlish, warmly
and irresistibly human—in short, all those things she so rarely is
elsewhere. Pavarotti, too, is tremendous fun as the lovesick Nem-
orino, and his singing of the show's hit tune, "Una furtiva lagrima,"
contains some of the best work of his career. Spiro Malas's Dr.
Dulcamara is a wonder of transparent, W. C. Fields–like hokum,
and Richard Bonynge's touch is as light-fingered as a pickpocket's.

The same team is responsible for an equally engaging recording of Donizetti's *Daughter of the Regiment* (London 414520-2
[CD])—indeed, the *very* recording in which Pavarotti pops all those
ringing high Cs.

Lucia di Lammermoor

Callas, Tagliavini, Cappuccilli, Ladysz, Philharmonia
Orchestra and Chorus, Serafin. Angel CDCB-47440
[CD].

More than any other of Gaetano Donizetti's sixty-odd operas,
which were often produced at the mind-boggling rate of eight to ten
per year (a contemporary caricature shows the composer seated at
a desk, his famous mop of hair askew, writing with two hands simultaneously), *Lucia di Lammermoor* is the archetypal representative of all that is best *and* most ridiculous in bel canto opera. As

theater, it is both grippingly effective and utterly absurd. The famous Sextet is one of the high-water marks of nineteenth-century ensemble writing, the long and demanding mad scene a silly and thinly veiled excuse for a twenty-minute coloratura concert. (Of course, it could be argued that Lucia's lengthy conversation with an equally energetic flute is no more preposterous than the goofy scene the recently stabbed Gilda, fresh from her gunnysack, is asked to deliver at the end of Verdi's *Rigoletto,* or the similarly exhausting vocal and dramatic tour de force the consumptive Violetta uses to conclude that same composer's *La Traviata.)* But then again, loving opera has always been dependent on a healthy disregard for common sense. And *Lucia di Lammermoor,* with the proper attitude and, more important, the proper cast, can be as rewarding an experience as the opera house has to offer.

Vocally, the most impressive Lucia of modern times was the young Joan Sutherland, whose 1959 London recording recalled the exploits of the almost mythic Luisa Tetrazzini, the great turn-of-the-century diva who today is best remembered for the chicken and spaghetti dish that bears her name. Dramatically and emotionally, the Sutherland Lucia was a rather different matter, and in her far less impressive remake with her husband Richard Bonynge, what were once merely Sutherland eccentricities had already become annoying clichés. The diction made almost every word incomprehensible, and that droopy, sad-little-girl delivery made you want to throw her down the nearest open manhole.

What the opera *should* be, as both a dramatic and vocal experience, is still best suggested by the classic recording made by Maria Callas. Like the Callas *Norma,* it is an exceedingly rich and beautiful characterization. It contains some of the finest singing Callas would ever deliver in a recording studio. The famous mad scene, for once, is not the unintentionally uproarious joke it usually is, but a riveting piece of theater cut from the same cloth as Shakespeare's scene on the blasted heath in *King Lear.* The rest of the cast, even the aging tenor, Ferruccio Tagliavini, is more than adequate. And the veteran Tullio Serafin gives us countless thrilling moments that confirm his reputation as one of the last of the great blood-and-thunder opera conductors. For Callas fans, or for anyone interested in making the rare acquaintance of *Lucia di Lammermoor* as convincing musical drama, this one is an absolute must.

Dukas, Paul (1865–1935)

The Sorcerer's Apprentice

New York Philharmonic, Bernstein. CBS MYK-37769 [CD], MYT-37769 [T].

Don't let any of those slightly smug and self-important music lovers who are going through that inevitable, pseudosophisticated "Trashing the Warhorses" phase of their development sway you. In spite of the fact this piece *did* serve as the backdrop for one of Mickey Mouse's greatest performances, in that otherwise turgid and self-conscious classic *Fantasia*, it is still one of the most dazzlingly inventive tone poems in musical history.

Of the twenty or so versions of the work that are currently available, the winner and still champ is Leonard Bernstein's early CBS recording. The conductor earns high marks for both wit and drama, and the performance also has a visual acuity that makes the playing extremely cinematic in the best possible sense of the word.

For those who might find the thirty-year-old recorded sound a trifle muddy—and it was not, even in its day, one of Columbia's more impressive sonic efforts—the ear-splitting, whistle-clean London recording with the Montreal Symphony and Charles Dutoit (421527-2 [CD], 421527-4 [T]) will melt the tweeters quite handily.

Dvořák, Antonín
(1841–1904)

Concerto in B minor for Cello and Orchestra

Feuermann, cello; National Orchestral Association, Barzin.
Philips 420776-2 [CD].

Fournier, cello; Berlin Philharmonic, Szell. Deutsche
Grammophon 429155-2 [CD], 429155-4 [T].

Du Pré, cello; Chicago Symphony, Barenboim. Angel CDC-
47614 [CD].

The events that led to the composition of this greatest of all
cello concertos are movingly documented in Josef Skvorecky's magnificent 1987 novel *Dvořák in Love* (Knopf), probably the finest
fictional treatment of the life of any composer. The Concerto's second movement was written as an elegy for the composer's sister-
in-law, the only woman with whom Dvořák was ever in love. In
fact, embedded in this poignant outpouring of grief is a quotation
from an early song Dvořák wrote for Josefina Čermáková, a few
years before he married her sister, Anna.

The Dvořák Cello Concerto has been brilliantly served in the
recording studio, beginning in 1929 with what remains the most
spellbinding realization of the solo part. In that classic recording by
cellist Emanuel Feuermann, the recorded sound was fairly dismal
even by the standards of the time, and the Berlin State Opera Orchestra under Michael Taube was barely equal to the task. Still, it
is this recording, more than any other, that demonstrates so conclusively why Feuermann, and not Pablo Casals, was the great cellist
of the twentieth century. The combination of bravado, patrician
phrasing, and flawless technique that Feuermann brought to the
Concerto has never been duplicated. The live performance from a
concert given in New York in 1940 with the National Orchestra
Association is just as memorable, the sense of occasion only height-
ening the breathtaking realization of the solo part. Hearing this fine
Philips restoration makes us realize anew what the world lost when
Emanuel Feuermann died during a routine operation in 1942, a few
months short of his fortieth birthday.

The modern recording which comes closest to the brilliance and passion of Feuermann's is that pointedly dramatic interpretation by Pierre Fournier and George Szell, recorded in Berlin in the 1960s and now available on Deutsche Grammophon. Fournier plays the solo part with fire, subtlety, and conviction, and Szell, who led the Czech Philharmonic in Casals's famous recording of 1937, gives what is arguably his most intense and involving recorded performance. (For a Feuermann-Szell recording in up-to-date sound, I would willingly trade my priceless baseball autographed by Mickey Mantle, 10 percent of my annual income, and my first-born male child.)

Jacqueline Du Pré's Angel recording with Daniel Barenboim and the Chicago Symphony is also very special. It is a red-blooded, slightly (but always persuasively) wayward interpretation in which the playing may owe something to that of her teacher Mstislav Rostropovich, but which fortunately lacks his tendency to vulgarity and self-indulgence. Barenboim, the cellist's husband, offers a sweepingly romantic yet sensitive accompaniment, and both the orchestra and recorded sound are absolutely first-rate.

Concerto in A minor for Violin and Orchestra

Perlman, violin; London Philharmonic, Barenboim. Angel CDC-47168 [CD], 4XS-37069 [T].

Somewhere between that Mount Everest of cello concertos and the foothills of his likable but hopelessly minor piano concerto lies the concerto Dvořák wrote for violin, a work that has never quite managed to challenge the popularity of the Bruch or Tchaikovsky concertos, though in terms of quality it is easily the equal of either.

Written for Brahms's great friend the Hungarian-born virtuoso Joseph Joachim, the piece cost Dvořák an unusual amount of time and anguish. The maniacally fastidious Joachim kept the score nearly two years, finally returning it with so many suggestions for "improvements" that Dvořák all but rewrote the solo part. The result—which Joachim never got around to actually playing—is one of the most broadly rhapsodic of nineteenth-century violin concertos, a lush, yearning, quintessentially Romantic work rounded off by a spirited rondo-finale whose principal theme, once heard, is all but impossible to forget.

Despite some fine recent releases—the teenage Japanese violinist Midori's stylish outing for CBS, and a swashbuckling Deutsche Grammophon recording by Shlomo Mintz—Itzhak Perlman's Angel recording from the 1970s still comfortably dominates the field. The most striking thing in the Perlman interpretation is the ease with which he evokes the "Bohemian" elements in the score. The playing, in fact, is so idiomatic that one wonders whether he might not have more than a few drops of Czech blood in his veins. Daniel Barenboim is an alert and able partner, and the remastered recorded sound more than holds its own with the best today.

Overtures (3); *Scherzo capriccioso*

Ulster Orchestra, Handley. Chandos CHAN-8453 [CD].

Although they usually turn up as filler on recordings of the symphonies, the three overtures Dvořák composed in 1891 were conceived—and should be presented—as a single, indissoluble work with the general title *Nature, Life, and Love.* The "Life" section— the *Carnival Overture*—became an instant sensation, and still overshadows the evocative *In Nature's Realm,* and what is, by far, the greatest panel of the triptych, the searing Shakespearean fantasy *Othello.*

Though *Carnival* has had more brilliant and daring performances—those by Rafael Kubelik, István Kertész, George Szell, and especially Fritz Reiner are not easily forgotten—the excellent Ulster Orchestra under Vernon Handley bring more than enough moxie to that pops concert favorite, and offer the strongest versions of the other two overtures currently in print. *In Nature's Realm* is the verdant tone poem the composer intended, and *Othello* seems the stuff of genuine tragedy, without once flirting with melodrama or hysterics. The interpretation of the *Scherzo capriccioso* that fills out the disc is also top drawer, as are the orchestral execution and recorded sound.

Quintet for Piano and Strings in A, Op. 81; Quartets (2) for Piano and Strings; Bagatelles

Firkusny, piano; Juilliard String Quartet. Odyssey MB2K-45672 [CD].

By any definition, these two dirt-cheap Odyssey CDs constitute an incredible bargain. Though not as well known, perhaps, as the *American* Quartet or the *Dumky* Trio, the A Major Piano Quintet is among the most attractive and accomplished of Dvořák's chamber works, which places it with the greatest chamber music of the Romantic era. The Piano Quartets are hardly less appealing, and the delectable Bagatelles, scored for the unusual combination of strings and harmonium, make a haunting physical sound unique in nineteenth-century music.

That dean of Czech pianists, Rudolf Firkusny, is obviously an ideal exponent of an idiom that has flowed through his veins since childhood. (As a very young boy, he played some of Janáček's music for the aging composer, who was mightily impressed.) The Juilliard Quartet prove to be perfect accomplices in an enterprise that will steal your heart without leaving you broke.

Serenade for Strings in E, Op. 22; Serenade for Winds in D minor, Op. 44

> Academy of St. Martin-in-the-Fields, Marriner. Philips
> 400020-2 [CD].

There has never been a day so wretched, a problem so insoluble, a night so long, a winter so bleak, a toothache so painful that one or the other of these enchanting works couldn't cure it. On those days when I walk in the door drained, disgruntled, disillusioned, full of contempt for all things human, and beating down an insane desire to kick the cat, I put on one of the Dvořák Serenades, make for the nearest chair, and within a few minutes a dippy grin— the external manifestation of a mood of avuncular forgiveness and beatific peace—invariably steals over my face. If only this inexhaustibly charming music were a little better known, many of the nation's psychiatrists would have to start looking for honest work.

Sir Neville Marriner's glowing Philips recording contains the most radiant performances of both Serenades on the market today. The string tone in the Op. 22 is the aural equivalent of a morning in early June; the wind playing in the Op. 44 is a marvel of individuality and character. (The thin, nasal twang of English oboes has never been one of my favorite sounds; here, I hardly notice.)

In a word, yummy.

Slavonic Dances, Opp. 46 and 72

Cleveland Orchestra, Szell. CBS/Sony 44082 [CD], Odyssey 34626/7 [T].

Royal Philharmonic, Dorati. London 430735-2 [CD].

Once, during the interval of a Cleveland Orchestra rehearsal at Severance Hall, a member of the orchestra greeted a visiting friend by saying, after carefully looking over his shoulder to see who might be listening, "Welcome to the American home of Bohemian Culture." And throughout his tenure with the orchestra, George Szell was an enthusiastic champion of the music of Dvořák, Smetana, and that Moravian giant, Leoš Janáček. Although born in Budapest, Szell had considerable Czech blood in his veins; he studied in Prague, and early in his conducting career was a familiar fixture in the Bohemian capital.

Szell's recordings of these popular works are the only ones that bear favorable comparison with Václav Talich's unsurpassable versions from the late 1940s. (Talich's pioneering recording from 1935, whose sound probably makes it a "collectors only" item, has surfaced on Music and Arts CD-658-1 [CD].)The playing of the Cleveland Orchestra is a wonder of brilliance and flexibility, and the conductor, while demanding the last word in virtuoso execution, never overlooks the music's wealth of subtle color and irrepressible charm.

From a somewhat less dizzying height, Antal Dorati's London recording is also very satisfying, especially if nearly flawless recorded sound or the compact disc format is an absolute must.

String Quartet No. 12 in F, Op. 96 *American*

Talich Quartet. Calliope CAL-9617 [CD], 4617 [T].

Written during a few days of the summer vacation the composer spent in the amiable, hard-drinking Czech colony of Spillville, Iowa, where he also completed the *New World* Symphony, Dvořák's *American* Quartet is only the most famous and colorful of those fourteen works which, taken together, constitute the most important contribution a nineteenth-century composer would make to the form after the death of Franz Schubert. Like the *New World* Symphony, the *American* Quartet was inspired by Dvořák's passionate love affair with the sights and sounds of the United States, although like the symphony, it does not contain, as has been so frequently suggested, a single American folk tune. (The subtitle, incidentally, was not the composer's, but instead the idea of a discreet publisher who sought to correct the brazen stupidity of an insensitive time. Shamefully, on the original title page, the F Major Quartet was called "The Nigger.")

With the warmly appealing recording by the Prague Quartet, available only in the sumptuous nine-CD box from Deutsche Grammophon (429193-2) that contains all of the composer's string quartets, this handsome Calliope recording by the Talich Quartet can be recommended without hesitation. The group, founded by a nephew of the great Czech conductor Václav Talich, plays with an engaging mixture of polish and youthful enthusiasm. Like the Prague and Smetana Quartets, they have this music in their bones, and unlike non-Czech groups, which tend to overemphasize the piece's "New World" color, they never forget that this great work is first and foremost an intensely Bohemian score. Also, their performance of the Op. 61 Quartet (No. 11) is so engaging that if you haven't begun to explore Dvořák's lesser-known chamber works, the urge to do so will probably be overwhelming.

String Quartets: No. 10 in E-flat, Op. 51; No. 12 in F, Op. 96 *American;* No. 13 in G, Op. 106; No. 14 in A-flat, Op. 105

> Panocha Quartet. Supraphon C37-7910 [CD] (Nos. 10 and 13); C37-7565 [CD] (Nos. 12 and 14).

If they stay together and stay healthy (to use an indispensable sportscaster's cliché), the young Panocha Quartet from Czechoslovakia should become one of the dominant chamber ensembles of the next quarter century. On the basis of the recordings they have made so far, and some firsthand experience hearing them on their last American tour, I am convinced they are already one of the finest quartets around.

Paradoxically for a quartet, their principal strength—aside from a highly evolved musicality and very sophisticated technique—is their unwillingness to forget their own individual identities for the sake of that mushy, pasteurized uniformity so many groups seem obsessed with these days. If they have a counterpart among the older outfits, it is the Borodin Quartet, another collection of rugged individualists who are not only instantly recognizable *as* individuals but who also add up to an even more appealing whole.

There are no better versions of these late Dvořák quartets currently available. The performances are understandably fresh and youthful, but are also (to coin a phrase) mature beyond their years. Only the Talich Quartet digs into this music with such abandon, authority, and finesse.

If this is the beginning of a cycle of *all* the Dvořák quartets, be prepared to drop some serious cash. You won't regret it.

Symphonic Poems (5)

> **Bavarian Radio Orchestra, Kubelik. Deutsche Grammophon 430074-2 [CD].**

Although they are not as consistently inspired as his symphonies and overtures, Dvořák's Symphonic Poems are mature, colorful settings of some of the wonderfully gruesome folk ballads collected by K. J. Erben: stories rife with murder, betrayal, dismemberment, and assorted mayhem—somehting for the whole family.

Rafael Kubelik's interpretations are on a par with the legendary recordings Václav Talich made in the early 1950s. A natural and arresting storyteller, Kubelik leads the listener through the gory plots so graphically that one need not necessarily know what's going on to enjoy them. (People with sensitive stomachs would probably not *want* to know.) The Bavarian Radio Orchestra responds with an idiomatic grace that recalls the Czech Philharmonic at the top of its form, and the recorded sound is as natural as it comes.

Symphonies (9)

> **Berlin Philharmonic, Kubelik. Deutsche Grammophon 423120-2 [CD].**
>
> **London Symphony, Kertész. London 430046-2 [CD].**

Fifty or even twenty-five years ago it would have been nearly impossible to convince the average music lover that there were really nine, as opposed to only three, Dvořák symphonies. Ironically enough, it was the composer himself who became the principal culprit in the misunderstanding, since he considered the F Major Symphony (No. 5) of 1875 his first mature work in the form and preferred to forget the rest. (He quite literally forgot a couple of the early works, neither of which would be performed during his lifetime.)

These days, there are perhaps as many as five Dvořák symphonies that have wormed their way into general awareness: in addition to the final three, the D Major (No. 6) has begun showing up on concerts with increasing frequency, as has the exuberant, rowdy No. 5, which finally seems to be shaking off the dust of more than a century of neglect.

The unique value of these two handsome CD boxes of all the Dvořák symphonies is the extent to which they demonstrate that the early pieces were not merely apprentice works or dry runs for what was to follow, but important, attractive, often inspired stages in the evolution of a great Romantic symphonist. While both István Kertész's and Rafael Kubelik's performances of the last four symphonies are among the very best available today, it is the special excitement they generate in the lesser-known works that makes the cycles the modern classics they are.

The Second, Third, and Fourth Symphonies contain a wealth —sometimes, an almost *embarrassing* wealth—of ingenious melodic ideas, and even the gabby, frequently clumsy *Bells of Zlonice* (No. 1) is made to seem the creation of a sleeping giant who is just on the verge of waking up. (Strangely enough, Kubelik had little affection for the First Symphony and only recorded it as a favor to Deutsche Grammophon to make the cycle complete. It was—and remains—one of the glories of his recording career.) The Berlin Philharmonic plays with its usual phenomenal precision, but also a warmth and freedom it rarely displayed during the Karajan era, and if you weren't told, you couldn't begin to guess the recording is more than twenty years old.

The Kertész interpretations, if marginally less idiomatic than Keublik's, are for the most part more vividly recorded. While in his phrasing and rhythmic thinking Kertész tends to be more straightforward than Kubelik, there is still an invigorating sense of freedom and spontaneity, with wonders from the London Symphony at every turn. A purely rational choice between these two incomparable cycles is nearly impossible to make. Fortunately, both are so reasonably priced that Dvořák-lovers, with minimal belt-tightening, can acquire them both.

Symphony No. 7 in D minor

**Concertgebouw Orchestra of Amsterdam, Davis. Philips
420890-2 [CD], 420890-4 [T].**

Given the fact that it *is* the man's greatest symphony—and, many would argue, his greatest work—you would think there would be a huge selection of first-rate recordings of the Seventh Symphony from which to choose. Think again. Compared to more than fifty recordings of the *New World* Symphony, the Seventh's total remains a mere dozen and a half—and some of those (by Järvi, Levine, and Maazel) run the scintillating gamut from ho to hum.

With the dramatic and darkly shaded interpretation that comes as part of Kubelik's superlative set, the best single-disc version now on the market is this Colin Davis recording for Philips. While Davis doesn't plumb the tragic depths as deeply as Kubelik—or Szell or Giulini in their badly missed recordings—his is a keen, powerful, elegantly organized performance that is superbly played and recorded.

An even finer version of the Eighth Symphony fills out this unusually desirable disc.

Symphony No. 8 in G; Symphony No. 9 in E minor, *From the New World*

**Cleveland Orchestra, Christoph von Dohnányi. London
421082-2 [CD].**

**Czech Philharmonic, Talich. Supraphon Crystal 11-0627-2
[CD] (No. 8); 11-0290-2 [CD] (No. 9).**

Unlike their recording of the Dvořák Seventh—which, admittedly, has been enthusiastically, even ecstatically, praised elsewhere—it was this recording of the Eighth, more than any other, that confirmed the Cleveland's reemergence as one of the world's great orchestras. Although standards were never allowed to slip during Lorin Maazel's unsettled and unsettling tenure as the orchestra's music director, the orchestra nevertheless played as though their hearts weren't quite in it. At the very least, the old Szell electricity was clearly gone.

Their splendid recording of the most amiable and openhearted of Dvořák's mature symphonies proved, triumphantly, that the Cleveland Orchestra's spirit, under Christoph von Dohnányi, has been thoroughly revived. Not since Szell has the orchestra given another conductor such awesome precision. But the healthiest indication that Dohnányi's was not to be a caretaker regime can be heard in the work of the middle and lower strings, who play with an even darker, more burnished quality than they did under Szell. The interpretation itself reminds me more than anything of Bruno Walter's immensely rewarding CBS recording, though one in which the Walter charm is matched by a Szell-like bite. For instance, in the rousing coda of the final movement Dohnányi makes a point that many conductors seem to miss: namely, that this three minutes of unbridled enthusiasm is nothing more than a thinly veiled Slavonic Dance.

On the other hand, if the quality of the recorded sound is not an issue, then the 1954 Talich recording will probably remain without equal in both this world and the next. Listen to only two minutes of the third movement and the ineffably sorrowful yet impish thing that he makes of it, and you'll understand why Václav Talich has always been regarded as the greatest Dvořák conductor of all time.

The same qualities that characterize both conductors' recordings of the Eighth Symphony can be heard in their very different versions of the *New World*. Dohnányi, in the best modern tradition, is completely unforced and natural, with rhythms that nonetheless have plenty of snap, and execution that is hair-raising in its perfection. Talich allows himself far more rhythmic liberties, and the result is an approach to phrasing which at times seems to mimic the inflections of speech. It is one of the most deeply communicative versions of the *New World* ever recorded and something breathtakingly close to representing Talich at the zenith of his art.

Trio No. 4 in E minor for Piano, Violin, and Cello, Op. 90 *Dumky*

Borodin Trio. Chandos CHAN-8445 [CD], ABTD-1157 [T].

The liner notes that tell you a *dumka*—of which *dumky* is the plural—is a kind of Czech dance (and I've never read a liner note that didn't) haven't got it quite right. A *dumka* isn't a dance at all, and the word isn't Czech, but Russian. Its literal meaning is a "passing through," as in ". . . this vale of tears," which Dvořák understood as meaning something essentially *sad*. (He may have associated it in his mind with an ancient form of song or poem that brooded, as lugubriously as possible, on the heroic deeds of a long-vanished past. This particular kind of brooding has always been a key element in the Czech national character: witness the ruminations of that Moravian neurologist Sigmund Freud, or the jovial fictions of Prague's foremost novelist, Franz Kafka.) As a matter of fact, Dvořák was never really certain *what* the word meant, but that's beside the point. What is important is that he was in the mood to write something *excessively* melancholy, and the *Dumky* Trio became just that.

Coupled with Smetana's equally disturbing piano trio, a work written in response to the death of his eldest daughter, this Borodin Trio recording is probably not the sort of thing you'd want to give to someone with even the mildest suicidal tendencies. Yet for deeply felt forays into two of the darker corners of Romantic chamber music, it exhibits a rare and sinister beauty that no other recording of either piece ever has. In the *Dumky*, the musicians come to terms with the frequent mood swings of the piece with the sensitivity of three adept psychiatrists; their performance of the Smetana unfolds as a long, unbroken cry of grief.

Though the playing may be "too intense for younger audiences," for the more experienced it should prove uncommonly rewarding.

Elgar, Sir Edward (1857–1934)

Concerto in E minor for Cello and Orchestra

Ma, cello; London Symphony, Previn. CBS MK-39541
[CD], IMT-39541 [T].

Anyone who has ever been sprung from an institution of higher learning has understandable feelings of affection and gratitude to Elgar for his best-known work. It is usually to the stirring strains of the *Pomp and Circumstance* March No. 1 in D, also known in England as "Land of Hope and Glory," that most high school and college inmates make their final, glorious escape. Though the average music lover still persists in thinking of him as little more than the stuffy, official musical voice of Edwardian England, Sir Edward Elgar was one of the last of the incontestably great Romantic composers. Finding one's way into Elgar's rich and occasionally overripe world certainly isn't easy. I should know. For it was only after years of mulish resistance that I finally embraced Elgar as one of my greatest musical passions.

There is no more rewarding way of jumping into the real Elgar than with his last major composition. The Cello Concerto, the only work in the literature that can be compared favorably with Dvořák's, was never better served than by the young Jacqueline Du Pré, who made her ardent, rhapsodic recording at the beginning of her fame in 1965, a recording that has been unaccountably withdrawn. Until it returns to circulation—as it most certainly must—Yo-Yo Ma's tautly expressive and phenomenally well played version with André Previn will fill the gap more effectively than any other. In additon to an Elgar Concerto of genuine stature, the recording offers what is probably the finest available account of another English masterpiece, the Cello Concerto of William Walton.

Concerto in B minor for Violin and Orchestra

Kennedy, violin; London Philharmonic, Handley. Angel
CD-EMX 2058 [CD].

Like the symphonies of Anton Bruckner, this longest and, many would say, noblest of all violin concertos has one minor flaw.

For in spite of its incomparably majestic length, it is still *much* too short. The Concerto dates from one of the most fertile periods of Elgar's creative life. Written for the Viennese violinist Fritz Kreisler during the waning years of the Edwardian era—a period that also saw the composition of Elgar's two symphonies—it was one of several key works in which Elgar tried to confine his flood of melodic invention and naturally expansive temperament within the limits of more rigid musical forms.

Apart from its sheer size (in most performances, the Concerto requires nearly fifty minutes to play), the work presents other challenging interpretative problems, chief among them an immense (and immensely original) accompanied cadenza in the final movement. In his 1932 recording with the sixteen-year-old Yehudi Menuhin, the composer demonstrated that the Concerto's difficulties are trivial when compared to its enormous rewards, and fortunately, after years of neglect, a new generation of violinists is beginning to agree.

The modern performance that most closely approximates the depth and authority of Sir Edward's classic interpretation can be found on an Angel recording by the admirable English violinist Nigel Kennedy. With a purity of tone and entrancing sweetness of spirit, Kennedy surmounts the Concerto's formidable problems in much the same way the young Menuhin had before him: by tossing them off as though they were, quite literally, child's play. Yet the real star of the show is the conductor, Vernon Handley, whose ability to highlight a wealth of striking local detail without ever losing sight of the work's overall sweep and architecture only confirms his reputation as one of the preeminent Elgarians of our time.

The Dream of Gerontius

Minton, Pears, Shirley-Quirk, King's College Choir, London Symphony Orchestra and Chorus, Britten. London 421381-2 [CD].

When Elgar wrote "This is the best of me" in the score of his setting of Cardinal Newman's mystical poem, he might also have written, "This is not only the best work written by an English composer in three centuries, but also the greatest oratorio written since the days of Handel."

To date, *The Dream of Gerontius* has had three unassailably great recordings: an impassioned account led by Sir John Barbirolli which is long out of print, the heroic version by Sir Adrian Boult now available in England on a pair of EMI CDs (47208-8), and this fascinating interpretation by Benjamin Britten, in which one great English composer pays homage to another.

Britten, like Barbirolli before him, represents something of a reaction to the "official" Elgar, as espoused primarily by Boult but which drew its inspiration and credibility from the performances the composer himself led late in life. This is the broad, expansive, *nobilmente* Elgar, the epitome of Edwardian dignity (some have said complacency), the Elgar of *The Apostles, The Kingdom,* and *The Dream of Gerontius,* that incomparable trilogy of "sublime bores."

Britten, who until relatively late in *his* life showed little or no interest in Elgar's music, found nothing that was even remotely boring in *Gerontius,* leading a performance in which grandeur and nobility, while never far from the surface, are decidedly less important than dramatic intensity. Tempos tend to be rapid, though never rushed; dynamic contrasts are vivid, though never overdone. There is a tingling sense of expectancy even in the more reflective moments of the score that makes it seem like something it shouldn't really be: a *Gerontius* that keeps its listeners on the edge of their seats.

The soloists are all excellent (although vocally, Pears had better days), and the huge choral forces respond like a chamber choir or with a rolling, full-throated Victorian roar, depending on what their extraordinary leader asks. With his Mozart recordings and versions of the Bach *Brandenburg* Concertos, this *Gerontius* suggests that England may have lost one of its greatest conductors when Benjamin Britten decided he preferred to compose.

The other panels of Elgar's sacred triptych, *The Apostles* and *The Kingdom,* are currently available in the best recorded performances they have ever received. In marked contrast to the Boult recordings, which took their own sweet (albeit noble) time in allowing these magnificent works to make their points, the new Chandos versions led by Richard Hickox invest the music with passion, urgency, and, above all, dramatic life. *The Apostles* (CHAN-8875/6 [CD], DBTD-2024 [T]) smolders with a sacred fervor that recalls the Verdi Requiem, and *The Kingdom* (CHAN-8788/9 [CD], DBTD-2017 [T]) perfectly captures the mood of rapt piety mixed with opulent turn-of-the-century decadence.

Enigma Variations

Royal Philharmonic, Previn. Philips 416813-2 [CD].
BBC Symphony, Bernstein. Deutsche Grammophon
416490-2 [CD].

With the passing of Sir John Barbirolli and Sir Adrian Boult,
many admirers of Elgar's music feared it would suffer the same fate
Frederick Delius's did following the death of Sir Thomas Beecham.
Of course, there was never any serious danger of that: unlike the
rarefied, specialized genius of his younger contemporary, Elgar's
was always the far more important and universal gift. Although no
major Delius conductor has emerged to take the place of the inimitable Baronet, the Elgar tradition continues to grow and flourish
in the hands of a brilliant new guard of sympathetic advocates,
whose brightest light is clearly André Previn.

As in his superlative recordings of the symphonies of Ralph
Vaughan Williams, Previn not only speaks the traditional Elgarian
language as though it were his native tongue but also — and wisely —
has never resisted the temptation to throw in a few new accents of
his own. While his early Angel recording of the *Enigma* Variations
was characterized by a refreshing openness and spontaneity, this
new version with the Royal Philharmonic is clearly the work of a
mature master. The vibrancy and sense of discovery have certainly
not vanished, but along with the still-youthful enthusiasm we can
hear a far more confident grasp of the larger ebb and flow of the
piece. Each of these inspired and inventive variations has great individual character and identity, yet that episodic quality which sab-
otages so many performances is nowhere to be found. In short, this
is the one *Enigma* on the market today in which the whole adds up
to considerably more than the sum of the admittedly striking parts.

Since the annual Grammy Awards ceremony is something of
a joke itself as far as classical recordings are concerned, and since
the prestigious Grand Prix du Disque competition lacks a category
for "Wackiest Recording of the Decade," I hereby announce the
winner of the first (and possibly annual) "Jimmy" Prize to Leonard
Bernstein, for the most insanely self-indulgent Elgar recording ever
made. Tempos, especially in the *Nimrod* variation, tend to be preposterously slow, and the rhythms are hauled around so arbitrarily
that even that King of the Score Maulers, Willem Mengelberg,
would have blushed. Predictably, this live BBC performance of the

Enigma Variations left the generally cheerless English critical establishment either totally befuddled or fit to be tied. And in truth, whatever else the goofy thing might be, it is certainly *not* the *Enigma* Variations. Perhaps it is a measure of the work's indestructible greatness or the force of Bernstein's hypnotic personality, but I treasure this delightful madness almost more than any other Elgar recording I own.

Pomp and Circumstance Marches (5); *Cockaigne* Overture; *The Crown of India* Suite

Scottish National Orchestra, Gibson. Chandos CHAN-8429 [CD], CBT-1012 [T].

This is the confident, public, tub-thumping Elgar, a man far removed from the thoughtful, melancholy Romantic who produced the Cello Concerto or the visionary mystic of *The Dream of Gerontius*. The supremely stirring *Pomp and Circumstance* Marches and the jingoistic *Crown of India* are the musical high noon of the Bristish Empire, the perfect reflection of a self-satisfied society celebrating the fact that it had stolen half the world fair and square.

Sir Alexander Gibson rouses his Scottish musicians to great heights of eloquence and enthusiasm in the Marches and the Suite, while *Cockaigne* (a cognate of "Cockney") crackles with working-class London life.

In another and possibly even finer Chandos recording (CHAN-8430 [CD], CBT-1013 [T]), the same forces (together with excellent soloists and a top-notch chorus) are equally persuasive in Elgar's *Coronation Ode,* in which the great striding tune of the D Major March first became "Land of Hope and Glory." Another masterwork of Elgarian occasional music, the wartime cantata *The Spirit of England,* is offered as a generous bonus.

Symphony No. 2 in E-flat

London Philharmonic, Boult. Angel CDM-64014 [CD].

With the dark and dramatic Symphony No. 1 in A-flat—which is now best represented by André Previn's powerful recording with the Royal Philharmonic (Philips 416612-2 [CD])—Elgar's E-flat Symphony is one of the summits of late-Romantic symphonic thought. With *The Dream of Gerontius*, it also represents much of what is best in Elgar: From the striding confidence of the opening movement through the ineffably poignant closing bars of the finale, it is a sort of gentlemanly and gently refined Götterdämmerung of the entire Edwardian era. As a matter of fact, the composer was already at work on the Symphony's emotional heart, the devastating Largo, when word reached him that the man who gave the age its name had died. This long, beautifully painful, inexpressibly moving elegy for Edward VII is one of the great farewells in all of music.

Sir Adrian Boult recorded the Elgar Second at least a half dozen times, and this final recording is easily the best. He invests the music with a dignity and significance no other conductor has been able to equal, but there is no hint of the stodgy standoffishness that occasionally marred his work in later years. The interpretation is as powerful as it is proper, as dramatic and colorful as it is beautifully shaped. The only other modern recording to match it was that feverish, tempestuous outburst by Sir John Barbirolli, a performance which, with Sir John's incomparable version of *The Dream of Gerontius*, is now shamefully out of print.

For those who *must* have the piece on cassette, only the stately, and occasionally stuffy, Chandos recording by Bryden Thomson and the London Philharmonic (ABTD-1162) can begin to approach the finish and nobility of the Boult.

Falla, Manuel de (1876–1946)

Nights in the Gardens of Spain

De Larrocha, piano; London Philharmonic, Frühbeck de
Burgos. London 410289-2 [CD].

Rubinstein, piano; San Francisco Symphony, Jordá. RCA
60046-4-RG [T].

When she first walks out on stage, Alicia de Larrocha looks
like nothing so much as a slightly plump, demurely elegant Barcelona housewife—which, when she is not off on one of her concert
tours, is precisely what she happens to be. Yet the moment she begins to play we are instantly ushered into the presence of one of the
great pianists of modern times. Her Mozart shimmers with crystalline purity and inner strength, and her Liszt is an exhilarating
amalgam of volcanic intensity and urbane sophistication, but it is
with the colorful, evocative music of her countrymen that de Larrocha is unique. It's unlikely that Isaac Albéniz, Enrique Granados,
or Manuel de Falla ever had a more sympathetic or persuasive interpreter of his piano music, and barring some unforeseen miracle,
they will probably never have one of this quality again.

In her most recent recording of Falla's exquisitely dreamy
Nights in the Gardens of Spain, de Larrocha plays with all the sensitivity and profound understanding that make her new London version of Albéniz's *Iberia* one of the classics of recent recording
history (see page 2). Unlike the many pianists who are unable to
resist the temptation of flooding the *Nights* with too much local
color, de Larrocha is able to approach it with the ease and assurance
of one who speaks its musical language fluently. Never has the music seemed more natural, or more naturally indebted to the piano
music of Ravel and Debussy, nor has there ever been a performance
so utterly spontaneous that it creates the illusion the soloist is simply
making all this up as she goes along. Rafael Frühbeck de Burgos
provides her with some richly idiomatic support, and the recorded
sound is breathtaking in its dynamic range and presence. Clearly,
this is the recording of the *Nights* that will dominate the catalogs
for years to come.

Artur Rubinstein's RCA recording, from the early 1960s, was
one of the best of his later efforts, and is the best cassette version

of the work currently available. The playing has a wonderful and easy grace, and it is supported admirably by Enrique Jordá's evocative accompaniment.

The Three-Cornered Hat; El amor brujo

Boky, mezzo-soprano; Montreal Symphony, Dutoit. London 410008-2 [CD].

In its intoxicating rhythms and harmonic language, its color, wit, and distinctive, highly original use of the resources of the modern orchestra, *The Three-Cornered Hat*—originally composed for Sergei Diaghilev's Ballets Russes—is the most important large-scale orchestral work ever written by a Spanish composer. All of its freshness and overt, provocative sensuality have remained intact for more than seventy years, and, with that masterpiece by a great French tourist, Bizet's *Carmen*, the ballet remains one of the most vivid of all musical distillations of the sights and sounds of Spain.

While *The Three-Cornered Hat* has never gone begging for first-rate recorded performances—Ernest Ansermet, who gave the work its world premiere in 1919, left a commandingly vivid interpretation in 1961, superseded by an even finer Angel recording by André Previn and the Pittsburgh Symphony two decades later—Charles Dutoit's recent effort for London captures more of the ballet's drama and atmosphere than any other.

The secret of the Dutoit performance lies in the perfect balance it projects between the sophistication and studied sensuality that are both so explicit in Falla's score. The rhythmic vitality Dutoit breathes into the more famous dances gives them a freshness that has probably not been heard since *The Three-Cornered Hat* was new. But it is in the less familiar music, which so often can seem like padding, that the performance really comes to life. For instance, the ballet's first bars, with those relentless timpani, castanets, and repeated cries of *Olé*, seem, in this performance, like some of the most inspired opening minutes any composer has ever written.

As always, the Montreal Symphony plays with tremendous dash and precision, and London's engineers, as they usually seem to do for Dutoit, set new standards for brilliance, warmth, and razor clarity of detail.

Fauré, Gabriel (1845–1924)

Dolly Suite; Pavane

Royal Philharmonic, Beecham. EMI CDM-63379 [CD].

Originally a work for piano four-hands—and heard to seductive advantage in that form on a Philips CD by the Labèques (420159-2)—the *Dolly Suite*, in the orchestration by Henri Rabaud, is one of the most enchanting of Fauré's inspirations. In Sir Thomas Beecham's magical hands, it emerges as a work of surpassing tenderness and fin de siècle charm.

Curiously enough, Beecham refused to approve the recording of the *Pavane*, for reasons that are difficult to explain. It may have had something to do with a flaw on the master tape: if you listen carefully, you'll hear the stereo drop out abruptly for the last two notes, which are recorded in monophonic sound. No matter, for this is easily the most rapt and diaphanous recording the *Pavane* has ever received. With equally unforgettable versions of Bizet's *Carmen* Suite, Saint-Säens's *Le Rouet d'Omphale*, and Debussy's *Prelude to the Afternoon of a Faun*, this is probably *the* indispensable French disc on the market today.

Bargain hunters should take note that Ernest Ansermet's lovely, if somewhat harshly recorded, versions of Fauré's *Pelléas et Mélisande* and *Masques et bergamasques* have now turned up on a London Weekend Classics CD (421026-2).

Requiem

Ashton, Varcoe, Cambridge Singers, City of London Sinfonia, Rutter (1893 version). Collegium COLCD-109 [CD], COLC-109 [T].

Battle, Schmidt, Philharmonia Orchestra and Chorus, Giulini (1900 fully orchestrated version). Deutsche Grammophon 419243-2 [CD], 419243-4 [T].

The French consider Gabriel Fauré the consummate musical incarnation of their culture—and certainly, no French composer ever produced a more cultivated body of chamber music, piano works, and songs—but for most non-French ears, Fauré, to use the tired metaphor, is the classic example of a rare, virtually priceless wine that simply refuses to travel. Outside his native country, his discretion, restraint, and natural reticence are still insufficiently appreciated. Then again, to expect anything but an educated Gallic audience to respond to the subtle delicacies of a song cycle like *La Bonne Chanson* is a little like expecting a non-German listener to fully grasp the more thorny lieder of Hugo Wolf.

Along with the melancholy and sinuously beautiful pops-concert staple the *Pavane,* one of the rare Fauré works that have enjoyed considerable popularity in the rest of the world is this gentlest and most reserved of the great nineteenth-century requiems. As in all his important music, the Fauré Requiem makes its subdued points without so much as wrinkling an inch of its immaculately polished surface. From first note to last, the music flows in an inevitable, unhurried way, offering not only quiet spiritual consolation but an extraordinary and original sonic beauty.

The Collegium recording, the first to present the work in the composer's original chamber music instrumentation, makes the strongest case for the Requiem that has yet been made. In fact, the reduced scale of the performing forces is such a perfect complement to the intimate nature of the music that one wonders why no one ever thought of recording it before. Both the singing and playing are engagingly fresh and youthful, and Collegium's spacious but detailed recording captures every nuance of an extremely subtle interpretation.

For those who prefer a Fauré Requiem with a little more meat on its bones, Carlo Maria Giulini's iridescent Angel recording of the 1900 orchestration, while maintaining the restrained poise of a fine chamber music performance, still overflows with old-fashioned romanticism and warmth.

Songs

Souzay, baritone; Baldwin, piano. Philips 420775-2 [CD].

From the days of Jean Lassalle and Victor Maurel (Maurel was the first Tonio in *I Pagliacci* and the man for whom Verdi wrote Iago in *Otello* and the title role in *Falstaff*) to more recent examples like Pierre Bernac and Martial Singher, France has been exceedingly generous in its production of world-class baritones. The last major representative of the species was Gérard Souzay, not only one of the finest singers of his generation but one of its greatest musicians.

This compilation of Fauré song recordings from 1960 and 1965 finds the physical sound of Souzay's silky instrument at its most captivating and the singer at the height of his expressive powers. His recording of *La Bonne Chanson*, Fauré's miraculous setting of nine love lyrics by Paul Verlaine, is probably the finest the cycle has ever received, although the individual items are no less graceful or deft. Souzay's unique gift was his ability to find an amazing variety of nuance in seemingly every note and word, without ever sounding fussy, mannered, or arch. Dalton Baldwin's model accompaniments help make this one of the most desirable song recitals currently available.

For the more adventurous, all of the songs on this album— together with every other *chanson* Fauré ever wrote—can now be found on an indispensable four-CD set from Angel (CDMD-64079). Although in these later recordings Souzay's voice is not ideally fresh, the artistry more than makes up for any defects; the remainder of the songs are covered by the indestructible Elly Ameling, the foremost recitalist of our time.

Finzi, Gerald (1901–1956)

Clarinet Concerto; *Love's Labour's Lost* Suite; Prelude for String Orchestra; Romance for String Orchestra

Hacker, clarinet; English String Orchestra, Boughton. Nimbus NI-5101 [CD].

Gerald Finzi is not one of the better-known twentieth-century British composers. His output was relatively modest (he died at the age of fifty-five), and he tends to be at his best in the music he wrote for the human voice, which is hardly the way to guarantee *any* composer's popularity. A recent ripple of interest in his music—he was never popular enough to enjoy a "revival"—has led to no fewer than four recordings of the 1948 Clarinet Concerto, one of Finzi's loveliest and most characteristic works.

Those—especially clarinetists themselves—who complain that too few important works have been written for the instrument really do need to hear the Finzi Concerto, which easily ranks with those of Carl Nielsen and Aaron Copland among the finest produced in this century. In fact, repeated exposure to its lush, almost Brahmsian opening movement, its deeply expressive Adagio, and the unbuttoned but unhurried finale has persuaded me that it may well be *the* clarinet concerto of modern times.

Alan Hacker, William Boughton, and company give the piece a polished, sensitive interpretation; if not quite the tour de force that Thea King makes of it in her recording for Hyperion (CDA-66001 [CD]), it is still a superb performance and a perfect introduction to a neglected masterwork. Also, the Hacker CD comes with first-rate versions of three other winning Finzi pieces, while King counters with an admittedly brave attempt at Sir Charles Stanford's hopelessly pompous Clarinet Concerto of 1902.

For St. Cecilia; Dies natalis; In terra pax; Magnificat

Langridge, Burrowes, Shirley-Quirk, Richard Hickox Singers, City of London Sinfonia, Hickox. London 425660-2 [CD].

As these four diverse and exceedingly accomplished works triumphantly prove, Finzi was one of the masters of twentieth-century sacred music. On a text by the great World War I memoirist Edmund Blunden, *For St. Cecilia* is in the resounding English tradition of St. Cecilia odes; the *Magnificat* is as rousing as it is succinct. The gems of the collection, though, are the two Christmas works: the rather stark but deeply moving *Dies natalis*, and the far more outgoing *In terra pax*, both of which are on a par with Benjamin Britten's finest Christmas music.

The performances led by Richard Hickox are affectionate, powerful, and completely natural, with exemplary contributions from all concerned.

Flotow, Friedrich von
(1812–1883)

Martha

Popp, Jerusalem, Ridderbusch, Nimsgern, Munich Radio
Chorus and Orchestra, Wallberg. Eurodisc 7789-2-RG
[CD].

Given the disturbing frequency with which the world's opera
companies are mounting revivals of dead-from-the-neck-up bel
canto howlers, and dark, unsingable downers by dour Finns, to say
nothing of the operas [*sic*] of Philip Glass, it's astonishing that Flotow's *Martha* shoulf be so scandalously ignored. Not only is it delightful theater, it abounds in memorable arias, from the several
unforgettable appearances of the English folk song "The Last Rose
of Summer" to the radiant and justly famous tenor aria "Ach so
fromm," which Caruso—to say nothing of every other significant
Italian tenor of the century—recorded as "M'appari."

As in his splendid recording of another neglected masterpiece,
Weinberger's *Schwanda the Bagpiper,* Heinz Wallberg leads a lush
and lively performance of the old charmer, with excellent contributions from most of the cast. The exceptions are Siegfried Jerusalem, well *beyond* excellent in his dashing portrayal of Lionel, and
Lucia Popp, whose intelligence, musicianship, dramatic flair, and
gleaming voice make her one of the great Lady Harriets history has
known.

To be investigated at once.

Françaix, Jean (1912–)

L'horloge de flore for Oboe and Orchestra

De Lancie, oboe; London Symphony, Previn. RCA 7989-2-
RG [CD], 7989-4-RG [T].

As they do to most right-thinking people, the perky, tuneful, mercilessly cheerful excretions of Jean Françaix—the A. A. Milne of French music—usually fill me with an irresistible urge to rip out daisies by the roots and hurl bricks at the nearest chirping bird. Except for *The Flower Clock*.

Written for John de Lancie, the former principal oboist of the Philadelphia Orchestra, *L'horloge de flore* is one of the most ingratiating and gracefully written of all modern oboe concertos and forms the centerpiece of an album that no lover of the instrument—or of elegant French music—can afford to be without. With suave and stylish accompaniments by André Previn and the London Symphony, de Lancie turns in equally definitive performances of the Ibert *Symphonie concertante* and the ethereal *Gymnopédies* by Erik Satie. As a bonus, the CD reissue includes a 1987 recording of the Strauss Oboe Concerto.

Franck, César (1822–1900)

Le Chasseur maudit

Boston Symphony, Munch. RCA 60695-2-RG [CD].

A fondness for Franck's splendidly gruesome *Chasseur maudit* (The Accursed Huntsman) usually accompanies similar passions for B horror-pictures of the 1940s (the ones with Rondo Hatton, Martin Kosleck, or both). The tone poem is one of the key works in an honorable line of black-schlock masterpieces that stretches back to Bach's "Mein Herze schwimmt im Blut" and looks forward to the Shostakovich Eighth.

In its sonically spruced-up format, Charles Munch's classic recording is more hair-raising than ever. It is the kind of loony, loose-limbed music, with a touch of unregenerate vulgarity, that always brought out the best in the conductor. The orchestra—especially the horn section—responds brilliantly, as do Victor's remastering engineers.

Sonata in A for Violin and Piano

Perlman, violin; Ashkenazy, piano. London 414128-2 [CD].

Mintz, violin; Bronfman, piano. Deutsche Grammophon 415683-2 [CD].

Like Leoš Janáček, who did not begin to produce his greatest music until he entered his seventh decade of life, Franck was a classic late bloomer among the major composers. He produced some shockingly dreadful music early in his career (*Hulda*, for instance, has a better than average claim to being the worst French opera of the nineteenth century, and *that's* saying something), and yet, toward the end, he found his own distinct voice in a tiny handful of masterworks that will probably endure forever.

Franck's Violin Sonata (known in some irreverent corners of the classical music radio trade as the Frank Sinatra) stands with those of Brahms and Schumann as one of the finest violin sonatas after those of Beethoven. As in all of Franck's most powerful and characteristic music, the work represents a conscious attempt to contain Romantic sentiment within formal classical structures, a tendency his French critics lambasted mercilessly, charging the composer with an unseemly and almost treasonous fondness for German formalism. (As preposterous as it might seem, many of those same critics took Georges Bizet's *Carmen* to task for being so obviously and slavishly "Wagnerian.")

While I still have the fondest memories of a long-vanished Decca interpretation by the fabulously musical Viennese violinist Erica Morini, Itzhak Perlman's London recording from the mid-1970s easily surpasses all currently available recordings of the work. Poised and elegant throughout, the playing of both the violinist and

Vladimir Ashkenazy is also shot through with a wonderful sense of dramatic urgency and immediacy. In their hands, for instance, the turbulent second movement emerges as one of the composer's greatest creations.

On a somewhat more reserved but no less compelling level, the more recent recording by Shlomo Mintz and Yefim Bronfman has much to recommend it, including youthful ardor, meticulous execution, and more up-to-date recorded sound.

Symphony in D minor

Chicago Symphony, Monteux. RCA 6805-2-RG [CD], 6805-4-RG6 [T].

There are people whose friendship I value and whose musical opinions I respect who absolutely cannot abide Franck's Symphony. (Curiously enough, they tend to be the same people who have an inexplicable revulsion for the music of Frederick Delius. Consequently, I never argue either subject with them, but instead tend to look their way with a mixture of benign sorrow and genuine confusion.) For if truth be told, what's *not* to like in this tuneful, brilliant, melancholy, triumphant work? It has something for everyone: despair, adventure, exuberance, romance, and an English horn solo in the second movement for which anyone who ever played the instrument, myself included, would cheerfully sell his grandmother to the gypsies.

For students of English horn playing, the legendary Laurence Thorstenberg gives one of the greatest performances of his incomparable career in this 1961 RCA recording. For those whose interests are a bit less parochial, Larry's luscious playing can be heard in what also happens to be the greatest recorded performance the Franck Symphony has ever been given.

If further proof were needed that Pierre Monteux was one of the most consistently satisfying conductors of the twentieth century, this stunning performance goes a long way to underscoring the point. With the youthful impetuosity that only this ageless octogenarian could muster, he levitates Franck's often problematical symphony almost to the level of those of Johannes Brahms. The first movement seethes with a barely containable intensity, the slow movement is a seamless, diaphanous love song, while the finale becomes a Tchaikovskian explosion of exuberance and romance. With his London Symphony *Daphnis and Chloë* and Boston Symphony version of Stravinsky's *Rite of Spring*—two works that Monteux introduced to the world—this is one of the principal monuments of a unique and irreplaceable talent.

Fucík, Julius (1872–1916)

Marches and Waltzes
Czech Philharmonic, Neumann. Teldec 42337 [CD].

In many of the more benighted corners of the planet, the Czech composer Julius Fucík is known as the John Philip Sousa of Bohemia. Those of us who know better refer to the March King as the American Julius Fucík. Best known for the immortal circus march *Entrance of the Gladiators,* Fucík also wrote many tunefully appealing waltzes which, if they don't exactly eclipse those of Johann Strauss II, are at the very least cut from the same entrancing cloth.

Václav Neumann proves to be an enthusiastic advocate of his countryman's music, and with the great Czech Philharmonic at its most precise and congenial, Fucík emerges as a composer of genuine character, originality, and charm. Besides, without a first-rate recording of his masterwork, what will you do if you suddenly acquire an elephant?

Gershwin, George (1898–1937)

An American in Paris; Concerto in F; *Rhapsody in Blue*

Golub, piano; London Symphony, Miller. Arabesque
Z-6587 [CD], ABQC-6587 [T].

At the very *least*, this is the greatest single Gershwin recording
ever made. Where it ranks among the great classical recordings of
the last twenty-five years only time will tell, though I suspect it will
rank very high. Among so many other things (peerless oboist, television star, and recording executive whose list of discoveries reads
like a *Who's Who* of American popular music), Mitch Miller is also
one of the most revealing and exciting conductors in the world today. This Arabesque recording of music by his friend George Gershwin may well be the crowning achievement to date in a long and
colorful career.

What Miller brings to Gershwin's music is an unusual combination of freshness and authority. But paradoxically, the freshness
comes from simply playing the music as the composer intended,
intentions Miller discovered firsthand while playing in the orchestra
for the composer's 1934 American tour, and in the original production of *Porgy and Bess.* Working from scores that Miller carefully marked from Gershwin's own interpretations and instructions,
the performances emerge from this astonishing recording sounding
like no others you've ever heard before. While infinitely more lyrical, expansive, and direct in their emotional expression, they are
also more intricate and subtle than those of any other Gershwin
recording on the market today. The important but rarely heard inner voices are coaxed out of the background with a startling clarity,
and the jazz inflections, for once, are not simply tossed in as cheap
effects but can clearly be heard for what they were all along: part
of the music's natural organic structure.

The playing of the London Symphony ranges from the merely
sensational to the absolutely terrifying—at times, the brass section
wails with the electrifying unanimity of purpose of the old Count
Basie band—and the technically spellbinding but intelligent and poetic playing of David Golub suggests that he is clearly one of the
finest pianists before the public today. For Gershwin lovers, the recording is an obvious necessity; for those who have never been able

to warm to the composer's more obviously "serious" music, this is an excellent opportunity to hear it—quite literally—for the very first time.

Piano Music

Bolcom, piano. Nonesuch 79151-2 [CD], N5-71284 [T].

The major qualitative difference between the songs of Franz Schubert and those of George Gershwin is that, by and large, Gershwin worked with better texts. The best of the songs he wrote to lyrics by his brother Ira *are* the enduring lieder of the twentieth century. Often, all that differentiates works like "An die Musik" and "The Man I Love" are their differing harmonic language and emotional content; as to their ultimate merit, five hundred years from now the connoisseur of art songs will probably be hard-pressed to choose between them.

In addition to the "Gershwin Song Book"—arrangements made by the composer himself of eighteen songs—this inviting Nonesuch recording gathers together most of Gershwin's music for solo piano in performances as stylish as they are unaffected.

An eclectic and frequently arresting composer in his own right, William Bolcom speaks Gershwin's musical language without any discernible accent: the frequently recorded Three Preludes sound more mysterious and rhythmically intriguing than they ever have before, and the *Rialto Ripples* are tossed off with a typically Gershwinesque wise-guy smile.

Porgy and Bess

Albert, Dale, Smith, Shakesnider, Marshall, Houston Grand Opera Orchestra and Chorus, De Main. RCA RCD3-2109 [CD], ARK3-2109 [T].

Although many of its arias have long since become popular standards (is there anyone who can forget his or her first encounter with "Summertime"?), Gershwin's last great achievement, *Porgy and Bess,* remains a neglected classic. Its initial run, while more than respectable for an opera, was disastrous by Broadway-musical standards, and ever since its ill-fated first production, *Porgy and Bess* has had the undeserved reputation of being a hard-luck show.

This handsome RCA recording by the Houston Grand Opera (the same adventurous company that more recently brought us John Adams's *Nixon in China,* whether we wanted it or not) proves conclusively that Gershwin knew precisely what he was about. For with the proper care and dedication—which does not necessarily mean the services of world-class voices or an internationally famous conductor—*Porgy and Bess* can clearly be heard as the closest thing we have to the Great American Opera.

Not since the path-breaking Columbia recording Goddard Lieberson produced in 1950 has any recorded version of the opera made such a convincing case for *Porgy and Bess*'s greatness. The entire cast is uniformly distinguished and enthusiastic, especially the bewitching Clamma Dale, and under John De Main's precise but freewheeling and expressive direction, this *Porgy* adds up to a very convincing musical and dramatic whole. If De Main misses the occasional inflection or the wonderfully sexy phrasing that made Lehman Engel's conducting such a joy on the old Columbia set, his vigorous sincerity is certainly to be preferred to Lorin Maazel's impeccably played and sung but rather cold and calculated runthrough for London.

To be fair, Simon Rattle's Angel recording (CDCC-49568 [CD]) has had critics tripping all over each other to see who could get in the most heartfelt Second Coming rave. (In one of the British publications—name withheld to protect the guilty—the critic kept referring to the wonderful contributions of "the coloured singers." One only supposed that the late twentieth century had arrived everywhere.) It *is* a fine, slick, jazzy production that has a good deal to offer, but not as much, I think, as the *Porgy* from Houston.

Gilbert, Sir William S.

(1836–1911) and

Sullivan, Sir Arthur

(1842–1900)

H. M. S. Pinafore

D'Oyly Carte Opera Company, Sargent (recorded 1930).
Arabesque Z-8052-2 [CD], A-9052-4 [T].

Iolanthe

D'Oyly Carte Opera Company, Godfrey. London 414145-2
[CD], 414145-4 [T].

The Mikado

D'Oyly Carte Opera Company, Nash. London 417296-2
[CD], 414341-4 [T].

Patience

D'Oyly Carte Opera Company, Godfrey. London 425193-2
[CD].

The Pirates of Penzance

D'Oyly Carte Opera Company, Godfrey. London 414286-2
[CD], 414286-4 [T].

Along with their inedible cuisine (who but they would even
consider *looking* at such emetics as "Steak and Kidney Pie" and
"Beans on Toast"?) and their public monuments (are there any
structures in the civilized world quite so ugly as the Albert Memorial

or the facade of Euston Station?), another of the great and presumably imperishable English traditions are the fourteen operas written by two of the strangest bedfellows in theatrical history, W. S. Gilbert and Arthur Sullivan. The myth that the two were close, inseparable friends is precisely that. From beginning to end, the relationship was characterized by mild mutual respect tempered by constant suspicion, distrust, and frequently open, albeit gentlemanly, contempt. In fact, all the two men had in common was an unshakable belief that each was prostituting his sacred talent for the sake of making money.

Those of us who are hopelessly drawn to the Gilbert and Sullivan operas tend to treat the affliction as any other incurable disease. For except among ourselves, to admit a passion for Gilbert and Sullivan is a bit like admitting to something slightly embarrassing, like being, to quote Sheridan Whiteside in *The Man Who Came to Dinner,* "the sole support of a two-headed brother."

For anyone similarly smitten, or for those who are thinking of taking the ghastly plunge for the very first time, the recordings listed above represent a fair cross-section of the D'Oyly Carte Opera Company's finest achievements. While the *Iolanthe, Mikado, Patience, Pirates,* and Godfrey-led *Pinafore* recordings are among the very best that the late and greatly lamented company founded by Gilbert and Sullivan themselves would ever make (John Reed, the last in the unbroken line of Savoy patter comics, is especially delightful, and Donald Adams is an incomparable Dick Deadeye and Pirate King), the 1930 *Pinafore* remains in a class by itself. The principal attraction here, aside from the buoyant conducting of the young Malcolm Sargent, is one of the few complete recorded performances left by the greatest Savoyard of all. After a career spanning more than fifty years, Sir Henry Lytton was the only Gilbert and Sullivan performer ever knighted for his services. Even the great Martyn Green could not approach the horrible perfection of Lytton's Sir Joseph Porter, K.C.B. Dramatically, it is a triumph of bumbling incompetence and unbridled lechery. Musically, it is absolutely glorious, thanks in no small part to an inimitable "voice" that can best be described as a cross between a soggy Yorkshire pudding and a badly opened beer can.

Glazunov, Alexander
(1865–1936)

Concerto in A minor for Violin and Orchestra; *The Seasons*

Shumsky, violin; Scottish National Orchestra, Järvi.
Chandos CHAN-8596 [CD], ABTD-1285 [T].

Of all the well-known composers, Nikolai Rimsky-Korsakov had, by far, the most hideous wife. And considering the dispositions of women like Frau Haydn and the dread Pauline Strauss, that's saying something.

At her husband's funeral in 1908, Madame Rimsky-Korsakov, with an atypical rush of human feeling (to say nothing of a completely unprecedented flash of perception), noticed that the deceased's prize pupil, a young man named Igor Stravinsky, was utterly disconsolate. In an effort to comfort him, the woman put her hand on Stravinsky's shoulder and said, "Don't despair. We still have *Glazunov*."

Such was the extent of Alexander Glazunov's reputation at the turn of the century, although we now tend to think of him primarily as Rimsky's acolyte and as the teacher of Dmitri Shostakovich. That he did not quite become what everyone thought he would—the towering giant of Russian music—came as a shock to everyone, except, perhaps, to the composer himself.

But then, too, neither was he the cut-rate Tchaikovsky he was widely considered only a generation ago. In the last few years, the musical world, especially the recording companies, has begun to reassess this minor but immensely attractive musical personality with some extremely gratifying results.

Not surprisingly, that indefatigable Estonian recording machine, Neeme Järvi, is in the vanguard of the current Glazunov revival. While neither recording of the composer's two most enduring achievements, the Violin Concerto and the ballet *The Seasons,* is the last word in delicacy or excitement, both are the best available versions of these once-popular works and might help steer the listener in the even more interesting direction of the Glazunov symphonies.

With the Bamberg Symphony and Bavarian Radio Orchestra, Järvi has recorded all eight of the completed symphonies for Orfeo (a ninth exists as a fragmentary single movement), and almost without exception, both the pieces themselves and the performances are sources of undiluted pleasure. For those who'd prefer to start slowly rather than investing in the entire set, the best place to begin is at the beginning, with the youthful, invigorating Symphony No. 1. Coupled with the brashly heroic Symphony No. 5 (Orfeo C-093101 [CD], M-093101 [T]), this is an excellent introduction to a body of work that deserves to be far better known.

Glière, Reinhold (1875–1956)

Symphony No. 3 in B minor, *Ilya Murometz*

BBC Philharmonic, Downes. Chandos CHAN-9041 [CD].

Best known for the ballet *The Red Poppy* and its (try as you will) unforgettable "Russian Sailor's Dance," Reinhold Glière was the Norman Rockwell of Soviet Socialist Realism, a man whose native musical conservatism (he was in fact irretrievably reactionary) fitted in perfectly with what the tone-deaf Joseph Stalin thought a "revolutionary" society ought to hear.

Glière's most important work, a mammoth programmatic symphony celebrating the life of a legendary Russian hero, is also his most controversial. The debate centers on just *how* bad the *Ilya Murometz* Symphony is.

Heavily edited, as it was in a famous recording by Leopold Stokowski, it was merely awful; given an uncut and committed performance—as it is here—it is *obscene*. Vulgar, vapid, stupid beyond description, it is a pathetic mélange of bathos, bombast, and empty, knuckleheaded gestures. It is also terribly loud and terribly long.

If you love *Ilya* as helplessly as I do, you will acquire this splendid, virtually note-complete recording without delay. (By the way, this is only the first installment in a series that promises to encompass all of Glière's major orchestral scores. The mind reels.)

For Glière in substantially smaller and marginally more charming doses, his two unusual concertos—one for harp, the other for coloratura soprano—have been reissued on an attractive London CD (430006-2). Joan Sutherland warbles magnificently through her lightweight confection, and Osian Ellis makes very light of the most challenging and completely agreeable harp concerto of modern times.

Gluck, Christoph Willibald
(1717–1787)

Orfeo ed Euridice

Horne, Lorengar, Donath, Orchestra and Chorus of the Royal Opera House, Covent Garden, Solti. London 417410-2 [CD].

Listening to this best known of Gluck's "reform" operas today, it is all but impossible to understand the violent passions it unleashed more than two centuries ago. In Paris, where Gluck had set up shop in 1773, the composer's insistence that drama, instead of florid singing, should be the true focus of the operatic stage generated heated public debates. As a matter of fact, it even provoked a number of private duels, in which many of his partisans and those of his principal rival, Nicola Piccinni, were killed. Today, of course, Gluck's revolutionary operas seem rather tame and timid stuff, largely because the reforms he inaugurated have long been accepted as elementary tenets of how opera should behave.

After Purcell's *Dido and Aeneas*, *Orfeo ed Euridice* is the earliest extant opera performed with any frequency today. Though the action is generally static, and the characters are little more than cardboard cutouts, *Orfeo* has some beautiful moments that still have the power to move us deeply, including the celebrated "Dance of the Blessed Spirits" and the haunting aria "Che farò senza Euridice."

With Dame Janet Baker's Glyndebourne Festival recording currently unavailable, the Solti recording is an acceptable, if not wholly satisfying, alternative. Vocally, Marilyn Horne makes an impressive hero: her deep, throaty sound and virile delivery are both positive assets in the role of Orfeo. If Pilar Lorengar, as Euridice, has seen better days—the characterization is surprisingly tentative and the sound is insecure and unfocused—then Sir Georg Solti, who would seem to be rather out of his element in this staid and stately music, gives one of the better recorded performances of his career. The conducting is as tasteful as it is pointed, and rarely—as in "The Dance of the Blessed Spirits"—has this music conveyed more genuine feeling or quiet charm.

Gounod, Charles (1818–1893)

*R*oméo et Juliette

> Malfitano, Kraus, Quilico, Van Dam, Bacquier, Capitole de Toulouse Orchestra and Chorus, Plasson. Angel CDCC-47365 [CD].

Poor Charles Gounod has fallen on decidedly hard times. Then again, it's rather difficult to work up any real sympathy for one of the luckiest musicians who ever lived. It was a major miracle that the man who was perhaps the tenth best French composer of his generation parlayed a gift for sugary melody into one of the greatest successes in the history of the operatic stage. His opera *Faust* was at one time performed with such monotonous frequency that a turn-of-the-century wag recommended that the Metropolitan in New York be renamed the "Faustspielhaus."

That *Faust* may finally be losing its viselike grip on the world's affections is suggested by the fact that there are currently only a handful of available recordings of it, and the best of those—with an uncomfortable Sir Colin Davis leading a stiff German orchestra and a largely hammy cast on Philips—is a turkey.

In marked contrast to the composer's immensely lucrative Goethe travesty, his setting of Shakespeare's *Romeo and Juliet* is a far less presumptuous and probably far finer work. With the proper cast, this genuinely touching but sadly neglected opera can make a very moving impression, as this superb Angel recording easily proves. While the two principals don't exactly efface the memory of the legendary performances Jussi Björling and the Brazilian soprano Bidú Sayão gave at the Metropolitan Opera shortly after the end of the war, both are exceptionally fine: Catherine Malfitano is a melting, delectably innocent Juliette, and the Romeo of the aging but always canny Alfredo Kraus is a triumph of interpretative savvy and consummate musicianship over a voice that has clearly lost its bloom.

Michel Plasson's conducting is consistently sensitive, supportive, and richly romantic. The orchestra plays wonderfully, and the recorded sound, especially in the compact disc transfer, is first-rate. Had these same forces turned their attention to *Faust,* that sadly shopworn opera might have been given, at least on records, another of its innumerable new leases on life.

Granados, Enrique

(1867–1916)

Goyescas Piano Suite

De Larrocha, piano. London 411958-2 [CD].

When the SS *Sussex* went down in the English Channel, torpedoed by a German U-boat in the second year of the Great War, she took with her one of the most original talents Spain had ever produced.

With his friend Isaac Albéniz, it was Enrique Granados who reawakened serious music in Spain, with a group of colorful, electric, rhythmically vibrant reactions to the etchings and paintings of Francisco Goya. The suite for piano, *Goyescas,* helped to establish the vocabulary and parameters of modern Spanish music, and has remained a pianistic tour de force to be undertaken only by the most fearless virtuosos. (Granados would later adapt the music into an opera by the same name, adding an orchestral *Intermezzo* that would eventually become his most familiar work.)

As in her most recent recording of Albéniz's *Iberia* (see page 2), Alicia de Larrocha is literally incomparable in this music. Other pianists have certainly tried to invest *Goyescas* with this kind of wit, passion, and insouciance, but none have ever come close. She makes it all sound so natural and preposterously easy that we need only sit back, relax, and enjoy the spells cast by one of the most beguiling sorceresses in living memory.

Grieg, Edvard (1843–1907)

Concerto in A minor for Piano and Orchestra

Perahia, piano; Bavarian Radio Orchestra, Davis. CBS MK-44899 [CD], MT-44899 [T].

One of the most apt but not completely flattering descriptions of the music of Edvard Grieg came from Claude Debussy, who called the diminutive Norwegian composer "a bonbon filled with snow." The implication, of course, is that along with the bracing Nordic freshness of his music, Grieg was essentially a miniaturist, a composer of delicious little trifles and nothing more. For more than a century, one of the most popular of all Romantic piano concertos has given the lie to the suggestion that Grieg was at his best only when he was thinking small. True, his finest work *does* tend to come in smaller packages, but this enduring classic also demonstrates that he was perfectly comfortable in large-scale forms as well.

From a recording made at a concert, Murray Perahia and Sir Colin Davis turn in a performance of uncommon dramatic power and interpretative finesse, one of those rare recordings in which everyone concerned seems to walk the tightrope between Romantic anarchy and modern control. The disciplined and completely unobtrusive German audience almost forgets to breathe, and the recorded sound is supremely transparent and warm.

If sound is not a major consideration, no recording has ever duplicated the poetry and insight of Dinu Lipatti's eternal 1947 performance, now available on a lovingly remastered Angel CD (CDH-63497).

Holberg Suite

Academy of St. Martin-in-the-Fields, Marriner. Argo 417132-2 [CD].

Written in 1884 for the bicentenary of the birth of Ludvig Holberg, the patriarch of Danish literature, the *Suite from Holberg's Time* is, after *Peer Gynt* and the Piano Concerto, the most popular and most frequently recorded of Grieg's larger works.

If the best possible recording is what you're after, then the choice is an easy one: this enchanting Marriner version in which you can almost smell the pine needles and taste the buttermilk. Now if only Argo (English Decca) could strike a deal with Deutsche Grammophon to piggyback Marriner's performance onto an exceptional Grieg recording by Neeme Järvi and the Gothenburg Symphony. That strenuously recommended release (419431-2 [CD]) brings you the finest available versions of the *Lyric Suite,* the Norwegian Dances, and the Symphonic Dances. Not only a great Grieg bash, but also a great buy.

Lyric Pieces for Piano

Gilels, piano. Deutsche Grammophon 419749-2 [CD].

Here are some of the most bewitching piano miniatures ever, in performances that are not likely to equaled, much less surpassed.

Emil Gilels might seem to be well outside his regular territory in this music, but his recording remains a standard against which all others will be judged. The playing reaches stratospheric heights, and the mixture of the familiar with the scarcely known works makes this one of the most desirable Grieg recordings ever made.

Anyone seriously devoted to this composer's piano music will find all of it—yes, *all* of it—on a monumental set of ten Bis compact discs (BCD-104/13) that features the gifted and apparently indefatigable Eva Knardahl. If her playing cannot really compare with Gilels's, it is not to be taken lightly, either. The interpretations are for the most part balanced, idiomatic, and unobtrusive, yet are not lacking in fire and individuality whenever the spirit moves her or the music demands. Not the least of the innumerable attractions of this gallant undertaking is the recorded sound. As we might expect from Bis, Robert von Bahr's small but maniacally perfectionist Swedish label, this is as close to being in a room with an actual piano as modern technology has come.

Peer Gynt (incidental music)

Hollweg, soprano; Beecham Choral Society, Royal
Philharmonic, Beecham. Angel CDM-69039 [CD].

Carlsen, Hanssen, Bjørkøy, Hansli, Oslo Philharmonic
Chorus, London Symphony, Dreier. Unicorn-Kanchana
UKCD-2003/4 [CD].

Like Tchaikovsky, who thoroughly despised his *Nutcracker* Suite, and Rachmaninoff, who often became violently nauseated at the prospect of having to give yet another performance of his C-sharp minor Prelude, Grieg was not especially fond of his most frequently performed work. In a famous letter written to the playwright Henrik Ibsen, he had this to say of the soon to be world-famous *In the Hall of the Mountain King:* "I have written something for the hall of the Troll king which smacks of so much cow dung, ultra-Norwegianism and self-satisfaction that I literally cannot bear to listen to it." In that, of course, Grieg has always been a minority of one. For the score he composed for a production of Ibsen's poetic drama *Peer Gynt* contains some of the best-loved moments in all of music.

For anyone who cut his or her musical teeth on the chestnuts from the two *Peer Gynt* Suites, the world premiere recording, from

Unicorn, of the complete incidental music will come as a major and unfailingly delightful surprise. (By the way, all the other recordings that claim to contain the "complete" incidental music are stretching the laws of truth in advertising. With Neeme Järvi's recent, and slightly less successful, Deutsche Grammophon recording, there are now precisely *two*.) Containing nearly an hour of unknown *Peer Gynt* music, the performance led by the fine Norwegian conductor Per Dreier makes for an enlightening experience, to say the very least. The "heavy hits" are all done to near-perfection, but it is the cumulative impact of the other, completely unfamiliar episodes that creates the more indelible impression. Far from being the light-weight collection of saccharine lollipops it can often become, the *Peer Gynt* music for once emerges as vivid and powerful drama. Dreier leads his forces with great individuality, charm, and authority; the Norwegian cast and chorus are consistently brilliant and idiomatic, and the playing of the London Symphony is above reproach.

The only serious flaw in this otherwise flawless recording is one that none of these dedicated performers could possibly control. For all its professionalism and devotion, it is simply *not* in the same stratospheric league with that vocally klutzy, harshly recorded source of wonder and despair Sir Thomas Beecham perpetrated a generation ago. In its new compact disc incarnation, this ageless performance seems even more magnetic and unsurpassable than ever. *Anitra's Dance* contains some of the most graceful playing ever captured in a recording studio, *The Death of Aase* becomes a muffled outcry of insupportable grief, and *Morning* dawns with a sylvan freshness that suggests the very first morning of the world. Yet it is in the *Hall of the Mountain King* that Beecham really makes us wonder what the composer's whining "cow dung" letter was all about. Unless, of course, Beecham read it too, and took that as his cue to do his best, in this macabre and terrifying performance, to scare a similar substance out of his listeners.

Grofé, Ferde (1892–1972)

Grand Canyon Suite

Cincinnati Pops, Kunzel. Telarc CD-80086 [CD], CS-30086 [T].

There is a special category of quasi-classical piece (one resists the term *semi-classical* since it immediately conjures up images of the 101 Strings and Mantovani) of which the *Grand Canyon Suite* seems to be the most stubborn survivor of all. Other examples include *Victory at Sea*, the *Warsaw Concerto*, the *Red Shoes* ballet (conducted in the movie by Sir Thomas Beecham), and one that never received anything like the attention it deserved: the suite from the music Norman Dello Joio composed for the CBS News series *Airpower*, which was recorded (and how!) by Eugene Ormandy and the Philadelphia Orchestra. For want of a term both more succinct and more descriptive than *semi-* and/or *quasi-classical*, let's call this stuff Music Serious Music Lovers Wouldn't Be Caught Dead Admitting They Liked, Even If They Did.

Apart from its intrinsic merits—which are considerable—Ferde Grofé's celebration of the world's most inspiring ditch was given enormous credibility by the advocacy of Arturo Toscanini, who loved this brilliantly effective tour of his favorite spot on earth. (Since it was also the vehicle of one of the Maestro's few palatable NBC Symphony recordings, one wonders why RCA didn't issue it, instead of those dreadful Beethoven, Brahms, and Verdi catastrophes, as part of the first installment of the Complete Toscanini on CD.)

Among modern recordings of the *Grand Canyon Suite*, none is more spectacular than Erich Kunzel's Cincinnati Pops outing for Telarc. Part of the gimmick (and who doesn't love a good gimmick, when it works?) is a second version of the *Cloudburst* movement which includes a frighteningly realistic recording of an actual desert thunderstorm captured by Telarc's engineers. The performance itself is an exceptionally fine one: the orgasmic climax of *Sunrise* is beautifully built, and *On the Trail* lopes along with just the right touch of innocent humor.

I wonder if Kunzel ever watched *Airpower*? (Apparently, the American conductor Davis Amos did. His version of Dello Joio's score, in an earnest though something less than soaring performance by the Krakow Philharmonic, is now available on Koch 3-7020-2 [CD], 3-7020-4 [T].)

Handel, George Frideric
(1685–1759)

Concerti Grossi (12), Op. 6

Academy of St. Martin-in-the-Fields, Brown. Philips 410048-2 [CD].

English Concert, Pinnock. Deutsche Grammophon 410897/ 9-2 [CD].

I somehow manage to shock people when I tell them I have always preferred the music of George Frideric Handel to that of Johann Sebastian Bach. I find Handel not only the far more appealing composer, but also the far more interesting man. Assiduously devoting his extramusical energies to prayer and the production of twenty-odd children, Bach seems to have been a classic seventeenth-century Lutheran homebody, whose life story makes for singularly boring reading. Handel, who was an internationally famous figure while Bach was still a provincial kapellmeister, was a mass of fascinating contradictions. In spite of his many physical and psychological afflictions—he was nearly felled by several major strokes, went blind at the end of his career, and for more than sixty years exhibited many of the classic symptoms of manic depression— Handel was nevertheless one of the healthiest composers in the history of music, a man whose many enthusiasms and vigorous love of life can be heard in virtually every bar of music he wrote.

Nowhere is the essence of Handelian exuberance and inventiveness more clearly in evidence than in these dozen concerti grossi he composed, largely for money, in 1739. (Dr. Johnson may have had Handel in mind when he framed one of the most irrefutable of all his aphorisms: "No man but a blockhead ever wrote except for money.") Though much of the thematic material was purloined from the works of other composers, the collection is full of an utterly original and irresistible beauty. The dance movements are as infectious as any written by a Baroque composer, the slow movements are often poignant and invariably memorable, and the slapdash, good-natured fugues remain as impressive as any Bach ever wrote.

Of all the fine recordings that are currently available, pride of place clearly goes to the elegant Philips set by the Academy of St. Martin-in-the-Fields. While detailed and scholarly, these non-period-instrument performances have none of the musty, stuffy, academic quality that has marred so many recent Handel recordings. Under Iona Brown, as they had for years under Sir Neville Marriner, the St. Martin's Academy plays with an appealing combination of bravado and finesse, and the Philips engineers have provided a warm but lively acoustic that is the perfect mirror of the performances themselves.

For the Baroque Authenticity Purists, Trevor Pinnock's only slightly less desirable Deutsche Grammophon recording offers a fine period-instrument alternative.

Concertos for Organ and Orchestra

Hurford, organ; Concertgebouw Chamber Orchestra, Rifkin. London 430569-2 [CD].

As a boy, my idea of ultimate torture—besides watching the deeply detested Chicago Cubs win the occasional game—was being made to sit still while someone was playing the organ. It undoubtedly had something to do with spending Sunday mornings languishing in a hot, stuffy Premethepiscobapterian church that smelled of dust and peppermint, while a sweet but hopelessly inept matron fumbled her way through hymn after ghastly hymn. To this day, it takes a lot to make me listen to the organ; Peter Hurford almost makes it a pleasure. Of course, he has a bit of help here from George Frideric Handel.

Handel's organ music could not be further removed from either the horrifying experiences of my youth or the leaden, insufferably self-righteous outpourings of many of the other Baroque masters. (Legend has it that Bach walked two hundred miles to hear Dietrich Buxtehude play; I would have *run* several miles in the opposite direction to have avoided it.) Even in the least of these works—and the general level of quality is phenomenally high—imagination and exuberance are to be found on every page, and Hurford's stylish, manly enthusiasm is difficult to resist. On a pair of medium-priced CDs, this is a tremendous amount of enjoyment for twenty bucks. If you can resist, your willpower is far more highly developed than mine.

Coronation Anthems (4)

Academy and Chorus of St. Martin-in-the-Fields, Marriner. Philips 412733-2 [CD].

If until very recently the House of Windsor has seemed one of the least interesting and dimmest-witted of Britain's royal families, the Windsors have been rocket scientists compared to the ill-starred and unlamented Hanoverian kings. George I, the founder of the line, not only refused to learn English during his reign but also succeeded in enraging his British subjects even more by refusing to trade in his German mistresses for English ones. His unstable grandson, George III, who suffered from recurrent bouts of madness throughout his life, was responsible for the loss of the nation's American colonies. In fact, the only significant accomplishment the entire dynasty can point to with pride was its employment of the Saxon composer George Frideric Handel, who produced for them some of the greatest ceremonial and occasional music ever written.

The magnificent Coronation Anthems are all that survive from the thoroughly bungled coronation of George II in 1727. At their first performance, the sequence of the hymns, together with most of the actual ceremony, was somehow thrown completely out of whack, thereby making it a typically Georgian event. Still, the anthems Handel provided are so stirring in their grandeur, so rich in their invention and execution, that upon hearing them even the most tenaciously republican of her former colonists might almost be tempted to ask Her Majesty to take us back.

Neville Marriner's Philips recording offers suitably grand, though never grandiose, performances of these imposingly noble works. The interpretation of the seven-minute *Zadok the Priest,* with its mysteriously hushed opening and thundering final fugue on the word *Alleluia,* is in itself worth more than the price of the recording. For anyone addicted to eighteenth-century pomp and circumstance, or who simply wants to be convinced that there *will* always be an England, this is a recording that cannot be passed up.

The Faithful Shepherd; The Gods Go a'Begging (suites arranged by Beecham); *Handel at Bath* (suite arranged by Allan Bennett)

> **Royal Philharmonic, Menuhin. MCA Classics MCAD-6231 [CD], MCAC-6231 [T].**

Rather than step out into the alley and try to settle *this* one again, suffice it to say that anyone who admires the works and pomps of that marvelous hybrid composer Handel-Beecham (a very close relative of Handel-Harty) will love these confections in the extremely tasty performances served up here by Sir Yehudi Menuhin. Handel-Bennett, while less distinguished, is still very endearing, as are the performances of the only *echt* Handel pieces on the program, the Overture and familiar "Arrival of the Queen of Sheba" from *Solomon.*

All that's needed now to propel us Baroque lowbrows into ersatz-Handel heaven is a CD reissue from Angel of Beecham's own recording of his masterpiece in the form, *Love in Bath,* which includes among its numerous wonders a trombone quotation of "Rule, Britannia" and an allegro setting of the famous *Largo.*

Messiah

> **Marshall, Robbin, Rolfe-Johnson, Hale, Brett, Quirke, Monteverdi Choir, English Baroque Soloists, Gardiner. Philips 411041-2 [CD].**

While his dramatic oratorios *Jephtha* and *Theodora* are probably finer works (Handel considered the chorus "He Saw the Lovely Youth" from *Theodora* his absolute masterpiece), *Messiah* has more than earned its status as the best-loved sacred work of all time. Its level of inspiration is astronomically high, its musical values phenomenally impressive, given the fact that the whole of the oratorio was dashed off in something under three weeks.

Although there are nearly two dozen *Messiah* recordings currently available, the catalog could easily stand to make room for one more that is no longer in print. Sir Thomas Beecham's famous recording of the stunning arrangement by Sir Eugene Goossens certainly deserves a compact disc face-lift. And until you've heard *Messiah* with Jon Vickers's singing, Beecham's racy tempos, and an orchestra that includes trombones, tubas, tam-tams, cymbals, snare drums, and gong, you haven't really lived.

A wonderful version of that greatest *Messiah* arrangement of all has finally been reissued by Deutsche Grammophon (427173-2 [CD]): Sir Charles Mackerras's loving interpretation of Mozart's German edition, in which the ingenious wind parts that were grafted on to Handel's string torso make for such an intoxicating amalgam of Christ and *Don Giovanni*. Perhaps the most beautifully played and sung of all *Messiahs* is Sir Colin Davis's Philips recording with the London Symphony, now reissued (420865-2 [CD]) on the company's medium-priced Silver Line series and *not* to be confused with his disappointing digital remake with the Bavarian Radio Orchestra.

John Eliot Gardiner's triumphant period-instrument version can be confidently mentioned in the same breath with any of the great *Messiah* recordings of the past. In fact, in many ways it is the most completely satisfying *Messiah* ever released. Using the reduced performing forces and older instruments that are common to almost every *Messiah* recording of the last decade, Gardiner nevertheless succeeds in projecting almost all of the oratorio's size and significance in a performance that is still very intimate in its physical dimension and sound. The soloists are all intelligent and musical, the chorus—in which Gardiner has wisely opted for sopranos instead of the more "authentic" boys—sings with joy and devotion, and the English Baroque Soloists, while they play with great precision and high-minded intensity, still give the unmistakable impression that they're all having an enormous amount of fun. Though nothing will ever make me part with my well-worn copy of the Beecham recording, the exultant new Gardiner version now joins that select circle of *Messiahs* I cannot do without.

Music for the Royal Fireworks

London Symphony, Szell. London 417694-2 [CD].

Cleveland Symphony Winds, Fennell. Telarc CD-80038
[CD].

It was through the arrangements for modern orchestra by the gifted Ulster composer and conductor Sir Hamilton Harty that Handel's *Music for the Royal Fireworks* and *Water Music* first became accessible to twentieth-century audiences. And although that curious hybrid composer Handel-Harty is now persona non grata in most musical circles, George Szell's gorgeous London recording from the mid-1960s proves just how ridiculous such snobbery is. The arrangements, though admittedly anachronistic, are as tasteful as they are exciting, and if you can bear the scorn of the Baroque-purist crowd, this recording will offer you countless hours of undiluted pleasure and delight.

Thanks to the classic series of recordings he made with the Eastman Wind Ensemble for Mercury, the name of Frederick Fennell is far more closely associated with Sousa marches than with Baroque Authenticity. Nevertheless, on this brilliant Telarc recording he leads the finest "authentic" performance of the *Royal Fireworks Music* currently available. Because, as its title implies, the work was originally intended for performance in the open and soon to be sulfur-clogged air, Handel's original scoring called for instruments that had a fighting chance of making themselves heard above the ruckus: a huge wind band dominated by oboes and bassoons. Fennell's forces make a spectacular noise on this high-tech recording. You can hear almost every buzzing vibration in that forest of double reeds, and the brass are so emphatic and lively you can nearly smell the valve oil. For audiophiles, Handel lovers, and anyone who has ever spent time in a high school band, this is an absolutely essential recording.

Ode for St. Cecilia's Day

Lott, Rolfe Johnson, English Concert and Chorus, Pinnock. Deutsche Grammophon 419220-2 [CD].

Like his oratorio *Israel in Egypt,* which can be heard on a superb Erato recording led by John Eliot Gardiner (ECD-88182 [CD]), Handel's setting of Dryden's "A Song for St. Cecilia's Day" is at once one of his most brilliant and shameful works: brilliant because it finds Handel the composer of choral music at the summit of his powers; shameful because all of the *Ode for St. Cecilia's Day,* as with most of *Israel in Egypt,* was cribbed from other sources. The oratorio drew its "inspiration" from several directions, whereas the thematic material of the *Ode* was stolen in its entirety from a collection of harpsichord pieces published by Handel's older contemporary Georg Muffat.

Of course, it is what Handel *made* of Muffat's melodies that matters, and with the *Ode to St. Cecilia's Day* he fashioned the finest of his smaller-scale vocal works. Though several of the arias that celebrate the patron saint of music are among the most exceptional Handel would ever produce—the gently insinuating "What passion cannot Music raise and quell?" and the hectoring "The trumpet's loud clangor" are only two—it is in its choruses that the *Ode* rises to its full greatness. For instance, the final fugue on Dryden's couplet "The dead shall live, the living die,/And Music shall untune the sky!" is among the principal treasures of Baroque music.

What Trevor Pinnock's period-instrument performance may lack in sumptuousness of sound it makes up for in stylishness and vigor. The reflective passages are brought off with the utmost sensitivity; the more boisterous items have an admirable snap and bustle.

Devotees of Handel's earlier Dryden ode, *Alexander's Feast,* will find it elegantly realized on a Philips recording (422053-2 [CD]) in a performance led by—surprise! surprise!—John Eliot Gardiner. *And* as long as you're browsing through the Handel section of your favorite store, you might just as well pick up Gardiner's exciting, illuminating, incorruptible versions of *Acis and Galatea* (Deutsche Grammophon 423406-2 [CD]), *Jephtha* (Philips 422351-2 [CD]), *Saul* (Philips 426265-2 [CD]), and *Solomon* (Philips 412612-2 [CD], 412612-4 [T]) and save yourself some extra trips.

Water Music

Los Angeles Chamber Orchestra, Schwarz. Delos DCD-3010 [CD].

My unremitting enthusiasm for the recording by the Los Angeles Chamber Orchestra has absolutely nothing to do with civic pride. The only Southern California cultural institutions for which I have a blind and uncontrollable passion are the Dodgers and Disneyland. This is, quite simply, the most thrillingly played of all recorded performances of Handel's popular score, and, by a comfortable margin, the craziest. The insanity here consists largely of what might best be described as virtuosity gone berserk. In a performance that features nearly as many added ornaments as notes in the score, Gerard Schwarz leads his brilliant ensemble through one of the great recorded bravura exercises of the last decade. The playing is dumbfounding in its swaggering effortlessness: listen especially to the LACO oboes and horns for some of the most breathtaking technical legerdemain to be heard on recordings today.

Among available tapes of the complete *Water Music*, Trevor Pinnock's affable period-instrument recording for Deutsche Grammophon (410525-4) is easily the preferred version.

Hanson, Howard (1896–1981)

Symphony No. 2, *Romantic*

Seattle Symphony, Schwarz. Delos DCD-3073 [CD].

One of the most embarrassing of the numerous embarrassing moments I have suffered during my radio career occurred at a small station in upstate New York in the mid-1970s, shortly after I introduced this moltenly beautiful symphony as being a work by "the late Howard Hanson." Midway through the first movement, the "late" Dr. Hanson phoned the station and proceeded to point out, in the most charming way imaginable, that my information was not entirely accurate.

For anyone who attended the National Music Camp at Interlochen, Michigan, the principal theme of the *Romantic* Symphony has many powerful associations. Since the late 1930s it has served to conclude every concert as the "Interlochen Theme" and was for years the signature theme of the camp's weekly NBC broadcasts. (More recently, Jerry Goldsmith used it to memorable effect at the end of his score for Ridley Scott's sci-fi thriller *Alien*.)

This Delos recording by Gerard Schwarz and his superbly trained Seattle Symphony is not only the finest recording of the *Romantic* we are likely to hear for the rest of the century, it is an interpretation whose sweep and energy rival those of the several recordings the composer made himself. The playing is as full of genuine sentiment as it is totally lacking in mawkish sentimentality, and the rhythmic tingle Schwarz wires into the jazzy sections of the final movement is a delight to hear. Offering equally convincing performances of the gorgeous *Nordic* Symphony and the rarely heard but deeply touching *Elegy in Memory of My Friend Serge Koussevitzky*, this is an important, exciting recording.

If anything, the subsequent releases in Delos's Hanson series have proved even more valuable. The greatest of the symphonies — the Third—together with the *Fantasy Variations on a Theme of Youth* and the Symphony No. 6 are all given gripping performances on Delos DE-3092 [CD]; the most personal work in the canon, the Fourth—called the *Requiem* because it was written in memory of his father—is paired on Delos DE-3105 [CD] with the outrageously beautiful *Lament for Beowulf,* one of the finest and most deeply moving choral works ever written by an American.

Harris, Roy (1898–1979)

Symphony No. 3

New York Philharmonic, Bernstein. Deutsche Grammophon 419780-2 [CD].

If Roy Harris was not the most original and important symphonist America has so far produced, the only other possible candidate for that distinction is William Schuman, whose Third Symphony is paired with Harris's here. This superb recording of two live New York Philharmonic performances of what are probably the finest symphonies both men composed affords us an excellent opportunity to make up our minds.

On balance, the Harris Third, which had a tremendous vogue during the 1940s, still seems the fresher and more startling work. And in its day, this concise, dramatic, and often soaringly lyrical piece attracted more than the usual New Music Crowd audience. Harris received fan mail on a regular basis from all sorts of people, including cab drivers, politicians, and baseball managers. The Schuman Third, while it may lack the Harris Symphony's apparent ease of inspiration, is nonetheless a starkly proud and powerful statement by a keen and frequently astringent musical mind. It may also be the better made of the two works, which, given Harris's fanatical approach to craftsmanship, is saying a very great deal.

Leonard Bernstein's invigorating interpretations of both symphonies will provide an ideal introduction to anyone who has yet to become familiar with these seminal works in the development of American symphonic thought. Though the conductor made some very fine studio recordings of both symphonies during his years with Columbia, the excitement of these concert performances easily outstrips the earlier versions'.

Harty, Sir Hamilton
(1879–1941)

Irish Symphony; A Comedy Overture

Ulster Orchestra, Thomson. Chandos CHAN-8314 [CD], ABTD-1027 [T].

The Ulsterman Sir Hamilton Harty is best known for being half of one of history's most celebrated hyphenated composers. It was Harty's joyous and accomplished arrangements for modern orchestra of Handel's *Royal Fireworks* and *Water Music* that introduced the composer to several generations of music lovers before the snobbish and pedantic period-instrument movement made such "tampering" unfashionable. In addition to elevating the Hallé Orchestra of Manchester to the very front rank of European ensembles, Harty was a charming and resourceful composer whose best works evidence a profound understanding of the possibilities of the modern orchestra and an abiding passion for his native Ireland.

An examination of Bryden Thomson's admirable cycle of Harty recordings should begin with *An Irish Symphony,* a beautifully made potpourri of traditional Irish airs, and the sparkling *Comedy Overture.* The performances by the Ulster Orchestra are so bracing and affectionate that most people will want to investigate other recordings in the Chandos series, beginning with the sturdy and tuneful Violin Concerto and thoroughly charming *Variations on a Dublin Air* (CHAN-8386 [CD]), followed by those two haunting vocal works that may well be Harty's finest achievements, *The Children of Lir* and the *Ode to a Nightingale* (ABR-1051 [T]), which also find the wonderful soprano Heather Harper at her most fetching.

Haydn, Franz Joseph
(1732–1809)

Concertos (2) for Cello and Orchestra

Schiff, cello; Academy of St. Martin-in-the-Fields, Marriner. Philips 420923-2 [CD], 420923-4 [T].

For reasons that are not so easy to explain, Haydn's D Major Cello Concerto has never been the basic staple of the cellist's rather limited solo repertoire it certainly deserves to be. Witness the fact that the C Major Concerto, which was not discovered until the 1960s in Prague, is nowadays heard almost as frequently. Perhaps it has something to do with the fact that neither concerto is a crowd-pleasing whiz-bang display piece, and that if orchestras are going to hire big-name players they generally want more drawing power than these modestly elegant eighteenth-century works are likely to supply.

Heinrich Schiff, partnered by a conductor with impeccable Haydn credentials, gives each of the concertos a vibrant, immaculately shaped performance: the C Major is especially graceful and lighthearted, but the D Major isn't far behind. Philips provides an unusually warm and natural acoustic for an unusually heartwarming release.

Concerto in E-flat for Trumpet and Orchestra

Marsalis, trumpet; National Philharmonic, Leppard. CBS MK-37846 [CD], IMT-37846 [T].

Though he was the literal father of the classical symphony and string quartet (the nineteenth century didn't call him "Papa" for nothing), few of the numerous operas, keyboard sonatas, or instrumental concertos Haydn composed throughout his life have ever been very popular, with the exception of the delightful and justly famous Trumpet Concerto. Along with its abundance of memorable melody and virtuoso fireworks, the Concerto is also a work of considerable historical significance. It was the first work by a major composer written for a newfangled contraption that was several generations ahead of its time: the initial, but not completely practical, incarnation of the *valved* trumpet.

When Wynton Marsalis's now famous recording was first released a few years ago, it was accompanied by an enormous amount of ballyhoo and hype. As the first classical recording by one of the finest jazz musicians of the younger generation, it promised little more than Barbra Streisand's ill-starred venture into art song, or the wonderful Cleo Laine's horrendous Frankenstein-Meets-the-Wolf-Man encounter with Schoenberg's *Pierrot Lunaire*. What it delivered, on the other hand, was one of the most stylish and spellbindingly brilliant recordings this beloved work has ever received.

Formidable competition comes from Gerard Schwarz on Delos and a majestic Deutsche Grammophon recording by the recently retired principal trumpet of the Chicago Symphony, Adolph Herseth, but Marsalis continues to set the standard for both lyric expressiveness and bravura display. The cadenzas he supplies are so electrifying that the playing would make the hair on a bald man's head stand on end.

The Creation

Mathis, Baldin, Fischer-Dieskau, Academy and Chorus of St. Martin-in-the-Fields, Marriner. Philips 416449-2 [CD].

One of the high-water marks in the sacred music of the Age of Enlightenment, *The Creation* is an innocent, dramatic, unaffected, and beautifully made celebration of the God of whom Haydn said so frequently, "When I think of Him, my heart leaps with joy." Even those who do not typically respond to lengthy religious works will find that *The Creation* overflows with such a wealth of inspired melodic and theatrical invention, only the most adamant of pagans are able to resist its glories. For instance, the choral outburst on the words "Let there be light" must certainly rank with the most exultant moments in all of music.

For the last thirty years, *The Creation* has led a charmed life on records. With the exception of Herbert von Karajan's last effort, a performance recorded at the 1982 Salzburg Festival that is so sinister in its calculation it would warm the cockles of an atheist's heart, there has really never been a *bad* recording of *The Creation*. Even Karajan's 1969 Deutsche Grammophon version has much to recommend it, especially the unbelievably moving singing of the tragically short-lived Fritz Wunderlich, captured in one of the final commercial recordings that incomparable tenor would make.

The most consistently rewarding version of the oratorio currently available is Sir Neville Marriner's masterly interpretation for Philips. Though the performance is essentially one of chamber proportions, the big moments still have a tremendous punch and weight. The Academy's playing is as alert and full of character as it has ever been on records, the singing of the three superb soloists, especially Dietrich Fischer-Dieskau, is refined without ever becoming precious or cute, and Philips's engineers have wrapped it all in warm yet brilliantly focused recorded sound. In short, if you have even the most latent of missionary tendencies, this is the recording of *The Creation* to try on your favorite unbeliever.

Mass No. 11 in D minor, *Nelson Mass*

Lott, Watkinson, Davies, Wilson-Johnson, English Concert
and Chorus, Pinnock. Deutsche Grammophon 423097-2
[CD], 423097-4 [T].

Most of the dozen great Masses Haydn composed date from
the final years of his extraordinarily productive career. The fact that
they contain some of the most wonderful music Haydn (or anyone
else, for that matter) ever wrote bears eloquent testimony to his
willingness to learn and grow.

For some peculiar reason, this phenomenal series of masterworks is currently badly underrepresented in the catalog. What I
have always considered the most inspired of the series, the *Har-
moniemesse*, has no adequate commercial recording, and even the
popular *Nelson Mass* has only recently been captured successfully
on compact disc by Deutsche Grammophon. (Sir Colin Davis's Philips version is strangely unsatisfying from a Haydn conductor of that
stature, and a Swiss performance—names withheld to protect the
guilty—from the small Claves label has all the energy of a soggy
Communion wafer.)

Leonard Bernstein's powerful CBS recording from the 1970s
is one that certainly deserves immediate transfer to compact disc.
The interpretation is both sensitive and highly charged, with brilliant singing and playing from everyone involved. Philips, by the
way, has already issued an electrifying live performance of the *Mass
in Time of War* (412734-2 [CD]), further persuasive evidence for
the argument that Bernstein was the finest Haydn conductor of his
time.

The period-instrument performance led by Trevor Pinnock is
among this accomplished musician's most successful yet. It is one
of high drama, soaring lyricism, and unflagging energy, all captured
in state-of-the-art recorded sound.

Sonatas for Keyboard

Brendel, piano. Philips 416643-2 [CD].

Bilson, fortepiano. Nonesuch 78018-4 [T].

Gould, piano. CBS M2K-36947 [CD].

They turn up, occasionally, as opening works on recitals—not being terribly demanding, they give the performer a chance to warm up—and they are heard on the radio from time to time, usually as a palate cleanser after a Mahler symphony. Haydn's keyboard sonatas (and he composed more than sixty) have never had the popular appeal of Beethoven's or even Mozart's, although the best of them are a constant source of astonishment.

Alfred Brendel has done more than anyone in recent years to bring this music some of the attention it has been denied during the last couple of centuries. His performances are enthusiastic, compelling, and quirky but always convincing and thoroughly personal; in fact, they represent some of the finest work this intelligent, versatile artist has yet done in the recording studio.

Malcolm Bilson is one of those rare period-instrument specialists who give the impression that they are following the lonely road of the fortepianist out of choice, rather than of necessity. He is a personable, magnetic performer who persuades us—as long as he is playing—that those tinny, tinkly sounds really *are* the only appropriate ones for the keyboard music of the period. His Haydn recordings are lively and entertaining, and only make us wish that more were generally available.

If not quite so perverse as his infamous Mozart recordings, the Gould interpretations of the late sonatas are completely insane. A stylistic amalgam of Bach and Prokofiev, Gould's Haydn is a strange and strangely appealing invention, proving that these underrated works—like all important music—are open to an almost limitless variety of points of view.

String Quartets (6), Op. 76

Tátrai Quartet. Hungaroton HCD-12812/3 [CD].

It was with the historic collection published as his Op. 20 that Haydn, in effect, invented the single most important vehicle of Western chamber music, the modern string quartet. In all the quartets he had written previously, the function of the viola, second violin, and cello was to support and embellish the first violin's solo line; with Op. 20, all four instruments began to become the equal partners they have remained ever since.

Of the eighty-two string quartets—from many of his earliest published compositions to the unfinished D minor fragment he was working on at the time of his death—none have proved to be more popular than the Op. 76 collection, which contains the *Quinten,* the *Sunrise,* and the *Emperor,* three of the most familiar of all string quartets.

As in all the performances from their complete Haydn cycle, the Tátrai play with a warm, idiomatic grasp of the material, in interpretations that manage to remain straightforward without ever sounding impersonal or dull.

Their recording of the pivotal Op. 20 collection is also highly recommended (Hungaroton HCD-11332/3 [CD]), as are their versions of the colorful Op. 33 set, which includes the *Joke* and the *Bird* (Hungaroton HCD-11887/8 [CD]).

Symphonies (104) (complete)

> Philharmonia Hungarica, Dorati. London 425900-2 (1–16); 425905-2 (17–33); 425910-2 (34–47); 425915-2 (48–59); 425920-2 (60–71); 425925-2 (72–83); 425930-2 (84–95); 425935-2 (96–104) [CDs].

In both its scope and level of accomplishment, Antal Dorati's justly famous cycle of the complete Haydn symphonies is one of the supreme achievements in the history of recorded music. Under the watchful eye of that greatest of Haydn scholars, H. C. Robbins Landon, Dorati and his musicians turned in a series of performances that were remarkable for their vigor, imagination, and consistency. The familiar symphonies reveal themselves with a wonderful sense of discovery and life, while the more obscure ones all tend to sound like preposterously neglected masterworks. The recorded sound from the 1970s is still exceptionally clear and warm, and Robbins Landon's program notes are among the most literate and enjoyable ever written. For offering so much enjoyment and enlightenment in such an attractive and economical package, London deserves everyone's heartfelt thanks.

Symphonies: No. 6 in D, *Le Matin;* No. 7 in C, *Le Midi;* No. 8 in G, *Le Soir*

> Academy of St. Martin-in-the-Fields, Marriner. Philips 411441-2 [CD].

In these appealing early works in which we hear the embryonic form of the classical symphony beginning to coalesce in the hands of its first great master, Sir Neville Marriner and the Academy give us an object lesson in both virtuoso display and interpretative charm. Although Trevor Pinnock and the English Concert are nearly as fine for Deutsche Grammophon (423098-2 [CD]), the lack of string vibrato eventually gets on the nerves and tips the scales to Marriner. (Not that they needed all that much tipping to begin with: early Haydn—for that matter, *any* Haydn—doesn't get much better than this.)

Symphonies: No. 88 in G; No. 92 in G, *Oxford*

Vienna Philharmonic, Bernstein. Deutsche Grammophon 413777-2 [CD].

Listening to any of his 107 works in the form (in addition to the 104 numbered pieces, there are 3 others we now know for certain were his), one is invariably tempted to paraphrase Will Rogers: "I never heard a Haydn symphony I didn't like." In no other body of work can one hear such a consistently high level of invention and craftsmanship, or a greater delight in the sheer act of creativity, as in that marvelous series of symphonies history's finest professional composer produced throughout his career.

Leonard Bernstein's Vienna recording of these two popular G Major symphonies is one of the most desirable Haydn recordings of the last decade. The interpretations are warm, witty, and, in the slow movements, unabashedly and unashamedly romantic. The *Oxford* Symphony has never sounded more lively or luxuriant on records, and this unbuttoned, brilliantly executed, yet meltingly tender performance of No. 88 is the only one that can be mentioned in the same breath with Wilhelm Furtwängler's famous, wonderfully screwball 1951 recording. It is currently available on compact disc, coupled with Schumann's Fourth Symphony (Deutsche Grammophon 427404-2 [CD]).

Symphonies 93–104, the *Salomon* (or *London*) Symphonies

Cleveland Orchestra, Szell. Odyssey MB2K-45673 [CD] (Nos. 93–98).

Concertgebouw Orchestra of Amsterdam, Davis. Philips
432286-2 [CD].

Here, in a pair of reasonably priced box sets, are the most
popular of the Haydn symphonies in performances that represent
the very highest standards of modern Hadyn conducting. The Szell
interpretations are phenomenally precise, with hair-trigger attacks
and releases and crisply immaculate phrasing, but they also bubble
over with an infectious good humor: the bassoon belch in the slow
movement of No. 93 must rank with the funniest musical effects
ever recorded; the famous slow movement of the *Surprise* Symphony has rarely sounded so mischievous. A minor hitch is the remastered recorded sound, in which all the original tape hiss
continues to fizz away and the upper strings are made to seem uncharacteristically brittle and dry.

On the other hand, the engineers at Philips lavished some of
their most richly detailed sound on Sir Colin Davis's performances,
which remain some of the most successful Haydn recordings ever
made. Although generally straightforward, all of the interpretations
have this conductor's stamp of intelligence and gentlemanly passion, and the Concertgebouw Orchestra ensures that they are
among the best-played versions on the market today.

Symphonies: No. 94 in G, *Surprise;* No. 96 in D, *Miracle*

Academy of Ancient Music, Hogwood. Oiseau-Lyre
414330-2 [CD], 414330-4 [T].

While the story of how the *Miracle* Symphony earned its name
is probably apocryphal (allegedly, the audience at the world premiere in London were so moved by the music that they rushed up
en masse to congratulate the composer a few seconds before a mon-
strous chandelier crashed into their recently vacated seats), and
while every Haydn symphony is a "surprise" symphony in one way
or another, in this delicious Oiseau-Lyre recording two of the composer's most popular works more than earn their subtitles. The
playing of Christopher Hogwood's spirited Academy of Ancient
Music really *is* quite miraculous in both symphonies, and the revelations in texture and balance that these period-instrument performances afford *are* a source of endless surprise. The winds play
with such individuality and character that you begin to suspect the

conductor must have swallowed an entire bottle of Sir Thomas Beecham pills, and Hogwood himself provides innumerable subtle comments from his chair at the fortepiano. The familiar slow movement of No. 94 has rarely seemed so sly or tensely dramatic, and the finale of the *Miracle* Symphony rushes off with such a flurry of unbridled high spirits and good humor that we can easily believe the old chandelier story might, after all, have been true.

Symphonies: No. 101 in D, *Clock;* No. 103 in E-flat, *Drum Roll*

Royal Philharmonic, Beecham. Angel CDB-62579 [CD].

Here is wily old Beecham again, in the process of sending all other Haydn conductors to school. Once, at one of those rehearsals that some canny engineers were wise enough to preserve on tape — it may well have been a rehearsal of the *Drum Roll* Symphony — Sir Thomas asked his timpani player whether the score didn't possibly call for cymbals and side drum too. When told it didn't, all he said was "What a pity," but in a pouty tone of voice reminiscent of a small boy who has just been told he can't go out and play.

The spirit of boyish playfulness that Beecham managed to preserve into his eighties bubbles over in these spirited recordings of two of his signature works. For instance, the second movement of the *Clock* ticks away with such mischievous glee, you almost suspect it's connected to a bomb. As always, the Royal Philharmonic plays so alertly for the old imp that we can see the tongue placed high in cheek when he uttered his famous pronouncement: "There are two golden rules for an orchestra: start together and finish together. The public doesn't give a damn what goes on in between."

Trios for Piano, Violin, and Cello, Nos. 24–31

Beaux Arts Trio. Philips 422831-2 (24–27); 420790-2 (28–31) [CDs].

Along with Antal Dorati's magnificent cycle of the complete Haydn symphonies for London, one of the major accomplishments of recent recording history was the Beaux Arts Trio's go-round of all forty-three of the Haydn piano trios. As valuable as the Dorati recordings certainly are (fully half of them remain the finest individual performances the symphonies have yet received), the Beaux Arts' may be even more so, for how many of us are familiar with even the best known of these inexplicably neglected works? Why history has treated the Haydn trios so shabbily is a perplexing mystery, since the best of them seem every bit as inventive and beautifully made as the finest of the composer's quartets.

Although still difficult to track down in this country, the complete recording of all the trios has recently been issued in Europe on nine jam-packed CDs. Listening to this incredible wealth of treasure over a period of a few weeks will only strengthen the conviction that Haydn was the finest professional composer who ever lived.

Hildegard of Bingen
(1098–1179)

Hymns and Sequences

> Gothic Voices, Page. Hyperion CDA-66039 [CD], KA-66039 [T].

Cleric, mystic, poet, playwright, naturalist, musician, and composer, Hildegard — later St. Hildegard — of Bingen was one of the most fascinating characters of the Middle Ages. In addition to writing extensively on theology and natural history, she maintained a voluminous correspondence with several popes and Holy Roman Emperors; she published a collection of her mystical visions in 1151, and wrote the morality play *Ordo virtutum*, which was accompanied by some eighty-seven plainsong melodies of her own devising.

As one of the first composers of either sex of whom we have an accurate record, Hildegard's historical significance goes without saying. Yet she was also a creative musician of genuine abilities, as this astonishing Hyperion recording of some of her hymns and sequences clearly shows.

For those who place listening to plainsong close to the bottom of their list of things to do (and how aptly named this numbingly dull stuff has always seemed), Hildegard's rare and hypnotic talent will come like a splash of cold water in the face. In the exquisite, innocent singing of the Gothic Voices, the simple melodies with their static drone accompaniments seem infinitely more varied, subtle, and resourceful than they have any right to be. They also possess an emotional and spiritual tranquillity whose calming spells are almost impossible to resist. (This from someone who respectfully gags on almost any form of early sacred music.)

An unqualified, and—for a pagan like me—completely surprising winner.

Hindemith, Paul (1895–1963)

Symphonic Metamorphosis on Themes of Carl Maria von Weber; *Mathis der Maler* (symphony); *Trauermusik* for Viola and String Orchestra

> San Francisco Symphony, Blomstedt. London 421523-2 [CD], 421523-4 [T].

In the generation since his death, Paul Hindemith's reputation has declined alarmingly. Once a leading voice of the twentieth-century avant-garde, a composer whose thorny, elegantly crafted experiments in dissonant counterpoint caused many to liken him to a modern Bach, Hindemith has now been unfairly dismissed as a stuffy "academic" composer who has little to say to a generation brought up on the mindless delights of minimalism.

While much of his music *can* seem rather dry and forbidding (although musicians love Hindemith, since he never wrote a piece that wasn't at least as much fun to play as it was to hear), the bulk of his reputation now rests on a scant handful of works, including the three Herbert Blomstedt and the San Francisco Symphony have recorded so successfully for London.

Among available versions of the symphony drawn from that most famous of all unknown twentieth-century operas, *Mathis der Maler* (the first production was canceled by the Nazis in 1934, causing Wilhelm Furtwängler to resign from the Berlin State Opera in protest), only the last commercial recording Jascha Horenstein ever made (Chandos CHAN-8533 [CD], ABT-1243 [T]) is clearly superior. But Blomstedt has no serious competition in the gravely eloquent *Trauermusik*, written for the funeral of King George V, or in the *Symphonic Metamorphosis*, which emerges with all its wit and color and most of its precision intact.

Since we are still in the midst of a major Hindemith drought as far as recordings are concerned, three others deserve to be mentioned: James De Priest's spotless versions of *The Four Temperaments* and *Nobilissima visione*, the haunting ballet based on the life of St. Francis of Assisi (Delos DCD-1006 [CD]); the deeply felt requiem on a text by Walt Whitman, *When Lilacs Last in the Dooryard Bloom'd*, in a moving performance led by Robert Shaw, who commissioned the work (Telarc CD-80132 [CD]), and the composer's own superlative versions of the Symphony in B-flat, the Concert Music for Strings and Brass, and *Nobilissima visione*, coupled with Dennis Brain's definitive recording of the Horn Concerto on Angel (CDH-63373 [CD]).

Hoffnung Music Festivals

Various artists, Hoffnung Festival Orchestra, various
conductors. Angel 63303-2 [CD].

It's all here, on a pair of shiny new compact discs: Chopin on tubas, "Let's Fake an Opera," Dennis Brain playing Mozart (albeit Leopold) on a garden hose, the *Leonore* Overture No. 4, the "perfectly straight" excerpt from Walton's *Belshazzar's Feast* conducted by the composer, as well as those two *magnum opera* the *Concerto*

Populaire, brilliantly pieced together from dozens of well-known piano concertos, and the *Horrortorio,* in which Dracula's daughter is wed to "that freak, that zombie, that unnatural growth," Frankenstein.

With all due respect to P. D. Q. Bach, it was the series of three musical festivals inspired by the incomparable and tragically short-lived English cartoonist Gerard Hoffnung which set a standard for murdering the classics that only Spike Jones, at his most inspired, could begin to approach. With a typically English combination of parchment-dry wit coupled with unbridled lunacy, the Hoffnung concerts made loving fun of virtually everything musical that could be made fun of, and did it with a touch that could be both extremely sophisticated and phenomenally crude.

Hoffnungians—those of us who have long since committed every note and nuance of this transcendent nonsense to memory—will be delighted by the quality of the CD transfers, which capture the sense of occasion far better than the old recordings did. For those who have never experienced this divine madness, I envy you your virgin run. Cherish it, for like your first romance, it is an experience that will never come again.

Holst, Gustav (1874–1934)

The Planets

London Philharmonic, Boult. Angel CDM-69045 [CD].

Every conductor who has ever tried to come to terms with this phenomenally popular score has had to do so under an enormous shadow. Even the composer himself, who made his own recordings during the 78 era, was no match for the man who led the world premiere of *The Planets* in 1918, and during the next six decades, Sir Adrian Boult would record the work no fewer than seven times.

Over the years, the legendary Boult interpretation changed very little. In fact, the tempos remained so consistent that the variance in timings from one recording to another amounted to no more than a few seconds—except, that is, in this final version, which the conductor recorded in his ninetieth year.

The conductor's last look at *The Planets* is one of the great modern orchestral recordings. Beginning with a *Mars* of such weight and menace that all other performances seem positively pacifist in comparison, Boult somehow manages to find new expressive possibilities that even he had previously overlooked. *Venus* is more subtle and dreamy, *Jupiter* roars with a Falstaffian good humor, and *Uranus* lumbers along with a wit and rhythmic point that no other recording can really begin to match.

Suites (2) for Military Band

> **Cleveland Symphonic Winds, Fennell. Telarc CD-80038**
> **[CD].**

Among old bandsmen (and even if they give it the snooty name of "wind ensemble," a band is still a band), the name of Frederick Fennell has been the stuff of legend for more than thirty years. An old bandsman himself—whose principal instrument, believe it or not, was the bass drum—Fennell made a classic series of Mercury records with the Eastman Wind Ensemble that were probably the finest band recordings ever. They not only forced the classical music establishment to take the "wind ensemble" more seriously, but also, along with their celebrated, spit-and-polish Sousa albums, gave many of the first recorded performances of some absolutely wonderful music.

While Fennell's Eastman versions of these first great classics of the modern band repertoire were indispensable in their day, his latest recording of Holst's magnificent Suites for Military Band is finer still. The Cleveland Symphonic Winds play with the same gusto and precision as the old Eastman crowd, and Fennell's interpretations, if anything, have become even more suave and energetic with the passage of time. If these marvelous performances fail to raise the hair on the back of your arms (or possibly even a lump in your throat), all that proves is that you've never experienced the indescribable thrill of sidestepping horse droppings at a brutal 120-beat-per-minute cadence during a Memorial Day parade.

Honegger, Arthur (1892–1955)

Le Roi David; Symphonies No. 2 and 4

L'Orchestre de la Suisse Romande, Ansermet. London
425621-2 (oratorio); 430350-2 (symphonies) [CDs].

Of that group of a half dozen rebellious young French composers who in the 1920s banded together, with the mercurial Jean
Cocteau as their spokesman, into a loose but like-minded confed-
eration called *Les Six*, only three went on to achieve lasting recognition as major composers. If Darius Milhaud possessed the most
robust and prolific talent, and Francis Poulenc the most rarefied and
individual gifts, then the most powerful and versatile voice in the
group belonged to Arthur Honegger.

His best music is characterized by a neoclassical formal economy in which driving rhythms, astringent harmonies, and a facile,
often very moving, Gallic lyricism are thrown together, forming a
very heady and original brew. His oratorio *Le Roi David* is one of
the most significant sacred works of the twentieth century, and his
five symphonies constitute one of the last largely undiscovered treasure troves of modern orchestral thought.

Given Erato's inexplicable decision to withdraw the superb
Honegger series led by Charles Dutoit, it is now Dutoit's old mentor
and the composer's friend, Ernest Ansermet, who has the last word
on the subject. *Le Roi David*, with its compressed and dramatic
retelling of David's life from his victory over Goliath through the
beginning of his reign as king, draws an alert and loving interpretation; the symphonies are given colorful and energetic readings
that remain among this conductor's best. As always, the playing of
Ansermet's Swiss radio orchestra is not ideally refined, but the recorded sound holds up very well. Ultimately, the bargain price and
the conductor's infectious enthusiasm for these scores should silence
most criticism.

Hovhaness, Alan (1911–)

Symphony No. 2, *Mysterious Mountain*

Chicago Symphony, Reiner. RCA 5733-2-RC [CD].

One of history's most prolific composers (it has been suggested that *profligate* might be a better description of his output), Alan Hovhaness is generally known for only two of his hundreds of mature works: *And God Created Whales*, which incorporated taped recordings of actual whale song, and *Mysterious Mountain*, which became famous through Fritz Reiner's Chicago Symphony recording. I have had enormous affection for the piece from the first moment I heard it, and for reasons that are not entirely musical.

I was playing the record one day when my paternal grandmother wandered in and asked what I was listening to. I had barely said "Hovhaness" when she fled screaming from the room, appalled at my rudeness. The composer's name bears a resemblance to an exceedingly vulgar Czech word for the by-product of a basic bodily function.

Contrary to the associations his name has for Czech speakers, Hovhaness's Symphony reaches misty heights that exert a powerful allure, especially in the sublimely peaceful opening movement. The performance is even more perfect than it seemed to me as a boy, and packaged with Reiner's glistening accounts of Stravinsky's *Song of the Nightingale* and Divertimento from *The Fairy's Kiss*—the recordings that may have led the composer to pronounce the Chicago Symphony, under Reiner, "the most precise and flexible orchestra in the world"—the CD represents an outstanding bargain.

Humperdinck, Engelbert

(1854–1921)

Hansel and Gretel

Schwarzkopf, Grümmer, Felbermayer, Ilosvay, Philharmonia
Orchestra, Karajan. Angel CDMB-69293 [CD].

Now that this best loved of all children's operas has finally
made its debut on compact disc, how appropriate it should be in
this magical recording from 1953 that captures more of the wonder
and wide-eyed innocence of *Hansel and Gretel* than any other performance ever has or ever will. Elisabeth Schwarzkopf and Elisabeth
Grümmer are unsurpassable as Humperdinck's immortal tykes, and
Herbert von Karajan's warm and glowing conducting provides a
depressing reminder of what a superlative musician that chilling,
arrogant wretch once was. The supporting cast sings with immense
character and devotion, and the original recorded sound has been
made to seem extraordinarily fresh and alive in the CD transfer.

Jeffrey Tate leads an outstanding modern *Hansel and Gretel*
on Angel (CDBC-54022 [CD]), which frequently approaches the
Karajan in terms of mystery and wonder. Although Barbara Bonney
and Anne Sofie von Otter are not quite as magical as their famous
rivals, they sing with exceptional beauty, and the recorded sound
is thrilling.

Husa, Karel (1921–)

Music for Prague 1968

Eastman Wind Ensemble, Hunsberger. CBS MK-44916
[CD], MT-44916 [T].

If you've become convinced that Contemporary Music now means either minimalist drivel or incomprehensible noise, you have yet to hear the music of Karel Husa, the major musical voice to have emerged from Czechoslovakia since Bohuslav Martinů, and one of the most powerful and original composers of our time. While his idiom is thoroughly, and often aggressively, modern, Husa is essentially a conservative: a composer who believes that music must carry enormous emotional and expressive burdens above and beyond the notes on the printed page. With his String Quartet No. 3, which won the 1969 Pulitzer Prize, Husa's most celebrated work to date has been *Music for Prague 1968*, which has so far amassed the astonishing total of more than seven thousand performances.

Written in reaction to the tragic events that engulfed the Czech capital in the fall of that year, *Music for Prague 1968* is a furious, brutally dramatic, and hauntingly beautiful evocation of a city and a people which, in the ten centuries prior to 1990, have known precisely twenty years of political freedom. With its vivid colors, brilliant craftsmanship, and searing intensity, this piece is one of the handful of authentic large-scale masterworks of modern times.

The Eastman Wind Ensemble performance, while a fine one, lacks the sweep and passion of the composer's own on a now-deleted Golden Crest recording. The recording to wait for is of a performance given February 13, 1990, when Husa, at the invitation of President Václav Havel, introduced it to the city for which it was written.

I once devoted a program to Husa's music which bore the purposefully provocative title "The Greatest Living Composer?" I should now confess what I *really* think: Lose the question mark.

Ives, Charles (1874–1954)

Symphony No. 2; Symphony No. 3, *The Camp Meeting;* *The Unanswered Question*

New York Philharmonic, Bernstein. CBS MK-42407 [CD].

Concertgebouw Orchestra of Amsterdam, Thomas. Sony Classical SK-46440 [CD] (Symphonies No. 2 and 3 only).

It was Leonard Bernstein's famous Columbia recording of the Second Symphony that almost single-handedly sparked the Ives revival of the 1960s. Prior to the release of that classic recording by the man who had led the work's world premiere more than a half century after it had been composed, Ives had been an obscure figure with a small but knowledgeable following. Within a few years, he was to become an American Original, a cult phenomenon, a composer who, in Bernstein's words, was "the Washington, Jefferson, and Lincoln of our music."

Now that the hoopla which surrounded the Ives centennial in 1974 has begun to fade into the distance like one of the those crackbrained parades that haunt his music, a more balanced guess at the stature of his achievement can finally begin to be made. Like another insurance executive who was also a diligent weekend artist, the Hartford poet Wallace Stevens, Ives possessed an important, original, and peculiarly American talent. And if, as his admirers claim, he was one of the most forward-looking composers of his generation—and he *did* anticipate many of the most significant trends in twentieth-century music, years and often decades before anyone else—there was also in Ives a good deal of the archetypal American Crank, a kind of musical Rube Goldberg raised to the nth degree.

The Second Symphony remains his most approachable and instantly likable work. In fact, it's difficult *not* to like a work whose principal themes include "Bringing in the Sheaves" and "Where, O Where, Are the Pea-Green Freshmen?"—a Yale student song that sounds like an impossibly civilized version of "Dixie"—and which concludes with a fabulous peroration on "Columbia," the Gem of the Ocean," flanked by reveille and the most spectacular orchestral raspberry (an eleven-note chord cluster) anyone ever wrote.

In its compact disc reissue, Bernstein's performance sounds more joyous, committed, and spirited than ever, and his versions of the *Camp Meeting* Symphony and the intriguing *Unanswered Question* should still be considered the definitive performances of both works. Though very fine, the conductor's more recent Deutsche Grammophon recording lacks some of the bite of the old Columbia outing.

Michael Tilson Thomas's more recent digital recording is also a tremendous amount of fun. While the performance may lack the last measure of Bernstein's savvy and gusto, this is the first commercial recording of the critical edition of the Symphony No. 2, and the playing of the Concertgebouw Orchestra, as playing per se, can't really be approached.

Washington's Birthday, Decoration Day, Fourth of July, Thanksgiving and/or Forefathers' Day (Holidays Symphony); Central Park in the Dark; The Unanswered Question

Chicago Symphony Orchestra and Chorus, Thomas. CBS MK-42381 [CD].

From the off-kilter barn dance in *Washington's Birthday* to the spendthrift use of an entire chorus to intone a single verse of "God! Beneath Thy Guiding Hand" in *Thanksgiving and/or Forefathers' Day*, the *Holidays* Symphony contains some of Ives's most characteristic and supremely eccentric inspirations.

Some of the pieces have had superb individual performances, most notably those of Leonard Bernstein, but it is this eye-opening recording by Michael Tilson Thomas and the Chicago Symphony that finally persuades us the *Holidays* are not only arresting parts but also an even more satisfying whole. (Ives himself indicated that he didn't care whether they were performed separately or as a unit; then, too, the only thing George Bernard Shaw would ever tell his actors was, "Speak the lines clearly and have a good time.") Never have the tempos and textures of the four pieces seemed so interconnected and interdependent, nor has any performance, at least in my experience, created the feeling of such an inevitable musical *and* dramatic flow.

The playing of the orchestra—from the barely audible opening of *Washington's Birthday* to the raucous march in *Decoration Day*, where the Chicago brass sound like the old Sousa band—is quite phenomenal, as is the recorded sound. With equally atmospheric performances of *Central Park in the Dark* and *The Unanswered Question*, this may be the most important single Ives recording yet made.

The finest recording of Ives's masterpiece, *Three Places in New England*—one of Michael Tilson Thomas's first—is now out on a Deutsche Grammophon compact disc (423243-2). To get it, you have to put up with Seiji Ozawa's rather lackluster walk-through of the Fourth Symphony, but the *Three Places* are done so magically that they're more than worth the price.

Janáček, Leoš (1854–1928)

The Cunning Little Vixen

Popp, Jedlička, Randová, Vienna Philharmonic, Mackerras.
London 417129-2 [CD].

Had Leoš Janáček died at the same age as Beethoven, he would be remembered today—if at all—as a very minor late-Romantic composer, conductor, and organist, whose name would occasionally turn up in the more complete biographies of his friend Antonín Dvořák. It was not until 1904, at the age of fifty, that he began to produce, apparently from out of nowhere, that startling series of works on which his reputation as one of the most powerfully original twentieth-century composers now rests. Janáček's sudden transformation from a provincial nobody into a modern giant is without precedent in the history of music. In the other arts, only William Butler Yeats's relatively late emergence as the great English-language poet of the twentieth century offers a similar example of such mysterious and wonderful growth.

The cornerstone of Janáček's achievement is his series of eleven operas, which are slowly being recognized as some of the most important works of the modern operatic stage. Their general acceptance was understandably delayed by the difficulty of the Czech language itself, and the fact that they are by definition untranslatable, since Janáček's musical language was intimately connected with the rhythms and inflections of Czech speech. Then, too, their subject matter is often so peculiar that theaters outside Czechoslovakia once thought them to be all but impossible to produce. For instance, the heroine of *Věc Makropulos* (*The Makropulos Case*—though a more correct translation would be *The Makropulos Thing*) is a 300-year-old opera singer; *Z mrtvého domu* (*From the House of the Dead*) is set in a czarist prison camp; and the cast of characters in *Příhody lišky Bystroušky* (*The CLV*) includes a dog, a badger, a cricket, a grasshopper, and a group described simply as "the various vermin." In spite of its profound and delightful eccentricity, *The Cunning Little Vixen* is neither nonsense nor simply another children's story, but one of the most bewitching and enchantingly beautiful operas ever composed.

Sir Charles Mackerras's grasp of the special power, charm, and expressive potential of Janáček's music is without equal in the world today. As a student, he studied the scores with the man who gave many of them their world premieres, the composer's friend Václav Talich. At this late date it is absurd to ask whether Mackerras, an American-born Englishman of Australian parentage, can possibly speak Janáček's language as idiomatically as a native; it is doubtful that any Czech conductor, except for Talich, has ever begun to speak it half so well.

Sir Charles's version of *The Cunning Little Vixen* is one of the greatest in an already triumphant series of Janáček recordings. He leads the Vienna Philharmonic through the difficult, delicate score as though it were no more challenging than an early Haydn symphony. The predominantly Czech cast is largely wonderful, especially since most of them drop the wobbly, intrusive vibrato that so many Eastern European singers are apparently taught from birth. Most wonderful of all, however, is the exquisite Vixen of Lucia Popp, one of the most hugely gifted sopranos of the last half century. Her passion, precision, and the extraterrestrial beauty of her physical sound make this one of the great characterizations of the last twenty years, and further make an already invaluable recording a completely indispensable one.

Unfortunately, a tape version is not currently available.

Jenůfa

Söderström, Popp, Randová, Dvořsky, Ochman, Vienna Philharmonic, Mackerras. London 414483-2 [CD].

Jenůfa was the first of Janáček's great operas, and it remains the most popular and instantly approachable. It is also, by a comfortable margin, the most conventional of all his works for the stage. Set in a sleepy Czech village, the direct but not-so-simple story of jealousy, vengeance, violence, and redemption is a dramatic amalgam of Smetana's *Bartered Bride* and Mascagni's *Cavalleria rusticana*. Musically, however, *Jenůfa* is an entirely different matter: a fresh, tuneful, and powerfully dramatic score in which one of history's major operatic composers first found his distinct and utterly original voice.

Like all the recordings in Sir Charles Mackerras's historic cycle of the Janáček operas, this is the *Jenůfa* that will probably dominate the catalogs until well into the next century. It is also one of those rare studio recordings that have all the immediacy and excitement of a live performance. Elisabeth Söderström—is there a finer Janáček heroine in the world today?—is both ineffably tender and witheringly powerful in the title role, and the rest of the cast, together with the orchestra and conductor, are all captured at the very top of their form.

If you are one of those people who are convinced, perhaps with good reason, that Opera came to a screeching halt with the death of Giacomo Puccini, give *Jenůfa*—especially this *Jenůfa*—a try.

Piano Music

Firkusny, piano. Deutsche Grammophon 429857-2 [CD].

Like his operas and orchestral scores, Janáček's piano works are the product of a wholly original musical mind. In all the pieces in this recital from the early 1970s, Rudolf Firkusny demonstrates why he is the foremost Janáček pianist history has so far known. The playing has a seamless perfection and an evocative magic that make this entrancing music spring to life in virtually every bar: *In the Mists* will probably never have a more refined and poetic performance; the Piano Sonata emerges with an uncommon sense of unity and depth. It's a pity that Book 1 of *On an Overgrown Path* couldn't be included, but the reissue returns fair value for the dollar, and the recorded sound holds up extremely well.

Sinfonietta; Taras Bulba

Vienna Philharmonic, Mackerras. London 410138-2 [CD].

Beginning with George Szell's stunning Cleveland Orchestra recording from the 1960s, Janáček's most popular orchestral work, the blazingly heroic *Sinfonietta*, has had some wonderful recordings. Currently, the piece is ably represented by Simon Rattle's cultivated but immensely stirring Angel recording, and a slightly scrappy but powerfully compelling Supraphon recording featuring Václav Neumann and the Czech Philharmonic.

As both an interpretation and a recording of demonstration quality, Sir Charles Mackerras's Vienna Philharmonic performance will be difficult to better for the foreseeable future. As usual, not even the most subtle detail of Janáček's complex language escapes this conductor's attention. The occasionally intricate rhythms and always complicated inner voicing are invested with a drive and clarity they have never been given before. The last time the Vienna Philharmonic brass (augmented for the occasion by a dozen extra players) were heard to play with such ferocious bite and mind-boggling unanimity was in Sir Georg Solti's famous recording of Wagner's *Ring*, made two decades ago.

The *Sinfonietta*'s inevitable companion work, the orchestral rhapsody *Taras Bulba*, is given an equally memorable performance. In fact, Mackerras invests it with such surging life and drama that some will be persuaded—as I must admit I always *have* been—that *Taras* may in fact be the more important and rewarding piece. At last check, there were no suitable tape versions of either work in the catalog.

Slavonic Mass (Mša glagolskaja)

Söderström, Drobková, Livora, Novák, Czech Philharmonic Orchestra and Chorus, Mackerras. Supraphon 10-3575 [CD].

Lear, Rössel-Majdan, Haefliger, Crass, Bavarian Radio
Orchestra and Chorus, Kubelik. Deutsche Grammophon
429182-2 [CD].

To call Janáček's *Slavonic Mass* one of the great sacred works
of twentieth-century music is as accurate as it is slightly misleading.
Written in the composer's seventy-second year, the *Slavonic Mass*
was originally thought to be a final act of contrition by a lifelong
agnostic. When a Prague music critic described it as being the work
of a "pious old man," the composer immediately shot back a post-
card with the single line, "Neither old nor pious, *young* man."

The unshakable faith the *Slavonic Mass* expresses with such
moving tenderness and medieval grandeur has to do less with the
composer's religious convictions, which were all but nonexistent,
than with his almost messianic belief in the survival of the Czech-
oslovak Republic, whose tenth anniversary in 1928 the *Mass* was
written to celebrate.

The Mackerras recording is one of the most successful in his
brilliant Janáček series: the playing of the Czech Philharmonic is as
vivid and emphatic as it has ever been on records; the soloists are
exceptional, the chorus alert and powerful, and the recorded sound
is shattering in its realism and impact. Rafael Kubelik's older Deutsche Grammophon recording still holds up remarkably well. Less
driven and more gently lyrical than the Mackerras version, it nevertheless has more than its share of electrifying moments. Bedřich
Janáček (whom I believe is no relation) is spellbinding in the titanic
organ interlude; in the *Mass*'s brazen postlude, the Bavarian Radio
Orchestra trumpets play with such wild abandon that you can almost see the musicians' tongues popping out of their instruments'
bells.

String Quartets: No. 1, *The Kreutzer Sonata;* No. 2, *Intimate Pages*

Smetana Quartet. Denon C37-7545 [CD].

Leoš Janáček was a man whose vigor and appetites remained
exorbitantly intact to the end of his long and unusual life. Taking
its cue from Smetana's famous E minor Quartet, *From My Life,* the
quartet subtitled *Intimate Pages* is one of music's most extraordinary autobiographical works. In it, the aging composer confessed

the pangs and torments of a hopeless love he had conceived for a much younger woman. (In truth, with his honeyed tongue and twinkling eye, Janáček ran into little rejection during what certain scandalized quarters of Bohemia and Moravia continue to regard as a legendary erotic career.) With the equally individual *Kreutzer Sonata,* based on the Tolstoy novella inspired by the Beethoven work, *Intimate Pages* is one of the most highly charged and original of twentieth-century chamber pieces. In the proper hands, both can easily seem to rank with the finest quartets of Bartók and Schoenberg.

With the Smetana Quartet, they are in just such hands. No more committed or impassioned performance of either work has yet been recorded: The Smetanas' intensity is such that at any moment you feel any one of the players may be on the verge of breaking a bow or snapping a string. Even in their live performances recorded a few years later for Supraphon, they would never match this level of beautifully controlled violence again. This is thoroughly adult music, meant for a thoroughly adult audience; if you qualify, enjoy.

Joplin, Scott (1868–1917)

Rags

Rifkin, piano. Nonesuch N5-71248 [T], N5-71264 [T], N5-71305 [T]. Angel 4DS-37331 [T].

Perlman, violin; Previn, piano. Angel CDC-47170 [CD], 4XS-37113 [T].

Well before Scott Joplin's music was belatedly made into a national institution in the hit movie *The Sting,* I had already become hopelessly addicted to his piano rags, thanks entirely to Joshua Rifkin. It was Rifkin's path-breaking series of Nonesuch recordings that all but introduced the world to the subtle, infectious, endlessly inventive music of a man who, in essence, transformed the musical wallpaper of turn-of-the-century bordellos into a high, and distinctively American, art. In any of his several recordings, Rifkin's self-effacing yet enormously colorful and individual interpretations are still the definitive solo piano versions of these works. No less delightful is the Angel recording of the arrangements for violin and piano, played with tremendous bite and enthusiasm by Itzhak Perlman and André Previn.

Unfortunately, the Deutsche Grammophon recording of Joplin's ragtime opera *Treemonisha* in the stunning performance led by Gunther Schuller is currently out of print. It badly needs to return to circulation on compact disc.

Josquin des Prés (c. 1450–1521)

Missa Pange lingua; Missa La sol fa re mi

Tallis Scholars, Phillips. Gimell CDGIM-009 [CD], 1585T-09 [T].

Though not normally an enthusiastic consumer of "monk music"—perhaps I saw the movie *Becket* once too often, or read too many cheerful books about the Spanish Inquisition as a boy—I must confess (so to speak) to an abiding admiration for the music of the greatest of the Flemish contrapuntists, Josquin des Prés. I feel a deep personal connection with him, not because he was one of the most venerated and influential composers of his era, but because he had a name that was as frequently mangled as mine is.

In the *Baker's Biographical Dictionary of Musicians*, Nicolas Slonimsky lists Després, Desprez, Deprés, Depret, Deprez, Desprets, Dupré, Del Prato, a Prato, a Pratis, and Pratensis as a few of the ways it was most commonly spelled, while Josquin—from the Flemish Jossekin, the diminutive of Joseph—was apparently mauled just as often.

The fabulous Tallis Scholars give loving performances of two of his finest Masses for Gimell, a small but exceptionally fussy English label that consistently produces some of the best-sounding recordings anywhere. The *Missa Pange lingua* is the more familiar of the two, but the *Missa La sol fa re mi* (which was *not* the basis for that wretched song in *The Sound of Music*) is equally captivating.

Kalinnikov, Vasily (1866–1901)

Symphonies (2)

Scottish National Orchestra, Järvi. Chandos CHAN-8611 [CD] (Symphony No. 1); CHAN-8805 [CD], ABTD-1433 [T] (Symphony No. 2).

The life of the Russian composer Vasily Kalinnikov reads like one of the more poignant short stories of Anton Chekhov. As a matter of fact, the two men were neighbors for a time at one of those Black Sea spas in the Crimea where both had gone to die of tuberculosis. Chekhov would be remembered as one of the giants of Russian literature, whereas Kalinnikov became one of the great "what ifs" of Russian music, a composer of tremendous talent and promise whose name is almost completely forgotten today.

After studying bassoon at the music school of the Moscow Philharmonic Society (he was forced to leave the more prestigious Moscow Conservatory because he was unable to pay the tuition), Kalinnikov managed to eke out a meager living playing in the city's theater orchestras. As a result of living most of his life in the squalor of the proverbial garrets and composing assiduously, a combination of overwork and undernourishment undermined his health; he died at Yalta two days before his thirty-fifth birthday.

While the Second Symphony of 1898 is a lovely work, the earlier G minor Symphony, written when he was twenty-nine, remains his masterpiece. Lyrical, exuberant, and utterly haunting—once heard, its principal themes will not be forgotten quickly—the symphony is one of the jewels of Russian late Romanticism, a work that ranks with any of the early symphonies of Glazunov, Tchaikovsky, or Rachmaninoff.

If not quite as exhilarating as the now-deleted recordings led by Evgeny Svetlanov, Neeme Järvi's versions are nonetheless devoted and bracing and certainly receive far better recorded sound.

Khachaturian, Aram

(1903–1978)

Gayane Suite; *Spartacus* Suite

Royal Philharmonic, Temirkanov. Angel CDC-47348 [CD].

One can only hope that wherever that happy-go-lucky music lover Joseph Stalin is roasting these days, he is exposed to a continuous dose of the ballet *Gayane*, Aram Khachaturian's subtle celebration of the joys of collective farming. Of course, it's easy to chortle at *Gayane* and its pile-driving "Sabre Dance," or to point out—with a chill—that this is what the Soviet government once hailed as ideal proletarian music, when Shostakovich and Prokofiev were catching hell. (Actually, Khachaturian himself also came under fire at the infamous Zhdanov Conference in 1948.)

For the most part, *Gayane* is good, clean Socialist Realist fun, with hummable tunes, plenty of local color, and a kind of childlike innocence that retains its freshness and seems immune to all manner of cynical trashing after nearly half a century of wear and tear. If Yuri Temirkanov's interpretations of the ballet's heavy hits—to say nothing of a blissfully truncated suite from the truly macabre *Spartacus*—are neither the most theatrical nor the most imaginative ever recorded, they are easily the best on the market today. The recording Kyrill Kondrashin made of *Gayane* and Dmitri Kabalevsky's *The Comedians* is all but screaming for a CD reissue from RCA.

David Oistrakh's definitive interpretation of the Violin Concerto, in a performance led by the composer, can now be found on

Mobile Fidelity/Melodiya (MFCD-899 [CD]), and the most elec-trifying Khachaturian recording ever made has finally appeared from RCA: that classic version of the Piano Concerto with William Kapell, Serge Koussevitzky, and the Boston Symphony (60921-2 [CD]), which makes the thing seem infinitely more musical and im-portant than it can possibly be.

Knussen, Oliver (1952–)

W*here the* Wild Things Are

Hardy, King, Harrington, Rhys-Williams, London Sinfonietta, Knussen. Arabesque Z-6535 [CD], A-7535 [T].

Needless to say, it is a bit too soon to tell what history, the Great Aesthetic Trash Compacter, will make of *Where the Wild Things Are*. My own suspicion is that the work will prosper as one of the enduring children's operas—if not precisely the late-twentieth-century equivalent of *Hansel and Gretel*, then at least something very close to it.

Oliver Knussen's setting of Maurice Sendak's tale of the archetypal Bad Kid and the Horrible (i.e., thoroughly lovable) Monsters is not only magnetic theater, but also highly inspired music-making. Knussen packs more mystery, enchantment, and pure fun into his forty minutes than many another operatic com-poser has been able to draw out of an entire evening; the soloists—especially Rosemary Hardy as the incorrigible Max—all seem ideal in their parts, and the composer-conducted performance is un-doubtedly definitive.

If you have any little wild things running around underfoot, sit them down in front of the speakers and see what they think. This aging Bad Kid loved it.

Kodály, Zoltán (1882–1967)

Dances of Galanta; Dances of Marósszek; Variations on a Hungarian Folk Song (Peacock Variations)

> Hungarian Radio Orchestra, Lehel. Hungaroton HCD-12252 [CD], MK-12252 [T].

After his friend and near-contemporary Béla Bartók, Zoltán Kodály was the most significant composer Hungary had produced since the death of Franz Liszt. Kodály began his career writing serious, and politely ignored, chamber works, but it was his discovery of Hungarian folk music in the early 1920s that transformed him into an internationally famous composer. Beginning with the folk opera *Háry János*, Kodály combined the unmistakable flavors of Hungarian folk song with a technique that owed much to Debussy and Ravel, and created some of the most refreshingly distinctive and original music of the twentieth century.

György Lehel leads some exceptionally fine and warmly idiomatic performances of the *Galanta* and *Marósszek Dances*. If his performance of Kodály's masterpiece, the *Peacock* Variations, is not quite a match for István Kertész's brilliant, but now withdrawn, London recording, it is easily the best available version in a shockingly uncrowded field.

Háry János

> Takács, Sólyom-Nagy, Gregor, Hungarian State Opera Orchestra and Chorus, Ferencsik. Hungaroton HCD-12837/8 [CD], MK-12187/9 [T].

Háry János Suite

> Cleveland Orchestra, Szell. CBS MYK-38527 [CD], MYT-38527 [T].

Though the Suite that Zoltán Kodály extracted from his 1926 folk opera *Háry János* remains his most universally loved and frequently recorded work, the opera itself is one of the treasures of the modern lyric theater. Its fantastic plot is a series of tall tales told by a retired hussar from the village of Abony Magna—the irrepressible Háry János—who after single-handedly defeating Napoleon and his legions has nearly as much trouble fending off the attentions of Napoleon's ardent wife.

Fortunately, the lone recorded performance of the complete opera is an extremely attractive one. Beautifully played and, for the most part, beautifully sung, the performance projects much of the opera's unique and unmistakable color. Since much of the humor is lost on non-Hungarian listeners, one can only hope that London will some day reissue István Kertész's dazzling recording from the early 1970s, which not only included all the opera's musical numbers but also featured the inspired Peter Ustinov in all the speaking roles.

For those who feel they don't really need to go beyond the popular *Háry János* Suite, George Szell's tender, flamboyant, meticulous, and uproarious CBS recording has never been equaled.

Korngold, Erich Wolfgang
(1897–1957)

Concerto in D for Violin and Orchestra

Heifetz, violin; Los Angeles Philharmonic, Wallenstein. RCA 7963-2-RG [CD], 7963-4-RG [T].

Perlman, violin; Pittsburgh Symphony, Previn. Angel CDC-47846 [CD].

A child prodigy whose accomplishments were compared to those of Mozart by no less an authority than Gustav Mahler, and the man who first brought genuine symphonic music to Hollywood films, Erich Wolfgang Korngold was one of the most fascinating musical figures of the twentieth century. His opera *Die tote Stadt* (The Dead City), begun when he was only nineteen, made him world famous, and his frightening abilities even convinced Richard Strauss that Korngold would inevitably supplant him as the century's foremost composer of German opera. Erich Leinsdorf's generally gorgeous recording, save for the wobbly singing of the hero, is finally back in circulation; buy it (RCA 7767-2-RG [CD], 7767-4-RG [T]) before it disappears again.

Forced to flee Europe after Hitler's annexation of Austria, Korngold eventually settled in Hollywood. There, with the scores for *Anthony Adverse, King's Row, The Adventures of Robin Hood, The Sea Hawk,* and other classic Warner Brothers films of the 1930s and '40s, he established the grammar and syntax of an entirely new musical language, whose influence can still be clearly and distinctly heard in the scores of John Williams and countless other film composers.

The Korngold Violin Concerto, whose thematic material was derived from several of his movie themes, is one of the most startlingly beautiful works in the instrument's repertoire. Sentimental, exciting, and unabashedly Romantic, it is as instantly approachable as it is impossible to forget. Although written for the Polish violinist Bronislaw Huberman, it was Jascha Heifetz who gave the work its world premiere and made the first commercial recording. Technically, of course, the playing is flawless; yet here Heifetz invests the music with a warmth and humanity that almost none of his other recordings possess. Itzhak Perlman's Angel recording is also exceptionally lovely. If in the quicksilver finale Perlman lacks the last measure of Heifetz's dizzying abandon, he milks the molten slow movement like the wonderfully shameless Romantic he has always been.

Film Music

National Philharmonic, Gerhardt. RCA 7890-2-RG [CD], 7890-4-RG [T].

Whichever Hollywood sage insisted that the greatness of film music was directly proportional to the extent to which you *didn't* notice it was an imbecile. One might just as well say that an actor's greatness may be measured by the extent to which you can't understand his lines. From almost the moment movies learned to talk, film music has been an integral part of the twentieth century's most characteristic art form. While a score can't save an awful picture, it can ruin a good one. On occasion—witness *Laura*, for instance —it can turn a fine film into a great one.

This collection of excerpts from Korngold scores was the first installment in RCA's phenomenally successful "Classic Film Scores" series, the brainchild of the composer's son, the late George Korngold.In addition to an expanded version of the music from *The Sea Hawk*, which in many ways is the musical equal of a Strauss tone poem, this reissue contains the famous *King's Row* fanfare, the germ from which seemingly half of all the film music written afterward would grow.

The National Philharmonic under Charles Gerhardt plays with fire and devotion, and the restored recorded sound is of demonstration quality.

Get out your handkerchiefs and prepare to swash those buckles. (Or is it buckle that swash?)

Orchestral Works

> **Northwest German Philharmonic, Albert.** CPO 999-037-2 *(The Snowman: Incidental Music; Dramatic Overture; Sinfonietta);* 999-046-2 *(Symphonic Overture; Much Ado About Nothing: Incidental Music; Piano Concerto);* 999-077-2 *(Baby-Serenade;* Cello Concerto; *Symphonic Serenade* for String Orchestra); 999-146-2 *(Straussiana;* Symphony in F-sharp; *Theme and Variations)* [CDs].

The first comprehensive recorded examination of Korngold's orchestral music from the small European label CPO provides the ideal means of better understanding this unique composer's achievement, and judging from the evidence these four handsome CDs present, the achievement was considerable. Even in the earliest works, produced when Korngold was not yet out of kneepants, one immediately detects a distinct, confident, and fully formed musical personality; in mature works like the Symphony in F-sharp, which Dimitri Mitropoulos called "the perfect modern score," one hears the heir of Mahler and Richard Strauss at the peak of his late-Romantic powers.

While there have been finer performances of individual works—the Violin Concerto is very well served by two classic recordings (see above), and the compelling debut recording of the

Symphony, with the Munich Philharmonic led by Rudolf Kempe, has just resurfaced on Varèse Sarabande (VSD-5346) — the series, as a whole, is a major triumph, offering carefully thought out, wholly sympathetic performances in beautifully rich recorded sound.

Kreisler, Fritz (1875–1962)

Violin Pieces and Arrangements

Perlman, violin; Sanders, piano. Angel CDC-47467 [CD].

In addition to being one of the great violinists of history, whose recordings of the Beethoven, Brahms, and Mendelssohn concertos remain unsurpassed in their Romantic daring and philosophical depth — all of which can now be found on an indispensable two-CD set from Pearl (GEMM-CDS-9362) — Fritz Kreisler was also the composer of some of the most enchanting music ever written for the instrument. Evergreen classics like *Caprice viennois,* *Liebesfreud,* and *Schön Rosmarin* were the apotheosis of turn-of-the-century Viennese charm and helped make their creator an immensely rich and famous man.

Nowhere does Itzhak Perlman reveal himself more clearly as Kreisler's natural heir than in this delectable recording of Kreisler miniatures and arrangements. While less free and arbitrary than the master (whose celebrated recordings from the 1930s and '40s keep slipping in and out of print), Perlman brings huge reserves of sensitivity and schmaltz to the proceedings, always drawing the fine but inviolable line between sentiment and sentimentality. Samuel Sanders is a wholly sympathetic partner, and the mid-70s recorded sound remains ideal.

Kurka, Robert (1921–1957)

The Good Soldier Schweik Suite

Atlantic Sinfonietta, Schenck. Koch 3-7091-2H1 [CD].

With Ernst Krenek's *Jonny spielt auf* and Jaromir Weinberger's *Schwanda the Bagpiper*, Robert Kurka's *The Good Soldier Schweik* has for years been at the top of my list of Neglected American Operas I Would Most Like to See. Completed shortly before Kurka's death from leukemia at the age of thirty-six, *Schweik* is a setting of Jaroslav Hašek's celebrated four-volume antiwar novel which introduced one of the classic characters of modern literature, a seemingly "feebleminded" Everyman who endures the lunacies of modern warfare with indestructible optimism and triumphant good humor.

Judging from the brilliant six-movement Suite that the composer extracted from the opera, Kurka—himself of Czech descent—captured the very essence of Hašek's darkly hilarious vision. In this sparkling performance by the Atlantic Sinfonietta under the late Andrew Schenck, it emerges as one of the unique works of modern American music: a memorable, tuneful, colorfully dramatic score—this in spite of the fact that the instrumentation calls for winds and percussion only.

Don't miss it.

Lalo, Édouard (1823–1892)

Symphonie espagnole for Violin and Orchestra

Perlman, violin; Orchestre de Paris, Barenboim. Deutsche
Grammophon 400032-2 [CD].

One of the most individual and restlessly inventive of all
nineteenth-century French composers, Édouard Lalo is now known
for only two apparently indestructible works: the D minor Cello
Concerto and the *Symphonie espagnole,* which is not, in fact, a
"symphony" at all but rather a form of the composer's own devising
that incorporates the structural elements of the concerto and the
suite. As one of the most inspired of all French musical tourist
works, *Symphonie espagnole* is to the brighter elements of Spanish
musical culture what Bizet's *Carmen* is to the darker side: a virtuoso
evocation of a specific time and place that few other works can
match.

With some vivid, expressive support from Daniel Barenboim
and the Orchestre de Paris, Itzhak Perlman here gives one of his
most buoyant and colorful recorded performances. Along with its
fabulous dexterity, the playing combines a bracing rhythmic vitality
with tasteful schmaltziness in a way that only Perlman, these days,
seems able to do.

The delectable opera *Le Roi d'Ys* more than deserves a listen
beyond its familiar overture and the famous tenor bonbon, "Vaine-
ment, ma bien-aimée"—and can be heard to excellent advantage in
a very fine performance led by Armin Jordan for Erato (2292
45015-2 [CD]). Lalo's only other well-known piece, the Cello Concerto, is now admirably served by a half dozen first-rate recordings,
the best of which features the impressive young Matt Heimovitz in
his debut recording (at age nineteen) for Deutsche Grammophon
(427323-2 [CD], 427323-4 [T]). His playing is both gutsy and sophisticated, and amazingly assured for a performer his age. The recording comes with an equally memorable performance of the
inevitable companion piece, the Cello Concerto No. 1 by Saint-
Saëns, as well as something we have needed for some time: an unimpeachable version of Bruch's *Kol Nidrei.*

Lehár, Franz (1870–1948)

The Merry Widow

Schwarzkopf, Steffek, Gedda, Wächter, Philharmonia
Orchestra and Chorus, Matačič. Angel CDCB-47177
[CD], 4AV-34044 [T].

He never quite scaled the golden heights of Johann Strauss's
Fledermaus, Gypsy Baron, or *Night in Venice*—the primary reason
his music has since been designated the summit of the Viennese operetta's "Silver Age"—but Franz Lehár was a charming and entirely
individual composer whose stage works represented the final, bittersweet sunset of one of the most endearing of all musical forms.
Though *Giuditta* and *The Land of Smiles* are probably finer works,
it was the effervescent and eternally glamorous *Lustige Witwe* that
became the only operetta in history (short of the Savoy operas of
Gilbert and Sullivan) to mount a serious popular challenge to the
absolute supremacy of *Die Fledermaus.*

   Even if Viennese operetta in general, or Lehár operettas in
particular, are not exactly your cup of *kaffee mit schlag,* I guarantee
you will find this ageless recording one of the most thrilling musical
experiences of your life. Elisabeth Schwarzkopf, the greatest
Marschallin and Mozart singer of her time, gives what may well be
the performance of her career as Hanna: regal, witty, sentimental,
and unbelievably sexy, the characterization all but leaps into your
living room. As a matter of fact, there have been only two or three
other opera recordings in history that begin to match the uncanny
sense of presence this one generates from its very first notes. The
admirable Nicolai Gedda and Eberhard Wächter also turn in something close to the performances of *their* careers, and under the inspired leadership of Lovro von Matačič, who casts what amounts
to a magical spell over the proceedings, this *Merry Widow* effortlessly swirls its way into the ranks of the greatest recordings of all
time.

Leoncavallo, Ruggiero
(1858–1919)

I Pagliacci

Callas, di Stefano, Gobbi, Panerai, La Scala Orchestra and
Chorus, Serafin. Angel CDCC-47981 [CD].

Since the days when Enrico Caruso virtually adopted Canio's
histrionic Act I aria "Vesti la giubba" as his signature tune, Leoncavallo's *Pagliacci*, with its inseparable companion piece, Mascagni's *Cavalleria rusticana,* has remained a staple of the operatic
repertoire. Based on an actual case that the composer's father, a
local magistrate, tried when Leoncavallo was a boy, *I Pagliacci* is
one of the two quintessential works of the slice-of-life verismo
school of Italian opera: a work in which the uncontrollable passions
of ordinary people result in a delightful mosaic of jealousy, betrayal,
and violent death.

The famous La Scala recording from the early 1950s is more
earthy and bloodcurdling than ever in its compact disc reincarna-
tion. Tito Gobbi is a wonderfully sly and malevolent Tonio, and the
Nedda of Maria Callas is unapproachable in its vulgar animal magnetism and dramatic intensity. Still, *I Pagliacci* has always been the
tenor's show, and it is this recording, perhaps more than any other,
that demonstrates what Giuseppe di Stefano *might* have been. As
it stood, he had probably the most brilliant career of the postwar
Italian tenors; had it been managed with greater intelligence and
care, it might have been *the* career since Caruso's. His Canio is
painted in very primary colors, and for the most part is very beautifully sung; still, for all its power, we can hear the unmistakable
signs that his incredible instrument had already seen its best days.

Of the more recent *Pagliaccis,* none are worth a damn. Placido
Domingo is fine on Philips, but the production is done in by the
fingernails-on-the-blackboard voice of Teresa Stratas and the limp
conducting of Georges Prêtre; Pavarotti grunts and bellows on London, and the Karajan recording on Deutsche Grammophon has to
put up with Karajan.

Liszt, Franz (1811–1886)

Concertos for Piano and Orchestra: No. 1 in E-flat; No. 2 in A

Richter, piano; London Symphony, Kondrashin. Philips 412006-2 [CD].

Composer, conductor, philosopher, ascetic, charlatan, religious mystic, prodigious sexual athlete, and, in all probability, the greatest pianist who has ever lived, Franz Liszt was the epitome of the Romantic musician: a restless bundle of ambition, nervous energy, and insatiable appetites. His influence on the development of nineteenth-century music was so enormous that it still remains difficult to assess. As a composer, he all but invented the tone poem, one of musical Romanticism's most enduringly popular forms. His experiments in thematic transformation were decisive in the leitmotif technique perfected by his son-in-law, Richard Wagner. And in churning out endless reams of fiendishly difficult piano music for use on his innumerable concert tours, he helped provide gainful employment for virtuoso pianists from his day to our own.

Liszt's Piano Concertos have long been staples of the concert repertoire, and each is a revealing glimpse at the two complementary, and often contradictory, sides of the composer's essential makeup: the brash, outgoing, self-indulgent E-flat Concerto, and the moody, poetic, introspective Concerto No. 2 in A.

No modern interpretations have ever captured more of the Concertos' poetry and barnstorming excitement than this sensational Philips recording by Sviatoslav Richter. On a purely technical level, they are among the most hair-raising piano recordings ever made. Yet along with the phenomenal virtuosity, Richter brings such a measure of grandeur and profundity to the music that those who were tempted to dismiss it as empty-headed bombast will never be tempted to do so again.

Far and away the best tape—in fact, one of the finest of all recorded pairings of the Concertos—is the Deutsche Grammophon version (423571-4) with Krystian Zimerman, also available on CD (423571-2). Though Zimerman's playing, per se, can't quite match the depth or brilliance of Richter's, the interpretations are poised and adult, and Seiji Ozawa is an admirable partner. The recording also includes a suitably spooky performance of the always tasteful *Totentanz,* a work that should never be listened to in a dark room or after having just consumed a pizza.

A Faust Symphony

Young, tenor; Beecham Choral Society, Royal Philharmonic Orchestra, Beecham. Angel CDC-63371 [CD].

A Faust Symphony is probably the most inspired of all musical treatments of Goethe's great philosophical play. It may also be Franz Liszt's masterpiece. Each of its three movements is an elaborate character sketch of the play's three central figures: a brooding, heroic, poetic movement devoted to the title character, a lyrical second movement called "Gretchen," and a finale devoted to Mephistopheles, in which Liszt, like Milton before him, could not resist giving the Devil all the best lines. One of the lengthiest and most challenging symphonies written up to that time, *A Faust Symphony* still makes tremendous demands on its interpreters, and the recording that is most successful in solving the work's innumerable problems is this one by Sir Thomas Beecham.

Originally released in the mid-1950s, the Beecham *Faust Symphony* is one of the conductor's finest recorded performances. Lyrical, pensive, impetuous, and shot through with a demoniacal wit, its only serious drawback was the rather shrill and harsh recorded sound, which the compact disc remastering has brilliantly managed to correct.

Hungarian Rhapsodies (19)

Szidon, piano. Deutsche Grammophon 423925-2 [CD].

Close to the top of my "Whatever became of . . ." list, just behind the Italian conductor-wunderkind of the 1950s, Piero Gamba, is the Brazilian pianist Roberto Szidon, who made a couple of recordings in the early 1970s and then seemed to vanish without a trace.

It took a certain amount of bravado to choose for one of his first recordings these popular works that everyone and his mother have been recording since time began. The results came as quite a jolt to HR collectors: not only were they among the most exciting performances heard in a generation, they brought a refined musicality to these frequently flogged warhorses that is almost never heard. A few individual performers (Cziffra, Kapell, Horowitz in his maniacal transcription of No. 2) have outscored Szidon at various points, but no more satisfying interpretation of the entire cycle has ever appeared. The playing has authentic poetry and finesse, plus electrifying moments of out-on-a-limb derring-do. This was clearly a major career in the making, and we can only wonder again what happened.

None of the recordings of the orchestral versions of the Rhapsodies are anything to write home about, so do yourself a favor and save the stamp.

Piano Sonata in B minor

Brendel, piano. Philips 410040-2 [CD].

Wild, piano. Etcetera KTC-2010 [CD].

Richard Wagner was especially fond of his father-in-law's only piano sonata. Shortly after Liszt sent him the manuscript, Wagner wrote back saying, "It is sublime, even as yourself." Though Johannes Brahms was also particularly keen to hear it performed, at the private concert that Liszt arranged in his honor Brahms showed his gratitude by falling asleep. Much of Liszt's piano music is little more than gaudy ephemera, but his B minor Sonata, with those of Schubert and Chopin, remains the Romantic era's most enduring contribution to the form, and one of that tiny handful of nineteenth-century piano sonatas that are every bit the equal of any Beethoven ever wrote.

Until London Records returns Sir Clifford Curzon's Homeric and inspired interpretation on a compact disc, the choice among available recordings of the work lies between the studied introspection of Alfred Brendel and the flamboyant virtuosity of Earl Wild. Brendel, whose link to the composer is a direct one (his teacher, Edwin Fischer, was a pupil of the Liszt pupil Eugen d'Albert), gives an immensely intelligent performance on his Philips compact disc. If Brendel's playing is not the last word in individuality or animal excitement, he nevertheless reveals the Sonata's complex structure with a disarming lucidity and ease. Earl Wild, though a bit less thoughtful than Brendel, makes the music flash and thunder like one of the hell-for-leather virtuosos of the past. Now, the ideal recording of the Liszt Sonata would be a combination of Wild's fire with Brendel's brains—which is *precisely* what Sir Clifford Curzon gave us two decades ago. (Got the message, London?)

Les Préludes (Symphonic Poem No. 3)

London Philharmonic, Solti. London 417513-2 [CD].

Chicago Symphony, Barenboim. Deutsche Grammophon 415851-2 [CD], 415851-4 [T].

Of the thirteen works with which Franz Liszt all but invented the tone poem, only *Les Préludes* is heard with any frequency today. Listening to Bernard Haitink's heroically ambitious cycle for Philips (now out of print) will quickly show you why. For in spite of the best of intentions and some of the best recorded performances any of these works are ever likely to receive, most of the Liszt tone poems are unmitigated junk. (It *is* difficult to think of another great composer whose ratio of trash to masterworks was quite as high as his.) Often as schlocky and bombastic as the rest, *Les Préludes* is saved in the end by its grandiose gestures, flood of memorable melody, and utter sincerity. Schlock it most certainly is, but of a wonderfully urgent and lovable variety.

Although Daniel Barenboim is extremely ardent in his version with the Chicago Symphony, Sir Georg Solti's recording with the London Philharmonic is probably more valuable. While the playing is undeniably exciting, rarely has *Les Préludes* been invested with such power and genuine nobility. Packaged with equally riveting and dignified performances of the rarely heard *Tasso* and *Prometheus,* this is probably the strongest case for the Liszt tone poems any single recording has ever made.

Mahler, Gustav (1860–1911)

Das Lied von der Erde

Patzak, tenor; Ferrier, contralto; Vienna Philharmonic, Walter. London 414194-2 [CD].

King, tenor; Fischer-Dieskau, baritone; Vienna Philharmonic, Bernstein. London 417783-2 [CD].

The popularity Gustav Mahler's music now enjoys would have been all but unthinkable a generation ago. Most of the symphonies remained unrecorded, and of those that were, many featured mediocre to wretched performances that could only begin to hint at the greatness contained in these noble, neurotic, enervating, and uplifting works. Today, recordings of the Mahler symphonies are nearly as common as those of Beethoven's, which is as it should be. For just as the Romantic symphony was born in that series of nine works Beethoven produced at the beginning of the nineteenth century, its convulsive, extravagantly beautiful death can be heard in the works Mahler wrote at the beginning of our own.

For most of his eighty-five years, Bruno Walter—Mahler's disciple and protégé—was the composer's most impassioned and indefatigable champion. Walter led the world premieres of the Ninth Symphony and *Das Lied von der Erde,* and he left recordings that remain some of the most telling and authoritative.

This famous 1952 version of the great symphonic song cycle *Das Lied von der Erde* is not only one of Walter's greatest recorded performances but one of the most intensely moving Mahler recordings ever made. The credit for this must be shared with the incomparable Kathleen Ferrier, whose haunting, richly sabled singing of the concluding "Abschied" has never been matched, and the superb Viennese tenor Julius Patzak, whose thin, leathery voice and consummate musicianship recall the art of another leather-voiced Viennese magician, Richard Tauber. But it is the conductor's gentle intensity that makes this one of the major triumphs in the history of the gramophone. All the passion and subtlety of this brilliantly executed interpretation can be heard with remarkable clarity in London's remastered recording. The compact disc is especially miraculous in the way it makes the original 1952 recording seem as though it had been completed the day before yesterday.

If more modern sound is an absolute necessity, Leonard Bernstein's Vienna Philharmonic recording, one of his very first with the orchestra, remains a noble and engrossing, if not entirely convincing, experiment. Tenor James King sings well enough and the orchestra goes out of its mind; the problem may lie in hearing a baritone sing the contralto's songs. Fortunately, the baritone is Dietrich Fischer-Dieskau at his most reserved, penetrating, and dignified. The principal selling point is Bernstein's rather unbelievable conducting, which he would certainly equal on records, but never surpass.

Songs of a Wayfarer; Kindertotenlieder; Rückert Lieder

Baker, mezzo-soprano; Hallé Orchestra, New Philharmonia Orchestra, Barbirolli. Angel CDC-47793 [CD].

Even in a career as long and memorable as Dame Janet Baker's, the performances captured on these recordings stand out as pinnacles of her vocal art. Never have the *Songs of a Wayfarer* sounded as Schubertian in their refinement, and *Kindertotenlieder,* while devastating in their sorrow, are at once tenderly consoling and totally lacking in self-pity.

Sir John Barbirolli was not only a great Mahler conductor but also a perfect partner for the mezzo-soprano; they seem to sense each other's needs and desires not simply bars but literally *pages* ahead of time, and yet move together so naturally that it sounds as though it were all being made up on the spur of the moment.

Dame Janet's Hyperion recording of the piano version (with Geoffrey Parsons) of the *Songs of a Wayfarer* plus some early Mahler rarities is recommended just as highly (CDA-66100 [CD]).

Symphony No. 1 in D

Concertgebouw Orchestra of Amsterdam, Bernstein. Deutsche Grammophon 427303-2 [CD], 427303-4 [T].

Completed when Mahler was only twenty-eight, the D Major Symphony—still known, in spite of the composer's violent objections, as the *Titan*—contains many of the key compositional ingredients of the mature Mahler style. Its Olympian length, the sheer size of the performing forces, the gentle Viennese charm, the obsession with death in the gallows humor of the funeral march, and the ecstatic, almost hysterical triumph of its closing bars are all significant portents of what was to come.

More than three dozen versions of the work are currently in print, but none can come within shouting distance of that overwhelming and endlessly inventive recording Jascha Horenstein made with the London Symphony in the late 1960s, now shamefully withdrawn. Available for a time on the Nonesuch label, and then on a Unicorn CD, it was one of the few studio recordings that managed to convey the on-the-spot sense of creation we encounter in only the most gripping live performances. A triumph of excess, exaggeration, and personality (and certainly no conductor ever made the final ten minutes seem more exultant or monumental), it was the Mahler First of a lifetime, and one we shouldn't have expected to be bettered any time soon.

Leonard Bernstein's final version *is* a recording of a gripping ("stupefying" would be far closer to the point) live performance. While the first two movements sound more serene and bucolic than usual—the Ländler is an amusing country-bumpkin affair—the Funeral March is straight out of Edgar Allan Poe (or possibly Alfred Hitchcock), and the finale is one of those apocalyptic firestorms that threaten to incinerate everything in sight.

Symphony No. 2 in C minor, *Resurrection*

Armstrong, soprano; Baker, mezzo-soprano; Edinburgh Festival Chorus, London Symphony Orchestra, Bernstein. CBS M2K-42195 [CD].

When Leonard Bernstein's second stereo recording of the *Resurrection* Symphony was first released, most of the critics jumped all over it for its alleged self-indulgence and exaggerations. Of course, to say that of *any* performance of this inherently self-indulgent and exaggerated work would have been a bit like busting a Sodom and Gomorrah city councilman for indecent exposure. In fact, the recordings of the *Resurrection* that fail most decisively— those by Kubelik, Maazel, and Sinopoli, for example—are those that try to make the work more polite, coherent, and civilized than it can possibly be. To his great credit, Bernstein simply yanks out all the stops and allows this paradoxical hodgepodge of pathos, bathos, banality, and nobility to speak eloquently, and unforgettably, for itself.

On cassette, that vastly moving, surprisingly straightforward RCA recording by Leopold Stokowski (ALK2-5392) is one of the finest that always unpredictable magician ever made.

Symphony No. 3 in D minor

> Procter, mezzo-soprano; Wandsworth School Boys Choir, Ambrosian Singers, London Symphony, Horenstein. Unicorn-Kanchana UKCD-2006/7 [CD].

> Ludwig, mezzo-soprano; Brooklyn Boys Choir, New York Choral Artists, New York Philharmonic, Bernstein. Deutsche Grammophon 427328-2 [CD], 427328-4 [T].

> Baker, mezzo-soprano; London Symphony Orchestra and Chorus, Thomas. CBS M2K-44553 [CD], M2T-44553 [T].

The longest symphony ever written by a major composer (and because of that fact, one of the few classical works that earns a place in *The Guinness Book of World Records*), the Third is obviously one of the more challenging Mahler symphonies to perform. In concert, it can make for an uncomfortable evening if the conductor has not done his homework; in the living room, it can offer countless excuses to turn off the receiver and see what's on TV.

And yet for all its daunting challenges, the Third has probably accounted for more important recordings than any other Mahler symphony, led by the three listed above. As extravagant as it may sound for such a work (the Mahler Third is hardly the Beethoven Fifth), I would suggest buying all three recordings, not only because I am unable to distinguish a clear-cut winner, but also because I would be unwilling—wild horses notwithstanding—to be dragged away from the other two.

The oldest of the three, Jascha Horenstein's famous utterance of a generation ago, seems only to grow in stature over the years. In terms of both sweep and detail, he hardly misses a trick. The first movement marches in with a beautiful relentlessness, and the finale, taken at a dangerously slow pace, more than justifies Horenstein's courage: here it sounds like the greatest single movement in all of Mahler.

The Bernstein recording, taped at a live performance, is also overwhelming. (Mark Swed, the critic I trust more than any other, was present at the concert and came away talking to himself.) The relatively dry acoustic can't compromise either the lush romance or the cumulative power of the performance; it is—as it should be—a thoroughly exhausting experience.

If Michael Tilson Thomas does not yet have the reputation of being a great Mahler conductor, then his version of the Third should change that immediately. Huge in scale, meticulous in its ornamentation, and bursting with energy, it more than holds its own with those of his older colleagues—which is to say with the finest Mahler recordings ever made.

Again, each of these triumphant releases is an unqualified winner. If you must narrow it down to only one, I suggest you toss a three-headed coin.

Symphony No. 4 in G

Raskin, soprano; Cleveland Orchestra, Szell. Sony Classical SBK-46535 [CD], SBT-46535 [T].

This most concise, charming, and popular of the Mahler symphonies is how most people find their way into the composer's music: it's the Mahlerian equivalent of Bruckner's *Romantic* Symphony. Yet like that other Fourth Symphony, the Mahler G Major is probably his least characteristic work. Genial, untroubled, and, except for a few dark moments in the third movement, completely lacking in any neurotic symptoms, the Fourth is as happy as Mahler can be and still remain Mahler. Even the inevitable presentiment of death in the finale is a singularly trusting and innocent vision of heaven through the eyes of a child.

This classic 1965 interpretation remains one of the most completely successful Mahler recordings ever made. With a charm and glowing humanity that many of his enemies rarely accused him of possessing, George Szell handles the music with a deceptively relaxed but always exceedingly firm grip. Climaxes—even the shattering one at the end of the third movement—merely seem to happen, and in fact the entire performance creates the illusion of unfolding by itself, without the intervention of human will.

Judith Raskin gives one of the most engrossingly spontaneous performances of her brilliant career in the final movement; the

Cleveland Orchestra has never been better, and in spite of some slightly intrusive hiss from the original analogue tapes, the compact disc restoration is remarkably fine.

Symphony No. 5 in C-sharp minor

Chicago Symphony, Solti. London 414321-2 [CD], 414321-4 [T].

Chicago still suffers from its age-old "Second City" complex, and is hence a place where superlatives tend to get thrown around more casually than anywhere else. The local Republican newspaper, the *Chicago Tribune,* calls itself "The World's Greatest Newspaper" on the masthead, hence the call letters of its television and radio stations, WGN. WLS, its Sears-owned competitor, is a reminder of "The World's Largest Store." Only in Chicago would things like the World's Tallest Building (the Sears Tower) or the World's Busiest Airport (O'Hare International) be pointed to as objects of civic pride, and only in Chicago would the city's orchestra, fresh from its first European tour, be cheered by a crowd who had probably not, for the most part, ever set foot in a concert hall, with banners proclaiming it (what else?) the World's Greatest Orchestra.

I was there in Orchestra Hall when Sir Georg Solti led an absolutely spellbinding performance of the Mahler Fifth during his first season as music director of the Chicago Symphony. The recording that was made several weeks later not only captured much of the overwhelming excitement of the interpretation, but also served to announce that the orchestra, after its stormy association with Solti's predecessor Jean Martinon, was at last back in form. They *do* sound very much like the World's Greatest Orchestra in one of the first recordings they made with their new music director. The woodwinds and brass negotiate this difficult music with supreme confidence and bravado, and the strings, both in the famous, gentle Adagietto and in the whirlwind finale, give Solti everything he asks for, which here amounts to the last word in excitement and finesse. Along with the playing itself (and this is, by a comfortable margin, the best-played Mahler Fifth ever released), Solti's interpretation is a subtle yet powerfully dramatic one, and the somewhat harsh sound of the original recording has been improved considerably.

Symphony No. 6 in A minor, *Tragic*

Vienna Philharmonic, Bernstein. Deutsche Grammophon 427697-2 [CD].

The Sixth Symphony occupies a unique position in Mahler's output as perhaps the most paradoxical work this endlessly paradoxical composer would ever produce. It is simultaneously the most objective and deeply personal of all his symphonies, the most rigorous in its formal organization, and the most devastating in its emotional effect. It is the only one of his ten completed works in the form (including *Das Lied von der Erde*) which, in its original version, adhered to the traditional format of the classical symphony, and the only one which ends on a note of catastrophic, inconsolable despair.

Bernstein's DG version of this dark masterpiece easily eclipses his earlier one for CBS, which in its day was the most compelling recorded performance available. Although the conductor's tempo in the first movement might seem a shade brisk to some, his shaping of the problematical finale is nothing short of masterly. The music rises heroically after each of the catastrophies signaled by one of those famous "hammer blows of fate"; the desolation he conjures in the final bars gives you the chilling feeling that someone has just walked on your grave. Thomas Hampson's beautifully sung *Kindertotenlieder* is the extremely attractive bonus.

Symphony No. 7 in E minor

Chicago Symphony, Abbado. Deutsche Grammophon 413773-2 [CD].

The Seventh is by far the most difficult of all the Mahler symphonies to approach and, finally, to love. In the mysterious Scherzo, flanked by two movements called *Nachtmusik*, the composer would write some of his most harmonically adventurous, forward-looking music. And if the opening movement presents more than its share of structural problems, the finale has always seemed, in comparison, utterly fragmented and frightfully banal.

In a pirated tape of a live London Symphony concert that has had a vigorous circulation in the underground market, Jascha Horenstein proved conclusively that the work's many problems are only surface deep. Not only was the conductor's grasp of the subtle, complex atmosphere of the three central movements amazing, he was also able to make the usually thin-sounding, patchwork finale seem as cogent and triumphant as the finale of the Mahler Fifth.

In his superb recording with the Chicago Symphony, Claudio Abbado accomplishes many of the same things. The first four movements—especially the Scherzo and second *Nachtmusik*—are invested with tremendous individuality and character, and the finale is perhaps the absolute high point to date in Abbado's admirable Mahler cycle. All the themes emerge as distinct and highly charged entities, which are carefully woven into a passionate and fabulously exciting whole. In fact, on repeated hearings of this elegantly thought out and brilliantly executed performance, the Seventh begins to join the Sixth, Eighth, and Ninth as one of the most powerful and original symphonies Mahler ever wrote.

Symphony No. 8 in E-flat, *Symphony of a Thousand*

Harper, Popp, Auger, Minton, Watts, Kollo, Shirley-Quirk, Talvela, Vienna State Opera Chorus, Vienna Singverein, Vienna Boys Choir, Chicago Symphony, Solti. London 414493-2 [CD].

Sir Georg Solti has said in print that he considers the Eighth the greatest of the Mahler symphonies, and on the basis of this stupendous Chicago Symphony recording, taped in Vienna, even the most rabid admirers of the Sixth and Ninth would be tempted to agree. On a singularly tight recording schedule (and the tension, at times, is almost palpable), Solti unleashes the grandeur of the music in a way that even Leonard Bernstein, in his famous London Symphony recording, is not quite able to match.

The performance of the opening movement, a setting of the medieval hymn *Veni, creator spiritus,* is almost withering in its joyous excitement, and the lengthy setting of the closing scene from Part I of Goethe's *Faust* is wonderfully operatic, in the best possible sense of the word. Solti loses no opportunity to exploit either the high drama or endless color of the score, from the hushed and sinister opening bars of the second movement to the vast and vastly moving chorus with which the Symphony concludes. The massed choruses sing with tremendous accuracy and enthusiasm, and the performance boasts the strongest collection of soloists of any

Mahler Eighth on the market today. Yet it is the superhuman playing of the Chicago Symphony that tips the scales, perhaps forever, in Solti's favor. Rumor has it that members of the Vienna Philharmonic who attended the recording sessions were deeply shaken by what they heard. Many left the hall speechless, while others were heard mumbling incoherently to themselves.

Symphony No. 9 in D

Concertgebouw Orchestra of Amsterdam, Bernstein. Deutsche Grammophon 419208-2 [CD].

Even before that historic series of concerts in May of 1920, when Willem Mengelberg presided over the first important festival of his friend's music, the Concertgebouw Orchestra of Amsterdam had begun the longest unbroken Mahler tradition of any of the world's major orchestras. The composer himself was a frequent guest conductor in Amsterdam, and in addition to Mengelberg's famous interpretations, those of his successors, Eduard van Beinum and Bernard Haitink, have gone a long way to cementing the Concertgebouw reputation as the finest Mahler orchestra in the world. Furthermore, the greatest Mahler conductor of recent times also appeared with them on a regular basis, and this live performance of the Ninth Symphony must now be counted with the three or four greatest Mahler recordings yet made.

In the two decades after his New York Philharmonic recordings became the principal impetus for the modern Mahler revival, Leonard Bernstein's approach to the composer's music both deepened and grew more extreme. The surface drama became increasingly turbulent (his detractors have called it "self-indulgent" and "overwrought"), while its deeper implications were plumbed with an understanding that was ever more lucid and profound.

This performance of the composer's most shattering work is a triumph of extremes. Where other conductors have been intense in this music, Bernstein is almost savagely so; where others have heard the last movement as Mahler's poignant farewell to life, Bernstein transforms it into the stuff of universal tragedy, a farewell to *all* life, possibility, and hope. In essence, the conductor's final version of this great work is as much Bernstein's Ninth as it is Gustav

Mahler's. For those who find the vision either too personal or too searingly painful to bear, Bernard Haitink's beautifully controlled recording with the same orchestra (Philips 416466-2 [CD]) is the best alternative.

Martinů, Bohuslav (1890–1959)

Nonet; *La Revue de cuisine;* Trio in F for Flute, Cello, and Piano

Dartington Ensemble. Hyperion CDA-66084 [CD].

With the work of his Polish near-contemporary Karol Szymanowski, the music of the Czech composer Bohuslav Martinů remains one of the last largely undiscovered treasure troves of twentieth-century music. Like Szymanowski, Martinů was a restless eclectic whose music nevertheless spoke with a unique and thoroughly original voice. In all of the more than four hundred works he eventually produced, one can hear the same quality that so impressed Igor Stravinsky in the music of Sergei Prokofiev: an elusive commodity Stravinsky called "the instant imprint of personality." If the Great Martinů Revival is not actually upon us yet, there has been some encouraging recent evidence—including the superb recording listed above—that it may be about to begin.

In addition to bringing us some of the finest performances of Martinů's chamber music that have yet been made, the invaluable Hyperion recording by England's Dartington Ensemble also provides a representative cross-section of the three major phases of Martinů's creative life. *La Revue de cuisine* (The Kitchen Revue) is a sassy, jazzy ballet produced during the composer's seventeen-year stay in Paris; the Trio in F, composed during Martinů's American exile in 1944, is one of the most Czech and ebullient of all his works. Yet the gem of the collection is the bright and deceptively simple-sounding Nonet, composed five months before the composer's death in 1959. In its serenity, melodic inventiveness, and structural elegance, it is easily one of the most nearly perfect and instantly enjoyable chamber works written since the end of the Second World War.

Symphonies (6)

Bamberg Symphony, Järvi. Bis CD-362 (Nos. 1 and 2); CD-363 (Nos. 3 and 4); CD-395 (Nos. 5 and 6) [CDs].

Neeme Järvi, the conductor of the Detroit Symphony (among other ensembles), is, to say the very least, an enigma. One of the most frequently recorded of contemporary conductors, he has plugged more holes in the catalog than a hundred little Dutchboys could. In repertoire that is either unknown or well off the beaten track, the burly Estonian tends to be vigorous, imaginative, and persuasive; on more familiar ground (witness his generally drab and uneventful cycle of the Dvořák symphonies), he often disappoints.

Among his most valuable contributions to date are the recordings of the six Martinů symphonies made for the Swedish label Bis. The decision to use the Bamberg Symphony as opposed to his own Gothenburg Orchestra was a wise one, resulting in idiomatic, intensely committed playing.

Martinů did not produce a symphony until he was fifty-two, so all six are the products of a fully mature musical personality. The First, a gleaming, rhythmically ingenious work commissioned by Serge Koussevitzky, was followed by the relaxed and rustic Second, Martinů's *Pastoral* Symphony. The Third is a brooding, violent, often desperate commentary on the events of World War II, while the Fourth, written in the spring of 1945, mixes joy, hope, and idyllic tenderness, and features a Largo that rivals the somewhat more familiar Largo from Dvořák's *New World* Symphony in depth and complexity. The Fifth is another of the composer's obstinately life-affirming statements, and the Sixth, the *Fantaisies symphoniques,* is the most ambitious and far-reaching of all his orchestral scores.

With playing and recorded sound that are both nearly perfect, this constitutes an ideal introduction to a major symphonic talent.

Mascagni, Pietro (1863–1945)

Cavalleria rusticana

Milanov, Björling, Smith, Merrill, Robert Shaw Chorale,
RCA Victor Orchestra, Cellini. RCA 6510-2-RG [CD].

Long before he died in abject poverty and disgrace—like Giacomo Puccini, he had been one of Mussolini's most ardent supporters—Pietro Mascagni was one of the most tragic figures in operatic history. At the age of twenty-six, he achieved world fame with *Cavalleria rusticana,* and for the next fifty-six years he was condemned to live out his life haunted by an overwhelming early success he was never able to repeat. "I was crowned before I was King" was the composer's own rueful assessment of his career, and history has been forced to agree.

While this lurid tale of betrayal and revenge has very little to do with "rustic chivalry," the literal translation of its title, *Cavalleria rusticana* has remained the most justly popular one-act opera ever written. Like Leoncavallo's *Pagliacci,* with which it is usually paired, Mascagni's masterpiece is the central work of the Italian verismo school. Like *Pag, Cav* explodes with vivid drama and raw emotions, though it also boasts a musical subtlety and sensitivity to character that only the best of Puccini's mature operas can begin to match.

The recording that captures more of the opera's finesse and earthiness than any other is this classic RCA recording from the mid-1950s, recently released on compact disc. Zinka Milanov was one of the century's great Santuzzas. Passionate, vulnerable, immensely feminine, she was also equipped with a voice as physically impressive as those of Leontyne Price and Rosa Ponselle. This recording catches her at something past her prime, but with her temperament and most of her instrument still intact, the interpretation still makes for an overwhelming experience. With the insouciant and spectacularly well-sung Turiddu of Jussi Björling, and the sensitive, richly powerful, garlic-laden conducting of Renato Cellini, this remains, for me, the only recording of the opera to own.

Since that other fine RCA recording with Placido Domingo has been withdrawn, presumably to be resurrected soon on compact disc, none of the modern versions can be recommended with any

239

enthusiasm. As with *Pag,* the *Cav* situation is pretty bleak, the choice coming down to Pavarotti sweating bullets on London or Karajan sliming his way through the thing on Deutsche Grammophon.

Massenet, Jules (1842–1912)

Manon

De Los Angeles, Legay, Dens, Borthayre, Berton, Chorus and Orchestra of the Opéra-comique de Paris, Monteux. Angel CDMC-63549 [CD].

At the time of his death in 1912, the suave and urbane Jules Massenet was one of the wealthiest composers who ever lived. His impeccably crafted, gently sentimental operas are among the finest and most popular ever written by a French composer. Audiences love them for their directness, dramatic realism, and inexhaustible flow of lovely melody. Singers love them because they are so carefully and gracefully written that even the most demanding Massenet role will invariably make even a fair or barely adequate singer sound exceptionally good.

With the reappearance of the classic Monteux *Manon,* one of the great operatic recordings returns to the catalog. Even those who normally do not respond to Victoria de los Angeles's singing (one opera-loving friend refers to her as "an air-raid siren with feet") cannot fail to be bowled over by the freshness and sheer dramatic ingenuity of the performance. Pierre Monteux's conducting is a wonder of panache and aching sensitivity, the rest of the cast is splendid, and the only real drawback is the rather fierce recorded sound.

Those who absolutely must have more up-to-date sound will find much to admire in Michel Plasson's suavely accomplished performance, also on Angel (CDCB-49610 [CD]). And Sir Colin Davis's utterly memorable version of *Werther* on Philips (416654-2 [CD]) remains, with the Monteux *Manon,* one of the most completely satisfying Massenet recordings ever made.

Maxwell Davies, Sir Peter

(1934–)

Eight Songs for a Mad King; Miss Donnithorne's Maggot

Eastman, speaker; Thomas, mezzo-soprano; Fires of
London, Maxwell Davies. Unicorn-Kanchana DKPCD-
9052 [CD].

On first hearing *Eight Songs for a Mad King,* most people are
flabbergasted. As well they should be, since it is the most frighteningly original musical work produced by an Englishman in this
century.

Employing some of King George III's actual demented ruminations, the piece is so grotesque, poignant, ridiculous, touching,
stupid, and powerful that it defies description. Julius Eastman, who
"interprets" the role of the king, is quite unbelievable: his repertoire
of sighs, shrieks, howls, and moans is astounding, as is his ability
to draw us into the mind of the character and make us feel genuine
compassion and concern.

Miss Donnithorne's Maggot, a similarly unhinging tribute to
the actual eccentric who provided Dickens with his model for Miss
Havisham in *Great Expectations,* has many intriguing moments,
but pales in comparison to the *Songs.*

I should admit that when I first heard this dizzy work, I was
convinced that everyone concerned with the project—composer,
performers, recording company executives—was in desperate need
of psychiatric care. I'm now fairly certain that *Eight Songs for a
Mad King* is a major twentieth-century masterpiece.

Mendelssohn, Felix (1809–1847)

Concertos for Piano and Orchestra: No. 1 in G minor;
No. 2 in D minor

**Perahia, piano; Academy of St. Martin-in-the-Fields,
Marriner. CBS MK-42401 [CD], MT-33207 [T].**

While far less familiar than the justly ubiquitous Violin Concerto, Mendelssohn's Piano Concertos are full of memorable ideas
and exquisite surface detail. And though they are easy on the ear
and psyche, they are by no means powder puffs: the stormy opening
movement of the G minor is as substantial as anything in Mendelssohn, and the slow movements of both Concertos are superbly
crafted and richly felt.

It's hardly surprising that such a fine Mozart pianist as Murray Perahia should be such a cunning advocate of these works,
which so clearly have their roots in the eighteenth century. Their
essentially classical poise and structure are not lost on him, nor does
he ignore that breath of early Romanticism that makes all of Mendelssohn's music what it is. Sir Neville Marriner, as always, is a
witty and generous partner, and the CD version comes with equally
impeccable performances of the Prelude and Fugue No. 1, the
Rondo capriccioso, and the *Variations sérieuses*.

A must for Mendelssohn lovers or Perahia fans.

Concerto in E minor for Violin and Orchestra

**Menuhin, violin; Berlin Philharmonic, Furtwängler. Angel
CDH-69799 [CD].**

**Lin, violin; Philharmonia Orchestra, Thomas. CBS MDK-
44902 [CD], MDT-44902 [T].**

This fresh, buoyant, eternally sweet-spirited work is probably
the best-loved violin concerto ever written. And in spite of the apparent effortlessness of its invention, the E minor Concerto had an
unusually long and painful gestation: from first sketch to finished
score, it occupied the usually deft and facile composer's attention
for the better part of six years.

Every important violinist of the century has recorded the work, and many of them more than once, but there is still something very special in Sir Yehudi Menuhin's 1954 recording with Wilhelm Furtwängler and the Berlin Philharmonic. Unlike their monumental interpretation of the Beethoven Concerto which fills out this unusually generous compact disc, the performance of the Mendelssohn is a marvel of quiet intimacy and elfin grace. Menuhin's playing (which in recent years has been seriously compromised by a neurological disorder) was never more poignantly innocent than it is here, and the conductor, who had only a few months to live, turns in one of the freshest and most impetuous of all his recorded performances.

Among more recent versions, the sensational debut recording by the Chinese-American violinist Cho-Liang Lin is not only the most exciting recording the Concerto has received in years, but also our first glimpse at what should undoubtedly develop into one of the great careers of the next generation. Like his contemporary the cellist Yo-Yo Ma, Lin is already a dazzlingly equipped musician. His technique is formidably seamless, and his musical personality is an engaging combination of outgoing bravado and introspective warmth. With the lush yet witty support supplied by the Philharmonia Orchestra and Michael Tilson Thomas, this is considerably more than a very impressive first recording by an important new artist. It is, with Menuhin's thirtysomething-year-old wonder, *the* recording of the Mendelssohn Concerto to own.

*E*lijah

Plowright, Finnie, Davies, White, London Symphony Orchestra and Chorus, Hickox. Chandos CHAN-8774/5 [CD], DBTD-2016 [T].

From its startling opening recitative, which actually begins before the dirgelike overture, through such powerfully dramatic choruses as "Hear our cry, O Baal," the oratorio *Elijah* is one of the great de facto Romantic operas: a gripping, lyrical, wonderfully theatrical work which, with a little lighting and makeup, could hold the stage as easily as the early Wagner operas.

The glowing performance led by the ever-imaginative Richard Hickox transforms *Elijah* into something very far removed from the sanctimonious Victorian monstrosity that Shaw used to complain about. This is vivid, utterly committed music-making as well as compelling theater: Mendelssohn's inspiration shimmers in every bar, and the drama is made to seem consistently immediate and real. Hickox's team of soloists is exemplary, and the exhilarating work of the London Symphony Chorus only confirms his growing reputation as the finest European choral director since the legendary Wilhelm Pitz.

For those in whom *Elijah* strikes a responsive chord, Mendelssohn's other major oratorio, *St. Paul,* is now available in the inspired performance Rafael Frühbeck de Burgos recorded in the mid-1970s (Angel CDMB-64005 [CD]).

A Midsummer Night's Dream (incidental music), Opp. 21 and 61

> Watson, Wallis, London Symphony Orchestra and Chorus, Previn. Angel CDC-47163 [CD].

> Mathis, Boese, Bavarian Radio Orchestra and Chorus, Kubelik. Deutsche Grammophon 415840-2 [CD], 415840-4 [T].

The famous overture Felix Mendelssohn composed for Shakespeare's festive comedy *A Midsummer Night's Dream* has a fair claim to being the greatest single musical work ever written by a teenager. Only Mozart and Schubert produced music of similar quality at a comparable age. The remainder of the incidental music Mendelssohn would write sixteen years later was also of a very high caliber, including the finest example of a form he would make forever his own, the quicksilver Scherzo, and one of the most famous five minutes in all of music, the stirring and, for many, bloodcurdling Wedding March, to whose famous strains countless freedom-loving people have trooped off to join the ranks of the Living Dead.

On records, André Previn has established a well-deserved reputation as one of the finest interpreters of the music of the major modern English composers, and of other big-name twentieth-century figures from Rachmaninoff and Prokofiev to Debussy and Ravel. That he is equally comfortable in the mainstream of the Austro-German tradition is amply documented by a recording like this one, in which he proves, quite conclusively I think, that he is the finest Mendelssohn conductor in the world today.

All of the familiar moments—the Overture, Scherzo, Intermezzo, Nocturne, and Wedding March—are invested with an exhilarating freshness and immensely individual character, while the less familiar set pieces and linking passages are given a weight and significance no other recording can begin to match. The spooky menace and rhythmic point of "You Spotted Snakes" are alone worth the price of the recording.

Rafael Kubelik's occasionally willful but thoroughly ingratiating performance on Deutsche Grammophon is clearly the first choice among all available cassettes.

Octet in E-flat for Strings

Academy of St. Martin-in-the-Fields Chamber Ensemble.
Philips 420400-2 [CD]. Chandos ABTD-1423 [T].

When I was sixteen I read something from the second volume of George Bernard Shaw's *Dramatic Opinions and Essays* that struck a painfully responsive chord:

> With the single exception of Homer, there is no eminent writer, not even Sir Walter Scott, whom I can despise so entirely as I despise Shakespeare when I measure my mind against his. It would positively be a relief to me to dig him up and throw stones at him.

At an age when I was wasting my life fighting acne and the oboe, yelling at girls, and trying to beat out three other guys for one of the two defensive-end spots on my high school football team, Felix Mendelssohn was composing his miraculously inspired E-flat Octet. After weeks of excruciating soul searching, leavened by the then major triumphs of making the team, and thereby attracting the attentions of an exceedingly cute cheerleader, I resolved to stop hating Mendelssohn by simply facing the irrefutable facts. I was a perfectly normal Midwest high school kid; he was a genius.

Nowhere is Mendelssohn's youthful brilliance revealed more felicitously than in the finest single work ever composed for this particular combination of instruments. The level of melodic inspiration and richness of ornamental detail is so phenomenal, the Octet is obviously the work of a mature master, not a boy of sixteen. Both of these superlative recordings capture almost all of the Octet's melting warmth and blindingly brilliant inspiration. In fact, a choice between them will depend largely on your preference for the tape or the compact disc format.

Overtures

London Symphony, Abbado. Deutsche Grammophon 423104-2 [CD].

Besides being the most complete collection of Mendelssohn overtures on the market—the standard *Midsummer Night's Dream, Hebrides, Ruy Blas, Fair Melusine,* and *Calm Sea and Prosperous Voyage* are joined by the thoroughly and perhaps deservedly obscure Trumpet Overture and Overture for Wind Instruments—this is also one of the most attractive Mendelssohn recordings currently in circulation.

As his classy set of the five mature symphonies demonstrates, Claudio Abbado is a Mendelssohn conductor of the very first rank: he responds fully and naturally to the zest and drama of the music, while taking great care with its delicate filigree. Each of the performances captures the special character and atmosphere of the individual pieces (the *Hebrides,* for instance, is marvelously gloomy), and the London Symphony plays as well as it has in years.

Songs without Words

Barenboim, piano. Deutsche Grammophon 423931-2 [CD] (complete); 415118-2 [CD] (excerpts).

Along with being able to hear the *William Tell* Overture without immediately thinking of the Lone Ranger, one of the acid tests of the true music lover is the ability to listen to Mendelssohn's "Spring Song" without breaking into fits of convulsive laughter. With the second Hungarian Rhapsody, it was pilloried in more cartoons of the 1940s and '50s than any other musical work, and its unaffected innocence *can* degenerate into saccharine ditziness if the performer fails to treat it like the delicate blossom it is.

Unlike so many performances of the *Songs without Words,* which have treated these magical, fragile miniatures like Victorian potted palms, Daniel Barenboim's reveal the wondrous little tone poems that lie buried beneath the decades of calcified interpretative treacle. While obviously affectionate, his interpretations have just enough twinkle of wit to prevent things from getting mushy. And even when the pianist does turn on the ooze, he does so with a charming fin de siècle graciousness—a pretty neat trick for a musician born in 1942.

If all eight sets seem like a bit much (though listening to them is precisely analogous to eating peanuts), a judicious selection, together with the three *Liebesträume* of Liszt and Schubert's *Moments musicaux,* are available on a single unusually enjoyable Deutsche Grammophon CD.

Symphony No. 3 in A minor, *Scottish*

London Symphony, Maag. London 433023-2 [CD].

Chicago Symphony, Solti. London 414665-2 [CD].

It is no accident that in Great Britain, Felix Mendelssohn is revered as one of the most important of all composers. In addition to writing the incidental music for Shakespeare's *Midsummer Night's Dream,* he supplied the oratorio-mad English with *Elijah,* one of the greatest nineteenth-century examples of their favorite form of musical entertainment. And with the *Hebrides Overture* and *Scottish* Symphony (the latter dedicated to Queen Victoria), he wrote two of the best and most popular of all musical travelogues based on British themes.

No recording of the *Scottish* Symphony has come within hailing distance of the astonishingly vivid and spontaneous performance by the London Symphony led by the Swiss conductor Peter Maag since it was first released more than thirty years ago. Impulsive yet highly polished, beautifully detailed yet sweepingly cinematic, the interpretation remains one of the great glories of the stereo era. Offering as it does Sir Georg Solti's brilliant Israel Philharmonic recording of the *Italian* Symphony (you simply will not believe the ferocious pace of the finale), this disc is one of the major bargains now on the market. Solti's slightly driven yet compellingly dramatic Chicago Symphony recording of the Third is the best alternative. With thrilling playing and dazzling recorded sound, this would be the first choice among all *Scottish* Symphony recordings, were it not for the once-in-a-lifetime combination of freshness and poetry Peter Maag found in the score so long ago.

Symphony No. 4 in A, *Italian*

Cleveland Orchestra, Szell. CBS MYK-37760 [CD], MYT-37760 [T].

More than any other work, it is the colorful, impeccably crafted *Italian* Symphony that best fixes Mendelssohn's place in the development of Western music. Essentially a classicist who was touched by the first winds of the Romantic movement, Mendelssohn reconciled eighteenth-century structural decorum with nineteenth-century emotionalism more comfortably than any other composer of his time. The *Italian* Symphony is one of the great transitional works of the early Romantic era, a piece whose formal organization is as tight as that of the symphonies of Haydn and Mozart, but whose expressiveness clearly points the way to Berlioz, Chopin, and Schumann.

The performance that most successfully projects both sides of the *Italian* Symphony's essential character is this immaculate and exciting CBS recording. Along with the highly buffed playing of the Cleveland, the finest Mozart orchestra of modern times, George Szell finds countless ways to remind us that this is also an intensely Romantic work. The Pilgrim's March, even at a rather brisk tempo, has a wonderfully melancholy grandeur, and in the concluding tarantella, taken at a breakneck clip, there are many dark and disquieting moments lurking beneath the swirling, giddy surface. With equally lucid and revealing performances of the best-known moments from the *Midsummer Night's Dream* music, this is one of the classic Mendelssohn recordings of the stereo age.

Trios (2) for Piano, Violin, and Cello

Golub, piano; Kaplan, violin; Carr, cello. Arabesque Z-6599 [CD].

Besides the phenomenal Octet for Strings, the two Piano Trios represent Mendelssohn's major achievement as a composer of chamber music. With their singing slow movements, sparkling Scherzos, and powerfully dramatic finales, both of these passionate, elegantly wrought works rank with the finest chamber music of the Romantic era.

Although for years the recordings by the Beaux Arts set the standard in both pieces, the newer versions by this brilliant trio of young Americans handily surpass them. A freshness in the approach and an effortlessness in the execution make the performances seem both utterly natural and thoroughly alive.

While the composer's six String Quartets are not on the same consistently high level as the Trios, they contain much wonderful music and can be heard in a very fine Deutsche Grammophon collection (415883-2 [CD]) by Stuttgart's Melos Quartet.

Menotti, Gian Carlo
(1911–   )

Amahl and the Night Visitors

> Soloists; Orchestra and Chorus of the Royal Opera House, Covent Garden, Syrus. MCA Classics MCAD-6218 [CD].

There was a time when Menotti-bashing was one of the opera lover's favorite indoor sports. I should know. For in those long-vanished days when I was snooty and arrogant and refused to admit that even *Norma* and *Lucia di Lammermoor* were music, Menotti seemed to me nothing more than a jumped-up Richard Rodgers, except that he couldn't write tunes that were nearly as good.

It wasn't this Christmas classic, or *The Consul,* or *The Medium* that belatedly drew me into this hugely underrated composer's web, but the shamefully ignored *Saint of Bleecker Street,* which follows Robert Kurka's *The Good Soldier Schweik* on the list of

Neglected American Operas I Would Most Like to See. (Unlike *Schweik*, whose irresistible suite is heard from time to time, *The Saint of Bleecker Street* was actually recorded and shows off all Menotti's gifts to their best advantage: the modest but authentic melodic genius, the ability to create living characters, the unerring sense of time, mood, and place, and the finely honed theatrical instinct that never seems to let him down.)

Lovers of *Amahl and the Night Visitors* (alas, admiration is about all I can muster) will be delighted with this handsome modern recording which, on every count—singing, playing, conducting, sense of life and atmosphere, and of course, recorded sound—is a dramatic improvement on the old 1951 TV soundtrack. For the sentimental, the original-cast version is now available on an RCA compact disc (6485-2-RG) and tape (6485-4-RG).

Messiaen, Olivier (1908–1992)

Turangalîla Symphony; *Quartet for the End of Time*

City of Birmingham Symphony, Rattle. Angel CDCB-47463 [CD].

To give credit where credit is due, Olivier Messiaen is the only composer of serious music whose work has ever made me throw up. I was listening to a new recording of *Vingt regards sur l'Enfant Jésus* (which one announcer of my acquaintance always translates on the air as "Give my regards to Jesus") when I felt that unmistakable feeling and made it to the restroom just in time. True, I was running a fever of 102 degrees; true, there was a particularly virulent form of intestinal flu making the rounds, and true, I *had* consumed an inhumanly large and greasy cheeseburger not an hour before. Nevertheless, I firmly believed that Messiaen was responsible, and I still believe it today.

Numerous respected musicians, and a fair-sized public, take Messiaen's mumbling mysticism and interminable bird calls seriously, so he can't be dismissed out of hand. Recently, for sins too horrible to mention, I assigned myself the penance of listening to Simon Rattle's recording of the endless *Turangalîla* Symphony. If you're drawn to this gibberish, you'll find the interpretation all you could possibly hope for: like André Previn's deleted Angel recording, the performance may even be far too good for the piece.

An older recording of that other Messiaen favorite, the knee-slapping *Quartet for the End of Time,* rounds out what is, for my taste, a far too generous release.

Milhaud, Darius (1892–1974)

La Création du monde

National Orchestra of France, Bernstein. Angel CDC-47845 [CD].

Contemporary Chamber Ensemble, Weisberg. Nonesuch 71281-4 [T].

One of the most prolific and entertaining composers that history has known, Darius Milhaud was also one of the largest. In fact, to find a composer of comparable girth, one has to go back to the late-eighteenth-century Bohemian composer and keyboard virtuoso Jan Ladislav Dussek, who became so obese toward the end of his career that his hands could no longer reach the keyboard of his piano. (Fortunately for posterity, Milhaud never learned to play the instrument, and thus was free to compose all his music while seated at a desk.)

La Création du monde (The Creation of the World), the jazz ballet written after the composer's encounter with American jazz in 1923, is probably Milhaud's finest and most characteristic work. It is given racy, vibrant performances in both the recordings listed above, and a choice between them will depend largely on your preference of format. The Bernstein compact disc also includes spirited interpretations of Milhaud's *Saudades do Brasil* and *Le Boeuf sur le toit*, the equally jazzy and surrealistic ballet whose scenario, by Jean Cocteau, calls for (among other things) a Paris gendarme to be decapitated by an overhead fan. The Weisberg tape comes with a superbly decadent version of another '20s "jazz" classic, the suite from Kurt Weill's *Threepenny Opera*.

Moeran, E. J. (1894–1950)

Symphony in G minor; *Overture to a Masque*

Ulster Orchestra, Handley. Chandos CHAN-8577 [CD], ABTD-1272 [T].

It is frankly astonishing that a work as fine as Moeran's G Minor Symphony should be so completely unknown outside of Britain. Brilliantly argued and crafted, with its roots firmly planted in British folk song, it is a work to stand alongside most of the Vaughan Williams symphonies, and it is one that would undoubtedly attract a large following were it simply to be played more often.

Given an unusually pointed and powerful performance by Vernon Handley and the fine Ulster Orchestra, the Symphony has a moiling, craggy intensity that recalls late Sibelius, although it has more than enough character and personality of its own. With an equally smashing account of the rambunctious *Overture to a Masque*, this is both an ideal introduction to an important, strangely neglected composer and an absolute must for lovers of modern British music.

Monteverdi, Claudio

(1567–1643)

Madrigals

Consort of Musicke, Rooley. Oiseau-Lyre 421480-2 [CD].

Though this anthology of works on frankly erotic themes is possibly not the most representative of the Consort of Musicke's irreproachable series of recordings of the Monteverdi Madrigals— more balanced collections include their versions of the complete Book 4 (Oiseau-Lyre 414148-2 [CD]), Book 5 (Oiseau-Lyre 410291-2 [CD]), or Book 6 (Virgin Classics VC-7-91154-2 [CD], VC-7-91154-4 [T])—none are more uplifting. As in Elizabethan poetry, the use of the phrase "to die" (and its many cognates) as a euphemism for achieving sexual climax was an honored convention among the Renaissance madrigal composers. Needless to say, there is nearly as much dying here (often accompanied by the most funky, salacious harmonies) as there was in the Papal Wars.

Anthony Rooley's singers make one feel like an honored guest at an immensely civilized orgy, and the rich but cozy recorded sound is close to ideal. Recommended only for those who are willing to practice safe listening.

Orfeo

Rolfe-Johnson, Baird, Dawson, von Otter, Argenta, Robson, Monteverdi Choir, English Baroque Soloists, Gardiner. Deutsche Grammophon 419250-2 [CD].

Jacopo Peri's *Dafne* predates it by a decade, but Monteverdi's *Orfeo* is now generally regarded as the first genuine opera, as the word is commonly understood today. Even though *Orfeo* is an extended vocal work that attempts to tell a continuous, coherent story, however, it is not "operatic" in the same sense *Carmen* and *Aida* are. The action, as in most operas before those of Mozart, tends to be static to the point of stagnation, and the characters are often less than two-dimensional. As a matter of fact, to the untrained ear, *Orfeo* can seem little more than a sequence of one- and two-part madrigals (if that's not a contradiction in terms), thrown together with exquisite imagination and taste.

John Eliot Gardiner's interpretation is every bit as persuasive as the recently deleted Angel version led by Nigel Rogers. As always, this most spirited of antiquarians finds the perfect balance between the demands of textual authenticity and the needs of human communication. The story unfolds crisply and cleanly, yet with ample amounts of drama and color, making it seem a far more modern and digestible experience than it usually is. All of the soloists, especially the virtuoso tenor Anthony Rolfe-Johnson, are exceptional, and Gardiner's Monteverdi Choir and English Baroque Soloists turn in their usual flawless performance.

*V*espro della Beata Vergine

Soloists, Philip Jones Brass Ensemble, Monteverdi Choir and Orchestra, Gardiner. London 414572-2 [CD].

The test of any performance of Monteverdi's *Vespers of 1610* is how many of the faithful remain awake at the end of the experience. Unlike *Messiah,* which contains many hit tunes to cling to and can thus be sampled, in pieces, like so many sacred chocolates, the *Vespers* must be swallowed and digested—all two hours of it—whole.

John Eliot Gardiner's performance, recorded in 1974, uses women's voices and modern instruments, making it one of the least "authentic" versions of the *Vespers* now available. Yet what might seem heretical to a Baroque purist will seem a delight to almost everyone else: the music emerges with a sweep and grandeur that none of the more scholarly recordings can begin to match. For anyone unfamiliar with this glorious score, here is the perfect introduction.

Mozart, Wolfgang Amadeus (1756–1791)

Once, when filling out an application for a summer job, on that line next to "other" under the heading of Religion, I wrote *Mozart*. The personnel officer was not amused, but then, I hadn't intended it as a joke. For there was a time when I was convinced that Mozart was at least as divinely inspired as Moses, Christ, the Buddha, Lao-tzu, or Mohammed, and I suppose I still am. For in no other works of the human imagination can the divine spirit be heard more distinctly than in the miraculous music this often vulgar, unpleasant, and difficult man produced during his pathetically brief thirty-five years. Were this book to do him justice, the section devoted to Mozart's music would take up more than half the total pages. What follows, therefore, is a painfully compressed selection.

The Abduction from the Seraglio

Auger, Grist, Schreier, Neukirch, Moll, Leipzig Radio Chorus, Dresden State Orchestra, Böhm. Deutsche Grammophon 423459-2 [CD].

As we learned from Miloš Forman's *Amadeus*, a stylized, brazenly inaccurate account of Mozart's life, which I have seen only 128 times, it was with *The Abduction from the Seraglio* that Mozart made his initial splash in Vienna, and through which he met the soprano Katharina Cavalieri (the original Constanze), with whom he may or may not have had a brief but toasty affair. (If true, that would have placed the soprano in some not terribly select company, for the composer of *Don Giovanni* certainly knew whereof he wrote.) In *The Abduction*, Mozart transformed the decidedly lowbrow entertainment called *Singspiel* into high art, a form to which he would return a decade later in *The Magic Flute*. In the process, he produced the first great opera of the German language and the earliest opera in *any* language that still commands a place in the standard repertoire.

With the classic Beecham recording waiting in the wings for its CD reissue, it might seem foolish to recommend any other *Abduction* now. And yet Karl Böhm absconds with so much of the opera's wit and warmth that even with Sir Thomas in the picture, this may not necessarily be the second choice.

In addition to a generally stronger cast and superior recorded sound, the primary strength of the Böhm performance is the singing of Arleen Auger. Her Constanze is a wonder of pert, innocent sexiness, which conceals a smoldering sensuality just beneath the surface. Vocally, she is equally impressive; her "Martern aller Arten," sung with breathless abandon and deadly accuracy, is among the most exciting performances this popular aria has ever received.

The forces of the Dresden Opera (the scene of Karl Böhm's rather shady activities during the war) respond with disciplined affection for their old führer, and the recorded sound is superb.

La clemenza di Tito

> Baker, Minton, Burrows, Popp, von Stade, Lloyd, Chorus
> and Orchestra of the Royal Opera House, Covent
> Garden, Davis. Philips 420097-2 [CD].

Mozart's final opera was one of the final examples of opera seria, a once-popular form that was already dying while Mozart's ink was still wet on the page. And although most representatives of the species do tend to be unendurably static and stultifying (it was opera seria that Tom Hulce, as Mozart, was castigating in *Amadeus* when he complained that the characters were so remote and lofty that they "shit marble"), *La clemenza di Tito* is a sublime masterpiece, though one perhaps better suited to the living room than to the operatic stage.

Sir Colin Davis and his unbelievably fine cast make a very strong case for the work. Dame Janet Baker has never seemed more agile or noble, and even the smallish roles are covered by singers of the stature of Frederica von Stade. The Covent Garden forces respond as enthusiastically as they ever have on records, and the remastered sound is exceptionally vivid.

Heartily recommended.

Concerto in A for Clarinet and Orchestra, K. 622; Sinfonia Concertante in E-flat for Violin, Viola, and Orchestra, K. 364

> Marcellus, clarinet; Druian, violin; Skernick, viola;
> Cleveland Orchestra, Szell. CBS MYK-37810 [CD],
> MT-37810 [T].

This is one of the most nearly perfect Mozart recordings ever made. Robert Marcellus, then the Cleveland Orchestra's principal clarinetist, gives a flawless, dramatic performance of the late and strangely uneven Clarinet Concerto, with some customarily precise and enthusiastic support provided by his colleagues under George Szell, and the gleaming version of the great Sinfonia Concertante is probably Szell's finest Mozart recording. Instead of using big-name soloists, the conductor wisely chose to place the Cleveland's immensely accomplished concertmaster and principal violist in the spotlight. The result is an interpretation of such total generosity and uncanny unanimity of purpose that even after thirty years, it must still be heard to be believed. For much of the time, the soloists seem like a single player with two sets of arms. Each of the beautifully wrought phrases is shaped with precisely the same dynamic shading and inflection, and even the tiniest details are never left to chance. For instance, the trill at the end of the second-movement cadenza is a miracle of timing and expressiveness. Szell's accompaniment is as energetic as it is patrician, and at the time the recording was made, the orchestra, as a Mozart ensemble, had no rival in the world.

Concerto in C for Flute, Harp, and Orchestra, K. 299; Flute Concerto No. 1 in G, K. 313

Galway, flute; Robles, harp; London Symphony, Mata.
RCA 6723-2-RG [CD], 6723-4-RG [T].

For most people, the choice of a recording of the finest work that Mozart composed for an instrument he thoroughly detested used to boil down to which of the various versions of the Flute and Harp Concerto James Galway or Jean-Pierre Rampal has so far made. Since yuppiedom's once-insatiable appetite for flute music has apparently begun to be sated (and why should this basically cold and inexpressive instrument have gotten so hot all of a sudden?), there are only four Galway versions listed in the current catalog and none for Rampal.

A far more shameless ham than his French colleague, Galway has also been a consistently finer player—wide vibrato, syrupy phrasing, penny-whistle antics and all. His RCA recording, while clearly a Galway show, is not the undiluted Ego-thon that many of his recent escapades have tended to be; the brilliant Marisa Robles more than holds her own, and we are even led to suspect that the conductor, Eduardo Mata, might have had a few things to say.

In RCA's Papillon Collection packaging, the performance comes with a flamboyant yet stylish interpretation of the G Major Concerto. Beware the RCA tape (AGK1-5442) which includes Galway's pointless, moderately offensive transcription of the Clarinet Concerto. It isn't quite so gruesome as Zamfir playing "Un bel di" on his wretched pan flute, but it will do.

Concertos (4) for Horn and Orchestra

Brain, horn; Philharmonia Orchestra, Karajan. Angel CDH-61013 [CD].

Tuckwell, horn; London Symphony, Maag. London 421199-4 [T].

Written for a man named Ignaz Leutgub (or Leutgeb), one of the most delightfully vulgar of Mozart's Salzburg cronies and the favorite butt of many of his practical jokes, the four Horn Concertos are among the most enchanting of all his works. From the evidence of the difficult solo parts, Leutgub must have been a virtuoso of considerable accomplishment. For as taxing as they are even for the modern performer, the Concertos were originally written for the waldhorn, an instrument without valves.

In their recent compact disc reissue, the classic recordings from the mid-1950s made by the legendary Dennis Brain are a moving, inspiring reminder of a man who was not only the century's finest horn player but also one of its finest musicians. The secret of Brain's art lay in the fact that his approach to the instrument was that of a great vocalist. His phrasing, command of dynamics, and dramatic coloration rivaled those of the finest Mozart singers of his generation. In fact, the slow movements of the Concertos become, in effect, hauntingly beautiful arias without words.

The modern recording that comes closest to duplicating Brain's achievement is the second of three recordings made thus far by Barry Tuckwell. With Peter Maag's incisive, sensitive support, Tuckwell gives the liveliest and most technically accomplished performances that have been heard on records since Dennis Brain's death. If they lack the final measure of depth and tenderness Brain brought to his famous recordings, they are still a magnificent accomplishment in their own right and are vigorously recommended.

Concertos (25) for Piano and Orchestra

**Perahia, piano and conductor; English Chamber Orchestra.
CBS MXK-42055 [CD], M3T-39044, M3T-42115,
M3T-39246, M4T-39689 [T].**

**Brendel, piano; Academy of St. Martin-in-the-Fields,
Marriner. Philips 412856-2 [CD].**

With the possible exceptions of his operas and last half dozen symphonies, it is in the series of piano concertos he wrote throughout his career that the full scope of Mozart's achievement can best be understood. From the earliest of these pieces, some of which were merely arrangements of the music of his teacher Johann Christian Bach, through the towering masterworks of his final years, the Concertos also offer the most dramatic evidence of Mozart's evolution from the most celebrated child prodigy in the history of music to the greatest composer who ever lived.

Each of these triumphant sets of the complete Piano Concertos is a milestone in the recent history of recording, and, as Murray Perahia and Alfred Brendel are among the most compelling Mozart performers of the last three decades, a choice between them will have to be made on personal rather than musical grounds. For those who respond to the "intellectual" approach to Mozart, Brendel's thoughtful, always self-possessed and disciplined playing serves almost all the Concertos exceptionally well. Like his teacher Edwin Fischer, Brendel is always acutely aware of the shape and architecture of the music. Everything is calculated—in the best possible sense of the word—to subordinate the individual details to the needs of the greater whole. Which is not to say that Brendel's playing is in any way academic or lacking in emotion. Whereas other pianists, including Perahia, can never let an especially grateful episode pass them by without embellishing it with the stamp of their own personality, Brendel always does. The result is many of the most satisfying and natural-sounding Mozart recordings available today.

Sir Neville Marriner's accompaniments are invariably invigorating, refined, and stylish, and the recorded sound, primarily from the 1970s, is both as brilliantly detailed and as warmly unobtrusive as the performances themselves.

Like Daniel Barenboim and Géza Anda before him, Murray Perahia serves as his own conductor in his consistently fascinating CBS set. As it turns out, the decision was a sound one, not only because the arrangement helps to underscore Perahia's essentially chamberlike approach to the Concertos, but also because his ideas are so firm, and intensely personal, that the presence of another musical personality would have simply gotten in the way.

If in the most general and oversimplified terms the Brendel recordings represent the modern classical vision of Mozart, then Perahia's are a bold and generally successful attempt to rethink the Romantic approach taken by the great pianists of a half century ago. In virtually all the recordings, Perahia finds something fresh and personal to say, especially in the slow movements, which are drawn out almost to the point of languor. The phrasing is consistently imaginative and spontaneous, and the physical sound of both the soloist and the orchestra, while decidedly hedonistic, also has a wonderful feeling of openness and inevitability. Though many listeners will find Perahia's performances a trifle precious and fussy, an equal number will consider them an endless source of discovery and delight.

A clear-cut choice between these two superb cycles is not an easy one to make. And needless to say, either of them, given the current highway-robbery pricing of compact discs, represents a substantial investment. The wise collector should probably just bite the bullet (or perhaps persuade one of the kids to take a part-time job at McDonald's), and acquire them both.

Piano Concertos: No. 19 in F; No. 20 in D minor

R. Serkin, piano; Cleveland Orchestra, Szell. CBS MYK-37236 [CD], MYT-37236.

Why the nineteenth century tended to take a rather dim view of Mozart remains one of music's most perplexing historical mysteries. Of course, that it chose to venerate its own, far lesser figures at his expense was nothing particularly unusual or new. The wholesale dismissal of the accomplishments of preceding ages was already a time-honored institution by the late fifteenth century: "The Dark Ages"—and for that matter "Renaissance"—were both terms that Renaissance propagandists coined.

Even so, how the Romantic era could have dismissed Mozart as that rococo lightweight with the powdered wig is all but impossible to fathom, especially given works like the D minor Piano Concerto, which, with *Don Giovanni,* Symphony No. 40, and the G minor String Quintet, is among the darkest outpourings of tragedy in all of music.

Having known each other since their student days, George Szell and Rudolf Serkin—an especially formidable combination in the music of Mozart, Beethoven, and Brahms—always managed to communicate with each other as if by some mysterious musical telepathy. Their performance of the D minor Concerto is one of the most profound and deeply serious ever recorded. Serkin's playing seethes with a brooding, impassioned intensity, and Szell's contribution, as usual, is a model of cooperative understanding which still maintains a distinct and potent personality of its own. The interpretation of the F Major Concerto is just as impressive, lending to what is often tossed off as a far lighter work an unexpected significance and weight.

Piano Concertos: No. 21 in C; No. 27 in B-flat

> Barenboim, piano and conductor; English Chamber
> Orchestra. Angel CDC-47269 [CD], 4AE-34485 [T].

Since its memorable appearance in Bo Widerberg's lovely 1967 film *Elvira Madigan,* the Concerto No. 21, or at very least its ravishing second movement, has become one of the most popular of all Mozart's works. It was always one of the best things in Daniel Barenboim's now-deleted cycle of the complete concertos for Angel. The fiery, poetic interpretation is a blissfully romantic one, and contains an achingly beautiful run-through of the slow movement almost guaranteed to break your heart.

The performance of No. 27 is equally memorable, and just as controversial. It is a huge and hugely dramatic reading, in which Barenboim seems intent on making the case that Mozart has a closer stylistic affinity with Schumann than with Haydn. While obviously not for purists, Barenboim's fearlessly red-blooded approach serves both works extremely well.

Piano Concertos: No. 23 in A; No. 25 in C

> Moravec, piano; Czech Philharmonic, Vlach. Supraphon
> 11-0271-2 [CD].

It was probably no accident that when the producers of *Amadeus* were casting about for a pianist to supply the music for the picture, they settled on Ivan Moravec. For a quarter of a century, this unassuming Czech musician has been one of the great Mozart interpreters of the modern era. His versions of these two popular concertos are graced with a unique poetry and insight. The playing is so effortless that we are constantly reminded of the composer's advice to future pianists, "Make it flow like oil." Joseph Vlach and the Czech Philharmonic provide exceedingly civilized settings for these gemlike performances, and the recorded sound remains admirably focused and warm.

Piano Concertos: No. 24 in C minor; No. 21 in C

Casadesus, piano; Cleveland Orchestra, Szell. CBS
MYK-38523 [CD], MYT-38523 [T].

The ideal companion piece to the stormy Concerto No. 24 in C minor is the equally troubled No. 20 in D minor. In that pairing, the most distinguished of all available recordings is one that the supremely gifted Clara Haskil made in 1960, a few months before her death. Now available on a compact disc from Philips (412254-2), the interpretations are a touching reminder of one of the most patrician yet curiously unassuming musicians of her generation.

On the other hand, as a *performance* of the C minor Concerto, none has yet to seriously challenge this classic recording by Robert Casadesus and George Szell. On the face of it, the Casadesus-Szell partnership—and they recorded many of the Mozart concertos together—must have seemed to many a rather peculiar one. On the one hand, there was Szell the fanatical perfectionist; on the other, the frequently inspired Frenchman whose approach to technical niceties could be shockingly cavalier. Yet somehow, together, their differences always seemed to cancel each other out.

Their version of the C minor Concerto is as poised and turbulent as any Mozart concerto recording ever made. While the soloist's contribution is not the last word in mechanical perfection, the playing communicates a sense of tragic grandeur no other performance does. Szell, as he did so often, rises not only *to*, but frequently *above*, the occasion. The conducting is so quick to pick up the music's dark and shifting moods, so tightly coiled in its pent-up intensity, that we can only wonder what kind of unspeakably shattering experience a Szell recording of *Don Giovanni* might have been.

Piano Concertos: No. 25 in C; No. 26 in D, *Coronation*

Ashkenazy, piano and conductor; Philharmonia Orchestra. London 411810-2 [CD].

If conclusive proof was ever required for the case that an artist's work need not necessarily reflect the circumstances of the artist's life, it is to be found in these two piano concertos, which Mozart composed during the last three years of his life. By any standard, these thirty-six months were a nightmare for the composer. His spendthrift wife was seriously ill, and the always fickle Viennese public had clearly grown tired of his music. He was living in abject penury, and his health, frail to begin with, was slowly succumbing to at least a dozen potentially fatal diseases. Depressed, discouraged, and racked by continuous pain, he nevertheless produced two of the greatest and most buoyantly extroverted of all his piano concertos during this period: the irrepressibly optimistic Concerto No. 25 and the magisterial *Coronation* Concerto.

As both soloist and conductor, Vladimir Ashkenazy is close to the top of his form in his recordings of both works. The performance of the *Coronation* Concerto, while capitalizing fully on the work's overtly ceremonial elements, makes it seem far more personal and significant than usual. On the other hand, Ashkenazy's interpretation of No. 25 is an irresistible explosion of gaiety and sunshine, made all the more brilliant by the lustrous playing of the Philharmonia Orchestra and the equally gleaming recorded sound.

Concertos (5) for Violin and Orchestra

Perlman, violin; Vienna Philharmonic, Levine. Deutsche Grammophon 419184-2 [CD].

Of all the incredible stories that form the Mozart legend, one of the most farfetched also happens to be absolutely true. Mozart was never taught how to play the violin. One day at the age of seven, he simply picked it up and that was that.

Within a year he was performing in public on a half-size instrument—on one momentous occasion before the Empress Maria Theresa herself. (Although he once sat on her voluminous lap, Mozart never thought very highly of the controversial monarch, who was said to be the real-life model for *The Magic Flute*'s sinister Queen of the Night; for her part, Maria Theresa dismissed the entire Mozart family as "useless people, running around the world like beggars.")

Written in Salzburg in 1775 when the nineteen-year-old composer was resting between concert tours, the five Violin Concertos are not only an arresting amalgam of the Italian, French, and German traditions he had absorbed during his travels, they are also, in their proud bearing and graceful melodic invention, a perfect reflection of late-Rococo tastes.

In this brilliant recording, Itzhak Perlman occasionally creates the impression that he is trying to disguise his own virtuosity, as if to suggest that too much technique might rob these youthful works of their freshness and charm. For the most part, he succeeds admirably, except in moments like the "Turkish" episodes from the finale of the A Major Concerto, when the sleeping volcano simply *must* blow its top. James Levine is an unassuming but never anonymous accompanist, and the Vienna Philharmonic is on its very best behavior—which is saying something in a city that consistently boasts the most dreadfully sloppy Mozart playing in the world.

Così fan tutte

> Schwarzkopf, Ludwig, Steffek, Kraus, Taddei, Berry,
> Philharmonia Orchestra and Chorus, Böhm. Angel
> CDMC-69330 [CD].

> Caballé, Baker, Cotrubas, Gedda, Ganzarolli, Van Allan,
> Orchestra and Chorus of the Royal Opera House,
> Covent Garden, Davis. Philips 416633-2 [CD],
> 416633-4 [T].

While it has never attained the popularity of *Don Giovanni*, *The Marriage of Figaro*, and *The Magic Flute*, the effervescent *Così fan tutte* certainly belongs in the company of the greatest operas Mozart—which is to say, anyone—ever wrote. Its lightweight but enchanting plot about the ever-present danger of female infidelity (the best approximation of the title is "So do they all" or "They're all like that") is not as male-chauvinist as it might seem, and Lorenzo da Ponte's witty and ingenious libretto drew from Mozart some of the most inspired music he would ever write for the stage.

Since as characters, the two romantic couples are as deliberately interchangeable as the four ditzy lovers in Shakespeare's *Midsummer Night's Dream,* and since the old misogynist Don Alfonso and the scheming maid Despina merely exist to move the delightfully complicated plot along, *Così fan tutte* is of necessity an ensemble opera, and probably the finest ever composed. It has its share of memorable arias, but its greatest moments are the duets, trios, and quartets in which operatic polyphony reached heights of inventiveness it would never again approach.

Among all the recordings the work has ever received, none can equal the wit, unanimity, and astonishingly generous give-and-take that can still be heard in the historic Angel recording from the early 1960s. Though all the principals are dazzling vocally and dramatically, Elisabeth Schwarzkopf and Christa Ludwig, as the sisters Fiordiligi and Dorabella, give two of the most delectable performances ever put on record, and the elfin yet ruefully world-weary Don Alfonso of Walter Berry is one of the great comic portrayals of modern times.

The more recent and extremely entertaining Philips recording offers some particularly captivating singing from Montserrat Caballé and Dame Janet Baker and spirited conducting from Sir Colin Davis, together with a tape option and more modern recorded sound.

Don Giovanni

Sutherland, Schwarzkopf, Sciutti, Alva, Wächter,
Cappuccilli, Frick, Philharmonia Orchestra and Chorus,
Giulini. Angel CDCC-47260 [CD].

Since the Giulini *Don Giovanni* was first released in 1963, there have no doubt been a few people who've waited for a finer recording of the greatest opera ever written. Good luck to them, and to those who await the Great Pumpkin, the Tooth Fairy, honest politicians, and anything worth hearing from Philip Glass.

In the title role, Eberhard Wächter may not have the animal magnetism and dramatic savvy of a Cesare Siepi or Ezio Pinza, but his performance is nevertheless exceptionally musical and intelligent, and very beautifully sung. And Wächter is the *weakest* link in the chain. All the other roles are represented by what still remain their finest recorded performances, from the suave, sweet-spirited Don Ottavio of Luigi Alva (who makes the character seem for once like something other than the mealy-mouthed chump he probably is) to the horrifying Commendatore of Gottlob Frick. Yet it is that incomparable trio of ladies, Elisabeth Schwarzkopf, Joan Sutherland, and Graziella Sciutti, together with the phenomenally inspired direction from the man in the pit, which levitate this *Don Giovanni* onto a plane shared by only a handful of opera recordings.

The Magic Flute

> Popp, Gruberová, Lindner, Jerusalem, Brendel, Bracht,
> Zednik, Bavarian Radio Orchestra and Chorus, Haitink.
> Angel CDCC-47951 [CD].

For Bruno Walter, *The Magic Flute,* not the Requiem, was Mozart's last will and testament. For in the characters of the questing hero Tamino, the noble priest Sarastro, and the vulgar, buffoonish bird-catcher Papageno, Walter saw the three essential components of Mozart's complex and often contradictory personality. Like most of the great conductor's speculations, this one carries a certain gentle authority, and in fact may contain more than a grain of truth. The most divinely simple of all his great operas, *Die Zauberflöte* affords some even more tantalizing grist for the speculation mill: Had he lived, would Mozart have continued the process of simplification heard here and in other later works? And if so, what effect would this new directness have had on the infant Romantic movement?

In his recording debut as an opera conductor, Bernard Haitink leads one of the warmest and most dramatic performances *The Magic Flute* has ever received. The unusually strong cast includes many of the finest living Mozart singers. Lucia Popp is an adorably sensual Pamina, Siegfried Jerusalem a subtle yet vocally exciting Tamino, and the Czech soprano Edita Gruberová, as the Queen of the Night, recalls the most brilliant and commanding German coloraturas of the past. In all, this is one of the great Mozart recordings of the last decade and will probably tower above the competition for years to come.

Surprisingly, there is no completely acceptable recording of the opera currently available on tape. Karl Böhm's Deutsche Grammophon recording (419566-4), while the strongest of all, is still a very mixed bag. On the one hand, it offers the magical Tamino of Fritz Wunderlich, and an imposing Sarastro in Franz Crass; on the other, it asks you to endure Roberta Peters's rather shrill Queen of the Night, and worse, the mugging and shameless hamming of Dietrich Fischer-Dieskau as Papageno.

The Marriage of Figaro

Schwarzkopf, Moffo, Cossotto, Wächter, Taddei, Vinco, Philharmonia Orchestra and Chorus, Giulini. Angel CDMB-63266 [CD].

The same qualities that make the Giulini *Don Giovanni* one of the classic operatic recordings of the stereo era can be heard to equally memorable advantage in his version of what is widely regarded as the greatest comic opera ever written. Though the contributions of the stunning cast cannot be praised too highly—for instance, the Countess of Elisabeth Schwarzkopf is in every way as great a creation as her Marschallin in Strauss's *Rosenkavalier*—it is Giulini's magical conducting that seems to place a stamp of immortality on the recording.

Only Erich Kleiber, in his famous, early stereo version for London (417315-2 [CD]), managed to draw as much from both the singers and from the score itself. Yet if the Kleiber performance offers an abundance of sparkling wit, vocal beauty, and effortless grace, the Giulini offers even more. Virtually every moment of the performance yields some startling yet utterly natural insight, and the ineffable purity Giulini conjures out of the Act IV finale makes it one of the most ethereally beautiful five minutes ever heard on a commercial recording.

Mass in C minor, The Great

Cotrubas, Te Kanawa, Krenn, Sotin, John Alldis Choir, New Philharmonia Orchestra, Leppard. Angel CDC-47385 [CD].

Apart from the unfinished Requiem, the C minor Mass is the most important of all of Mozart's choral works, and the equal to the finest of that towering series of Masses his friend Franz Joseph Haydn completed at the end of his career. Like the Requiem, *The Great* C minor Mass is a dark and disturbing work, full of uncharacteristic doubts and unsettling tensions.

Raymond Leppard leads an extremely humane and civilized interpretation of the work in a performance that features both a choir and orchestra of chamber proportions. The soloists are all very individual and moving; Kiri Te Kanawa gives us one of her finest recorded performances. Her singing, as well as that of Ileana Cotrubas, is as physically beautiful as any to be heard on records today, and she also invests the music with a character and sense of involvement most of her recordings rarely reveal.

Piano Sonatas (17)

Barenboim, piano. Angel CDZE-67294 [CD].

No one has ever suggested that Mozart's piano sonatas are in any way comparable in stature or importance to the concertos he wrote for the instrument; with a couple of exceptions—the A minor Sonata, K. 310, and the eternally popular A Major Sonata, K. 331— they are relatively unimportant in his output. Of course, the operative word is *relatively*. In absolute terms, they are as instructive and enjoyable as any keyboard works written between Bach and Beethoven, and for undemanding, "easy" listening (a phrase we Serious Music types are supposed to deplore), they are worth five times their weight in Vivaldi concertos.

Since the days when only Arthur Schnabel and Walter Gieseking seemed interested in playing them (Gieseking's peerless Angel set from the early 1950s really does need to be issued on compact disc without delay), there has been an explosion of Mozart sonata recordings, with superb complete cycles from András Schiff, Mitsuko Uchida, and Ingrid Haebler, among others, including a largely unheralded series from Peter Katin on the small Olympia label which includes some of the most enjoyable performances of all.

On balance, though, the immensely individual and richly redblooded interpretations by Daniel Barenboim continue to dominate the field. If he doesn't make the mistake of looking for hidden Beethoven in these generally modest pieces, he doesn't coddle them either. In other words, the playing is neither forced nor deliberately understated. There is also a sense of perfect balance between style and substance in the performances, greatly enhanced by unusually natural recorded sound.

Quartet in F for Oboe and Strings, K. 370

Mack, oboe; Cleveland Orchestra Ensemble. Crystal CD323 [CD], C-323 [T].

One of the principal glories of twentieth-century American wind playing—which by common consent is now regarded as the most vital and distinguished in the world—is the incomparable sound of the American oboe, the final stage in the evolution of an instrument that began life as the raucous business end of the medieval bagpipe. Essentially a fusion of the flexibility of the French school with the strength and solidity of the German sound, it came to final fruition in the example and precept of Marcel Tabuteau, the longtime principal oboist of the Philadelphia Orchestra and professor of music at the Curtis Institute, and in the playing of the first great native-born virtuoso, Mitch Miller.

The greatest of Tabuteau's pupils, longtime principal of the New York Philharmonic, and in the opinion of many the finest player who ever drew an incredibly deep breath, the legendary Harold Gomberg, recorded this alpha and omega of the instrument's chamber literature twice: once in the 1950s for American Decca, and again toward the end of his career for Vanguard. Until the latter is returned to circulation (and with such a treasure at their disposal, how *could* Vanguard reissue that limp essay in the art of wobbling by André Ladrot?), lovers of the Mozart Quartet will have to make the best of a bad situation.

Quintet in A for Clarinet and Strings, K. 581

Shifrin, clarinet; Chamber Music Northwest. Delos DCD-3020 [CD].

Mozart thoroughly despised the flute and the tenor voice, but his initial reaction to the recently invented clarinet was love at first sound. He encountered it at the court of Mannheim in the late 1770s, and during the next decade he would produce the first great works written for the instrument: the E-flat Trio, K. 498, and the most popular of all his chamber works, the great A Major Clarinet Quintet.

From the recording made during the 78 era by the legendary English clarinetist Reginald Kell to that poignant little performance with a group of captured Chinese musicians led by Major Charles Emerson Winchester III (David Ogden Stiers) in the concluding episode of "M.A.S.H.," the Quintet has received countless memorable performances over the years, and is currently represented by at least a half dozen superlative recordings.

Less well known than his glamorous near-contemporary Richard Stoltzman, David Shifrin is every bit his equal, as this sterling Delos recording clearly shows. Physically, Shifrin's sound is as large and as beautiful as any in the world today. Musically, he is one of the most imaginative and individual performers of his generation, mixing an attractive, instantly recognizable musical personality with an unerring sense of decorum and good taste. Though cast on a somewhat grand and Romantic scale, Shifrin's interpretation is also superbly detailed and intimate. With sensitive and enthusiastic support from four of his Chamber Music Northwest colleagues, and dazzling recorded sound, this is easily the most appealing recording the Quintet has received in at least a dozen years.

Currently, Stoltzman's recording with the Tokyo Quartet (RCA 60723-4-RC) is the best of the available tapes.

Quintet in E-flat for Piano and Winds, K. 452

Perahia, piano; English Chamber Orchestra members. CBS MK-42099 [CD], IMT-42099.

In an otherwise chatty letter written to his father around the time of the Quintet's premiere, Mozart said he considered it the finest work he had written up to that time. Not the finest *chamber* work, mind you, but the finest work, period. And the music he had written up to that time included most of the string quartets, all the Masses (except the Requiem), and all but the last three symphonies.

Among its many admirers was the young Beethoven, who just happened to produce a quintet for the same combination of instruments—piano, oboe, clarinet, bassoon, and horn—in the exact same key. (Recording company executives will always be grateful to Beethoven for his thoughtfulness: the Op. 16 Quintet invariably serves as the companion piece for the Mozart, as on this CBS release.)

Murray Perahia's bracing, eventful performance with the winds of the English Chamber Orchestra has much in common with his versions of the Mozart piano concertos. Although Perahia is clearly the leader of the band—the piano is the dominant voice, as it was certainly meant to be—the four wind players are given an unusual amount of freedom in terms of texture and phrasing, and all seem to fall in happily with Perahia's plans. Neil Black, the finest oboist the British have produced since Leon Goossens, is especially stylish and playful, but his ECO colleagues aren't far behind. With an equally spry and sensitive account of the Beethoven (which, if it can't compare with the Mozart, is still a very impressive work for a rude, uncouth kid from the Rhineland), this is one of the most enjoyable chamber music recordings in years.

Quintets (6) for Strings

Gerecz, Lesueur, Grumiaux Trio. Philips 416486-2 [CD].

Sandwiched between the C minor Quintet, which he arranged from his unsettling Serenade for Winds, K. 388, and the Quintet in E-flat, his last significant chamber work (completed a few months before his death), are two of Mozart's greatest compositions in any form: the sunny Quintet in C, K. 515, and its tormented companion piece, the Quintet in G minor, K. 516. Cast in the composer's favorite "tragic" key, the G minor Quintet is one of music's most desperate outcries, the work—in Alfred Einstein's vivid phrase—"of a lonely man surrounded on all sides by the walls of a deep chasm."

If other recordings may have plumbed that chasm more dramatically, none have done it with greater understanding or more sheer beauty than that accomplished ensemble led by the Belgian violinist Arthur Grumiaux. In fact, in all these sublime works one can hear some of the purest and most responsive chamber-music playing ever recorded.

Whenever an eminent critic of my acquaintance feels himself in danger of buying a surplus Sherman tank and giving the human race what it probably deserves, he heads for a cabin in the woods armed only with mineral water and cassettes of these performances.

So far, he has always returned restored and refreshed, with renewed hope for the species. Considering what even used tanks must be going for these days, this recording may be one of your shrewder long-term psychotherapeutic investments.

Requiem

Price, Schmidt, Araiza, Adam, Leipzig Radio Chorus, Dresden State Orchestra, Schreier. Philips 411420-2 [CD], 411420-4 [T].

After Fritz Wunderlich, who died in a tragically senseless household accident at the age of thirty-six, Peter Schreier was probably the most gifted tenor to have come out of Germany since the end of the war. Like Wunderlich, he possessed a voice of uncommon physical beauty during his prime, and even after it began showing signs of wear and tear his intelligence easily compensated for what time had taken away. Now, as Schreier's singing career draws to a close, he is proving to be an equally polished and sensitive conductor.

Schreier's Philips recording of the great unfinished Requiem is as perceptive and powerful as any recorded performance has ever been. Tempos are judiciously chosen; the brilliantly disciplined chorus sings with equal amounts of gusto and devotion, and the Dresden State Orchestra has been honed to a fine cutting edge. Yet as in his stunning recording of Bach's *St. Matthew Passion,* it is with his stellar quartet of soloists that Schreier gets the most electrifying results. Perhaps it is simply because he has a natural understanding of their needs and problems, or perhaps it is because *they* know they are singing for one of the greatest singers of his time, but each of these fine singers—particularly Margaret Price—gives one of the most impressive recorded performances of his or her career. Philips's recorded sound is as warm and dramatic as the performance itself, rising to shattering heights in the *Dies irae,* while fading to a hushed whisper in the *Lacrimosa.*

Serenade No. 6 in D, *Serenata notturna;* Serenade No. 7 in D, *Haffner*

Prague Chamber Orchestra, Mackerras. Telarc CD-80161 [CD].

Few people begin what Voltaire called "that dull meal at which dessert is served at the beginning" as memorably as did the offspring of one of Salzburg's most prominent families, for whose marriage Mozart composed the *Haffner* Serenade. Like most of the composer's lighter occasional works, this one contains deep and unsuspected riches: within its eight diverting movements is a de facto violin concerto.

Oldřich Viček, the concertmaster of the Prague Chamber Orchestra, acquits himself admirably in the demanding solo part, and Sir Charles Mackerras never loses sight of the essentially frivolous—albeit divinely frivolous—nature of the music. From first to last, this is a spirited, good-natured romp characterized by sprightly tempos, pointed rhythms, and uncomplicated emotions. As a generous bonus, the recording comes with an equally persuasive account of the *Serenata notturna*.

Although Mackerras's companion version of the *Posthorn* Serenade (No. 9) is also outstanding, it isn't *quite* as outstanding as Sir Neville Marriner's performance on Philips (412725-2 [CD]). In the outer movements, the Academy of St. Martin-in-the-Fields have never sounded more lively and alert, nor have they ever seemed as cultivated as they are in the darkly fragile Andantino.

As superb a *Posthorn* as this certainly is, the irresistible performances of the two little Marches, K. 335, very nearly steal the show.

Serenade No. 10 in B-flat, *Gran partita;* Serenade No. 11 in E-flat; Serenade No. 12 in C minor

Chamber Orchestra of Europe, Schneider. ASV
CDCOE-804 (No. 10); CDCOE-802
(Nos. 11 and 12) [CDs].

Even counting the *Music for the Royal Fireworks*, the Dvořák D minor Serenade, the Holst suites, and that score of deathless masterworks by John Philip Sousa, these three Mozart serenades are probably the greatest music ever written for winds. In its variety, invention, and sheer humanity, the *Gran partita* is one of the best arguments ever put forward for being alive—and at nearly an hour, it is *still* too short. The E-Flat Major Serenade is all but a dictionary definition of geniality, while its C minor companion piece is one of the most mysterious works Mozart ever wrote. (We know nothing about the occasion for which he produced this turbulent outburst, whose complexity and depth of emotion are so at odds with what is supposed to be an essentially lightweight form. Nor can we guess how it must have been received by its first audience. It would be similar to a modern audience trooping off to see a Neil Simon comedy and being treated to something on the order of *King Lear*.)

Without making too much of the May-December metaphor, the combination of the young, enthusiastic Chamber Orchestra of Europe and the sage, vastly experienced Alexander Schneider must account for some of the special chemistry of these glowing performances. The kids and the Old Man get on like a house afire, with results that are so wide-eyed *and* knowing it reminds you of one of the key lines from Masters's *Spoon River Anthology:* "Genius is wisdom and youth."

Serenade No. 13 in G, K. 525, *Eine kleine Nachtmusik*

Columbia Symphony, Walter. CBS MYK-37774 [CD], MYT-37774 [T].

Recordings of this imperishable charmer come and go, but none has ever seriously challenged that miracle of freshness and amiability Bruno Walter recorded in the final years of his career. If the strings of the Columbia Symphony are not as clean and precise as they could have been, or the remastered recorded sound still retains its tubby bottom and hissy top, what does it matter? The music unfolds with such affectionate deftness and spontaneity, you'll almost suspect the ink was still wet on the page.

In addition to this most ingratiating of all recorded versions of the Serenade, the album also features vintage Walter interpretations of the *Impresario, Così fan tutte, Marriage of Figaro,* and *Magic Flute* Overtures, together with the moving, important, yet rarely heard *Masonic Funeral Music.*

Sonatas (16) for Violin and Piano

Goldberg, violin; Lupu, piano. London 430306-2 [CD].

These elegant, deeply musical recordings of the mature Violin Sonatas were the fruits of a unique collaboration. The concertmaster of Wilhelm Furtwängler's Berlin Philharmonic who, despite the conductor's impassioned defense of his Jewish musicians, was forced to flee Nazi Germany in 1934, Szymon Goldberg was also, for a time, the violinist of a famous string trio whose other members were cellist Emanuel Feuermann and *violinist* Paul Hindemith. When he recorded the Mozart sonatas in 1975 with the then young Romanian pianist Radu Lupu, Goldberg was in his mid-sixties, a player of vast experience and understanding with almost all his technique intact.

Though other teams, such as Perlman and Barenboim, have brought more color and flash to these marvelous works, no recordings have ever presented the Sonatas more naturally or shown so much mutual respect and affection as these. For just as the youthful pianist is inspired to play with a burnished wisdom, so the playing of the aging violinist seems infused with a springlike glow. The result, in short, is a series of performances as ageless and timeless as they are undeniably beautiful.

String Quartets Nos. 14–19, *Haydn* Quartets

Quartetto Italiano. Philips 416419-2 [CD].

Chilingirian Quartet. CRD 3362/4 [CD], 4062/4 [T].

Begun in 1782 after a nine-year period during which he composed no string quartets at all, the six works that Mozart wrote under the influence of, and eventually dedicated to, his friend Franz Joseph Haydn constitute one of the great summits in the history of chamber music. Haydn himself was overwhelmed by his young friend's touching act of homage. It was this music that led Haydn to tell Mozart's father, "I swear before God and as an honest man, that your son is the greatest composer known to me, either in person or by reputation."

Collectors who would like to buy the six Quartets together in a convenient package now find themselves in one of those difficult quandaries the recording companies seem to take such delight in. The most charming and completely memorable versions of the *Haydn* Quartets, those classic performances by Quartetto Italiano, are now available only as part of an eight-CD box from Philips, which also brings us superb performances of the rest of Mozart's twenty-three quartets. To be sure, this represents a substantial outlay of money, but this "medium-priced" set (and how long will it be before compact disc prices start becoming rational?) actually is a bargain in the long run. Compared to the hit-and-miss six-CD set with the Amadeus Quartet on Deutsche Grammophon, the all-important pleasure-per-dollar ratio is extremely high.

Of the recordings that feature the *Haydns* all by themselves, the lively, insightful interpretations by the Chilingirian Quartet are probably the most consistently rewarding. The Salomon Quartet's period-instrument cycle for Hyperion is also an exceptionally fine one, if you can get past their rather nasal sound and don't mind scaring the bejesus out of every cat in the neighborhood. (Actually, feline entrails haven't been used in fiddle strings for years.)

String Quartets Nos. 21–23, *Prussian* Quartets

Alban Berg Quartet. Teldec 43122 [CD], 43122 [T]; 42042 [CD], 42042 [T].

These recordings of Mozart's final string quartets, written for the king of Prussia as one of the composer's last futile attempts to gain a suitable permanent position, were among the first that introduced us two decades ago to Vienna's Alban Berg Quartet. In retrospect, the introduction was as prophetic as it was auspicious: with 20-20 hindsight we can perceive just what sort of group this world-class ensemble would become.

The playing is as fresh and unaffected as it is meticulously balanced and blended, an early taste of the paradoxical calculated spontaneity that has characterized their best work ever since. The *Prussian* Quartets have rarely been invested with so much precision and vitality, and the version of the first of the *Haydn* Quartets that fills out the release—the G Major Quartet, with its breakneck fugal finale—is the kind of giggling wonder that is impossible to hear without a broad grin creasing the stoniest face.

Symphonies: Nos. 1–20

Academy of St. Martin-in-the-Fields, Marriner. Philips 416471-2 [CD].

Sir Neville Marriner's admirable set of the early symphonies, the opening volume of Philips's epic Complete Mozart Edition—a 45-volume, 179-CD collection of the man's *entire* output—offers refreshingly vibrant and consistently stylish interpretations of the first twenty numbered symphonies, together with eleven other equally agreeable works. Mozart's early essays are clearly juvenilia—although, being *Mozart's* juvenilia, virtually every scrap has something enchanting or revealing to say. Expect no hidden masterworks here, just a fascinating glimpse into the evolution of the most extraordinary genius the world has ever known.

Symphonies: No. 25 in G minor; No. 28 in C; No. 29 in A

> **Prague Chamber Orchestra, Mackerras. Telarc CD-80165 [CD].**

At an age when most teenage boys are beginning to think about whom to ask to the junior prom, Mozart was busy writing music like this for his boss, the reactionary Prince Archbishop of Salzburg. On hearing the "Little G minor" Symphony for the first time, His Eminence's only comment was, "Far too modern."

This trio of youthful works—surely the greatest symphonies ever written by an adolescent—have had no finer recorded performances than these by Sir Charles Mackerras and the Prague Chamber Orchestra. Benjamin Britten's famous versions of 25 and 29 were exceptionally dramatic and resilient, but Mackerras yields nothing to those classic interpretations in terms of sparkle or elegance; besides, the Brittens are now long out of print.

As in the other releases in his exceptional Mozart symphony series, Mackerras takes the middle ground between the grand opulence of a Walter or a Klemperer and the desiccated stinginess of period-instrument recordings. The orchestra, using modern instruments, is of chamber proportions, but the slightly reverberant acoustic creates the impression of space and depth without sacrificing any of the detail. Tempos tend to be brisk but judicious, and the execution is as meticulous as it is exuberant. With No. 28 tossed in for *very* good measure, this amounts to nearly eighty minutes of world-class music-making—a best buy in anybody's book.

Symphonies: No. 35 in D, *Haffner;* No. 39 in E-flat

> **Cleveland Orchestra, Szell. CBS MYK-38472 [CD], MYT-38472 [T].**

Nowhere are George Szell's considerable skills as a Mozart conductor more conspicuously on display than in his recordings of these two amiable symphonies. From its thrilling opening flourish, the performance of the *Haffner* crackles with unfailing energy and transcendent wit; No. 39 strides serenely through its comfortable progress as in a pair of old but very fine shoes given a spanking new shine. The Cleveland Orchestra proves again that it was the finest Haydn-Mozart ensemble of its time, and the remastered sound, while slightly shrill, is perfectly adequate.

Symphonies: No. 36 in C, *Linz;* No. 38 in D, *Prague*

> Vienna Philharmonic, Bernstein. Deutsche Grammophon
> 415962-2 [CD], 415962-4 [T].

Leonard Bernstein's vision of these two popular symphonies by Mozart has much in common with his final recordings of the music of Haydn. Shunning the chamber dimensions and drier sound favored by younger conductors in recent years, Bernstein's Mozart remains a bracing anachronism. The interpretations are ripe and richly Romantic, characterized by luscious textures, extreme but always persuasive tempos, powerfully dramatic gestures, and forward thrust. The opening of the *Prague* Symphony has never sounded more vividly operatic (after all, it *was* written at the same time as *Don Giovanni*), nor has the *Linz* ever sounded quite so exhilarating or rhapsodic. In recent years, the Vienna Philharmonic has rarely played better for anyone. In fact, it is only the sense of electric excitement which hints that the recordings were made during concert performances.

Symphonies: No. 40 in G minor; No. 41 in C, *Jupiter*

> Philharmonia Orchestra, Klemperer. Angel CDMD-63272
> [CD].

With their transcendentally serene and good-natured companion piece, No. 39 in E-flat, the G minor and *Jupiter* Symphonies form a trilogy that represents the high-water mark of eighteenth-century symphonic thought. In these great and mysterious works (why or for what occasion Mozart wrote them has never been known) the classical symphony reached its final stage of perfection. After Mozart, there was no place left for the form to go, other than through the bold and convulsive experiments of Beethoven, which signaled the beginning of the symphony's inevitable end.

Otto Klemperer's monumental performances from the early 1960s have a fair claim to being the greatest recordings each of the last two symphonies has ever received. It is not simply the breadth of the interpretations that makes them so extraordinary, for other conductors have adopted tempos in the outer movements that are nearly as slow. It is the conductor's Olympian insight, whether in probing the depths of despair in No. 40, or the heights of the *Jupiter's* exultation, that gives the performances a unique sense of scale and scope. There have been more turbulent recordings of the G minor Symphony, and more exciting readings of the *Jupiter,* but there are none that capture more of the tragedy and triumph of Mozart's farewell to the symphony than these.

If Klemperer's Mozart is to your taste—for *my* hard-earned money, his Mozart conducting ranks with Beecham's and Walter's as the greatest we are ever likely to hear—this four-CD set combines these two recordings with versions of eight of the other late symphonies in one convenient, not-to-be-missed box.

Variations for Solo Piano (complete)

Barenboim, piano. Angel CDCC-54362 [CD].

This handsome three-CD set is obviously not to be digested over the course of one or two evenings, but, like Boswell's *Life of Johnson,* is to be dipped into indiscriminately whenever the spirit needs a quick fix of civilizing charm. From famous sets like the twelve variations on "Ah, vous dirai-je, Maman" to oddities like the six variations on "Mio caro Adone" by Antonio Salieri, Daniel Barenboim is here as consistent and imaginative as he was in his magnificent cycle of the piano sonatas, bringing to each set a sense of eager discovery that makes even the least of them seem unique.

Mussorgsky, Modest

(1839–1881)

Boris Godunov

Vedernikov, Arkhipova, Koroleva, Sokolov, Shkolnikova,
USSR Radio and Television Orchestra and Chorus,
Fedoseyev. Philips 412281-2 [CD], 412281-4 [T].

In any of its several versions — the two by the composer himself and the famous revision made by a well-intentioned friend —
Boris Godunov is not only the most powerful and original Russian
opera ever written but also one of the most relentlessly gripping
theatrical experiences of the operatic stage. Since the days when
Feodor Chaliapin's famous, overwhelming interpretation made it a
major box-office attraction in the West, most listeners have come
to know *Boris* through Rimsky-Korsakov's brilliant arrangement.
While that wizard of the late-Romantic orchestra deserves the lion's
share of credit for the opera's subsequent popularity, in Mussorgsky's 1872 revision the opera emerges as a cruder, rougher, and
more starkly original piece.

For years, we have needed an absolutely convincing recorded
performance of Mussorgsky's final revision, and this admirable
Philips recording is probably as close as we are likely to get in the
foreseeable future. The greatest strengths in the performance are
precisely what they need to be: the intensely dramatic conducting
of Vladimir Fedoseyev, and the broodingly powerful Boris of Alexander Vedernikov. Other basses — Chaliapin, Alexander Kipnis,
Boris Christoff, George London — have brought finer voices and
more refined musicality to the part, but in the big scenes, Vedernikov more than delivers the goods. The Clock Scene is especially
unhinging in the way Vedernikov slowly begins losing his grip, and
in Boris's Farewell and Death, he is perhaps more credible (and
genuinely moving) than any performer since George London. The
supporting cast is generally excellent, though the Pretender is more
wobbly and inadequate than usual. In the massed choral scenes (and
in *Boris,* as in Puccini's *Turandot,* the chorus is at least as important
as any of the opera's other major characters) the USSR Radio and

Television Chorus sings magnificently, with that characteristic Russian combination of wild exuberance and ink-black despair.

*K*hovanshchina

Lipovsek, Burchuladze, Atlantov, Haugland, Borowska, Kotscherga, Popov, Chorus and Orchestra of the Vienna State Opera, Abbado. Deutsche Grammophon 429758-2 [CD].

Set against the backdrop of the political turmoil that swept Russia at the time the forward-looking Peter the Great ascended to the throne in 1689, *Khovanshchina* is in many ways a more ambitious opera than *Boris Godunov* and, in most respects, far less universal. Essentially a sweeping historical panorama, it lacks the cohesiveness, to say nothing of the riveting central character, that animates Mussorgsky's masterpiece. But in its best moments—the lovely prelude "Dawn on the Moscow River," the wonderfully suggestive "Dance of the Persian Slaves," the thrilling choral passages, the deeply poignant closing scene in which the Old Believers opt for a *Götterdämmerung*-like immolation rather than renounce their faith—*Khovanshchina* clearly springs from the same source of inspiration which yielded that greatest of Russian operas.

Captured during actual performances at the Vienna State Opera, Claudio Abbado's *Khovanshchina* is one of the conductor's finest recordings. Aided by an alert and sensitive cast, he infuses the often episodic action with an uncharacteristic urgency and sense of purpose. Apart from the occasional cough or stomping entrance, the live recording only heightens the sense of drama and occasion.

For anyone even remotely interested in Russian opera, this is an indispensable recording.

*P*ictures at an Exhibition

New York Philharmonic, Bernstein. CBS MYK-36726 [CD], MYT-36726 [T].

Richter, piano. Philips 420774-2 [CD]. Odyssey YT-32223 [T].

Either in its original piano version or in the familiar orchestration Serge Koussevitzky commissioned from Maurice Ravel in 1922, *Pictures at an Exhibition* is among the most inventive and original works ever written by a Russian composer. Beginning with the pioneering recordings by Koussevitzky and Arturo Toscanini, the Ravel edition of the *Pictures* has probably received more great recordings than any other twentieth-century orchestral score.

One of Leonard Bernstein's earliest recordings after assuming the directorship of the New York Philharmonic in 1958 also remains one of his best. It was also the most impressive stereo recording CBS (then Columbia) had made up to that time. Bright and richly detailed, with a particularly solid and resonant bottom end, the physical sound remains astonishing in its compact disc transfer, and Bernstein's performance, after thirty-some years, remains the one to beat. In no recording do all the individual pictures emerge with such character and clarity, from the heavy ponderousness of the "Ox-cart" section to the delicate humor of the "Ballet of the Chicks in Their Eggs." Yet it is with the final two portraits that Bernstein leaves the competition at the museum door. The "Hut on Fowl's Legs" is a wonder of demonic fury and intensity, and the performance concludes with the most thrilling and majestic "Great Gate of Kiev" ever put on records. The explosive version of *Night on Bald Mountain* that accompanies the *Pictures* makes it seem like a very wild evening indeed.

Among recordings of the original piano suite, none—not even Vladimir Horowitz's famous Carnegie Hall recording, or the gleaming new version by the recent Tchaikovsky Competition winner Barry Douglas—can be mentioned in the same breath with Sviatoslav Richter's historic 1960 recording. In spite of the relatively drab and distracting recorded sound (it was taped at a recital in Sofia, Bulgaria, on a night when the entire city, apparently, was dying of terminal smoker's hack), there has never been a version of the *Pictures* to match it. It is not only the most electrifying performance Mussorgsky's suite is ever likely to receive, but also one of the dozen greatest recordings any modern pianist has made of *anything*.

Songs (complete)

Christoff, bass; Labinsky, Moore, pianists; ORTF Orchestra, Tzipine. Angel CHS-63025 [CD].

If Mussorgsky had written nothing but the music contained in this collection, he would still be remembered as one of history's most powerfully original composers. Like the Dostoyevsky novels or the Chekhov plays, Mussorgsky's songs create a reality both unmistakably Russian and thoroughly universal. With the lieder of Hugo Wolf, they are also the most disturbingly "modern" of nineteenth-century art songs, not simply because they tend to avoid the great traditional Romantic subjects of love and nature, but because in their essentially ironic vision of human experience they anticipate the defining attribute of the twentieth-century mind.

Recorded in the late 1950s, Boris Christoff's tour of this dark, sarcastic, satiric, frequently beautiful universe is one of the major achievements in recording history. Like Chaliapin and Alexander Kipnis before him, the great Bulgarian bass is the kind of consummate singer-actor who is able to capture the full measure of the composer's range, from the black humor in the famous "Song of the Flea"—for which he produces the most menacing laugh since Chaliapin's—to the delicate nostalgia of "Sunless" and the *Nursery Songs.*

Lovers of lieder, Mussorgsky, and great singing will have replaced their worn LPs the day this three-CD set hit the stores. Everyone else should get a copy now.

Nicolai, Otto (1810–1849)

The Merry Wives of Windsor

Mathis, Wunderlich, Frick, Bavarian State Opera Orchestra and Chorus, Heger. Angel CDMB-69348 [CD].

A book on the subject of German Comic Opera might be a bit more involved than one on, say, Irish Erotic Art. But not by much. For if you discount the southern Germans (i.e., the Austrians), and those works that seem to capture German wit at its rapierlike best (believe it or not, the second most frequently performed of all operas in Germany, after Weber's *Freischütz,* is Albert Lortzing's *Zar und Zimmermann*), there's isn't a lot to be said.

Friedrich von Flotow, composer of *Martha*, was French in all essential characteristics but birth, as was the cellist from Cologne who moved to Paris as a boy and called himself Jacques Offenbach. Richard Strauss's *Rosenkavalier* has its comic moments, to be sure, but its prevailing mood is one of wistful melancholy. And the less said about more recent attempts the better, from Schoenberg's relentlessly unfunny *Von Heute auf Morgen* to Henze's sneering *Der junge Lord*, both of which tend to go over like lead bratwursts.

Which leaves Otto Nicolai's bubbly, ingenuous *Merry Wives of Windsor*, which had its first performance two months before the composer's premature death. The fifth and final opera by the founder (in 1842) of the Vienna Philharmonic, *Die lustigen Weiber von Windsor* can be one of the most instantly likable of all German operas, especially in a performance as high-spirited as this one. The Falstaff of Gottlob Frick is one of that cavernous bass's most telling creations (unlike Verdi's endlessly lovable fat knight, Nicolai's version of Sir John also has a slightly sinister side), and as the young lovers, Edith Mathis and Fritz Wunderlich are impossible to fault and even more difficult not to adore. Robert Heger's conducting is crisp, finely detailed, and amusing, and the early-'60s recorded sound is surprisingly vivid and alive.

Nielsen, Carl (1865–1931)

Choral Works (*Hymnus amoris;* Motets; *The Sleep; Springtime in Funen*)

> Soloists, Copenhagen Boys' Choir, Danish National Radio Choir and Orchestra, Segerstam. Chandos CHAN-8853 [CD], ABTD-1470 [T].

Whenever you find yourself in the midst of a romantic campaign with an object who refuses to melt, introduce him/her/it to Nielsen's *Hymnus amoris* and relax. For years, a singularly ugly friend of mine (if you pushed his face into a big wad of dough you'd get gorilla cookies) has been using the ploy with astonishing success. Just put it on and prepare to be jumped.

In addition to the heart-dissolving beauties of the *Hymn of Love,* this loveliest of all Nielsen albums offers the entrancing *Springtime in Funen,* the challenging and dramatic *The Sleep,* and the gravely beautiful Motets. Both the performances and the recorded sound are ideal.

Symphonies: No. 3, *Sinfonia espansiva;* No. 5

Royal Danish Orchestra; New York Philharmonic, Bernstein. CBS MK-44708 [CD].

For a time during the mid-1960s, it seemed to many that the late-Romantic Danish composer Carl Nielsen was belatedly going to join his Finnish contemporary Jean Sibelius as one of the last and most popular practitioners of modern symphonic form. Though the Nielsen revival has obviously begun to lose momentum in recent years (there were once *two* complete recorded cycles of all six symphonies; today there are none), Nielsen's remains a charming, provocative, and utterly original voice, especially in the *Sinfonia espansiva,* the first of the three major symphonies on which most of his future reputation will be based.

It's difficult to imagine a more inspired performance of it than the one on this CBS recording, which did so much to advance the Nielsen revival. Leonard Bernstein's enthusiasm for the work is as obvious as it is infectious. The Royal Danish Orchestra catch fire in what is probably the finest performance they have given in their collective memory, from their thunderous exuberance in the swaggering opening movement to the way they assault the normally flaccid finale as though it were an undiscovered masterwork of Johannes Brahms.

Bernstein's version of the Fifth, if not quite so overwhelming, still sets a standard for commitment and intensity that has yet to be approached. In this fabulously difficult work, the New York Philharmonic responds with one of its pluckiest performances; Bernstein inspires the snare-drummer to play with the verve and individuality of an Art Blakey, and CBS's engineers almost succeed in disentangling the Symphony's complex web of sound.

Symphony No. 4, *Inextinguishable*

San Francisco Symphony, Blomstedt. London 421524-2 [CD], 421524-4 [T].

Even the bungled acoustics of its horrid new concert hall cannot obscure the fact that the San Francisco Symphony, under Herbert Blomstedt, has entered its Golden Age. In less than a decade, this unpretentious musician has so completely rejuvenated the old band that it now must rank among the world's very best: the woodwinds play with grace and character, the brass is a model of fearless solidity, and the strings exhibit that burnished warmth which suggests a fine German orchestra at the top of its form.

Blomstedt's new version of the Nielsen *Inextinguishable* is one of his most impressive recordings to date: an interpretation of high tension, soaring lyricism, and withering drama, thrillingly played and recorded. In fact, it is the only recent *Inextinguishable* that can be mentioned in the same breath with Jean Martinon's classic RCA recording with the Chicago Symphony.

The performance of the Fifth Symphony that fills out the CD is every bit as strong.

Wind Chamber Music (complete)

Bergen Wind Quintet, et al. Bis CD-428 [CD].

When he isn't busy being epic and heroic, i.e., "expansive" and "inextinguishable," Nielsen is at his absolute best doing charming little things, as in his naively disarming songs (Angel has a moral obligation to reissue the Danish tenor Aksel Schiøtz's immortal recordings) and the brief masterworks contained on this treasurable Bis CD.

The centerpiece is clearly the great Wind Quintet of 1922 (which, along with Hindemith's *Kleine Kammermusik* and the Wind Quintet of Arnold Schoenberg, are surely the twentieth century's most important examples of the form), but the other items are no less appealing, from the Allegretto for Two Recorders to that inspired study in tongue-in-cheek winsomeness, the *Serenata in vano*. The Bergen Wind Quintet and their friends play this music with unquenchable enthusiasm and grace, and the Bis recorded sound, as usual, is close to perfection.

Among recordings of the two wind concertos Nielsen lived to complete (he had planned to compose one each for the five friends who gave the Quintet its premiere), the Bis version (CD-321 [CD]) of the unsettled and far-reaching Clarinet Concerto is easily the finest to date. Ole Schill's effortless handling of the all-but-impossible solo part is a marvel, as is the conducting of Myung-Whun Chung, whose Nielsen cycle with the Gothenburg Symphony is now about halfway to completion.

Aurèle Nicolet's Philips recording (412728-2 [CD]) of the Flute Concerto is still the best available. The French virtuoso plays with an attractive blend of crystalline aloofness and rhapsodic dash, and is given surprisingly nimble support by the Leipzig Gewandhaus Orchestra and Kurt Masur.

To round out a collection of all three Nielsen concertos, Cho-Liang Lin's CBS recording (MK-44548 [CD], MT-44548 [T]) of the Violin Concerto is easily the most startling that has so far appeared. The playing of both the soloist and the Philharmonia Orchestra under Esa-Pekka Salonen is so fiercely committed that this curiously underrated piece seems at very *least* the equal of the far more familiar work that fills out the recording: the Violin Concerto of Jean Sibelius.

Novák, Vítězslav (1870–1949)

Slovak Suite; South Bohemian Suite

Czech Philharmonic, Vajnar. Supraphon CO-1743 [CD].

There is a kind of piece with which everyone in classical music radio is familiar, and which some of us—especially the patient, gallant people who man the switchboards—have come to dread. These might be called, for want of a better phrase, the "What-was-that?-Where-can-I-buy-it?-What-the-hell-do-you-mean-it's-out-of-print!" recordings, those odd, offbeat obscurities that seem to affect listeners like catnip. Morton Feldman's mesmerizing *Rothko Chapel* is one such work that will invariably light up the phone banks; the *Slovak Suite* by Vítězslav Novák is another.

A student of Dvořák whose early work was vigorously praised by Johannes Brahms, Novák—like his friend Josef Suk—was among the last of the Bohemian late Romantics, composers who were deeply influenced by Dvořák's example but who also managed to make highly individual statements of their own. Like Suk's youthful Serenade for Strings, the *Slovak Suite* is so warmhearted, subtle, sophisticated, and opulent that it will have the most jaded listener sighing for more. (If you can persuade someone in the store to audition the CD for you, tell him or her to cue up the movement called "Two in Love." If they don't sell out their stock and take another half dozen orders for more, I would be greatly surprised.)

Both the *Slovak Suite* and the equally hypnotic *South Bohemian Suite* are given definitive performances by the Czech Philharmonic, who used to play Novák's music as standard repertoire items when they were led by the composer's friend and drinking buddy, the great Václav Talich. František Vajnar is no Talich, but his interpretations are loving, generous, and beautifully lit.

Offenbach, Jacques
(1819–1880)

Gaîté Parisienne

Pittsburgh Symphony, Previn. Philips 411039-2 [CD].

Like *Les Sylphides* and *La Boutique fantasque,* those ersatz ballets arranged from the piano music of Chopin and Rossini, *Gaîté Parisienne,* Manuel Rosenthal's inspired adaptation of melodies from the Offenbach operettas, still tends to raise eyebrows (and many noses) among the Serious Music set. Though as a smug and jaded musical curmudgeon I yield to no one in my arrogance or pickiness, I've never understood how it's possible *not* to like this dazzling confection, especially in a performance as lively and charming as this.

The ballet has received numerous fine recordings, including one by Rosenthal himself, but none can approach the urbane wit and Gallic grace of this superb Philips recording by André Previn. All the great set pieces—the Barcarole from *The Tales of Hoffmann,* the "Can-Can" from *Orpheus in the Underworld*—are given the most lively and affectionate performances imaginable. In fact, the recording is a triumph of bracing rhythms, inventive phrasing, and tasteful sentimentality from beginning to end.

Overtures

> Philharmonia Orchestra, Marriner. Philips 411476-2 [CD].

Many of the best-loved of Offenbach's overtures—*Orpheus, La Périchole, La Belle Hélène*—are not, strictly speaking, his own work. Like Sir Arthur Sullivan, Offenbach frequently left much of the actual business of arranging and orchestrating the tunes from the operettas to others. Since the overtures were rarely more than potpourris, he would simply indicate which melodies he wanted in which order and then proceed to get on with more important things, such as writing or producing his next project or chasing after his next amour.

Sir Neville Marriner captures the spirit of these immortal trivialities perfectly, largely because he is able to maintain a light, flippant-sounding touch without making any of it *seem* trivial. The Philharmonia Orchestra is coaxed into that rare, wonderfully paradoxical state of relaxed alertness, and the recorded sound is superb.

The Tales of Hoffmann

> Sutherland, Domingo, Tourangeau, Bacquier, Cuénod,
> Orchestra and Chorus of Radio Suisse Romande,
> Bonynge. London 417363-2 [CD].

Throughout his long and lucrative lifetime as the father of the operetta (his astonishing output of tuneful, racy musical satires earned him the sobriquet "The Mozart of the Boulevards"), Jacques Offenbach dreamed of writing a single, serious opera that would be the crowning achievement of his career. With *The Tales of Hoffmann,* finished a few months before his death (which occurred while the work was in rehearsal for the first production), the diminutive German-born cellist turned lighthearted French composer realized his goals. Though overshadowed in popularity by Gounod's once-ubiquitous *Faust,* Offenbach's immortal adaptation of stories by the German Romantic writer E. T. A. Hoffmann is the only French opera which, in the quality and consistency of its inspiration, can be mentioned in the same breath with *Carmen* and Debussy's *Pelléas et Mélisande.*

This stunning London recording from the early 1970s is still the single most satisfying recorded performance *Hoffmann* has ever received. Joan Sutherland, who undertakes all four of the opera's heroines, has never been more impressive. While Antonia and Giulietta are a trifle lacking in character, both are splendidly sung. As the doll Olympia, however, Sutherland turns in a virtuoso tour de force of such staggering dimensions that even those of us who do not count ourselves among her most rabid fans come away in a state of slack-jawed amazement. As the opera's several villains, Gabriel Bacquier is as suavely malevolent as any singer who has ever undertaken the roles, but the gem of the production is Placido Domingo's Hoffmann. For nearly two memorable decades now, Domingo's achievements have rivaled those of the greatest tenors of the century's Golden Age. Vocally and dramatically, this Hoffmann is one of his most impressive creations, a performance which—if it hasn't already—will one day become the stuff of legend.

Orff, Carl (1895–1982)

Carmina Burana

Armstrong, English, Allen, St. Clement Danes Boys Choir,
London Symphony Orchestra and Chorus, Previn. Angel
CDC-47411 [CD], 4AM-34770 [T].

Like acne, or an insatiable lust for Milk Duds, *Carmina
Burana* is a juvenile affliction most people eventually outgrow. As
that torrent of unspeakably dull and repetitious music clearly
proved, Carl Orff was not just a one-work but a one-*idea* composer.
This astonishingly simple, musically primitive setting of some
bawdy medieval lyrics can be a dazzlingly effective experience the
first couple of times you hear it. It is only after repeated encounters
that the vulgarity and yawning vapidity of *Carmina* really begin to
get on a person's nerves.

For those who have an affection for this trash (and I must
admit that *I* always have), André Previn's Angel recording is one of
the finest ever made. To his credit, Previn does nothing to cheapen
the work further than its composer already has, but instead constantly seeks out its humor, limited subtlety, and frequently engaging wit. Which is not to say that the performance attempts to
housebreak *Carmina Burana*. For at the end, we are thoroughly
convinced that this is music a gland would write, if only it could.

Pachelbel, Johann (1653–1706)

Kanon in D

Stuttgart Chamber Orchestra, Münchinger. London
411973-2 [CD], 411973-4 [T].

What violent emotions Pachelbel's sweet little *Kanon* continues to provoke! It is now one of the most frequently recorded of all classical works, but there are those of us who still can't quite understand what all the shouting is about. At best, Pachelbel was a third-rate Baroque nonentity who occasionally rose to the level of the second-rate in some of his organ music. And though the *Kanon* was composed more than a century before Napoleon showed the world what *really* heavy ordnance could do, it still unquestionably qualifies as *large bore.*

If you really *must,* Karl Münchinger leads the Stuttgart Chamber Orchestra in a tender yet admirably disciplined performance on London. The compact disc version is especially useful, in that you can program the *Kanon* to repeat again and again, thus saving yourself untold thousands of dollars by putting off that frontal lobotomy you had planned.

Paganini, Niccolò (1782–1840)

Caprices (24) for Unaccompanied Violin

Perlman, violin. Angel CDC-47171 [CD], 4XS-36860 [T].

Unlike his rather lumpy and charmless violin concertos, the Paganini Caprices are among the most intriguing works ever written for the violin, by the man who was, by all accounts, its greatest master. Stories of Paganini's virtuosity are legion. For a week after a concert in which he played the whole of Beethoven's *Kreutzer* Sonata on a single string, he was the talk of Paris; when his driver asked for a considerable raise since his master was becoming so famous, Paganini readily agreed, provided he be driven everywhere on a single wheel.

Musically and technically, this recording made by Itzhak Perlman in the early 1970s has yet to be bettered. The playing is as sensitive as it is audacious, and for once even the most difficult of the individual pieces emerge with a color and freshness that suggest miniature tone poems, instead of mere excuses for wanton virtuoso display.

Concerto No. 1 in D for Violin and Orchestra

Kaplan, violin; London Symphony, Miller. Arabesque Z-6597 [CD], ABQC-6597 [T].

Having written off this piece years ago as feeble, empty-headed fluff, I must now recant completely. Then again, I never understood that Paganini's popular D Major Concerto was in reality a miniature Rossini opera without words. At least that's the way Mark Kaplan and Mitch Miller make it seem in this electrifying recording.

Though Kaplan is not yet as well known as some of his more widely publicized female colleagues, he proves conclusively here that he more than deserves to be. Technically, he is on a par with any violinist in the world today; musically, he is already a highly evolved personality, whose daring and bravado are matched only by his intelligence and wit.

Throughout the Paganini, and the blazing performance of the Wieniawski D minor Concerto that accompanies it, he treats the dog-eared classics as music, not simply as a convenient vehicle for showing us what he can do. With a shrewd conductor who also adopts, or perhaps inspired, that refreshing attitude, both of the tired old warhorses are up and running like thoroughbreds from the opening bars.

In spite of formidable competition in both pieces, these recordings leave all others in the dust.

Paine, John Knowles

(1839–1906)

Symphonies (2)

New York Philharmonic, Mehta. New World NW-374-2
[CD] (Symphony No. 1; *As You Like It* Overture); NW-
350-2 [CD], NW-350-4 [T] (Symphony No. 2).

John Knowles Paine was the John Greenleaf Whittier of American music. Portland-born and Berlin-trained, Paine looked to European models for precept and sustenance, and except for certain titles like *Columbus March and Hymn,* his is no more distinctly American music that "Maud Muller" is an especially American poem. Although formal and derivative, Paine's two Symphonies — the first ever published by an American composer — are richly imagined, elegantly crafted, moving, manly, and surprisingly memorable works. Admittedly, it has scant competition, but Paine's Second Symphony in A—called *Im Frühling* as a nod to his beloved Schumann—is easily the strongest American symphony produced during the nineteenth century. If the earlier work in C minor is less determined and individual, it is still full of clever touches and fine tunes and more than repays repeated hearings.

It is difficult to imagine more eloquent champions than Zubin Mehta and the New York Philharmonic, who give both symphonies and the snazzy *As You Like It* Overture top-drawer performances, captured in admirably lifelike recorded sound.

Palestrina, Giovanni

(c. 1525–1594)

Missa Papae Marcelli

Tallis Scholars, Phillips. Gimell CDGIM-339 [CD].

It's the gloomy winter of 1563, and the Council of Trent, concerned that the whacked-out new church music is taking everyone's mind off the meaning of the words being sung, is about to outlaw the use of polyphony—music in which several voice parts are heard simultaneously. (If the old monotonous monophonic chants were good enough for Pope Gregory and the boys, then by Jesu, they should be good enough for us!)

At which point young Giovanni Pierluigi, who's from the town of Palestrina, just outside Rome (actually, at thirty-eight he isn't all *that* young), bursts in with the manuscript of his latest polyphonic Mass, which is not only utterly gorgeous but so skillfully written that you can understand every single syllable. The Council relents, decides that polyphony is not the work of the Devil, and the subsequent history of Western music—from Bach to the Beatles—is assured.

It would make a terrific movie. In fact, it *did* make an intriguing opera: Hans Pfitzner's somewhat long-winded but erratically inspired *Palestrina,* which can be heard to great effect in a 1973 Deutsche Grammophon recording that has now been released on three generously packed compact discs (427417-2). The only problem with one of music's most dramatic stories is that it almost certainly never took place. Polyphonic music was saved in 1563 because of the viselike pressure put on the Council by the music-loving Emperor Ferdinand I, not because the prelates were impressed with Palestrina's work.

Be that as it may, the most famous Mass of the church's greatest composer has never sounded more, well, heavenly than it does in this transcendent performance by the Tallis Scholars. The starkly beautiful *Vox Patris caelestis* by the Tudor composer William Mundy and Gregorio Allegri's catchy *Miserere* (which with time may become the ecclesiastical Pachelbel *Kanon*) round out one of the best recordings of sacred music available today.

Parry, Sir Hubert (1848–1918)

Symphony No. 3 in C, *The English;* Symphony No. 4

London Philharmonic, Bamert. Chandos CHAN-8896 [CD],
ABTD-1507 [T].

It isn't *quite* true that no significant music was produced by
native-born English composers between the death of Henry Purcell
in 1695 and the appearance of Elgar's first undoubted masterpiece,
the *Enigma* Variations, in 1899: the Savoy operas of Gilbert and
Sullivan are among the most valuable theatrical commodities ever
devised by the mind of man, and the symphonies and choral works
of that eminent Victorian, Sir Hubert Parry, are clearly those of an
important composer, possibly even a major one.

Best known for that stirring anthem *Jerusalem,* Parry was a
musician cut from the same cloth as his younger contemporary Elgar. There is a stately, and occasionally self-satisfied, Victorian
grandeur in his best pages, coupled with a natural vigor and deep-
seated melancholy, that make him an appealing and completely approachable "private" composer as well.

Parry's Third Symphony, finished in 1889 and called *The English* because of its many folklike melodies, is an ideal introduction
to his vaguely Elgarian yet still utterly individual world. If anything,
the Fourth Symphony is an even finer work, bursting with ideas and
a dignified energy.

The London Philharmonic under Matthias Bamert play these
marvelous works with an ease and confidence that almost suggests
they are standard repertoire items; in fact, the performances make
such a strong case, you almost wonder why they aren't. The other
recordings released thus far in their Parry symphony cycle are just
as enjoyable: the Symphony No. 2, *The Cambridge,* offered with the
resourceful Symphonic Variations (CHAN-8961 [CD], ABTD-
1553 [T]), and the agreeably Brahmsian Symphony No. 5 paired,
appropriately, with the *Elegy for Brahms* (CHAN-8955 [CD],
ABTD-1549 [T]).

More impressive than any of the symphonies, though, are the
deeply moving "sinfonia sacra," *The Soul's Ransom,* and the politely sensuous *Lotus Eaters,* on a text by Tennyson—two of Parry's
greatest choral works, which draw from Bamert his finest recorded

performances to date. Packed onto another Chandos CD (CHAN-8990) lasting nearly eighty minutes, this is a release that no one interested in choral and/or English music can afford to miss.

Pärt, Arvo (1935–)

Arbos; Pari Intervallo; An den Wassern zu Babel; De Profundis; Es sang vor langen Jahren; Stabat Mater

> Various soloists, Hilliard Ensemble, Hillier. ECM 831959-2 [CD], 831959-4 [T].

The music of the Estonian composer Arvo Pärt resembles the bumblebee: by all the laws of aerodynamics neither should be able to fly, and yet somehow, preposterously, they do. To call Pärt a minimalist is both accurate and misleading. Although he seems to adopt many of the static, lifeless procedures of Philip Glass and that crowd, his *real* source of inspiration would appear to be the hypnotic stasis of Gregorian chant. In Pärt's music, there is little in the way of development of musical ideas—in fact, there are few *ideas* at all. Somehow, though, he manages to wring genuine substance and feeling from his stubbornly thin materials: his gravely austere setting of the *Stabat Mater,* for instance, is absolutely bewitching, and the brief *An den Wassern zu Babel* has a stark grandeur that utterly belies its modest size.

The performances sound definitive.

Piston, Walter (1894–1976)

Symphony No. 2

**Boston Symphony, Thomas. Deutsche Grammophon
429860-2 [CD].**

In addition to being a great musical pedagogue whose pupils
included Leonard Bernstein and whose books *Harmony* and *Orchestration* remain standard texts, Walter Piston was one of the
finest of all American composers. His music combines an Italianate
lyricism (the family name was Pistone) with a ruggedly virile individuality that often suggests the rocky coast of his native Maine.
At his best, as he is in the powerful, exquisitely crafted Second Symphony of 1943, Piston reveals himself as one of our most important
symphonists and an immediately appealing, instantly recognizable
voice. In this flawless and exhilarating performance by Michael Tilson Thomas and the Boston Symphony, the Piston Second is the
centerpiece of an invaluable American album that also contains Paul
Zukofsky's electrifying recording of William Schuman's Violin
Concerto and a once-in-a-lifetime interpretation of Carl Ruggles's
overwhelming *Sun-Treader.*

Gerard Schwarz's hugely successful Piston series for Delos is
highlighted by a splendid recording of the Fourth Symphony, the
Serenade for String Orchestra, and the *Three New England Sketches*
(DE-3106 [CD]), and the composer's most popular work, the suite
from the ballet *The Incredible Flutist,* is now represented by a col-
orful, high-voltage performance by Leonard Slatkin and the St.
Louis Symphony, coupled with an equally fine account of the Sixth
Symphony (RCA 60798-2-RC [CD]).

Ponchielli, Amilcare

(1834–1886)

La Gioconda

Callas, Barbieri, Amadini, Poggi, Silveri, Neri, Turin Radio
Orchestra and Chorus, Votto. Fonit-Cetra CDC-9 [CD].

Caballé, Baltsa, Pavarotti, Milnes, Hodgson, London Opera
Chorus, National Philharmonic, Bartoletti. London
414349-2 [CD].

The next time you're at a party with people who really think
they know a lot about opera, challenge any one of them to relate,
in its simplest terms, the plot of *La Gioconda*. In retrospect, it's
almost impossible to fathom how the future librettist of Verdi's
Otello and *Falstaff* and the composer of *Mefistofele*, Arrigo Boito,
could have come up with such a hopelessly confusing pile of gibberish, or how Amilcare Ponchielli, a composer of limited abilities,
could have fashioned from it one of the most powerful and enduring
works of the Italian operatic stage. *La Gioconda* would have a decisive influence on almost every Italian opera that followed, including the later operas of Verdi and those of Ponchielli's most
celebrated pupil, Giacomo Puccini.

For more than three decades, the only Gioconda has been that
of Maria Callas. It is one of the most gripping of all her recorded
characterizations and one that seems to inspire everyone around
her, from the other principal singers to every member of the chorus
and orchestra, to give his or her absolute best. The recorded sound,
from a 1952 broadcast, is surprisingly lively and realistic.

The only real modern competition for this classic recording
comes from the splendid London set, which counts among its principal strengths recorded sound of astonishing clarity and presence,
and one of the finest performances Luciano Pavarotti has given in
years. The rest of the cast, apart from Montserrat Caballé's rather
stiff and unimaginative heroine, is generally excellent, and Bruno
Bartoletti—like Antonino Votto on the Fonit-Cetra set—conducts
like a man possessed.

Poulenc, Francis (1899–1963)

Concert champêtre for Harpsichord; Concerto in G minor for Organ, Strings, and Timpani

Malcolm, harpsichord and organ; Academy of St. Martin-in-the-Fields, Brown. London 425627-2 [CD].

If ever a composer wrote music that bore an uncanny resemblance to the way he actually looked, it was the tall, gangly, always slightly off-kilter Francis Poulenc. There is a pervasive and goofy oddness in all the work this deft, graceful, and highly original composer produced. Had he been just a little less peculiar, he might have been as important as Debussy; as it stands, he is responsible for some of the major French art songs of the twentieth century and is, perhaps, France's major modern composer of sacred music.

Two of Poulenc's most entertaining and individual works are given superb performances on this brilliant London recording. George Malcolm does yeoman service as the soloist in both concertos; Iona Brown's accompaniments are as stylish and musical as one could wish. In the best of all possible worlds, the performance of *Concert champêtre* might have been a touch more coquettish, but it—like that of the Organ Concerto—is easily the finest now available.

Gloria in G

Carteri, soprano; French National Radio Orchestra and Chorus, Prêtre. Angel CDC-47723 [CD].

Composed only two years before his death, Poulenc's *Gloria* is one of his most consistently inspired, touching, and exhilarating works. Not since Haydn had anyone set the *Laudamus Te* quite so joyously, and the work's closing bars easily rank with the most divinely inspired moments composed in this century.

Not only was Georges Prêtre's Angel recording the first to be made of this great modern sacred work, it was done with the composer himself in attendance. Only Leonard Bernstein, in a CBS recording now available on CD (MK-44710), found the same immensely appealing combination of fun and devotion in the *Gloria*, although for the most part the Prêtre interpretation is far more charming and, hence, far more French. The recording has the further advantage of having been made with the composer on hand. It's a sensation that is impossible to explain in words, but while listening to the music, you can actually feel his presence.

L'Histoire de Babar (le petit éléphant)

Ustinov, narrator; Paris Conservatory Orchestra, Prêtre.
Angel 4XS-36644 [T].

Having spent my childhood devouring pictorial histories of music and the Second World War, and having no children of my own yet (of whom I'm aware), I'm a fairly recent Babar convert. A friend introduced me to Jean de Brunhoff's plucky pachyderm through a Christmas gift of *Le Roi Babar,* and I've been hooked ever since. (I can sing the *Chanson des éléphants* in my sleep—"Pata Pata, Ko Ko Ko" and so on—but enough of that.)

The orchestral version of Poulenc's sweet but by no means gooey setting of the original Babar story is memorably served by Peter Ustinov on this Angel cassette (but *where,* may I ask, is the CD, please?). The reading of the English translation is as sly as it is tender and wise, avoiding even a hint of condescension; Georges Prêtre and the orchestra are excellent, and the recorded sound is fine.

Piano Music

Rogé, piano. London 417438-2 [CD], 417438-4 [T].

Poulenc's piano music, like his *chansons,* has attracted far too few major interpreters. In the case of the songs, that's almost understandable: the memory of performances by the composer and Pierre Bernac (Poulenc's longtime lover and the man for whom many of the best of them were written) remains vivid and indelible, and few singers are anxious to go up against such a legend. Then too, the songs have a quivering, elusive enchantment that makes them extremely difficult to perform well, as do many of the composer's finest piano works.

For the uninitiated or the unconvinced, Paul Crossley's heroic survey of the complete piano music for CBS (M3K-44921) may prove a bit intimidating, especially when it comes time to fork over the cost of three full-priced CDs. The set is more than worth the expenditure, since Crossley is a subtle, imaginative pianist whose performances are as astute as they are enjoyable.

Pascal Rogé's London recording might prove a far more manageable introduction. In addition to including some of Poulenc's most important and characteristic piano works—the three *Mouvements perpétuels,* the *Novelettes,* and a judicious sampling of the mercurial *Improvisations*—the playing is fairly sensational, full of capriciousness, sentiment, and Poulencian wisecracking, all captured in remarkably realistic sound.

Praetorius, Michael

(1571–1621)

Terpsichore Dances

> London Early Music Consort, Munrow. Angel CDM-69024 [CD].

When the extravagantly gifted David Munrow died by his own hand in 1976, the cause of early music lost one of its most devoted and appealing advocates. As committed to the "authentic" performance of Renaissance and medieval music as any musician of his generation, Munrow was also a great entertainer and a compelling performer, as this stupendous 1973 recording of music by Praetorius clearly shows.

Rarely have the famous *Terpsichore* Dances sounded more lively, lovely, or utterly infectious, and the lesser-known but stunningly beautiful motets from *The Muses of Zion* here emerge as one of the most important vocal collections of the period.

If, like a highly respected critic and my sometime tennis partner, you are usually tempted to dismiss Renaissance dance fare as "village idiot music," this wonderful monument to David Munrow's towering talent will make a believer out of almost anyone.

Prokofiev, Sergei (1891–1953)

Alexander Nevsky (cantata)

Cairns, mezzo-soprano; Los Angeles Master Chorale, Los Angeles Philharmonic, Previn. Telarc CD-80143 [CD].

The way to come to Sergei Eisenstein's 1938 film *Alexander Nevsky* is *not* through a modern recording of the cantata that Prokofiev cannibalized from his score for it. I should know. After committing Fritz Reiner's interpretation to memory but never having seen the picture itself until I entered college, I eagerly made my way to one of Ann Arbor's little revival houses in the late 1960s, fully prepared for one of the cinematic experiences of my life. And so it proved to be.

With growing incomprehension, I sat through the sloppy editing, the hammy acting, the inexcusable "humor," and the execrable sound, until the fateful moment when I turned to my date, a beaded, willowy quasi-hippie named Heather (I still think it should be against the law for parents to name their children after anything that can be found in a field), and asked, far more loudly than I had intended, "What *is* this shit?" I was resoundingly booed by the cognoscenti, and retired from the theater in disgrace.

To this day, I fail to understand *Nevsky*'s status as one of the milestones of cinema. An OK Stalinist propaganda orgy, sure: The scene where the comic-book Teutonic Knights throw the kids into the fire is grisly and disturbing, though tame stuff indeed compared to what would actually happen three years later. But a great film? If so, I have no idea what the term "great film" could possibly mean. From the wretched soundtrack, which was nonetheless unable to disguise an inept, hideously out-of-tune performance, it would be hard to tell that Prokofiev did indeed produce a wonderful score; for that we can thank the recording companies, who with various versions of the *Alexander Nevsky* Cantata have given this thrilling piece a life of its own.

As splendid as Reiner's classic recording is, the fact that he used an English text all but cripples the performance. The words—in a perfectly accurate translation—are so irretrievably silly, and the diction of Margaret Hillis's Chicago Symphony Chorus is so flawless, that even the most sympathetic listener (as I have always been) is hard pressed not to crack up.

Among the Russian versions of *Nevsky,* in which gems like "Arise! Arise! Ye Russian folk,/In battle just to fight to death!" are mercifully blocked by the language barrier, André Previn's Telarc recording, if not quite so vibrant as his older outing with the London Symphony, is clearly the first choice. Previn's *Nevsky* has become much darker and richer over the years, and the Philharmonic's deeper voices—the lower strings and brass, and the orchestra's exceptional bass clarinetist, David Howard—respond with a wonderfully menacing rumble. Yet the performance also has its moments of blazing, flood-lit grandeur: "Alexander's Entry into Pskov" will push your speaker's tweeters—to say nothing of your neighbor's patience—to their absolute limit.

Christine Cairns sings her solo beautifully, and the chorus, like the orchestra, is enthusiastic, responsive, and, when the score requires, very, *very* loud. As we have come to expect from Telarc, the recorded sound is miraculous.

Concerto No. 3 in C for Piano and Orchestra

Graffman, piano; Cleveland Orchestra, Szell. CBS MYK-37806 [CD], MT-37806 [T].

The most popular of Prokofiev's five piano concertos has received numerous first-rate recordings since the composer himself left his historic account of this profound, ebullient piece in the 1930s. Incidentally, that exhilarating performance with the London Symphony conducted by Piero Coppola (grandfather of the film director) can now be found on Pearl (GEMM CD-9470 [CD]). The greatest modern performance of the Third Concerto is on this CBS recording, which also includes equally gripping run-throughs of the audacious First Concerto and the Third Piano Sonata. This generously packed reissue includes some of the finest playing Gary Graffman ever did in a recording studio, and is further cause for lament that that brilliant career was cut short by a neurological disorder. In both concertos, the accompaniment George Szell provides is spellbinding, and the late-1960s recorded sound is still more than adequate.

Concertos (2) for Violin and Orchestra

Mintz, violin; Chicago Symphony, Abbado. Deutsche Grammophon 410524-2 [CD].

No two works will better explain Prokofiev's position as one of the most popular of all twentieth-century composers than these magnificent violin concertos, written just before and immediately after his long, self-imposed exile from the recently created Soviet Union. While the youthful D Major Concerto (No. 1) is one of the freshest and most original works Prokofiev had produced up to that time, the G minor Concerto is among the greatest modern works for the instrument. Lyrical, dramatic, sardonic, and overflowing with that utterly distinctive melodic personality which makes all of Prokofiev's music unique, the Second Concerto ranks with the finest of all the composer's mature works, which is to say, with the finest music written since the turn of the century.

The Israeli violinist Shlomo Mintz is an ideal advocate of both these wonderful works. His technique and temperament easily overcome all the formidable challenges the music presents. The accompaniments provided by Claudio Abbado are as poised and passionate as one could hope for, and Deutsche Grammophon's recorded sound is something close to ideal.

An outstanding tape by the Russian violinist Dmitri Sitkovetsky with Sir Colin Davis and the London Symphony is currently available from Virgin Classics (VC-7-90734-4). In fact, the playing is so explosive and idiomatic, many will feel the CD version (VC-7-90734-2) gives Mintz, Abbado, and company an extremely exciting run for their money.

Lieutenant Kijé Suite; *Love for Three Oranges* Suite; Symphony No. 1, *Classical*

> Philadelphia Orchestra, Ormandy. Odyssey MBK-39783 [CD].

During the many years when he was one of the world's most frequently recorded conductors, Eugene Ormandy never made a finer recording than these versions of three of Prokofiev's most popular scores. Even if the interpretation of the *Classical* Symphony leaves out the final measure of sassy wit, and the outer movements of the *Love for Three Oranges* Suite could use a touch more maniacal energy, none of the pieces has ever been better played in a recording studio. At almost every turn, Ormandy's great orchestra manages some wonder of unanimity or solo display. At Odyssey prices, this is a phenomenal bargain that must not be missed.

For those who are interested in *Kijé* alone, the magic of two performances from the 1960s has never been surpassed. George Szell's CBS recording (MYK-38527 [CD], MYT-38527 [T]) is coupled with that finest of all recorded performances of Kodály's *Háry János* Suite (see page 215), and Fritz Reiner's dazzling RCA recording (60176-2 [CD], 60176-4 [T]) accompanies that conductor's incomparable—though, alas, English-language—version of *Alexander Nevsky*.

Prokofiev's endlessly inventive opera has finally received an adequate recording: a sparkling French-language production of *L'Amour des trois oranges* by the Lyon Opera under Kent Nagano (Virgin Classics VC-7-91084-2 [CD], VC-7-91084-4 [T]). Those who have long suspected from the evidence of the famous suite that *The Love for Three Oranges* must be one of the great twentieth-century operas will be heartened to discover that they were absolutely right.

Peter and the Wolf

Perlman, narrator; Israel Philharmonic, Mehta. Angel CDC-47067 [CD], 4DS-38189 [T].

You have to be an irredeemably crusty curmudgeon not to respond to the warmth and wonder of Prokofiev's best-known work. Like *Hansel and Gretel, Peter and the Wolf* transcends the traditional limits of a conventional "children's work"; its simplicity can be grasped and loved by the tenderest of musical ears, while its immense wit and sophistication can appeal to the most refined of musical tastes.

For years, the most delectable of all recordings of the work featured a wonderfully sly narration (complete with some marvelously personal sound effects) by Michael Flanders, a performance that can still be found on a Seraphim cassette (4XG-60172). Since that recording will probably never appear on compact disc—and, in fact, may disappear altogether at any moment—the best alternative for the foreseeable future is this fine Angel recording by Zubin Mehta. Though superbly played by members of the Israel Philharmonic, by far the best thing about the recording is the endearing narration by Itzhak Perlman, who somehow manages to transform Prokofiev's Grandfather into a Jewish Mother without doing a significant disservice to either the spirit or the letter of the score. A sparkling performance of Saint-Saëns's *Carnival of the Animals* rounds out this extremely desirable release.

Piano Sonatas Nos. 6–8

Pogorelich, piano. Deustche Grammophon 413363-2 [CD] (No. 6).

Pollini, piano. Deustche Grammophon 419202-2 [CD] (No. 7).

Richter, piano. Deustche Grammophon 423573-2 [CD] (No. 8).

Written between 1942 and 1944 during the darkest days of the Great Patriotic War, Prokofiev's wartime piano sonatas are not only his most important works for the instrument but are also, conceivably, the most significant contribution to the form made by a twentieth-century composer. Formidably difficult and emotionally exhausting, they place enormous burdens on both the performer and the listener. While only the most courageous virtuosos need bother to approach them, an immense technique is not enough: they all plumb depths that require a considerable expressive maturity and an unusual degree of self-knowledge.

The three Deustche Grammophon recordings—and what a civilized thing it would be for the company to repackage them on a single disc!—are among the respective pianists' finest achievements, especially Ivo Pogorelich's spellbinding version of No. 6, the A Major Sonata, in which this largely self-indulgent punk for once seems nothing of the kind. Maurizio Pollini, too, proves in the Seventh that in addition to a rarefied poetic sensibility he also possesses a thunderous technique, whereas Sviatoslav Richter is simply being Richter in his astounding live performance of Eighth Sonata— which is to say, the greatest pianist of his time.

Romeo and Juliet (complete ballet)

Boston Symphony, Ozawa. Deustche Grammophon 423268-2 [CD], 423268-4 [T].

At the Paris premiere of his Second Symphony in 1925, Prokofiev is alleged to have turned to a companion and asked the rueful question, "Can it be that I really *am* a second-rate composer?" Any of a dozen works will answer that, including what may well be the greatest full-length ballet ever written.

Romeo and Juliet is not only a worthy successor to *Swan Lake* and *The Sleeping Beauty*, it is superior to both in many significant respects. The level of melodic and rhythmic invention is generally more inspired than it is in either Tchaikovsky masterpiece, and as drama it is far more immediate, cogent, and profound. It is not the path-breaking work that Stravinsky's *Rite of Spring* clearly was, but as an old-fashioned epic on the grand scale, nothing like it would emerge from twentieth-century Russia.

With André Previn's superlative Angel recording temporarily out of circulation, Seiji Ozawa's excellent version with Boston will fill the gap more than adequately. Here, this frequently glib conductor resists doing his usual traffic cop routine: the playing has genuine bite and a feline grace, and climaxes rise to splendidly noisy proportions. The Boston Symphony brilliantly covers any inadequacies in the interpretation with playing the likes of which one never hears at the ballet.

Among single-disc versions (although since DG fits the entire ballet on two CDs, an excerpts album hardly seems worth the trouble), Joel Levi's Cleveland Orchestra recording for Telarc (CD-80089 [CD]) is the most desirable since Erich Leinsdorf's stunning but now deleted Boston Symphony anthology for RCA.

String Quartets (2)

Chilingirian Quartet. Chandos CHAN-8929 [CD], ABTD-1531 [T].

Unlike Shostakovich, whose cycle of fifteen string quartets encompassed most of his creative life and represented, after the symphonies, his finest achievement, Prokofiev was curiously indifferent to the form, producing only two quartets during his entire career. Although they have yet to enter the standard quartet repertoire, both are strong and individual pieces, redolent with Prokofiev's unmistakable melodic quirkiness and wit.

The Chilingirians make a virtually airtight case for both works. The more difficult First Quartet of 1930 nearly comes off as the more musically incisive of the two, but the folksiness of the wartime Second Quartet casts the more appealing spell. The recorded sound is every bit as fine as we have come to expect from Chandos's adept engineers.

Symphonies (7)

French National Radio Orchestra, Martinon. Vox Box CDX-5001 [CD] (Symphonies 1, 4, 5, 7, *Russian Overture; Overture on Hebrew Themes*); CDX-5054 [CD] (Symphonies 2, 3, and 6).

Of all the recordings released during the composer's centennial year of 1991 (his death went practically unnoticed, as it fell on the exact same day as Joseph Stalin's), none was more welcomed than this phenomenal bargain. For little more than what it costs to buy a single full-priced CD, one can enjoy Jean Martinon's idiomatic and understanding Prokofiev cycle on four generously packed compact discs.

By far the strongest performances are of precisely what one would want: the elusive and difficult middle symphonies. No more persuasive or understanding versions of Nos. 2, 3, 4, and 6 currently exist, and if Martinon and his game French orchestra face serious competition in the other works, these are still extremely enjoyable readings that will please all but the most fanatically discriminating tastes. Excellent notes and remastered sound.

Symphony No. 5 in B-flat

Israel Philharmonic, Bernstein. CBS MK-35877 [CD].

Since it first began to be known in the late 1940s, the Fifth has remained the most popular, and is probably the most important, of the composer's seven symphonies. Like the equally celebrated Fifth Symphony of Dmitri Shostakovich, it is one large-scale symphonic work to have emerged from the Soviet Union that seems destined to occupy a permanent place in the standard repertoire, and rightly so. For the Prokofiev Fifth, like the Shostakovich, is a big, powerful, intensely dramatic, and unmistakably *Russian* composition that will probably continue to move and inspire audiences well into the next century, and beyond.

Though the Prokofiev Fifth has had some memorable recordings in the last thirty years—André Previn's classic London
Symphony performance is easily the best available tape (Seraphim
4XG-60434), and in Leonard Slatkin's amazing St. Louis Symphony recording (RCA RCD1-5035 [CD]), the orchestra sounds
like the Berlin Philharmonic in overdrive—this last entry from
Leonard Bernstein is easily the most overwhelming recording this
popular work has yet received. Bernstein's earlier New York Philharmonic recording was a controversial one a quarter of a century
ago. Suffice it to say that his interpretation only grew more personal
and powerful over the years: tempos are all on the extreme side, as
is the emotional content of what can often be heard as a rather cool
and sardonic work. Bernstein builds some of the most tremendous
climaxes heard on commercial recordings of the modern era. The
Scherzo whips by with a tremendous sense of urgency, and the finale
contains some of the most exhilarating moments that this
conductor—which is to say *any* conductor—ever left in a commercial recording.

Ptaszynska, Marta (1943–)

Jeu-parti for Vibraphone and Harp

> Rutkowski, vibraphone; Mazurek, harp. Olympia OCD-324
> [CD].

I should confess that I have not exactly memorized Marta
Ptaszynska's *Jeu-parti* for Vibraphone and Harp, nor do I expect to
do so any time soon. It is the composer's all-but-unspellable (and
for most people, unpronounceable) name that instantly captured
my attention. For obvious reasons, my heart immediately goes out
to anyone with a difficult surname, and I would hate to think that
Ptaszynska's worthy music might go unheard simply because a prospective buyer would be too linguistically intimidated to ask for it.

So if you're afraid you might get tongue-tied or otherwise embarrass yourself in the record store, simply open the book to this page, point to the woman's name, and say, "I want the *Jeu-parti* for Vibraphone and Harp by *her*." (Asking for it by number is no fun, and five will get you ten that the salesperson won't have a clue about how to pronounce it either.)

Better still, this album devoted to percussion music of contemporary Polish composers also features the recording premieres of works by Krzysztof Baculewski, Zbigniew Bargielski, Pawel Buczynski, Andrzej Krzanowski, and Zbigniew Penherski, together with pieces by the older and more established Witold (not to be confused with the lesser-known Zbigniew) Rudzinski and Kazimierz Serocki.

Again, I bought the recording not only because I think all us unpronounceables should stick together, but also because I wanted a companion album to Olympia OCD-316, which features piano music by—among others—Andrzej Dutkiewicz, Marian Borkowski, Artur Malawski, Zbigniew (not to be confused with the better-known Witold) Rudzinski, Tadeusz Szeligowski, and Romuald Twardowski.

Puccini, Giacomo (1858–1924)

La Bohème

De los Angeles, Björling, Amara, Merrill, RCA Victor Orchestra and Chorus, Beecham. Angel CDCB-47235 [CD], 4X2G-6099 [T].

This astonishing recording—certainly one of the greatest commercial recordings ever made—was thrown together at the last possible moment and, in fact, was very nearly never made at all. For more than thirty years it has been the standard recording of Giacomo Puccini's most popular opera, and will undoubtedly remain so for as long as recordings are made.

Apart from a superlative cast (Victoria de los Angeles and Jussi Björling are especially wonderful as the lovers), most of the real magic of this most magical of all Puccini recordings comes from the pit. Several volumes could be written about the special insights, beautifully shaped phrases, aching tenderness, and surging passion Sir Thomas Beecham finds in Puccini's score. No one has ever made the love music bloom so effortlessly, or captured more of the high spirits or bitter tragedy of the work than Beecham did on what was an impossibly tight recording schedule. Robert Merrill, the superb Marcello, once told me that Sir Thomas caused great consternation by insisting that his duet with Björling, "Ah Mimi, tu più non torni," be recorded again, even though time was running out and the first try had seemed to be a virtually perfect performance. Later, when the producer, who could hear no difference in the two versions, asked the conductor why he had insisted on a second take, Beecham replied with characteristic glee, "Oh, because I simply *love* to hear those boys sing it!" That this very special recording *was* a labor of love from beginning to end is as obvious now as on the day it was first released.

La fanciulla del West

Neblett, Domingo, Milnes, Howell, Orchestra and Chorus
of the Royal Opera House, Covent Garden, Mehta.
Deutsche Grammophon 419640-2 [CD].

Many people continue to wonder why *The Girl of the Golden West*, Puccini's major effort between *Madama Butterfly* and *Turandot*, has never caught on. It certainly got off to a galloping start at its Metropolitan Opera premiere: Arturo Toscanini—temporarily on speaking terms with the composer—was in the pit, and the principals included the dream trio of Emmy Destinn as Minnie, Enrico Caruso as Dick Johnson, and Pasquale Amato as Jack Rance.

Although the opera has always had its passionate advocates (and I include myself among them), the problem is so obvious that it hardly seems worth mentioning: *La fanciulla del West,* in spite of its many wondrous beauties, is really, *really* dumb. And it's not that the action, based on a play by *Butterfly*'s author David Belasco, is either foolish or implausible; in many ways, it is one of the better dramatic constructs Puccini was given to work with. *Fanciulla*'s central impossibility, at least for American audiences, is the language. How are we to credit a literal horse opera in which the miners, cowboys, and Indians all sing in Italian? (The acid test is the first scene of Act II. If you can listen to Billy Jackrabbit and his squaw Wowkle grunting and ugh-ing at each other in between bouts of flawless Italian and not burst out laughing, you have my undiluted admiration.)

This Deutsche Grammophon recording makes the strongest case for the opera since the magnificent 1958 London set with Renata Tebaldi and Mario del Monaco, which is now available on a pair of compact discs (421595-2). While still a stunner—Tebaldi's Minnie is arguably the most finely crafted of all her Puccini heroines—the older recording yields to the newer one on a pair of important points: the far more sensitive and sympathetic Johnson of Placido Domingo and the more expressive, imaginative conducting of Zubin Mehta.

Madama Butterfly

Tebaldi, Bergonzi, Cossotto, Sordello, Santa Cecilia Academy Orchestra and Chorus, Serafin. London 411634-2 [CD], 411634-4 [T].

That this radiant, heart-stopping opera was a fiasco at its world premiere in 1904 still seems impossible to most opera lovers today. We forget that the audience at Milan's La Scala was not exactly anxious to embrace a love story between an occidental and a fifteen-year-old Japanese girl, and that the composer (as he later admitted) had made a serious miscalculation in the structure of his new work. What we now know as the second and third acts of the opera were once a single, uncomfortably lengthy act that would have tested the patience of even the most ardent of the composer's admirers.

As one of the best-loved operas ever written, *Madama Butterfly* has had more than its fair share of memorable recordings, but none was ever more poignant than this classic 1958 version, with the sumptuous Renata Tebaldi in the title role. Tebaldi's Cio-Cio-San is a marvel of dramatic evolution, from the innocent child of the opening scene to the towering, tragic heroine of the opera's final moments. The supporting cast, especially the beautifully sung Pinkerton of Carlo Bergonzi and the vastly resourceful Suzuki of the young Fiorenza Cossotto, could not have been improved upon.

Tullio Serafin's conducting is its usual admirable amalgam of sensitivity, understanding, and dramatic bite, and the original late-1950s acoustics have held up surprisingly well.

Manon Lescaut

> Callas, di Stefano, Fioravanti, La Scala Orchestra and Chorus, Serafin. Angel CDCB-47392 [CD], 4AVB-34019 [T].

It was no accident that onstage the Callas–di Stefano love scenes always had the fiery ring of truth: All of them had been rehearsed many times behind closed doors. The singers' offstage love affair not only made good grist for the tabloid mills, it gave their musical moments together a magic no other operatic duo of the 1950s could even approximate.

Manon Lescaut, Puccini's first major success as a composer, provided the vehicle for one of the best of their recorded collaborations, with Maria Callas at her most penetrating and believable and Giuseppe di Stefano at his most musical and refined. (There are many who still remember him as a kind of bellowing, lyric-tenor version of his great contemporary, the bellowing *tenore da forza* Mario del Monaco. Here di Stefano displays both the ardor and vocal sophistication—to say nothing of the naturally beautiful physical sound—that led many to predict a career as long and brilliant as Beniamino Gigli's.)

The always reliable Tullio Serafin catches fire and turns in the best-conducted *Manon Lescaut* yet recorded, and even the mono sound proves no serious distraction: from the opening scene we are caught up in the poignant drama and are soon swept away.

La Rondine

> Te Kanawa, Domingo, Rendall, Nucci, Ambrosian Opera Chorus, London Symphony, Maazel. CBS M2K-37852 [CD].

During a visit to Vienna in 1912, Puccini was asked by an enterprising Austrian publisher to write a Viennese operetta. Presumably, what the publisher had in mind was a kind of *Madama*

Butterfly meets *Die Fledermaus*. The result was *La Rondine*, the lightest and least performed of the composer's mature works.

Though certainly no *Bohème*, *La Rondine* (The Swallow) is just as certainly not the misbegotten disaster its detractors have always claimed it to be. If the opera is not exactly riddled with unforgettable Puccinian melodies, the tunes are still ingratiating enough to be worth anyone's time. Moreover, the characters are likable, the action is swift and sure, and the orchestral fabric is full of wonders from the composer's top drawer.

This recording makes by far the strongest case for the piece that any version ever has. Kiri Te Kanawa's luscious voice is ideally suited to the heroine, Magda, an appealing cross between Violetta and the Merry Widow, and Placido Domingo lavishes his usual care and intelligence on a role that is far more interesting than it otherwise might seem. Although Lorin Maazel's conducting is not ideally subtle and relaxed, he still coaxes some marvelous playing from the London Symphony as well as skilled contributions from the rest of the cast.

There are really no excuses left for not exploring this charmer.

*T*osca

Callas, di Stefano, Gobbi, La Scala Orchestra and Chorus, de Sabata. Angel CDCB-47174 [CD], 4AV-34047 [T].

If there ever was such a thing as a perfect opera recording, this is it. It features, among other things, Maria Callas, the greatest Tosca of the modern era, the most elegantly sung of tenor Giuseppe di Stefano's heros, and a villain—the Baron Scarpia of Tito Gobbi—that will stand your hair on end. But what puts this *Tosca* on a level that will probably not be approached is the conducting of Victor de Sabata. Though not as well known as his near-contemporary Arturo Toscanini, de Sabata, I think, was always the finer conductor. Like Toscanini's, his dramatic sensibilities were very highly developed, yet unlike the Maestro, de Sabata had an immensely complex musical mind that not only probed the music with greater depth but allowed it sufficient space to breathe. His conducting throughout this inspired recording is nothing less than miraculous, from the soaringly beautiful support he lends to the love music to that chillingly violent moment in the second act when the evil Baron finally "gets the point."

In short, this is a classic recording no opera lover can afford to be without.

Il trittico (Il tabarro; Suor Angelica; Gianni Schicchi)

Donath, Popp, Seiffert, Panerai, Munich Radio Orchestra, Patané. Eurodisc 69043-2-RC [CD].

One hit, one near-miss, and a dud: not a bad average, unless your name happens to have been Giacomo Puccini. *Il trittico*, the composer's trilogy of one-act operas that had its premiere at the Met on December 14, 1918, has rarely been presented in that form since. *Gianni Schicchi*, the comedy, was a resounding success from the beginning and is frequently heard alone. Though the melodramatic curtain raiser, *Il tabarro* (The Cloak), is enjoyably gruesome and direct, nothing, apparently, will ever save *Suor Angelica*—the literal weak sister of the set—although some very great divas have given Puccini's nun-with-a-past a try.

You might think that with all its big-name talent—Renata Scotto, Ileana Cotrubas, Marilyn Horne, Placido Domingo, and Tito Gobbi—the CBS recording would have the field to itself. Much of the reason the upstart Eurodisc version knocks the giant off so easily has to do with the conducting of Giuseppe Patané. Unlike Lorin Maazel, a competent stick-waver but little more, the Italian constantly searches out—and usually finds—precisely the right color or mood the moment demands.

In addition to the exemplary conducting, the Munich *Trittico* features some striking individual performances: the droll, sharply drawn Schicchi of Rolando Panerai is more than a match for Gobbi's legendary characterization, and if Lucia Popp can't quite save the feckless Angelica, she makes her an exceptionally lovely thing to hear.

Turandot

Sutherland, Pavarotti, Caballé, Pears, Ghiaurov, John Alldis Choir, London Philharmonic, Mehta. London 414274-2 [CD], 414274-4 [T].

The emergence of *Turandot* as an opera whose popularity has begun to challenge that of Puccini's other major works is a relatively recent phenomenon. For years, all anyone ever knew about *Turandot* was the beautiful third-act aria "Nessun dorma," and the fact that the opera remained unfinished at the time of the composer's death. For all its obvious flaws and inconsistencies (the unfinished love duet would have undoubtedly been the crowning achievement of Puccini's career, and the problems with the hero's character would have unquestionably been ironed out had the composer been given time to revise the score), *Turandot* is a great opera—as daring, original, and phenomenally beautiful a work as Puccini ever wrote.

When it was first released in the early 1970s, this now legendary London recording shocked the opera world. What was Joan Sutherland, the reigning bel canto diva of her time, doing recording a role that she never had, and obviously never would, sing on stage? Whatever the reasons, the gamble paid off handsomely. As Puccini's icy princess, Sutherland gave one of her finest recorded performances. The interpretation is full of fury, dramatic intensity, and—in the final scene—a startling warmth and femininity that have never been this singer's strongest suits. Similarly, Luciano Pavarotti, who recorded the role of Calaf before he ever sang it onstage, is brilliant as the Unknown Prince. Unlike the work of the Pavarotti of recent years, who seems to shout and croon his way through almost every performance, this is not only an interpretation by a great tenor in his prime but a sad reminder of what a vulgarian this once-electrifying artist has allowed himself to become.

Though I have never been Zubin Mehta's greatest fan, here he delivers one of the finest performances of his career. No detail in Puccini's astonishing orchestration is overlooked, and the conducting is as tenderly lyrical as it is compellingly dramatic. If you have yet to make the acquaintance of what may well be the composer's masterpiece, this is the *Turandot* for you.

Also very special is RCA's Rome recording made during the summer of 1960 and now available on both CD (RCD2-5932) and cassette (AGK3-3970). The chief glories of this memorable performance are the molten Calaf of Jussi Björling (who manages to transform "Nessun dorma" into "Nessun-ah dorma") and the powerful Birgit Nilsson in the title role. Although the Rome Opera House forces are clearly no match for London's superbly disciplined group, Erich Leinsdorf brings a measure of soaring lyricism to the score that Mehta can't quite match.

Purcell, Henry (1659–1695)

Dido and Aeneas

Norman, Allen, McLaughlin, Kern, Power, English
Chamber Orchestra and Chorus, Leppard. Philips
416299-2 [CD], 416299-4 [T].

More than any other recording of the last generation, this new
version of *Dido and Aeneas* demonstrates why this incredible work
by the thirty-year-old Henry Purcell is the oldest of all operas that
can still hold a place in the standard repertoire today. Under Raymond Leppard's inspired direction, the work leaps to life in a way
that it rarely has on commercial recordings. Jessye Norman's Dido
rivals those of Kirsten Flagstad and Janet Baker in its depth and
intensity, and Thomas Allen is the most manly and heroic Aeneas
I can remember hearing. For those who usually find this greatest of
English operas too thin in its characterization, or too slight in its
development, this magnificent and luxuriant new version will probably change their minds.

The Fairy Queen

Soloists, Monteverdi Choir, English Baroque Soloists,
Gardiner. Deutsche Grammophon 419221-2 [CD].

Not an adaptation of the epic poem by Edmund Spenser
(which of course would have made it *The Faerie Queen*, as well as
something that would have been at least two days long) but of
Shakespeare's *Midsummer Night's Dream*, this ridiculously underperformed "semi-opera" contains some of the most miraculous music Purcell ever composed. Tuneful and fanciful, with a gossamer
lightness and extraordinary rhythmic life, *The Fairy Queen* should
be far more familiar, and undoubtedly would become so were it
routinely given performances as vital and engaging as this.

With his customary blend of unassailable scholarship and
boyish enthusiasm, John Eliot Gardiner misses no opportunity to
underline the manifold glories of the score, yet does so with a deftly
unobtrusive hand. The only other Purcell recording quite like it is

318

Gardiner's now-deleted Erato version of *King Arthur*, the most important of Purcell's collaborations with another seventeenth-century giant, John Dryden. In both recordings Gardiner makes an extremely convincing case that *each* work is in fact the composer's masterpiece, and with both he reminds us with a renewed sense of wonder and tragedy what music lost when Henry Purcell died at the age of thirty-six.

Music for the Theater

Kirkby, Nelson, Bowman, Hill, Covey-Crump, Keyte, Thomas, Academy of Ancient Music, Hogwood. Oiseau-Lyre 425893-2 [CD].

More than six hours of the incidental music Purcell composed for various largely forgotten plays might be too much of a good thing for most people, yet these classic recordings by the Academy of Ancient Music remain a source of unalloyed delight. Christopher Hogwood's soloists prove ideal accomplices, with vocal timbres skillfully adjusted to match the sound of the antique instruments.

Rachmaninoff, Sergei
(1873–1943)

The Bells (choral symphony)

Troitskaya, Karczykowski, Krause, Concertgebouw Orchestra and Chorus, Ashkenazy. London 414455-2 [CD].

Outside the English-speaking world, where he has always been something of an embarrassment to the literary establishment, Edgar Allan Poe is widely regarded as a major figure in modern poetry. In France, for instance, where one sees more statues to his memory than to that of Shakespeare, his reputation is enormous, thanks largely to the passionate advocacy of Charles Baudelaire. The great Frenchman's translations are markedly superior to their models, perhaps because Poe's poetry tends to lose so much in the original.

Working from an excellent Russian translation of Poe's noisiest masterpiece, Rachmaninoff fashioned a dramatic, volatile, supremely colorful cantata that easily ranks among his greatest works. To date, *The Bells* has had no finer or more inspired recording than Vladimir Ashkenazy's impulsive version for London. As with André Previn's inexplicably withdrawn Angel recording, Ashkenazy brings just the right combination of expansiveness and control to the interpretation, together with a sense of unpredictability that the Previn lacks. With superb soloists, to say nothing of the great Concertgebouw Orchestra and flawless recorded sound, this is *The Bells* that should ring yours admirably.

Concertos for Piano and Orchestra (4); *Rhapsody on a Theme of Paganini*

Wild, piano; Royal Philharmonic, Horenstein. Chandos 8521/2 [CD].

In one form or another, these thrilling recordings have remained in circulation since the mid-1960s, when they were originally recorded for *Reader's Digest*. The American pianist Earl Wild and the dapper, impulsive Russian-born conductor Jascha Horenstein had never worked together before, though it would be difficult to gather that from this finest integral recording of the Rachmaninoff Concertos ever made.

The success of the project rested primarily on the almost perfect fusion of two surprisingly similar musical temperaments; for in spite of the differences in their ages and backgrounds, the youthful soloist and the aging conductor were from the same arch-Romantic mold.

Even more than the composer's own recordings with Stokowski and Ormandy and the Philadelphia Orchestra, or Ashkenazy's cycles with Haitink and Previn, the electricity Wild and Horenstein generated together remains unique. On records, only a handful of pianists can match Wild's thunderous impetuosity in this music, and the conductor brought the same sort of measured lunacy and passionate brinkmanship to the accompaniments that can be heard in his famous Mahler recordings.

With beautifully remastered recorded sound that completely belies its age, this is an ideal choice for anyone who wants all four Concertos and the *Paganini Rhapsody* in a convenient, hugely exciting, and unusually economical package.

Concerto No. 2 in C minor for Piano and Orchestra

Richter, piano; Warsaw Philharmonic, Wislocki. Deutsche Grammophon 415119-2 [CD].

Graffman, piano; New York Philharmonic, Bernstein. CBS MYK-36722 [CD], MYT-36722 [T].

Although the composer himself, who was certainly one of the great pianists history has so far known, left a series of famous, authoritative recordings of all his major works for piano and orchestra, no recording of his most popular concerto has ever generated more sheer wonder or excitement than Sviatoslav Richter's famous version from the mid-1960s. Interpretatively, the performance is something of a madhouse. Tempos are invariably extreme, from the slowest of Adagios to a breakneck clip in the final movement that will leave most listeners panting on the floor. Yet as eccentric as the interpretation certainly is, it is also utterly convincing, thanks to the technique and temperament of the foremost pianist of our time.

For those who prefer a cassette of this high-cholesterol classic, Gary Graffman's version with Leonard Bernstein remains as polished as it is poetic, with one of the finest modern versions (in fact, my favorite) of the *Rhapsody on a Theme of Paganini* as the extremely attractive filler.

Concerto No. 3 in D minor for Piano and Orchestra

Horowitz, piano; New York Philharmonic, Ormandy. RCA RCD1-2633 [CD].

Some very reliable rumors insist that Rachmaninoff stopped playing his D minor Concerto in public shortly after he heard it performed by the young Vladimir Horowitz. And for the better part of fifty years, the Rachmaninoff D minor was a cornerstone in what was surely the tiniest concerto repertoire any major pianist has ever possessed. Though I have always felt about Horowitz much the same way I feel about his father-in-law, Arturo Toscanini, and his near-contemporary Jascha Heifetz, give the man his due: In this particular music, no pianist of the century has ever come close. Of course, for something approaching the ultimate in hair-raising piano fireworks, the 1951 studio recording Horowitz made with Fritz Reiner and the RCA Victor Orchestra (RCA 7754-2-RC [CD], 7754-4-RC [T]) surpasses this 1978 live performance. But as a souvenir of one of the century's most phenomenal technicians, this recording belongs in almost every collection.

The Isle of the Dead; Symphonic Dances

> **Concertgebouw Orchestra of Amsterdam, Ashkenazy. London 430733-2 [CD].**

Best known for his once-ubiquitous piano music, during his lifetime Sergei Rachmaninoff was equally celebrated as a composer of orchestral music and songs. The dark and richly atmospheric *Isle of the Dead,* one of the most accomplished of all his compositions, and the four Symphonic Dances, his last major work, have never been served more brilliantly than in this London recording by the Concertgebouw Orchestra under Vladimir Ashkenazy. The Symphonic Dances were actually composed for and dedicated to Eugene Ormandy and the Philadelphia Orchestra—the last of their several recordings can still be found on Odyssey (YT-31246 [T])—but Ashkenazy's version is in every way more colorful, rhythmically vibrant, and intense. For those who are still persuaded that the heart of Rachmaninoff's output was the Prelude in C-sharp minor and the syrupy *Vocalise,* these wonderful performances of a pair of masterworks should come as an extremely pleasant surprise.

P iano Music

> **Rachmaninoff, piano. RCA 7766-2-RG [CD], 7766-4-RG [T].**

This collection of twenty-five shorter works and transcriptions offers convincing evidence that Sergei Rachmaninoff was one of the greatest pianists of whom we have an accurate record. For a composer of such overtly Romantic music, Rachmaninoff the pianist was strikingly modern in his outlook and technique. In these recordings, made between 1925 and 1942, the year before his death, he takes surprisingly few liberties: the approach is generally free of rubato and other rhythmic distortions, and any suggestion of nineteenth-century rhetoric is conspicuously absent. The playing itself ranges from the revelatory to the spellbinding. The famous C-sharp minor Prelude is done in the darkest possible tones, with a feeling of completely detached understatement; the technical legerdemain in encores like the *Midsummer Night's Dream* Scherzo will stand your hair on end.

An exciting and invaluable document.

Preludes (23) for Piano

Ashkenazy, piano. London 414417-2 [CD].

Incredibly enough, given their wealth of invention, emotional and musical variety, and fabulous melodic richness (as with a Chopin melody, a Rachmaninoff tune can be maddeningly impossible to forget), only one completely successful recording of all twenty-three of these miniature miracles has been made, this London version by Vladimir Ashkenazy. The pianist is uncannily successful in drawing out the special character of each of the individual pieces, and, in general, the playing has a wonderful audacity, mixed with a lyrical tenderness and engaging wit. Though the Ashkenazy compact discs should be snapped up by anyone interested in stupendous piano playing or the music itself, Hyperion's set by Howard Shelley—which is also available on tape (CDA-66081/2 [CD], KA-66081/2 [T])—offers a fascinating and distinctly *non*-Russian second opinion. Some of the interpretations might seem a bit odd—the famous C-sharp minor Prelude lumbers along like a brontosaurus with bad knees—but even the oddest of Shelley's ideas are strangely persuasive, as is Hyperion's ultrarealistic sound.

Sonata in G minor for Cello and Piano

Harrell, cello; Ashkenazy, piano. London 414340-2 [CD].

After suffering his famous nervous breakdown at the turn of the century and undergoing hours of autosuggestion at the hands of an eminent Moscow physician named Dahl—"You will compose again . . . You will write a piano concerto . . . You will write with great facility . . ."—Sergei Rachmaninoff broke his creative logjam with the C minor Piano Concerto, which he gratefully dedicated to his therapist. The same resurgence of creativity that would lead to one of Rachmaninoff's best-loved works would also produce one of his finest, the Cello Sonata, which followed the Second Piano Concerto by only a few months.

There are those who suggest the Sonata may be Rachmaninoff's masterpiece, and it's easy to hear why. In this intimate yet turbulent work, the composer avoids most of the rhetorical pitfalls that can sabotage his other large-scale pieces; there is no hint of empty gesture or padding, and no suggestion that the music has been overcomposed. Instead, the Sonata's emotions—most notably its aching melancholy—are expressed with a disarming honesty and directness.

Lynn Harrell and Vladimir Ashkenazy are both subtle and explosive in this seethingly dramatic recording; the music is never allowed to degenerate into self-pity (in lesser hands, it certainly can), and the result is a pleasant mixture of freshness and doom. The encores are also handled quite magnificently, especially the often cloying *Vocalise,* which here sounds entrancingly virginal and sweet.

Symphony No. 2 in E minor

London Symphony, Previn. RCA 60791-R-RV [CD], 60791-4-RV [T].

There are two ways of viewing Rachmaninoff's E minor Symphony: as a late-Romantic dinosaur, completely out of step with its time, or as one of the lushest and loveliest symphonies ever written. Both views are correct. Compared to what was going on in music at the time it was written (1907), Rachmaninoff's finest orchestral work was a complete anachronism, a throwback to an era when unabashed sentiment was not yet a cause for embarrassment. For all its old-fashioned sentimentality, however, the Symphony is also an utterly genuine expression of the essence of the Romantic spirit.

For instance, if there is a Romantic symphony with a lovelier slow movement than the famous Adagio of this one, it has yet to be discovered.

André Previn has so far recorded the Symphony three times, and although his finest version, a London Symphony recording for Angel made in the mid-1970s, has been withdrawn, his first outing for RCA has now been reissued to fill the gap. Aside from a few standard cuts, the performance has all the thrust, exuberance, and compassion of the later recording, and what it may lack by way of the final measure of confidence, it makes up for with youthful exuberance and panache. An equally fine interpretation of *The Rock,* one of the composer's most strangely underrated and underplayed scores, is the generous filler.

Symphony No. 3 in A minor

**Concertgebouw Orchestra of Amsterdam, Ashkenazy.
London 410231-2 [CD].**

If an enthusiasm for this majestic anachronism is inexcusable (for who, aside from the Hollywood film composers, was producing this kind of deep-pile, wall-to-wall lushness in 1936?), then I beg to be excused. The Third Symphony, like the Second, is so hopelessly likable that I've never been able to understand those who shun it. I'd even go so far as to suggest that people who aren't moved at least in some small way by the great subordinate theme of the first movement (the one that sounds so much like the folk song "Shenandoah") are probably capable of *anything:* drowning puppies, eating babies, attending Philip Glass concerts . . .

Vladimir Ashkenazy whips up the Concertgebouw Orchestra into a fine Russian frenzy from the opening bars and never apologizes or attempts to housebreak the Symphony into something it isn't. Instead, in the words of Dostoyevsky, he lets it all hang out—which it does magnificently.

Vespers for Contralto, Tenor, and Unaccompanied Mixed Chorus

**Robert Shaw Festival Singers, Shaw. Telarc CD-80172
[CD].**

Composed only two years before the October Revolution, Rachmaninoff's *Vespers* of 1915 was probably the last important sacred work written in Russia; soon, such impulses would be totally subsumed in a state-controlled "spirituality" that would lead to countless deathless masterworks in praise of Stalin, the Motherland, and the latest hydroelectric dam.

Although we don't usually think of Rachmaninoff as a composer of sacred music, the *Vespers* contains moments of extraordinary depth and beauty: the evocation of the spirit—and often, it seems, the letter—of the Eastern Orthodox worship is uncanny, especially of those dark, unmistakably Russian services that combine awe and terror in roughly equal doses.

Although not as idiomatic as several Soviet recordings that have appeared over the years (and where else in the world can one find those rumbling, impossibly resonant basses?), Robert Shaw's performance is the best Western recording this singular masterpiece has yet received. Predictably, Shaw's forces are technically flawless, and they also manage to inject an unusually high percentage of the ineffable "spook element" into the score. The recording is suitably rich and warm.

Ravel, Maurice (1875–1937)

Alborada del gracioso; Boléro; Rapsodie espagnole; La Valse

> Montreal Symphony, Dutoit. London 410010-2 [CD], 410010-4 [T].

For anyone interested in four of Ravel's most popular showpieces in state-of-the-art performances and recorded sound, it would be difficult to improve upon this, one of Charles Dutoit's most impressive recordings to date. The playing of the Montreal Symphony is quite sensational: *La Valse* and *Rapsodie espagnole*, in particular, are barn-burners; *Boléro* has rarely sounded so sensual *and* civilized, and the brief *Alborada del gracioso* is an unmitigated delight. Superlatives fail me on this one. Buy it, and enjoy.

Concertos (2) for Piano and Orchestra

De Larrocha, piano; London Philharmonic, Foster. London 417583-2 [CD].

Ravel completed both of his piano concertos in 1931. They would prove to be his last major works, and the composer himself considered them his most important ones. (Ravel's pronouncements on his own music, like those of any composer, should be taken with a few pounds of salt, however. He once said, of *Boléro,* "I have written only one masterpiece. Alas, it contains no music.") The jazzy, elegant G Major Concerto, consciously written in the spirit of the Mozart concertos, and the dramatic Concerto for the Left Hand, produced for the Austrian pianist Paul Wittgenstein, who had lost his right arm during the First World War, are certainly *among* Ravel's finest and most enduring efforts. Apart from being a brilliant solution to an impossible technical challenge, the Concerto for the Left Hand is an endlessly imaginative and resourceful work (who but Ravel would introduce the soaring principal theme on the contrabassoon?). In addition to its wit and gaiety, the G Major Concerto contains one of Ravel's most ethereal inspirations, a seamless love song that recalls a Bach arioso.

Beginning with Marguerite Long, who introduced the G Major Concerto in 1932, both works have enjoyed a singular run of first-rate female interpreters, including their greatest living exponent, Alicia de Larrocha. From her thunderous entrance in the Concerto for the Left Hand to those otherworldly musings in the G Major's slow movement, there is virtually nothing in either concerto that she doesn't do better than anyone else. Lawrence Foster's accompaniments are similarly stylish, as is the remastered recorded sound.

Daphnis and Chloë (complete ballet)

Montreal Symphony, Dutoit. London 400055-2 [CD].

Ordinarily, London's withdrawal of Pierre Monteux's classic recording of the work that is widely regarded as Ravel's masterpiece could be viewed as an act of insensitivity bordering on criminal negligence. It was Monteux who introduced this spellbinding work to the world in 1911, and it was his recording, from the early days of the stereo era, that no one ever seriously expected to be surpassed. Although for historical reasons alone, London never should have even considered dropping it from its catalog, Charles Dutoit's stupendous recording takes at least some of the sting out of London's unforgivable crassness.

In many ways, this initial installment in Dutoit's fabulous Ravel series is still the most impressive. The dynamic range of both the performance and the recording is phenomenal, from the most delicate whispers in Ravel's diaphanous orchestration to the thunderous outbursts in the orgiastic final scene. Dutoit's command of the idiom is as complete and masterly as that of the greatest Ravel conductors of the past, and the playing of his impeccable orchestra cannot be praised too extravagantly. Clearly, this is already one of the milestones of the early digital era.

L'Enfant et les sortilèges

> Ogéas, Gilma, Berbié, Herzog, Sénéchal, Maurane, Rehfuss, French National Chorus and Orchestra, Maazel. Deustche Grammophon 423718-2 [CD].

In no other work was this most childlike of composers more obviously himself than in the enchanting one-act opera *L'Enfant et les sortilèges* (The Child and the Things of Magic). Working from an inspired text by Colette, Ravel not only fashioned one of his most mercurial scores, he also probed more surely and deeply into the mystery and magic of childhood than any composer ever had before. Only the considerable difficulties involved in staging this phantasmagorical work have prevented it from being more generally recognized as one of the supreme masterworks of modern opera.

Though *L'Enfant* has had indifferent luck in the theater, it has fared very well in the recording studio. The ideal reissue would have been the shimmering Angel recording led by André Previn, but Lorin Maazel's version from the early 1960s is very nearly as fine. The cast is an unusually strong one, featuring singers whose high level of vocal accomplishment is matched by their skillful projection of character. Yet the real star of the show is that strangely inconsistent conductor, who here seems to dip back into his own childhood for an interpretation the technical adroitness of which is matched only by its sense of wonderment.

The same company recorded Ravel's other one-act opera, *L'Heure espagnole,* at almost the same time with equally memorable results (Deutsche Grammophon 423719-2 [CD]). Both belong in any serious collection.

Introduction and Allegro for Harp, Flute, Clarinet, and String Quartet

Allen, harp; Wilson, flute; Shifrin, clarinet; Tokyo String Quartet. Angel CDC-47520 [CD].

The highlight of this recording, which is essentially a showcase for the talent of the lovely American harpist Nancy Allen, is the performance of Ravel's Introduction and Allegro, surely one of his most finespun inspirations and one of the most beautiful of twentieth-century chamber works. Allen and flutist Ransom Wilson are especially effective in drawing out the Introduction's dreaminess and gaiety, with excellent support from the rest of the high-powered talent. The Ravel and Debussy miniatures that fill out the album are also handsomely done.

While I generally disapprove of using serious music as background noise, aural wallpaper, or for any other nonmusical purpose (such as a sleeping pill or an aphrodisiac), this is one of those recordings which, when slipped on after a particularly miserable day, will make almost anyone human again.

Pavane for a Dead Princess; Mother Goose; Le Tombeau de Couperin; Valses nobles et sentimentales

Montreal Symphony, Dutoit. London 410254-2 [CD].

With the two brilliant recordings listed above, these stunning interpretations of four other popular works by Ravel all but complete Charles Dutoit's triumphant Ravel cycle. Versions of the two piano concertos with Pascal Rogé (London 410230-2 [CD]) are the only modern performances worthy of comparison with Alicia de Larrocha's hair-raising recording from the mid-1970s (see above).

As in his performances of *Daphnis and Chloë, Boléro, La Valse,* and the rest, Dutoit breathes an incredible freshness and vigor into these familiar works. For once, the famous *Pavane* does not come off as a cloying wad of sentimentality, and the other works are given performances as refined as they are exciting. Rarely have the closing bars of *Mother Goose* sounded so imposing, or the fabulously difficult music that begins *Le Tombeau de Couperin* been tossed off with such apparent ease. Again, London's engineers have provided Dutoit with demonstration-quality recorded sound, and again, the Montreal Symphony sounds like nothing less than one of the greatest orchestras in the world.

Piano Music (complete)

Crossley, piano. CRD 3383/4 [CD].

Like his witty, sensitive survey of the complete Poulenc piano music for CBS (see page 301), Paul Crossley's Ravel omnibus is one of the most engaging recordings of French piano music to have been released in years. While several individual performances might be preferred—Vladimir Ashkenazy's civilized yet immensely colorful *Gaspard de la nuit* for London (410255-2 [CD]), or Vlado Perlemuter's technically suspect but uniquely authoritative *Miroirs* for Nimbus (NI-5005 [CD])—each of Crossley's polished, stylish, refreshingly self-effacing interpretations ranks with the very best available today.

As a colorist, Crossley has much in common with that master of impressionistic understatement, Walter Gieseking; as a technician, his performances recall the pure, unobtrusive beauty Alicia de Larrocha brings to her Ravel recordings. *Le Tombeau de Couperin* has an almost Mozart-like poise and elegance, and in the gnarlier moments of *Valses nobles* and *Miroirs* Crossley has plenty of ready technique at his disposal. CRD's recorded sound is as pristine and luminous as the performances themselves.

String Quartet in F

See Debussy String Quartet, page 122.

Respighi, Ottorino (1879–1936)

Ancient Airs and Dances for Lute (3 sets); *The Birds*

Australian Chamber Orchestra, Gee. Omega OCD-1007 [CD].

Although the Sydney and Melbourne Symphonies—to name the two ensembles that are probably best known "Up Over"—have each made fine recordings, this may be the *finest* orchestral recording to have come out of Australia. If the Australian Chamber Orchestra's recordings of Schubert symphonies with Sir Charles Mackerras and an album of Strauss and Stravinsky with Christopher Lyndon Gee suggested they were a top-notch outfit, then this version of four popular Respighi works proves they are one of the great chamber orchestras of the world.

The competition in both *The Birds* and the popular *Ancient Airs and Dances* suites is ferocious. Sir Neville Marriner's recordings with the Academy of St. Martin-in-the-Fields and the Los Angeles Chamber Orchestra, to say nothing of Antal Dorati's classic version with the Philharmonia Hungarica, have set a standard in the *Ancient Airs* that many of us thought would never be approached. Similarly, wonderful recordings of *The Birds* have appeared and vanished, including a surprisingly nubile interpretation from Eugene Ormandy that CBS really can't afford *not* to reissue.

So along comes this recording by Gee and his plucky Aussies that blithely mops the floor with all of them. Not only are the performances extremely sophisticated, especially in the subtly shifting colors of the *Ancient Airs,* they also manage to convey a sense of discovery, wonderment, and enthusiasm that few recordings by professional musicians ever do. The recorded sound, like the playing itself, is impeccable, so much so that further Omega releases by the ACO are awaited with the keenest interest.

La Boutique fantasque

Toronto Symphony, A. Davis. Sony Classical MDK-46508 [CD], MDT-46508 [T].

Like those other classic pastiche ballets, Stavinsky's *Pulcinella* and Vincenzo Tommasini's adaptation of some Scarlatti sonatas called *The Good-Humored Ladies,* Respighi's *Boutique fantasque* is a startlingly successful fusion of two distinct styles and centuries. And nowhere is the orchestral genius of Ottorino Respighi more clearly evident than in this fizzing, luxurious concoction arranged from the melodies of Rossini.

Under Andrew Davis's inspired direction, the Toronto Symphony dance their way through this sparkling music as though they were one of the great orchestras of the world. No detail of the subtle, imaginative orchestral tissue escapes their attention, and the ballet's inner life emerges in a rush of joyous energy. The recorded sound is as sumptuous as the orchestration. The equally attractive fillers (Bizet's *Jeux d'enfants* and *L'Arlésienne* Suite No. 2) and Sony's medium price make this extremely difficult to turn down.

The Fountains of Rome; The Pines of Rome; Roman Festivals

Philadelphia Orchestra, Muti. Angel CDC-47316 [CD].

How unfortunate it is that this tremendously gifted composer had virtually no musical conscience or taste. (I have always thought it no accident that the word *pig* can be found within his name.) A wizard of the modern orchestra, and Italy's only significant non-operatic composer of the prewar era, Ottorino Respighi is best remembered for this triptych of tone poems celebrating the sights and sounds of his beloved Rome. Respighi's command of orchestration rivaled that of any composer who has ever lived, which is largely why these three pieces of unadulterated trash rank with the most popular orchestral showpieces of the twentieth century. (And like everyone else who has ever fallen under their vulgar spell, I love all three to distraction.)

Though nothing will ever make me give up my cherished RCA recording of the *Fountains* and *Pines* by Fritz Reiner and the Chicago Symphony (RCD1-5407 [CD]), the performances on Riccardo Muti's Angel recording are very much in that rarefied league. In addition, Muti gives us a spine-tingling run-through of the grisly *Roman Festivals,* my own nomination as the greatest single piece of musical schlock produced by anyone in the last hundred years. (The only other possible contender, Richard Addinsell's *Warsaw Concerto*, was written for a movie and only accidentally took on a macabre life of its own.) As in so many of their recent recordings, the playing of the Philadelphia Orchestra really must be heard to be believed. The last vestiges of Eugene Ormandy's "Philadelphia Sound" were all but eradicated by his dynamic successor. And while Muti may not be the most consistently profound or interesting conductor before the public today, he certainly deserves enormous credit for having revitalized a great American orchestra.

*M*etamorphosen modi XII; Belkis, Queen of Sheba (suite)

Philharmonia Orchestra, Simon. Chandos CHAN-8405 [CD].

One of the marks of true genius is its infinite capacity to renew, rejuvenate, and surpass itself. *Metamorphosen* is an academic, agreeably turgid series of variations on a medieval tune, but the music from *Belkis, Queen of Sheba* is something very special, even for Respighi.

Compared to *Belkis, Roman Festivals* is the *St. Matthew Passion*. The suite from this 1934 biblical ballet (and what one wouldn't give to hear the whole thing!) is so smarmy, so brazenly crude, so ineluctably vile, that *schlock* is a poor and trifling word to describe it. At this stratospheric level, trash ceases to be mere trash, and *Belkis* is a kind of final apotheosis of Respighian vulgarity. It's hardly surprising that the composer died only two years later. What was left to be done?

It goes without saying that I loved every millisecond of it, especially in Geoffrey Simon's resolutely wanton interpretation. The Philharmonia Orchestra comports itself like a band of shameless harlots, and the Chandos engineers capture every grunt and groan to perfection.

Rheinberger, Joseph

(1839–1901)

The Star of Bethlehem (Christmas cantata) for Soprano,
Baritone, Chorus, and Orchestra

Streich, soprano; Fischer-Dieskau, baritone; Bavarian Radio
Chorus, Graunke Symphony Orchestra, Heger. Carus
83.111 [CD].

The first composer of note to have emerged from the Duchy
of Liechtenstein, Joseph Rheinberger is remembered today (if he is
remembered at all) for some of the most fastidious and handsomely
made organ music of the nineteenth century. The two concertos and
twenty sonatas keep flitting in and out of the recording catalogs,
and still show up on concerts and recitals from time to time. What
Rheinberger *should* be remembered for is *Der Stern von Bethlehem*,
a touchingly innocent, sweet-spirited work that has somehow managed to escape becoming the Christmas classic it assuredly deserves
to be.

This fetching recording, which was available for a brief time
in the 1960s from Angel, is a charmer from beginning to end. Without so much as a wink of condescension, Robert Heger and his
dedicated forces make their way through this guileless little masterwork as though it were entitled to the same care and devotion
usually lavished on the *Christmas Oratorio*. The result is one of the
most captivating sleepers in recent memory.

Rimsky-Korsakov, Nikolai

(1844–1908)

Capriccio espagnol

New York Philharmonic, Bernstein. CBS MYK-36728
[CD], MYT-36728 [T].

CBS won't exactly make bargain hunters ecstatic with this
skimpy release, which combines Rimsky's Spanish travelogue with
Tchaikovsky's *Capriccio italien*. Even in the long-vanished LP days
that kind of "radical cheap" packaging would have been ballsy;
given today's CD and tape prices, it took—as my grandmother used
to say—some *real* stones.

On the other hand, the performances are vintage early Bernstein and are thus, in terms of sheer animal excitement, extremely
difficult to surpass. *Capriccio espagnol*, which was the original filler
for the conductor's *Pictures at an Exhibition*, is as seductive and
vibrant as ever; the solo display—most notably from the orchestra's
oboist, Harold Gomberg—matches anything from the rival Philadelphia Orchestra's heyday, and the closing bars flash by in a blind-
ing swatch of local color.

Scheherazade

Chicago Symphony, Reiner. RCA RCD1-7018 [CD].

Royal Philharmonic, Beecham. Angel CDC-47717 [CD].

It's difficult to think of anyone who better deserves the title
of History's Greatest Minor Composer. Saint-Saëns actually predicted that that was how posterity would remember *him*, but he was
forgetting about the work of this Russian near-giant. An orches-
trator and teacher of genius (his brilliant edition saved his friend
Mussorgsky's *Boris Godunov* from oblivion, and his best-known
pupil, of course, was Stravinsky), Rimsky-Korsakov never quite
grasped the greatness that always seemed to be just within reach.
For moments, even for entire acts of dazzling operas like *Le Coq*

d'or, Mlada, or *The Snow Maiden,* you can hear him on the verge of actually *doing* it, and then, inevitably, the music draws back at the very last.

By that same token, *Scheherazade,* one of history's most colorful and beautifully made orchestral scores, is also, in a sense, one of its most heartbreaking. It is a work that never quite adds up to much more than the sum of its fabulous parts: an elegant, vivid, brilliant, clever, colorful piece, but never a great one.

Among the many memorable recordings *Scheherazade* has had over the years, none has ever made it seem closer to being a great piece than the performance recorded in the late 1950s by Fritz Reiner and the Chicago Symphony. In spite of formidable competition from Sir Thomas Beecham and the Royal Philharmonic, whose legendary interpretation recorded at about the same time remains the last word in individuality, charm, and staggeringly inventive solo display, Reiner's combination of near-perfect execution, finesse, and unadulterated sex makes this—by a whisker—*the* performance of *Scheherazade* to own. The original recorded sound has been dramatically improved for the compact disc, which, as a bonus, includes that most electrifying of all recordings of Debussy's *La Mer* (see page 119).

Suites from the Operas (*Christmas Eve; Le Coq d'or; The Legend of the Invisible City of Kitezh; May Night; Mlada; The Snow Maiden; Tsar Saltan*)

> Scottish National Orchestra, Järvi. Chandos CHAN-8327/9 [CD].

As Dmitri Shostakovich may or may not have pointed out in *Testimony* (the authorship of the controversial memoirs is still in question), for more than a decade Rimsky-Korsakov suffered from a debilitating emotional disease called Piotr Ilyich Tchaikovsky. "Tchaikovsky kept Korsakov from composing, interfered simply by existing," Shostakovich (or someone) observed. "For ten years, Rimsky-Korsakov couldn't write an opera and after Tchaikovsky's death he wrote eleven operas in fifteen years. And it's interesting to note that this flood began with *Christmas Eve.* As soon as Tchaikovsky died, Korsakov took a theme already used by Tchaikovsky and rewrote it his way."

Whoever proposed the theory, it does have a dreary and peculiarly Russian ring of truth; for with the passing of his archantagonist, Rimsky-Korsakov did enter the most fruitful period of his creative life, producing the bulk of the music on which his reputation, at least in Russia, continues to rest.

Why his operas have never gained a significant toehold in the West remains a baffling mystery. Some, like *Le Coq d'or,* are as masterly as any Slavic opera short of Smetana's *Bartered Bride* and Mussorgsky's *Boris Godunov,* and many of them—as this gorgeous series of recordings from Chandos will show—contain some of his most distinctive and original music, from the eerie mystery of the *Invisible City of Kitezh* to the delightful *Christmas Eve,* whose stirring Polonaise is alone worth the price of admission.

This is possibly the best, and certainly one of the most valuable, of the many recordings the rather overexposed Neeme Järvi has made. Honed to a fine edge, the Scottish National Orchestra cuts through the formidable difficulties of this music with ease, and the conductor has a genuine knack for revealing both its obvious and hidden treasures. Those with a sweet tooth for *Scheherazade* will have a fine time gorging themselves on these equally tasty goodies; the more shameless gluttons will also want Järvi's more workmanlike, yet utterly worthy, versions of *Antar* and the other two symphonies, the *Capriccio espagnol,* and the *Russian Easter Overture,* all shoehorned onto a pair of Deutsche Grammophon compact discs (423604-2).

Rodrigo, Joaquín (1901–)

Concierto de Aranjuez for Guitar and Orchestra

Williams, guitar; English Chamber Orchestra, Barenboim.
CBS MK-33208 [CD].

Angel Romero, guitar; London Symphony, Previn. Angel
CDC-47693 [CD], 4AM-34716 [T].

Like the dippy Pachelbel *Kanon,* Joaquín Rodrigo's *Concierto de Aranjuez* has become a big classical hit in the last dozen years, and its popularity is richly deserved. Written with the great Andrés Segovia in mind, Rodrigo's *Concierto* is easily the finest such work ever composed for the instrument: a work that not only exploits virtually all of the rather limited expressive possibilities of the guitar, but also provides us with one of the most haunting of all musical evocations of the sights and sounds of Spain.

To date, John Williams has recorded the *Concierto* no fewer than four times, and it is his version with Daniel Barenboim and the English Chamber Orchestra that is still the most completely satisfying recording the piece has ever received. Technically, Williams is without equal among living guitarists, and here, as in all his recordings, he tosses off the *Concierto*'s formidable difficulties as though they didn't even exist. Yet unlike his other versions, this performance has a freshness and spontaneity that no other recording can begin to match. Thanks, no doubt, to Barenboim's rich and flexible accompaniment, Williams is allowed to phrase and emote with a freedom he has rarely shown on records before or since. As the interpretation is currently available only as compact disc, the Angel Romero–André Previn recording for Angel would be my first choice among available tapes. Romero's playing is nearly as brilliant and refreshing as Williams's, and instead of the Villa-Lobos Guitar Concerto that comes with the Williams recording, this one offers the more conventional (and desirable) coupling of Rodrigo's equally enchanting *Fantasia para un gentilhombre.*

Concierto madrigal for Two Guitars and Orchestra; Concierto Andaluz for Four Guitars and Orchestra

The Romeros, guitars; Academy of St. Martin-in-the-Fields, Marriner. Philips 400024-2 [CD].

It has been suggested that with the *Concierto de Aranjuez* of 1939, Rodrigo stumbled upon a formula so successful that he was content to build a career out of rewriting the piece indefinitely. Even if this were perfectly true (which it isn't, quite), who could possibly care? Only the naive or the very young tend to prefer the idea of originality to the reality of cleverness, since the latter is a precious, hard-won skill and the former, for all practical purposes, simply doesn't exist. Besides, if an idea is a good one and the market will bear it, by all means, use it again. Bach, Handel, Rossini, Stravinsky, and numberless other lesser figures never felt any qualms about re- cycling their own, as well as other composer's, ideas; and the com- poser of *Star Wars* and other hugely successful film scores has grown wealthy and famous by scrupulously avoiding *any* musical idea that might even remotely be called his own. (The list of com- posers and specific works that have "inspired" John Williams is a long and eclectic one and would make a fascinating little book; at very least, it might be turned into a documented monograph that the powers that be at ASCAP might be interested to read.)

If they *are* warmed-over versions of *Concierto de Aranjuez*, then *Concierto madrigal* and *Concierto Andaluz* prove what every mother knows, to wit, that leftovers can often be every bit as delicious—if not more so—than the original meal. These gracefully melodious and instantly assimilable works are thoroughgoing de- lights, especially in performances such as these. The gifted, extrovert Romeros play the concertos as though they had been written spe- cifically for them—which, as a matter of fact, they were.

Sir Neville Marriner's accompaniments and Philips's recorded sound are worthy of both the soloists and the music itself.

Rossini, Gioacchino

(1792–1868)

The Barber of Seville

Callas, Alva, Gobbi, Philharmonia Orchestra and Chorus,
Galliera. Angel CDCB-47634 [CD].

Despite some formidable competition from the beautifully
sung and brilliantly recorded Philips recording led with high and
obvious zest by Sir Neville Marriner (411058-2 [CD], 411058-4
[T]), this imperishable Angel release, for all its flaws, remains the
most enchanting and infectious recorded performance of the
world's most popular opera buffa. The supporting cast is consistently excellent, especially the irreplaceable Tito Gobbi and the exceptionally suave Almaviva of Luigi Alva, and the star of the show,
Maria Callas, in one of her rare comic roles proves that she was
every bit as successful a comedienne as she was a tragic heroine.
Listen, especially, to the way she teases the phrases in "Una voce
poco fa," and you'll begin to understand why we Callas cuckoos
immediately begin to salivate at the mere mention of the woman's
name. Although niggling cuts have been made throughout the performance and the recorded sound is not up to today's standards,
there is a sparkling, good-natured sense of fun in this famous interpretation that will probably never be captured in a recording studio again.

La Cenerentola

Baltsa, Araiza, Alaimo, Raimondi, Ambrosian Opera
Chorus, Academy of St. Martin-in-the-Fields, Marriner.
Philips 420468-2 [CD].

Rossini's daffy retelling of the Cinderella story is proof positive that there was always more to the composer than a handful of
overtures and *The Barber of Seville*. Until the bel canto revival of
the 1950s and '60s, it certainly might have seemed that those were
his only works, for the simple reason that the florid vocal writing

in operas like *Cinderella* is so daunting that most singers simply opted for the better part of valor. To compound the problem, the title role, like that of Isabella in *L'Italiana in Algeri,* is written for a coloratura contralto, which is about as common these days as articulate vice presidents or two-headed sheep. (For that matter, *true* contraltos of any kind are an all but extinct species. If you don't believe it, dig out any of Ernestine Schumann-Heink's old recordings and try to find even the vaguest approximation of that sort of instrument today.)

The only solution in such a vocally benighted age as ours is a mezzo with the range and agility of an Agnes Baltsa. Though she is not entirely believable as Rossini's helpless waif—the size and power of the voice place it roughly in the dreadnought class—Baltsa's energy and accuracy more than save the day. With stylish contributions from Francisco Araiza and Ruggero Raimondi, and the bubbly conducting of Sir Neville Marriner, *La Cenerentola* emerges as the uproarious masterpiece many are only now discovering it to be.

In *L'Italiana in Algeri,* an even funnier opera (not witty, not amusing, but bust-a-gut-laughing *funny*), Baltsa and Raimondi are even more impressive, while Claudio Abbado's conducting, like Marriner's, is an essay in the art of comic timing. The sense of presence in this Deutsche Grammophon recording (427331-2 [CD]) is exceptional, as is the playing of the Vienna Philharmonic.

Overtures

Academy of St. Martin-in-the-Fields, Marriner. Philips 412893-2 [CD].

Orpheus Chamber Orchestra. Deutsche Grammophon 415363-2 [CD].

London Symphony, Abbado. Deutsche Grammophon 419869-2 [CD].

Philharmonia Orchestra, Giulini. Angel CDM-69042 [CD].

London Classical Players, Norrington. Angel CDC-54091 [CD], 4DS-54091 [T].

Chicago Symphony, Reiner. RCA 60387-2-RG [CD], 60387-4-RG [T].

The seven familiar overtures and one oddity (*Otello*) in Sir Neville Marriner's collection are all that survive from one of the more quixotic projects in recent recording history: the complete survey of the surviving Rossini overtures that circulated for a time on a set of four Philips LPs. It would be good to have *all* those performances transferred to CD. For in addition to some genuinely arcane material (the *Demetrio e Polibio* Overture remains my favorite), the interpretations—as can be gathered from this sampling—were bursting with vitality and an unmistakably Rossinian sense of humor.

Humor and vitality also characterize the performances by the Orpheus Chamber Orchestra. In what may still be the group's finest recording to date (and given their list of outstanding releases, that's saying a very great deal), they demonstrate fairly conclusively that a conductor's baton is the cheapest instrument there is.

Among recordings made by Italian conductors, those by Claudio Abbado and Carlo Maria Giulini are the most appealing. Aside from being superbly idiomatic, each brings out the lovely singing quality of the music and more than a little of its whiplash excitement. For instance, the Giulini *William Tell* goes out in such a spectacular cloud of dust that a colleague of mine—after a stunned pause of several seconds—announced on the air: "And just think, he was originally going to call it *Pavane for a Dead Princess*."

Roger Norrington and his plucky London Classical Players offer a series of hair-trigger performances on period instruments that manage to sound neither pendantic nor stodgy. The conductor's tempos have an exhilarating bite and lift, the orchestral fabric a wonderfully piquant edge.

Finally, as performances or recordings, no versions of these popular works have ever superseded the scintillating recordings Fritz Reiner and the Chicago Symphony made in 1958. The brass play with an awesome grandeur and solidity, the strings are rich yet nimble, and the woodwinds have all the personality of characters straight out of commedia dell'arte. This is a gifted conductor and the great American orchestra of its time captured at the height of their powers in phenomenally remastered recorded sound.

Sonatas for Strings

Camerata Bern. Deutsche Grammophon 413310-2 [CD].

The question of how one of the laziest composers in history managed to accomplish so much in so little time (after the premiere of *William Tell,* he retired to a life of indolence at the age of thirty-seven) is answered in part by these six miraculous little works: he got a *very* early start. Composed when Rossini was only twelve, the String Sonatas, like the equally precocious Wind Quartets, reveal a talent almost as highly evolved as Mozart's was at a comparable age.

If you have a youthful musical underachiever in your household, these glistening performances by Camerata Bern might just do the trick: the wunderkind will either be spurred on to greater efforts by the young Rossini's example, or will be discouraged completely. Either way, you can't lose.

William Tell

Pavarotti, Freni, Milnes, Ghiaurov, Ambrosian Opera Chorus, National Philharmonic, Chailly. London 417154-2 [CD].

Shortly after its triumphant first production at the Paris Opéra in 1829, *William Tell* began to fall victim to the editor's blue pencil. Within the year, performances were being trimmed ever more drastically. There is a famous story that has one of the composer's ardent admirers telling him, "I heard Act Two of *William Tell* at the opera last night." "What?" Rossini is alleged to have replied. "The whole of it?"

The whole of this uneven work that Rossini consciously intended to be his masterpiece can last upwards of five hours in the theater. It is far more easily—and profitably—digested in the comfort of one's living room, especially in as compelling a production as this one. Opting for Italian instead of the original French, Riccardo Chailly leads a fiery, deeply committed, handsomely sung performance that makes one overlook the opera's excessive length. (When consumed an act at a time, it doesn't seem excessive at all.) All of the principals are excellent, particularly Sherrill Milnes in the title role, and London's top-of-the-line 1978 recorded sound remains breathtaking.

Ryba, Jakub Jan (1765–1815)

Czech Christmas Mass

Soloists, Czech Philharmonic Chorus and Orchestra,
Smetáček. Fidelio CD-1809 [CD].

This vastly productive, thoroughly miserable composer—he
wrote more than 120 Masses alone and died by his own hand at the
age of forty-nine—was one of the first Bohemians to write serious
music to Czech texts. As such, Ryba has belatedly begun to be recognized in Czechoslovakia as one of the most important precursors
of Smetana and the other members of the national school.

An utterly enchanting Mass setting interspersed with a folksy
retelling of the nativity tale, the *Czech Christmas Mass* is probably
Ryba's masterpiece. Disarming, simple, and completely unaffected,
it is—like Rheinberger's *Star of Bethlehem* (see page 334)—a work
that could easily become one of the best-loved Christmas classics if
only given half a chance.

Václav Smetáček and his forces make a wholly sympathetic
case for the piece: the performance glows with good will and innocent warmth, and the recorded sound, while slightly distant, is
otherwise superb.

Saint-Saëns, Camille
(1835–1921)

Carnival of the Animals

New York Philharmonic, Bernstein. CBS MYK-37765
[CD], MYT-37765 [T].

Ironically enough, it was for a work he refused to have performed in public during his lifetime that the vastly prolific and once enormously popular Camille Saint-Saëns remains best known today. While much of his tuneful, ingratiating, always impeccably crafted music has apparently begun to lose its grip on the modern imagination, the ageless *Carnival of the Animals* has never gone begging for first-class recorded performances.

I have some very vivid memories of a Leonard Bernstein Young People's Concert in which it was first explained to me that the cuckoo was represented by the clarinet, the swan by the cello, and so forth. I bought the Bernstein recording soon afterward (one of the first records in my collection that did *not* have an erotic cover) and have cherished the performance ever since. Bernstein brings an obvious and unmistakable enthusiasm to both his narration and to the music. The soloists and the orchestra play with passion and devotion, and the early-1960s recorded sound is still very serviceable. In its most recent incarnation, the performance comes with an equally memorable—and when the horns get wound up, terrifically scary—interpretation of Prokofiev's *Peter and the Wolf*.

Concertos (5) for Piano and Orchestra

Rogé, piano; London Philharmonic, Philharmonia
Orchestra, Royal Philharmonic, Dutoit. London
417351-2 [CD].

To use a grating contemporary phrase, the five Saint-Saëns piano concertos are very user-friendly works, meaning, among other things, that they are very easy to access. (This gradual pollution of the language through daily wear and tear is what the

345

French poet Paul Valéry was thinking about when he was asked what poets really *did*. "That's simple," he said. "Each night you have to take a ten-franc whore and try to turn her into a virgin.")

Pleasant, shallow, unstintingly professional, and as easy on the mind as they are on the ear (for a man like Saint-Saëns, requiring his listeners to think simply wouldn't have been civilized), they rank with the Tchaikovsky suites and the Vivaldi concertos as some of the greatest elevator music ever written.

Pascal Rogé releases all their genuine charm without trying to turn them into something they're not. For instance, in the popular Second Concerto, which pianists are often tempted to inflate into something larger than it can really become, he maintains a decidedly laissez-faire interpretative touch, which compromises neither the work's essentially lighthearted character nor its moments of virtuoso display. Charles Dutoit is an equally levelheaded advocate of this music, providing accompaniments that give the composer and the listener precisely what they want.

Among recordings of Saint-Saëns's other instrumental concertos, Yo-Yo Ma is at his most elegant in his version of the A minor Cello Concerto; Cho-Liang Lin and Michael Tilson Thomas give us what is easily the most electric performance of the Third Violin Concerto ever recorded, and possibly the most exciting Saint-Saëns recording now in print. Sony has sensibly rereleased these exceptional recordings—together with Cecile Licad's fine performance of the Second Piano Concerto—on a single CD (MDK-46506) and tape (MDT-46506).

Danse macabre; Le Rouet d'Omphale; Phaéton; Carnival of the Animals

> Philharmonia Orchestra, Dutoit. London 414460-2 [CD], 414460-4 [T].

What would have made this an even more welcome addition to the catalog is a recording of the last of Saint-Saëns's four tone poems, *La Jeunesse d'Hercule,* instead of the surprisingly lackluster run-through of *Carnival of the Animals* that accompanies the other three. But no matter, for these are the most articulate and individual versions of *Danse macabre* and *Omphale's Spinning Wheel* in a generation, and even the slightly stuffy *Phaéton,* in Dutoit's tactful face-lift, seems fresher than it ever has before.

Samson et Dalila

Domingo, Obraztsova, Bruson, Lloyd, Thau, Chorus and Orchestre de Paris, Barenboim. Deustche Grammophon 413297-2 [CD].

After *Carmen* and *Faust*, *Samson et Dalila* has been the most enduringly popular of all French operas, in spite of the fact that it took a surprisingly long time to catch on. When a single act was given in Paris in 1875, two years prior to the Weimar premiere, critics chided it for its lack of memorable melody and its mundane orchestration. Of course, in addition to its lavish spectacle, exotic orientalisms, and moving human drama, *Samson*'s wealth of unforgettable, luxuriantly scored melody is what has kept it alive all these years.

Of the available recorded *Samsons*, Daniel Barenboim's version is by far the best compromise. Placido Domingo makes an imposing, gloriously sung hero, and Barenboim's conducting misses none of the score's grandeur (the big choral scenes are especially thrilling) and very few of its more subtle details. The problem is Elena Obraztsova, who is curiously sexless as the Philistine sexpot.

Rita Gorr, on a competing Angel set, makes a sensationally vivid Dalila, but that performance is seriously marred by Georges Prêtre's unimaginative conducting. The long-rumored Dutoit version may change the picture completely, but until then, this generally exciting (and moderately priced) effort will do.

Symphony No. 3 in C minor, *Organ*

Hurford, organ; Montreal Symphony, Dutoit. London 410201-2 [CD].

Zamkochian, organ; Boston Symphony, Munch. RCA 60817-2-RG [CD], 60817-4-RG [T].

The only one of Saint-Saëns's symphonies that is ever performed these days owes much of its current popularity to the recording industry. In the mid-1950s, when the record companies were casting about for "sonic spectaculars" to show off the revolutionary wonders of stereo, the *Organ* Symphony began to enjoy a new lease on life. Along with Paul Paray's wonderful Mercury recording with the Detroit Symphony, Charles Munch's classic

Boston Symphony recording dominated the catalogs for decades. It had fire, a healthy measure of Munchian madness, stupendous playing from the orchestra, and recorded sound to raise the roof—which it still does in its compact disc reissue. In fact, the Munch recording would remain the obvious first choice were it not for the even more extraordinary interpretation led by Charles Dutoit.

What makes the Dutoit such a great performance is as easy to hear as it is difficult to describe. In its simplest terms, this is the one recording of the *Organ* Symphony that actually makes the piece sound like what it most assuredly is *not:* a great work. The conductor captures most of the Symphony's color and dramatic gestures, but for once the gestures seem internal and natural, as opposed to the empty, bombastic postures that they probably are. In short, along with its freshness, intelligence, and subtlety, this is the only version of the *Organ* Symphony in my experience in which we seem to be hearing music of genuine grandeur, instead of something merely grandiose.

Satie, Erik (1866–1925)

Piano Music

Rogé, piano. London 410220-2 [CD], 410220-4 [T].

Whether the arch-eccentric Erik Satie was an important composer or merely a fascinating crank is really beside the point. Since the 1960s he has attracted an ever-widening public, and for the time being he should be taken as seriously as the relatively brisk sales of Satie recordings would seem to demand.

Aside from the famous crackpot titles ("Desiccated Embryos," "Flabby Preludes for a Dog," and "Sketches to Make You Run Away" must be the choicest), the celebrated publicity stunts (for the premiere of his ballet *Parade*, Picasso painted a huge sign on the curtain which read, "Erik Satie is the greatest composer in the world. Anyone who disagrees with this statement is kindly asked to leave"), and the unquestioned influence he had on younger French composers, Satie was essentially a gifted, if largely unlettered, dilettante whose most inspired creation was his own bizarre public image.

Pascal Rogé's recital of some of the composer's best-known works will go a long way to making at least partial believers out of the more devout Satie skeptics, like me. The beautifully austere and justly popular *Gymnopédies* are given serenely rapt performances, and the versions of the six *Gnossiennes, Embryons desséchés* (which isn't quite as good as its title), and miniatures like *Je te veux* and the *Bureaucratic Sonatine* are hardly less inspired. A second volume (421713-2 [CD], 421713-4 [T]) in what presumably will be an ongoing Satie series is just as memorable, though in the case of this composer, more can quickly turn out to be much, *much* less.

Among recordings of the Debussy orchestrations of the first and third *Gymnopédies*, the most desirable is probably Michel Plasson's on Angel with the Toulouse Capitole Orchestra (CDC-49471 [CD]). Although Charles Dutoit, Georges Prêtre, and Leonard Slatkin all lead more successful performances per se, Plasson's come as part of a generous all-Satie album, which includes the ballets *Parade* and *Relâche,* together with other orchestrations by Milhaud and Poulenc.

Scarlatti, Domenico
(1685–1757)

Keyboard Sonatas

> Pinnock, harpsichord. Deutsche Grammophon 419632-2 [CD].
>
> Pinnock, harpsichord. CRD CD-3368 [CD], 4068 [T].
>
> Yepes, guitar. Deutsche Grammophon 413783-2 [CD].

An exact contemporary of George Frideric Handel and Johann Sebastian Bach (1685 was one of the great vintage years in the history of music), Domenico Scarlatti was to the harpsichord what Chopin would later be to the piano: the first important composer to study the special characteristics of his chosen instrument, and then write music specifically designed to show off its individual character and peculiar strengths. His output of keyboard music was as prodigious as it was inspired. In 1971, a facsimile edition of the complete music for keyboard was published in eighteen densely packed volumes. The truly devoted and/or demented can now acquire all 555 of them on a set of thirty-four (34) Erato compact discs (45309-2), wheelbarrow not included.

It's a great pity that all the recordings featuring the father of modern Scarlatti scholarship, Ralph Kirkpatrick, are now out of print. His book *Scarlatti,* published in 1953, not only instantly became the standard work about the composer, but also helped clear up the centuries-old muddling of the order of composition of Scarlatti's numerous works. Kirkpatrick's performances were predictably enthusiastic and sympathetic, as are those of Trevor Pinnock, whose several recordings for Deutsche Grammophon and CRD are also models of modern Baroque scholarship and musical sensitivity.

For those who don't give a hang about authenticity, the wonderfully delicate and entrancing arrangements by the Spanish guitarist Narciso Yepes are almost impossible to resist. (I once knew someone who absolutely hated them, but he eventually became an ax murderer or a politician, I can't remember which. In any event, none of his friends were terribly surprised.)

Schmidt, Franz (1874–1939)

Symphony No. 4

Vienna Philharmonic, Mehta. London 430007-2 [CD].

The Viennese have an abiding affection for the music of Franz Schmidt, an Austrian composer who was an exact contemporary of Arnold Schoenberg and a spiritual descendant of Anton Bruckner and Gustav Mahler. It was while studying in Vienna with Hans Swarowsky that Zubin Mehta came to love Schmidt's music, and his interpretation of the composer's mighty Fourth Symphony might make you love it as well.

Although echoes of Schmidt's great predecessors can be heard throughout this late-Romantic masterpiece, it presents a personality and point of view very much of its own. More closely argued than Bruckner, less neurotic than Mahler, the Fourth is a work of enormous sweep and power that commands the listener's attention from beginning to end. Mehta inspires the Vienna Philharmonic to play the Symphony as no other orchestra in the world possibly could, and the recorded sound is both sumptuous and detailed. Mehta's gleaming Los Angeles Philharmonic version of Schoenberg's Chamber Symphony No. 1 comes as an attractive and altogether appropriate bonus.

Those who find themselves responding to this strangely overlooked composer—as those who respond to Bruckner and Mahler undoubtedly will—should waste no time investigating two other superb Schmidt releases: Neeme Järvi's Chandos recordings of the Second Symphony (CHAN-8779 [CD], ABTD-1415 [T]) and Third (CHAN-9000 [CD], ABTD-1582), both of live concert performances with the great Chicago Symphony in full cry.

Schoenberg, Arnold

(1874–1951)

Cello Concerto (after Harpsichord Concerto of Georg Matthias Monn)

Ma, cello; Boston Symphony, Ozawa. CBS MK-39863 [CD].

As much as I am tempted to ride this personal hobbyhorse into the ground, I will resist making any emotional (and they would be thoroughly heartfelt) appeals on behalf of the music of Arnold Schoenberg, the most significant composer of the twentieth century, and probably the *best* composer since Johannes Brahms. The Schoenberg debate will continue to rage long after all of us are gone and forgotten. (Why is it that in writing of Schoenberg, one always, and almost automatically, slips into such cheerful images and turns of phrase? Perhaps because this melancholy figure remains the most thoroughly misunderstood composer in history.) In fact, the great bogeyman of the early twentieth-century avant-garde, the man whose experiments with atonality, serialism, and the twelve-tone technique "destroyed" music as we know it, was in fact the most conservative composer since Bach: an arch-Romantic who perceived—correctly—that if Western music were to go on at all, it needed an entirely new language. (The five-hundred-year-old system of triadic tonality that had made such music possible had simply worn out.)

Even if you shudder at the mere mention of Schoenberg's name, you probably won't be able to resist the Cello Concerto, a work so puppy-dog friendly that even the most musically shy five-year-old can embrace it with pleasure. Beginning with a happy little tune that bears a striking resemblance to "Rule, Britannia," Schoenberg's adaptation of a harpsichord concerto by the eighteenth-century Austrian composer Georg Matthias Monn is one of his most impressive essays in virtuoso orchestration: bells tinkle, the woodwinds jabber, and the solo instrument is all but asked to stand on its head. Although the cello part is allegedly one of the most difficult ever written for the instrument, Yo-Yo Ma glides through it with ease and obvious relish, and Seiji Ozawa's contribution could not have been more sympathetic or alert.

A more substantial but equally unthreatening work, the Concerto for String Quartet and Orchestra, presents Schoenberg the pedagogue showing Handel, in one of his occasionally slipshod Op. 6 concerti grossi, how the thing *really* ought to have been done. Listening to one great master gently wagging his finger at another—and producing a freestanding masterpiece in the process—is a delightfully amusing experience, particularly in the witty, openhearted performance by the American String Quartet and the New York Chamber Orchestra led by Gerard Schwarz (Nonesuch 79145-2 [CD], 79145-4 [T]).

Five Pieces for Orchestra

Berlin Philharmonic, Levine. Deutsche Grammophon
419781-2 [CD].

After leading the American premiere of the Five Pieces for Orchestra in Boston, the misanthropic German conductor Karl Muck announced with his customary tact, "I can't tell you whether we've played *music,* but I assure you we've played every one of Schoenberg's notes, just as they were written." Curiously, there are still those who entertain similar doubts about this modern masterpiece, more than eighty years after it was composed. With *Pierrot Lunaire,* the monodrama *Erwartung,* and the closing moments of the Second String Quartet, the Five Pieces represent the summit of Schoenberg's experiments with nontonal (he detested the word *atonal*) music: a work of stupefying originality and beauty that should be heard as frequently as the *Eroica* Symphony or *The Rite of Spring.*

In one of his best recordings in years, James Levine leads the Berlin Philharmonic in a subtle, powerful, superbly colored performance of this early Schoenberg masterpiece, in which the musical argument becomes very nearly as lucid as anything in the music of Schoenberg's favorite composers, Mozart and Brahms. With equally loving and perceptive versions of Berg's Three Pieces for Orchestra and Webern's Six Pieces, Op. 6, this is now the best single-disc collection of orchestral music by the three giants of the Second Viennese School.

Now then, if the same forces would only move on to one or two other Schoenberg items, like the Op. 31 Variations (which the Berlin Philharmonic introduced under Furtwängler in 1928), the orchestral versions of the Chamber Symphonies, the Violin Concerto (with Perlman), the Piano Concerto (with Pollini), *A Survivor from Warsaw* (which might take some guts), the brief but delectable *Begleitungsmusik zu einer Lichtspielszene* (Accompaniment to a Cinema Scene), and the rarely heard Suite in G for Strings, I could die a happy man.

Gurrelieder

> Norman, Troyanos, McCracken, Klemperer, Tanglewood Festival Chorus, Boston Symphony Orchestra, Ozawa. Philips 412511-2 [CD].

Gurrelieder, Schoenberg's magnificent orchestral song cycle/ oratorio, is both the perfect introduction to his early style and one of the last great masterpieces of Romantic music. If you are one of those people who turn up their noses at the mere mention of Schoenberg'sname, *Gurrelieder* might just be the medicine to cure you of a most unfortunate ailment.

While this Philips recording is not the ideal *Gurrelieder*, it is, for the most part, a very good one. The strongest things about it are the Tove of Jessye Norman, the speaker of Werner Klemperer, the playing of the Boston Symphony, and the excitement a live performance always generates. James McCracken struggles heroically with one of the most difficult tenor parts ever written, but this is not an especially comfortable or attractive performance, and the usually reliable Tatiana Troyanos is unexpectedly wobbly as the Wood Dove. Seiji Ozawa, as usual, leads an interpretation that scores very high marks for the beauties of its physical sound and the attention to detail, but that nevertheless tends to gloss over the more profound elements in the music. Still, in spite of its flaws, this recording belongs in every collection, especially since a *Gurrelieder* from Carlos Kleiber or Klaus Tennstedt is *not* on the horizon and probably shouldn't be expected any time soon.

Alas, the performance is not currently being offered on cassette.

Moses und Aron

> Mazura, Langridge, Bonney, Haugland, Chicago Symphony Orchestra and Chorus, Solti. London 414264-2 [CD].

There will always be a special place in hell for the well-known foundation (name withheld to prevent all right-thinking people from sending them several letter bombs per day) that turned down Arnold Schoenberg's modest request for sufficient funds to complete his oratorio *Jacobsleiter*, and one of the great unfinished works in musical history, *Moses und Aron*. (This same foundation, by the way, regularly doles out hefty grants to feckless boobs who, to quote my grandfather, if they had to take a trip on brains wouldn't have to pack a lunch.) Be that as it may, even without the music of its third act (the composer did complete the moving text), *Moses und Aron* easily ranks with the most intriguing and important of all twentieth-century operas. Were it given performances like this one on a regular basis, it might become, if not another *Bohème*, then at least a work that would be performed with something approaching the frequency it deserves.

Sir Georg Solti, in one of the finest recordings he has made since the completion of London's Vienna *Ring*, places both the opera and Schoenberg where they properly belong. It has often been suggested that Schoenberg only wanted to rewrite the music of Johannes Brahms for the twentieth century. The suggestion is ludicrous, of course, but it contains at least a grain of truth. For Schoenberg, even in the most advanced of his twelve-tone works, remained an unrepentant Romantic to the very end. Unlike the other fine recordings of *Moses und Aron* (by Pierre Boulez and Michael Gielen, both out of print), it is the Solti version that most clearly recognizes the Romantic elements in this rich and moving opera and makes them work. Rarely, for instance, has the most famous moment in the score, "The Dance Around the Gold Calf," sounded more lurid (in fact, the entire scene is a triumph of prurient interest, as the composer intended), and never have the difficult principal roles been more effortlessly or beautifully sung.

The Chicago Symphony, as always, is miraculous in its poise and execution, and the recorded sound is stunning in its warmth and detail. Be warned, *Moses und Aron* is no *Aida;* still, it is a very great work that will repay in abundance any investment of time and energy the listener is willing to make.

Piano Music (complete)

Pollini, piano. Deutsche Grammophon 423249-2 [CD].

I suspect that the reason Schoenberg's piano music turns up so rarely on recitals has less to do with the resistance of the audience than it does with the perfectly understandable unwillingness of pianists to play it. There is nothing about this important, serious music that could possibly attract a shallow or self-serving performer, and pianists—bless them—are no more profound or altruistic as a group than any of the rest of us.

Like the composer's friend and longtime champion Eduard Steuermann, whose old Columbia recordings were among the great documents of modern music-making, Maurizio Pollini is one of those rare performers who are able to grapple with the music on its own uncompromising terms and yet make it seem as though they were doing it out of love and not some misplaced sense of duty. The performances are as sensitive and dramatic as his interpretations of Beethoven, Schubert, and Chopin, and should win these passionate, rarefied, uniquely lyrical works many friends.

*P*ierrot Lunaire

DeGaetani, speaker; Contemporary Chamber Ensemble, Weisberg. Nonesuch 79237-2 [CD], 71251-4 [T].

Stravinsky's *Rite of Spring* and Schoenberg's *Pierrot Lunaire* are the two great watersheds of modern music. The latter is a piece of such staggering originality and inventiveness that it still seems as though it might have been written yesterday, instead of the year 1912.

This classic recording with Jan DeGaetani and Arthur Weisberg's Contemporary Chamber Ensemble on Nonesuch is the closest thing we have yet had to an ideal realization of *Pierrot Lunaire*. DeGaetani, who made her formidable reputation by singing the most impossibly difficult contemporary music as though it had been written by Stephen Foster, weaves her way through Schoenberg's eerie, mysteriously beautiful *Sprechstimme* as though she were telling us stories from Mother Goose (which, after all, is not that far removed from what the *Pierrot* speaker is supposed to do). The highest praise that can be lavished on the accompaniment she receives from Weisberg and company is that it is altogether worthy of this legendary modern performance.

*S*tring Quartets (5)

LaSalle Quartet. Deutsche Grammophon 419994-2 [CD].

Like so many of his major works, Schoenberg's Quartets have been shrouded in misunderstanding and neglect for so many decades that coming to them for the first time can make for both a bewildering and exhilarating experience. The early D Major Quartet of 1897, with its echoes of Dvořák and Schubert, is among the most buoyant and approachable of all Schoenberg's works; the first and fourth of the numbered Quartets have much to recommend them, and the middle two rank with the masterworks of modern chamber music. The Second Quartet, in whose final movements Schoenberg first abandoned traditional harmony, is among his most boldly original works—in addition to the nontonal experiments, there is a haunting part for soprano voice—and the Third Quartet, one of his finest twelve-tone scores, erupts with a passionate intensity not far removed from the smoldering mood of *Erwartung*.

It is good to have the sensitive, impassioned recordings by the LaSalle Quartet back in circulation, for as performances they have even more to communicate on a human level than the more technically dazzling versions by the Juilliard Quartet, no doubt slated for CD reissue by CBS/Sony. In addtion to the Schoenbergs, this four-CD box offers the major works for string quartet by Berg and Webern, including what is probably the finest *Lyric Suite* since the old Dial recording by the Kolisch Quartet. For lovers of contemporary chamber music, this is a major cause for rejoicing.

Verklärte Nacht

English Chamber Orchestra, Ashkenazy. London 410111-2 [CD].

Santa Fe Chamber Music Ensemble. Nonesuch D4-79028 [T].

The early *Verklärte Nacht* (Transfigured Night), written by a largely self-taught twenty-six-year-old composer, is one of the most amazing works in the history of nineteenth-century music. (And as with Brahms, the composer he admired most of all, the ratio of masterworks to lesser pieces in Schoenberg's output is extraordinarily high.) The lush sonorities, the wealth of ornamental detail, the advanced harmonic thinking, and the expressive confidence of the work completely belie the composer's youth and relative lack of experience. Had Schoenberg never written another note of music, he would still be remembered, for this piece alone, as one of the most fascinating voices of the entire late-Romantic era.

Among recordings of the orchestral version of *Verklärte Nacht,* the London release by the strings of the English Chamber Orchestra led by Vladimir Ashkenazy is enormously rich and atmospheric. The playing has all the expansiveness and freedom that have characterized most of this conductor's recent work, and a clarity and discipline that continually remind us of *Verklärte Nacht's* inception as a string sextet.

Among recordings of the original version of the piece, the Nonesuch release recorded at one of the Santa Fe Chamber Music Festivals remains unapproached. In fact, the only significant drawback to this otherwise virtually perfect recording (which is coupled with a blazing account of a late Schoenberg masterpiece, the great String Trio) is that it has yet to be issued on compact disc.

Schubert, Franz (1797–1828)

Impromptus (8) for Piano

Perahia, piano. CBS MK-37291 [CD], IMT-37291 [T].

Like Mozart and Mendelssohn, Franz Schubert was one of the authentic miracles of Western art. At sixteen, he composed the first great German *lied,* "Gretchen am Spinnrade," and in the remaining fifteen years of his tragically brief life became not only the undisputed master of German art song (he wrote more than seven hundred), but also the most important composer of symphonies, chamber music, and piano sonatas after his hero and idol, Beethoven. Though the two men lived in Vienna for years, the almost pathologically modest and self-effacing Schubert never screwed up the courage to meet the older man. He did serve as a pallbearer at Beethoven's funeral in 1827, which took place a scant twenty months before his own. No other composer, including

Mozart, had a greater or more facile gift for melody, and none—not even the indefatigable giants of the Baroque era—was more prolific. The two sets of Impromptus are among the most charming and characteristic of Schubert's piano works, and all have been served handsomely on records since the 78 era. On the basis of this CBS recording, Murray Perahia must be considered one of the great Schubert interpreters in the world today. The playing has a light, direct openness that is genuinely refreshing, but also plenty of *Schwung* and sinew whenever the music demands. In fact, these popular works have probably not been in better hands since the days of Arthur Schnabel and Edwin Fischer.

Octet in F for Strings and Winds

Academy of St. Martin-in-the-Fields Chamber Ensemble.
Chandos CHAN-8585 [CD], ABTD-1276 [T].

This sublimely entertaining chamber work, which in some performances can last very nearly as long as Beethoven's Ninth Symphony, is as much fun as eight musicians can have with their clothes on. (Rumors of an Octet au naturel given at a well-known music festival in Southern California continue to prove groundless. The festival's director told me in confidence that though they were certainly open to the idea, it was not only impossible to find a clarinetist who was willing to appear in that condition, but also one whom relatively normal people would be willing to look at.)

As in their Philips recording made in the late 1970s, the Academy of St. Martin-in-the-Fields Chamber Ensemble gives a performance for Chandos in which both the simplicity and sophistication of Schubert's great score are given full rein. Mechanically, the playing is all but flawless; yet it is the sheer *enjoyment* we hear in the playing that makes the recording stand out. For years, Angel's recording with the Melos Ensemble, now available in England on an EMI compact disc, set a standard I thought would never be approached. This one joins it at the very top of any list.

Piano Sonatas: in C minor, D. 958; in A, D. 959; in B-flat, D. 960

Pollini, piano. Deutsche Grammophon 419229-2 [CD].

Though Schubert produced some twenty piano sonatas over the course of his career, he was never really comfortable with the form. It was only with these last three, written during the final year of his life, that Schubert, the incomparable miniaturist of the Impromptus and *Moments musicaux,* produced some large-scale piano works which in their depth and quality rival any that his revered Beethoven ever wrote. Not since Arthur Schnabel (who once said, "I play Beethoven to make my living; Schubert I play for love") have these works had a more probing or poetic interpreter than Maurizio Pollini. If other performances of the C minor Sonata have unleashed a more torrential strength, Pollini stands virtually alone in evoking the bitter tragedy of the A Major, and the heroic grandeur of the Sonata in B-flat. While all the interpretations are full of the special insights (his detractors would call them "mannerisms") that have made Pollini the most deeply personal keyboard artist of his generation, the occasional eccentricities are far outweighed by the extraordinary depth and beauty of this set.

Quintet in A for Piano and Strings, *Trout*

Curzon, piano; Vienna Octet. London 417459-2 [CD].

Like his near-contemporary Solomon, Sir Clifford Curzon was one of the most physically unprepossessing of the great modern pianists, looking like a cross between a Talmudic scholar and an Oxford don. But Curzon possessed a blazing technique and a temperament to match. His penchant for canceling appearances eventually became legendary, and in my own personal experience only the high-strung Byron Janis backed out on more concerts for which I had tickets in hand. (A musical wit once suggested that the pianist's management should announce, "Mr. Curzon is available for only a limited number of cancellations this season.")

Nonetheless, when Curzon came to play—as he did in this celebrated 1958 recording of the *Trout* Quintet—all grumbles about his personal quirks were silenced. The playing is both completely relaxed and supremely magisterial, with a bracingly vigorous account of the Scherzo to keep the listeners on their toes. Combined with a loving account of the *Death and the Maiden* Quartet, this is a bargain that few can afford to pass up.

Quintet in C for Strings, D. 956

Ma, cello; Cleveland String Quartet. CBS MK-39134 [CD], IMT-39134 [T].

From works like the sublime and serene C Major Quintet, it would be impossible to deduce that the last eighteen months of Franz Schubert's life were an inexpressible nightmare. Dying of syphilis, the composer was nonetheless able to churn out a body of work of such unearthly beauty and purity that the only creative period like it was that equally astonishing *annus mirabilis* of the English poet John Keats.

While the great Cello Quintet has had many distinguished recordings over the years, beginning with an unforgettable account by the old Hollywood Quartet dating from the mid-1950s, no recorded performance has been more sensitive or moving than this CBS release by cellist Yo-Yo Ma and the brilliant Cleveland Quartet. One of the most impassioned and committed of all recent recordings of the work, this is also one of the most polished and meticulous. The attentive and generous contribution made by the "fifth wheel" offers further evidence that Yo-Yo Ma is the most breathtakingly complete cellist of his generation, and with good playback equipment, the amazingly lifelike recorded sound will almost persuade you that the players are in your living room.

Rosamunde (incidental music)

Von Otter, soprano; Chamber Orchestra of Europe, Abbado. Deutsche Grammophon 431655-2 [CD].

Once on the air, in introducing a work by Anton Rubinstein, I addressed the old Romantic legend that that fiery Russian composer and pianist, because of his astonishing physical resemblance to Beethoven, was in fact the great man's illegitimate son. I pointed out that as Beethoven had died in 1827 and Rubinstein was born in 1829 this would have been extremely difficult, given the fact that in the 1820s there were no sperm banks in the city of Vienna, other than Helemina von Chézy. Not only would this giftless clown supply the transcendentally stupid libretto that would completely scuttle *Euryanthe*, the grandest of Carl Maria von Weber's operas, she would also give Franz Schubert the material for one of his worst theatrical disasters, a play called *Rosamunde,* which closed after only two performances.

Claudio Abbado's masterly recording of the *Rosamunde* incidental music is a sheer delight from beginning to end. The Chamber Orchestra of Europe plays this enchanting music with just the right combination of youthful zest and mature gentility, and the soprano and chorus are utterly delectable. Given wonderfully lifelike sound by the Deutsche Grammophon engineers, this is easily one of the best Schubert recordings of the decade.

*D*ie schöne Müllerin

Fischer-Dieskau, baritone; Moore, piano. Deutsche
Grammophon 415186-2 [CD].

Unlike his half dozen operatic projects, which came to nothing or ended in disaster, Schubert's setting of twenty interrelated lyrics by the irredeemably minor poet Wilhelm Müller is one of the most successful music dramas ever written. In this simple, loosely structured tale of a wandering young miller who falls in love, is spurned by the title character (The Fair Maid of the Mill), and finally commits a Romantic suicide by drowning himself in a brook, Schubert fashioned history's first great song cycle and one of the two supreme masterpieces in the form.

Although there have been some memorable recordings of *Die schöne Müllerin* over the years—in many ways, the famous 1941 recording by the Danish tenor Aksel Schiøtz has never been surpassed, and that other celebrated wartime recording by Julius Patzak is now available on a Preiser CD (93128)—Dietrich Fischer-Dieskau's several recordings are all impressive, most notably the now-withdrawn 1962 version for EMI, followed closely by this 1972 remake for Deutsche Grammophon.

Unlike some of the baritone's later recordings, which are ruined by archness and a host of exasperating mannerisms, his third version of the cycle still finds the voice at its freshest and fullest (thereby eliminating the need to posture, primp, and snort) and captures one of the greatest musical storytellers since John McCormack was in his prime. The unerringly perceptive, quietly inventive accompaniments of the great Gerald Moore are the stuff of which legends are made.

Songs

Although it is still difficult to offer any coherent recommendation of Schubert song recordings, the task is certainly easier than
it was a couple of years ago. Even though the major companies now
seem intent on reissuing *everything* on CD, this pleasantly profligate
policy does not seem to extend to lieder, which continue to appeal
to a relatively small but rabid crowd. Unbelievably, only *one* of
Hermann Prey's Schubert recordings other than a Denon version
(C37-7240) of *Winterreise* is to be had anywhere at any price: an
engaging recital of Goethe settings from the small Saphir label (INT-
830.837 [CD]). Apparently, no one at the several recording companies that have dealt with the baritone over the years has heard
that he is—no kidding, guys—one of the greatest Schubert singers
in history and, in the opinion of many of us, the foremost lieder
specialist to have emerged since the end of the war.

If the Prey situation is surprising, that of Hans Hotter is a
scandal. It is as if that noblest German bass of his generation, whose
recordings of Schubert came closest to sounding the ultimate depths
and most profound stillnesses of the composer's heart, simply never
existed. The wonderful Austrian company Preiser, which specializes
in historic vocal reissues, has released one CD (93145), but again,
for an artist of Hotter's stature, this is inexcusable. By that same
token, the wonderful and still vigorously active Dutch soprano Elly
Ameling remains woefully underrepresented: only three of her Philips recordings have made the jump to CD (410037-2, 416294-2,
and 420870-2), although there is an attractive, if somewhat redundant, recital of sixteen songs available from Etcetera (KTC-1009
[CD], XTC-1009 [CD]).

On the brighter side, things on the Fischer-Dieskau front are
definitely looking up. In addition to that ageless *Schöne Müllerin*
(see above), two other Angel recordings from the 1950s and '60s
have also resurfaced on compact disc: a dandy *Schwanengesang*
with Gerald Moore (CDMC-63559), and a lovely recital of some
of the best-known songs (CDM-69503), in which the singing is so
effortless and unaffected that those who only know the barking,
hammy "Fish" of recent years will hardly believe it's the same
singer. And finally, Orfeo provides perhaps the most telling recording of all: a group of sixteen songs from an exhilarating recital the
baritone gave with Moore at the 1957 Salzburg Festival (C-140101
[CD]). As singing, as drama, as human communication, it captures
a unique musical force at its most compelling.

A two-CD set from Angel (CDHB-63040) preserves the famous recordings the silvery-voiced Elisabeth Schumann made between 1927 and 1949, though to add further insult to injury, no recital albums by either Schumann's great friend and contemporary Lotte Lehmann or their incomparable successor Elisabeth Schwarzkopf are currently in print.

Gerard Souzay's collection of twenty-two songs from the early to late '60s on Philips (422418-2 [CD]) is one of the most exciting reissues to date. In addition to the suave, almost disturbingly handsome voice of one of the great lieder singers of the modern era, the recording features an intelligent mixture of some of the best-loved songs with some of the least familiar. The eerie, darkly sexual, quasi-homicidal, and almost totally unknown "Der Zwerg" (The Dwarf) is as great a Schubert song recording—as great a lieder recording—as any that has ever been made.

Finally, Hyperion's quixotic and largely successful series that will attempt to record *all* the songs has already yielded several clear winners. Volume 1 (CDJ-33001 [CD]) finds Dame Janet Baker at the height of her mature interpretative powers and the voice showing only the slightest signs of wear and tear; Volume 3 (CDJ-33003 [CD]) offers the lovely mezzo-soprano Ann Murray in beautiful voice, and on Volume 4 (CDJ-33004 [CD]) Philip Langridge continues to demonstrate that he is one of the most intelligent and musical Schubert singers in the world today.

All in all, things could be worse.

String Quartets (15)

Melos Quartet. Deutsche Grammophon 419879-2 [CD].

In addition to providing beautifully thought out and handsomely executed versions of the more familiar later quartets, the principal value of this attractive six-CD set is the warmly graceful performances the Melos give of the early ones. While obviously not in the same league as the masterworks Schubert would compose toward the end of his life, they are astonishingly confident and tuneful pieces that deserve to be far better known. These gifted German musicians miss no opportunity to underscore the charm and innocence of the music, and if the remastered sound tends to be a trifle distant and harsh, that is the only minor reservation about an otherwise splendid release.

String Quartets: No. 13 in A minor; No. 14 in D minor, *Death and the Maiden*

Alban Berg Quartet. Angel CDC-47333 [CD], 4DS-38233 [T].

As in their recordings of the Beethoven quartets, Vienna's Alban Berg Quartet are all but impossible to better in these performances of these great last quartets of Schubert. The ensemble's almost obscenely beautiful physical sound has never been captured to more thrilling effect (the hushed yet paradoxically full-bodied *pianissimos* of which they are capable continually remind me of the high notes that only Leontyne Price in her prime could pop out with such bewitching ease), but as always in their recordings, the Bergs offer us considerably more than a collection of pretty sounds. The *Death and the Maiden* Quartet (so called because one of its movements is a set of variations on Schubert's song of that name) has rarely sounded this dark and disturbing (there are, of course, ample doses of light and life as well), and the great A Minor Quartet explodes with a dramatic intensity that no other recording can match. The sound that Angel's engineers have supplied is as opulent as the performances. For Schubert lovers, or simply anyone interested in two of the greatest string quartets written after those of Beethoven, these are absolute musts.

Symphonies: No. 3 in D; No. 5 in B-flat; No. 6 in C, *Little C Major*

Royal Philharmonic, Beecham. Angel CDM-69750 [CD].

Like her onetime Prague neighbor, Franz Kafka, my grandmother held a fairly dark view of the human condition. For instance, she was persuaded that virtually all useful wisdom was contained in the old Czech beatitude "Blessed are they who expect nothing, for they shall not be disappointed." She was also a devout believer in the Czech time payment plan (100 percent cash down, *no* easy monthly installments) and was firmly convinced that there was no such thing as a "bargain." She lived to be ninety-four.

Had she lived to be 109—as well she might have, if it hadn't been for that final pileup on her fully paid-for though, as she often complained, ridiculously overpriced Harley-Davidson—she might have admitted that bargains *do* exist. For here are three of Schubert's most endearing early symphonies in the finest recorded performances they are ever likely to receive on one "medium-priced" compact disc.

As far as Sir Thomas Beecham was concerned, early Schubert was merely an extension of Mozart and Haydn (which, to a large degree, it indeed was), and he treats the music with the same easy wit and amiability. Which is not to say that he sees them as warmed-over versions of the *Surprise* and *Haffner* Symphonies. Never forgetting for a moment that even as a boy Schubert was one of the great masters of melody, Beecham caresses the glorious tunes with an affection and knowledge of breath that suggest a great lieder specialist. As always, the Royal Philharmonic give the impression they would do anything for their unpredictable founder, and the recorded sound from the late 1950s is fine. Alas, the recording is becoming difficult to find domestically. It is definitely worth the time and expense to import it, if necessary, directly from any of the large English mail order houses. (Addresses can be found in *The Gramophone* magazine.)

Anyone hunting for comparable versions of the other early symphonies will find that the Deutsche Grammophon compact discs by Claudio Abbado and the Chamber Orchestra of Europe come closest to approximating the Beecham spell. The relaxed yet buoyant romps through Nos. 1 and 2 are especially enjoyable (423652-2), while the performance of the *Tragic* (No. 4) is both weightier and more supple than those we usually hear. Although this disc (423653-3) comes with the best modern recording of the Third Symphony, the Beecham remains in a universe by itself.

Symphony No. 8 in B minor, *Unfinished*

Vienna Philharmonic, Solti. London 414371-2 [CD].

With Bruno Walter's timeless recording temporarily out of print (slated for reissue, no doubt, on one of Sony's medium-priced or bargain labels), Sir Georg Solti's version of Schubert's best-loved symphony will fill the bill nicely until its inevitable return. As always, the conductor gets the very best out of this frequently crotchety orchestra: the strings glow with a burnished intensity; the winds play with point, self-assurance, and enormous individuality. The interpretation itself is virile and straightforward, with the characteristic Solti drama and color. In fact, for many this will be more than a stopgap, especially those who prefer the *Unfinished* on the more heroic, driven side.

Symphony No. 9 in C, *The Great C Major*

Berlin Philharmonic, Furtwängler. Deutsche Grammophon 427405-2 [CD].

Orchestra of the Age of Enlightenment, Mackerras. Virgin Classics VC-790708-2 [CD], VC-790708-4 [T].

Schubert's final completed symphony can be a very problematic work. Since the *Great* of the sobriquet refers as much to its massive length as to the divinity of its melodic inspiration, the Ninth Symphony can degenerate (and often has) into nothing more than a collection of Sunday school tunes. Wilhelm Furtwängler's eternal recording from the early 1950s is the one version of the piece that makes it seem as structurally sound, and dramatically inevitable, as the Beethoven Ninth. The performance is a triumph of Furtwänglerian brinkmanship at its most magical. The unwritten, yet electrifying, accelerando that leads out of the Introduction to the first movement's principal theme, the spring in the Scherzo's rhythm, and the headlong forward thrust of the finale make this one of the most exciting orchestral recordings ever.

Among performances led by conductors from *this* planet, Sir Charles Mackerras's lively period-instrument version for Virgin is both a fascinating experiment and a completely winning interpretation. The sound of the antique (and fake-antique) instruments, while often spare and stark, is never unpleasant or abrasive, and the ensemble's blend of enthusiasm and professionalism is a joy. My only reservation is in supporting a group with the consummate, yea, *cosmic* pomposity to call itself "The Orchestra of the Age of Enlightenment." As the enlightened Dr. Johnson said, "The name sucks, and there's an end on't."

Trios for Piano, Violin, and Cello: No. 1 in B-flat, D. 898; No. 2 in E-flat, D. 929; Nocturne in E-flat, D. 897; Sonata Movement in B-flat, D. 28

Golub, piano; Kaplan, violin; Carr, cello. Arabesque Z-6580-2 [CD], ABQC-6580-4.

This divine music has had more than its fair share of outstanding recordings, beginning with a still electrifying (if technically and interpretatively wayward) performance of the Trio No. 1 by the *always* electrifying and wayward Cortot-Thibaud-Casals Trio from 1926. A decade later, an even more fabulous version of the Trio No. 2 appeared, featuring violinist Adolf Busch, his cello-playing brother Hermann, and son-in-law to be, Rudolf Serkin. Since then, all of the leading groups—Beaux Arts, Suk, Borodin—have come to terms with these cornerstones of the trio literature, as have some superb ad hoc ensembles like Rubinstein-Heifetz-Feuermann and Rubinstein-Szeryng-Fournier.

That these recent recordings by Golub-Kaplan-Carr are so superb will come as no surprise to anyone familiar with their versions of the Brahms trios (see page 88); what *might* be surprising is how easily these three young musicians place all previous recordings in the shade. Mechanically, the playing is impeccable, as is the individual and collective musicianship. Yet it is the unusual combination of wisdom and freshness—qualities so central to the music itself—that makes the interpretations such revelations.

In addition to the two rarely heard miniatures, the performance of the Trio No. 2 concludes with two fourth movements: the finale as it was published and is usually performed, together with the original version, which contains 100 bars of very worthy music that Schubert persuaded himself to cut.

*W*anderer Fantasie

Rubinstein, piano. RCA 6257-2-RC [CD].

Even when Sviatoslav Richter's overwhelming Angel recording from the early 1960s is released domestically (it can be found in Europe on an EMI compact disc), Artur Rubinstein's startling performance from the same period won't have to yield an inch. While not known as a Schubert specialist, Rubinstein was uniquely equipped to probe one of the most influential and forward-looking of the composer's works. For in his rhapsodic, possibly *overly* Romantic performance, Rubinstein draws the obvious parallel to the music that can trace its roots to this path-breaking composition: the piano music of Schumann, Liszt, and his beloved Chopin.

The performances of the B-flat Sonata and the last two Op. 90 Impromptus that fill out the disc are also superb, but it's this *Wanderer*—possibly the *Wanderer* of a lifetime—that counts.

*W*interreise

Prey, baritone; Bianconi, piano. Denon C37-7240 [CD].

Hotter, bass; Moore, piano. Angel CDH-61002 [CD].

There aren't too many vocal works that can make Mahler's *Kindertotenlieder* or the Shostakovich Fourteenth Symphony seem cheerful in comparison, but that greatest of all song cycles, Schubert's *Winterreise,* is one of them. In the entire lieder repertoire, nothing can match the heartbreaking despair of this "Winter Journey" based on twenty-four poems by Wilhelm Müller; even the relatively bright moments, like "Der Lindenbaum," which has almost acquired folk-song status, are shot through with desolation and foreboding. And yet, like *King Lear, Winterreise* is neither self-pitying nor self-deluding. It is an unflinchingly courageous look at a horrible truth, and as such, a central musical catharsis of the Western imagination.

Hermann Prey's interpretation of *Winterreise* has been a classic of the recital platform for more than a quarter of a century. On stage, he typically performs it by itself, without preamble or encores and often, it is said, without taking any bows. It is a mature and completely selfless conception, dark without being dour, tragic with no hint of lugubriousness, effortless yet never glib. While none of his several recordings manages to fully capture the kind of devastating experience this *Winterreise* can be in the concert hall, the most recent version comes very close.

Hans Hotter's classic recording is also indispensable, but only for those who are willing to look directly into the black heart of absolute despair. More than any other singer, Hotter elevates this music to the shattering heights of Greek tragedy, in one of the most chilling vocal recordings ever made and one of the most courageous.

Schuman, William (1910–1992)

New England Triptych; Judith (choreographic poem);
Variations on "America" (orchestration of organ work
by Charles Ives); Symphony No. 5

Seattle Symphony. Schwarz. Delos DE-6115 [CD].

The music William Schuman produced over a period of more
than fifty years represented the fusion of an essentially late-
Romantic temperament, a commanding modern intellect, and perhaps the most highly evolved sense of craftsmanship of any
American composer of his time. One of his greatest advocates, Leonard Bernstein, provided a succinct summary of Schuman's art:
"vitality, optimism, enthusiasm, long lyrical line, rhythmic impetuosity, bristling counterpoint, brilliant textures, dynamic tension."
All of these qualities can be heard in the four works contained on
what may very well be the most completely successful Schuman recording yet released.

In the capable hands of Gerard Schwarz and his finely honed
Seattle Symphony, the *New England Triptych* and the orchestration
of Ives's *"America" Variations* emerge with a point and presence
they have rarely enjoyed in the recording studio; the rarely heard
choreographic poem *Judith* and the magnificent Fifth Symphony are
revealed as modern American masterworks.

For anyone interested in American music, this is a cause for
serious rejoicing.

Schumann, Robert (1810–1856)

Carnaval; Fantasiestücke, Op. 12; Waldscenen

Rubinstein, piano. RCA 5667-2-RC [CD].

Nowhere is the genius of this purest and most tormented of the German Romantics heard to better advantage than in his works for solo piano. Beginning with *Carnaval,* which in 1834 announced the arrival of a major new composer, Robert Schumann began to evolve an entirely novel form of piano music: a large structure made up of many smaller parts that were tied together by a single, unifying poetic idea. Within this loose-knit "literary" framework, which allowed for the widest possible range of musical expression, Schumann produced the most fanciful, wildly imaginative piano works written up to that time. Compared to Schumann, Liszt (aside from the great B minor Sonata) was a purveyor of empty bombast, and Chopin was a broken record stuck in the same gloomy groove, a mood that H. L. Mencken aptly described as "two embalmers doing a post-mortem on a minor poet; the scent of tuberoses; autumn rain."

Until that most phantasmagorical of all *Carnaval* recordings returns to circulation—a version from the early '50s by the English pianist Solomon—Artur Rubinstein's RCA recording from the mid-1960s will probably remain unchallenged. The playing has ample color and sentiment, and just the right amount of rhythmic flippancy to make the individual pieces leap into life. The "Chopin" section is particularly lovely in its quiet restraint, and the final March of the Davidsbündler (Schumann's society of young, iconoclastic champions of the highest ideals in life and art) against the Philistines (represented by a mean-spirited little waltz) is unusually exciting.

Another Rubinstein recording (RCA 6258-2-RC [CD]), which features the pianist's unforgettable interpretations of *Kreisleriana* and the *Fantasia* in C is, if anything, even more successful, while CBS recordings by Murray Perahia offer subtle, spontaneous, and richly expressive versions of the *Davidsbündlertänze* and the Op. 12 *Fantasiestücke* (MK-32299 [CD]), as well as performances of *Papillons* and the Symphonic Etudes (MK-34539 [CD], MT-34539 [T]) in which poetry drips from every bar.

Concerto in A minor for Cello and Orchestra

Ma, cello; Bavarian Radio Orchestra, Davis. CBS MK-42663 [CD], MT-42663 [T].

Until Sir Edward Elgar unveiled his masterpiece in the form in 1919, this soaring work by Schumann had the field to itself as the World's Second-Best Cello Concerto. Even now, the choice of which of these very different works should be ranked just behind the B minor Concerto of Antonín Dvořák is largely a matter of personal taste: whether one prefers the passionate lyricism of the Schumann or the Elgar's depth and starkly beautiful despair.

For years, the glowing early recording by the young Jacqueline Du Pré stood alone among all versions of the Schumann Concerto, and still does on an Angel cassette (4AE-34490). Like her performance of the Elgar Concerto, this winsome, ebullient interpretation will remain one of her most enduring monuments; we can only wonder nervously why Angel is waiting to transfer it to compact disc.

Yo-Yo Ma's cultivated performance for CBS will hold the fort more than adequately until that happens. Along with an unusually civilized (perhaps a bit *too* civilized) reading of the Concerto, the CD comes with equally refined versions of Schumann's complete music for cello and piano, in which Ma is given admirable support by his friend Emanuel Ax.

Concerto in A minor for Piano and Orchestra

Bishop-Kovacevich, piano; BBC Symphony, Davis. Philips 412923-2 [CD].

Like Edvard Grieg's A minor Concerto, a work with which it is almost invariably paired on recordings, the Schumann Piano Concerto represents something close to the finest work the Romantic era produced in the form. Moody, sensual, and heroic, it was also one of Schumann's greatest achievements with music cast on a larger scale. Like his admired Chopin, Schumann is still accused of being a miniaturist, incapable of sustaining extended forms; works like the Piano Concerto and the four symphonies triumphantly lay *that* nonsense to rest.

Neither the inspired, albeit slightly insane, version by Sviatoslav Richter and Lovro von Matačič nor the poetic and impulsive mid-'50s recording by Solomon is currently available, but Stephen Bishop-Kovacevich and Colin Davis prove to be as persuasive in this warhorse as they are in the performance of the Grieg Concerto that accompanies it. Although the playing has an exhilarating Romantic waywardness about it, the Concerto's structure—to say nothing of its countless little details—is kept under admirable control. The immaculately balanced early-'70s recorded sound barely shows its age.

Dichterliebe; Liederkreis, Op. 39

Fischer-Dieskau, baritone; Eschenbach, piano. Deutsche Grammophon 415190-2 [CD].

When in 1840 a cigar-chomping, beer-guzzling, foul-mouthed womanizer named Robert Schumann settled down to the joys of what his near-contemporary Friedrich Engels called "that leaden boredom known as domestic bliss," not only the composer's life but also the history of art song would be altered forever. After a protracted legal struggle with his bride's domineering father, Schumann found that his marriage to Clara Wieck unleashed an astonishing outburst of creativity, that "Year of Song" in which he wrote most of the works that established him as Schubert's first great successor as a master of German lieder.

Schumann's sensitivity to the infinite shades of meaning in any text was extraordinary, helped no doubt by the fact that the composer, in his youth, had intended to become a poet. At Schumann's best, only Schubert and Hugo Wolf are his legitimate peers; even Brahms, Mahler, and Strauss, as important as their songs most certainly are, cannot really begin to approach the scope or quality of Schumann's achievement.

This Deutsche Grammophon recording by Dietrich Fischer-Dieskau is not only one of the best introductions to this tender, turbulent universe, it is also a genuine bargain. In addition to superlative recordings of Schumann's most important cycles, the frequently bitter and desperate Dichterliebe (A Poet's Love) and the marvelous Op. 39 Liederkreis (literally, Song Cycle) on poems of Joseph von Eichendorff, Fischer-Dieskau and his responsive partner Christoph Eschenbach offer up beguiling performances of seven of the Myrthen songs.

While Schumann is also being seriously affected by the protracted and frustrating lieder drought we're passing through (when the best collections of individual songs feature beefy operatic types like Margaret Price and Jessye Norman, you *know* we're in trouble), a Deutsche Grammophon recording (415519-2 [CD]) by Brigitte Fassbänder, daughter of the gifted baritone Willi Domgraf-Fassbänder, should be snatched up immediately. In addition to honest, attractively sung versions of a half dozen individual items and the Heine *Liederkreis,* Op. 24, the soprano and the shrewd, gently efficient Irwin Gage offer the finest available version of Schumann's great song cycle *Frauenliebe und -leben* (Woman's Love and Life). Though feminists have taken exception to this by-product of mid-nineteenth-century male chauvinism—the text, by a *man,* wouldn't you know it, says that a woman's purpose is to love and serve her husband—the sweetly sentimental songs are so entrancing that you wind up not caring what the wretched words say.

Kinderscenen

> Moravec, piano. Supraphon 11-0359-2 [CD], Nonesuch 79063-4 [T].

Ivan Moravec's performance of Schumann's greatly beloved suite of childhood recollections as captured by Nonesuch is probably the most beautiful ever recorded. Its wide-eyed innocence is matched only by its technical perfection, and it is one of several recordings which make the convincing case that as a tonal colorist, Moravec is the late-twentieth-century equivalent of the legendary Walter Gieseking. Listen, especially, to the utterly unaffected yet gently devastating performance of the famous "Träumerei," or the ambling miracle he makes of the celebrated opening bars of the piece, which have been pressed into service in films such as *My Brilliant Career* and *Sophie's Choice.*

The more recent Supraphon recording is every bit as distinguished; it comes with somewhat inappropriate—though magnificently turned out—partners, Bach's Chromatic Fantasy and the B-flat Major Sonata of Mozart.

Quartet in E-flat for Piano and Strings; Quintet in E-flat for Piano and Strings

> Beaux Arts Trio; Rhodes, viola; Bettelheim, violin. Philips 420791-2 [CD].

In addition to the three string quartets that popped out within a few weeks' time, both these vibrant works date from 1842, which musicologists have called "The Year of Chamber Music," possibly because Schumann produced more important chamber music in 1842 than at any other time of his life. (At college, my astronomy professor, the distinguished Hazel Losh, once amazed us all by pointing out the big red spot which can be seen in Jupiter's southern hemisphere and saying, with a perfectly straight face, "Now this is what we professional astronomers call 'The Big Red Spot of Jupiter.'")

While the Quartet is a spectacularly fine piece, the Quintet is Schumann's greatest chamber work. Not only is it one of the most fruitful and compelling of all his compositions—I've never met anyone yet who could keep his feet from tapping in the dynamic final movement, or his jaw from going slack during the incredible double fugue—but also one of the most surprisingly original. For oddly enough, prior to 1842, no one had ever written a significant work for piano and string quartet.

The Beaux Arts Trio and company are at once meticulous and enthusiastic in both works, and the recordings are vivid and warm. It could be argued that the playing doesn't have the abundance of "character" that Glenn Gould and Leonard Bernstein brought to their wildly peculiar collaborations with the Juilliard Quartet, available on a CBS CD (MPK-44848). On the other hand, the "Beaux-os'" performances are recognizably those by musicians from planet Earth.

Scenes from Goethe's "Faust"

Fischer-Dieskau, Pears, Harwood, Shirley-Quirk, Vyvyan, Aldeburgh Festival Chorus, English Chamber Orchestra, Britten. London 425705-2 [CD].

During a climactic moment in Song of Love, MGM's lavish, high-cholesterol biography of Schumann, Paul Henreid, as the composer, is happily conducting a big choral work when he begins hearing a disturbing, high-pitched noise. Since the producers could hardly tell audiences in 1947 that this was the initial symptom of the hideous venereal disease that would eventually drive Schumann mad, they tried to sidestep the issue in another, unintentionally uproarious scene. The brave Clara (Katharine Hepburn) emerges from her husband's study with a worried-looking medico who has just examined him. To the equally worried-looking Brahms (Robert Walker), she delivers the classic line: "Johannes, the doctor thinks that Robert may be suffering from *melancholia.*"

The stirring music Henreid was conducting was the *Scenes from Goethe's "Faust,"* one of the least-known of the composer's major works and, in its best pages, one of the most inspired. The reissue of Benjamin Britten's enthusiastic and deeply committed 1973 recording makes one wonder, all over again, why this generally magnificent score isn't heard more often. Anyone with an interest in Schumann and/or Romantic choral music should investigate this one immediately.

Symphonies (4)

Amsterdam Concertgebouw Orchestra, Haitink. Philips 416126-2 [CD].

While there have been performances of the individual symphonies that offer more flair and color—George Szell's recording of the *Spring* and Fourth symphonies is especially riveting (CBS MYK-38468 [CD], MYT-38468 [T]), and Carlo Maria Giulini's Los Angeles version of the *Rhenish* (Deutsche Grammophon 400062-2 [CD]) is unique in its poetry and adult passion—the most consistently satisfying set of Robert Schumann's four great symphonies is this one led by Bernard Haitink. The interpretations are utterly free of exaggeration: tempos are judicious; textures are beautifully controlled and balanced, and throughout all these carefully judged, meticulously executed performances is a sense of inevitability and rightness few modern recordings can equal. Compared to some of the more strong-willed recordings on the market (those by Levine, Bernstein, and Furtwängler, as well as those mentioned above), Haitink might at first seem a trifle colorless and bland. With repeated exposure, however, his maturity and enormous dignity, together with the fabulous playing of the orchestra, more than carry the day.

Scriabin, Alexander

(1872–1915)

Symphonies (5)

Philadelphia Orchestra, Muti. Angel CDC-54251 [CD].

Even by the transcendentally self-indulgent standards of late-Imperial Russia, Alexander Scriabin was an extravagant figure: a musician, poet, philosopher, and mystic who sought to unite music, poetry, drama, and dance into a new visionary art form he called the "Mystery." Less an aesthetic principal than a theological one, the "Mystery" was intended to be an all-embracing new gospel into which the whole of human experience would be subsumed, a kind of artistic equivalent of Einstein's elusive unified field theory.

Needless to say, no one—including Scriabin himself—was precisely certain what any of this mumbo-jumbo meant, yet it led to some of the most interesting, and understandably decadent, music to have emerged from the final years of the Romanov dynasty. Scriabin is at his intensely overwrought best in the final three symphonies, which were naturally given the histrionic subtitles *Divine Poem, Poem of Ecstasy,* and *Prometheus, the Poem of Fire.*

While they are not the most completely persuasive recordings these problematical works have ever received—another conductor of the Philadelphia Orchestra, Leopold Stokowski, left some hair-raising interpretations during the 78 era—Riccardo Muti's performances are alert, sensuous, and wholly sympathetic. The two early symphonies come off equally well (no finer recording of either has ever been made), and the playing of the orchestra is a wonder at every turn.

Those who respond to Scriabin's rarefied, deeply personal vision will also want to acquire Vladimir Ashkenazy's brilliant and knowing accounts of the ten Piano Sonatas, now crammed on a pair of medium-priced London CDs (425579-2). If not the ideal performances of all these challenging works—Horowitz virtually owned the final two (CBS MK-42411 [CD]), while Nos. 3 and 5 served as the vehicles for perhaps the most provocative recordings Glenn Gould ever made (CBS M3K-42150 [CD])—they still present a balanced, musical, and immensely well played vision of an exceptionally interesting body of work.

377

Shchedrin, Rodion (1932–)

Carmen Ballet (after Bizet), for Strings and Percussion

**Bolshoi Theatre Orchestra, Rozhdestvensky. Eurodisc 7933-
2-RG [CD]. Odyssey/Melodiya YT-34613 [T].**

In the pre-*glasnost* 1960s, some imaginative press people on
both sides of what used to be called the Iron Curtain were trying
to pass Rodion Shchedrin off as the latest incarnation of the classic
Russian enfant terrible, whose predecessors included Sergei
Prokofiev and Dmitri Shostakovich. And there probably *were* people in positions of power who were shocked by Shchedrin's music—
but they were those who would have been shocked by the music of
Lawrence Welk.

The "new Shostakovich" was in reality an irremediably conventional, extremely well-behaved composer: if not a Party hack
like Marian Koval, Mikhai Chulaki, or Tikhon Khrennikov, then
still a man whose music was unlikely to offend the most reactionary
apparatchik's grandmother. (How subversive could someone be
who in 1969 produced a cantata called—and surely you can whistle
its principal themes, can't you?—*Lenin in the People's Heart?*)

The *Carmen Ballet*, Shchedrin's most "original" work to date,
is a cutesy though frequently inspired arrangement for strings and
a ridiculously overstocked percussion section of familiar themes
from the Bizet opera. After a half dozen exposures its charm begins
to wear a little thin, but it's fun to hear every couple of years or so.
In spite of the fairly harsh recorded sound, Gennadi Rozhdestvensky's barn-burner of a performance is the preferred one.

Shostakovich, Dmitri

(1906–1975)

Concerto No. 1 in C minor for Piano, Trumpet, and Orchestra; Chamber Symphony; Preludes

Kissin, piano; Moscow Virtuosi, Spivakov. RCA 7947-2-RC [CD], 7947-4-RC [T].

Yevgeny Kissin is one of the latest in that seemingly inexhaustible line of gifted young pianists with which the Soviet Union has peacefully bombarded the world since a diminutive firebrand named Vladimir Ashkenazy burst on the scene in the mid-1950s. Kissin, who like his predecessors seems to have unlimited reserves of technique and temperament, is extremely well suited to both the wiseacre exuberance and unexpected tenderness of Shostakovich's most familiar concerto. Vladimir Spivakov and the more or less aptly named Moscow Virtuosi give the kid admirably pointed support and are equally efficient in the Chamber Symphony, arranged by Rudolf Barshai from Shostakovich's dramatic String Quartet No. 8.

For those who believe in the Shostakovich Cello Concertos—I have little faith in them myself—Heinrich Schiff and the Bavarian Radio Orchestra led by the composer's son Maxim offer a polished, authoritative version of the First Concerto and the only available recording of the somewhat aimless Second (Philips 412526-2 [CD]).

String Quartets (15)

Borodin Quartet. Angel CDC-49266/70 [CD].

If there was ever the slightest doubt that the fifteen string quartets of Dmitri Shostakovich rank not only with the major chamber works of the twentieth century, but with the most significant works in the form since Beethoven, this triumphant cycle by the Borodin Quartet should lay it to rest. Begun in 1935, when the composer already had four symphonies to his credit, the Quartets eventually became, as they had for Beethoven before him, the vehicle for expressing the most private of all his thoughts and emotions. (Nevertheless, Shostakovich vigorously discouraged any suggestion that the symphonies were the public statements of the "official" Shostakovich, and that the Quartets were the ruminations of the introverted, painfully shy man within. However, given that some of the early Quartets are genuinely symphonic in their structure and expression, and some of the later symphonies are almost chamberlike in their size and proportions, the oversimplified generalization seems to fit.)

For a time, a superb series of all fifteen Quartets in performances by England's Fitzwilliam Quartet was available domestically on Oiseau-Lyre. As fine as those interpretations certainly were, they have now been superseded by this incredible, and probably historic, version by the Borodin Quartet. Having studied with the composer extensively (they were his favorite chamber ensemble after the celebrated Beethoven Quartet, which gave most of these works their world premieres), the Borodins bring an incomparable authority and understanding to the music that no other ensemble can begin to rival. They also possess one of the most individual physical sounds in the musical world today: a sound at once rich and sparse, pointed and flexible, from a collection of clearly defined individuals who work as a completely unified, indissoluble whole.

With the exception of the autobiographical Eighth Quartet, with its programmatic allusions to the Second World War and quotations from many of the composer's previous works, none of these extraordinary pieces has yet to enter the standard chamber repertoire, nor are they likely to do so any time soon. Still, they represent as individual and uncompromising a body of work as has been produced so far in this century, from the formal complexity of the early quartets to the wrenching, often lugubrious death throes of the final entries in the series. The Quartet No. 15, for instance, is a series of six unrelentingly gloomy Adagios, all cast in the key of E-flat minor. In short, while this is certainly not a series of recordings that will appeal to admirers of the *1812 Overture* and *Victory at Sea,* it represents one of the most daring and significant recording projects of the last decade. At present, there would seem to be no plans to release these amazing performances on cassette. Which means we will have to content ourselves with one of the first authentic milestones in the brief history of the compact disc.

Symphony No. 1 in F

London Philharmonic, Haitink. London 414677-2 [CD].

There is a case to be made that Dmitri Shostakovich never wrote a more audaciously original work than this youthful masterpiece, submitted as a graduation exercise to the Leningrad Conservatory and composed when he was only eighteen. In it, many of the Shostakovich hallmarks—the sardonic humor, the grand gestures, the often brilliantly eccentric orchestration—are clearly in evidence, together with a freshness and almost palpable joy in the act of composition that none of his fourteen subsequent symphonies would ever really recapture. (Within several years of its premiere, the First Symphony had made Shostakovich a world-famous figure, and hence, from the mid-1920s onward, a man Soviet officialdom would try to keep on an increasingly tight leash.)

Bernard Haitink's excellent London recording is easily the first choice among all versions on compact disc. Less immediate and personal than the Bernstein recording on Deutsche Grammophon, it is nevertheless a powerful, deeply committed reading, and one that is exceptionally well played and recorded.

Vladimir Ashkenazy's London recording with the Royal Philharmonic (425609-4 [T]) is the best of the scant and disappointing collection of tapes.

Symphony No. 5 in D minor

New York Philharmonic, Bernstein. CBS MYK-37218 [CD], MYT-37218 [T].

Not to be confused with their second recording of perhaps the most famous twentieth-century Russian symphony (a performance taped on tour in Tokyo in 1979), this is the celebrated recording Bernstein and the Philharmonic made two decades earlier, after returning from a highly publicized tour of the Soviet Union. The reasons this remains the most satisfying of all recordings of the Shostakovich Fifth—a work that Bernstein's mentor, Serge Koussevitzky, found as indestructible and universal as the Fifth Symphony of Beethoven—are as clear today as they were when the recording was first released.

Bernstein's interpretation succeeds because he views the Symphony not as an ironic or paradoxical work, but rather as one that marks the culmination of the nineteenth-century Russian symphonic tradition. Which is not to say, exactly, that he treats the work as though it might have been written by a harmonically advanced Tchaikovsky, but that *does* seem to be the overall impression he wants the Symphony to make. From the crushing opening statement of the principal theme, through the unusually expansive (and expressive) Adagio, to the giddy, helter-skelter finale, this is a Shostakovich Fifth that is as direct, vibrant, and openhearted as any large-scale orchestral work any Russian ever composed.

And if, in light of some of the more recent performances of the work, Bernstein's view might seem a bit *too* Romantic and literal, it should be remembered that the composer often said Bernstein was his favorite American interpreter. The New York Philharmonic plays as well as they ever have in their history, and the recorded sound—especially in the compact disc version—barely shows its age.

Symphonies: No. 6 in B minor; No. 11 in G minor, *The Year 1905*

Concertgebouw Orchestra of Amsterdam, Haitink. London 411939-2 [CD].

Even though the Sixth Symphony has no subtitle and the Eleventh is officially known as *The Year 1905,* either of these profoundly pessimistic works could easily be called "Music to Go Out and Shoot Yourself By." The Largo of the Sixth—regarded by some as the greatest slow movement in Shostakovich—is so full of angst and unrelieved anguish that the two slight and apparently lighthearted movements which follow it come off as a sinister, horribly unfunny joke. And while ostensibly a programmatic lament for the abortive 1905 uprising, the Eleventh afforded the composer a convenient outlet for his all but limitless disillusionment and disgust with life. These are harrowing, courageous works that are not intended for casual listening. In their searing honesty they also tend to validate the old Spanish proverb that insists the only two things that cannot be looked at directly are the sun and the truth.

As in all the recordings from his magnificent Shostakovich series, Bernard Haitink brings enormous integrity and seriousness of purpose to both performances. The rather loosely organized Eleventh, which can sometimes seem like little more than above-average film music, has rarely sounded as unified or meaningful, and the playing of the Concertgebouw Orchestra is wondrous, as always.

Symphony No. 7 in C, *Leningrad*

Chicago Symphony, Bernstein. Deutsche Grammophon 427632-2 [CD].

Thanks to conductors like Bernard Haitink, Paavo Berglund, Mariss Jansons, Gennadi Rozhdestvensky, and Neeme Järvi, all of whom have made dignified, searching, musical, or illuminating recordings of the composer's most controversial symphony, the once wildly lionized, once savagely pilloried *Leningrad* seems well on the way to a general rehabilitation, to use an expression from the bad old post-Stalinist days. Though it can never recapture the phenomenal popularity it enjoyed as a symbol of Soviet resistance during the Second World War, the *Leningrad* is being widely accepted now as a serious, substantial, worthwhile work.

Don't believe it for a moment.

Béla Bartók, who parodied the famous first-movement march theme so mercilessly in his *Concerto for Orchestra,* was absolutely right: The *Leningrad* is seventy minutes of shallow, grossly manufactured, spur-of-the-moment junk that no amount of interpretative devotion can redeem.

Leonard Bernstein, in this live recording with the Chicago Symphony, refuses to take the revisionist view of the *Leningrad* Symphony, with predictably pleasurable results. The only *enjoyment* to be had in this bellicose nonsense lies in accepting it for the trash it is and having a good, messy wallow. In a performance even more agreeably vulgar and theatrical than his old New York Philharmonic recording, this is precisely what Bernstein allows us to do.

Symphony No. 8 in C minor

Concertgebouw Orchestra of Amsterdam, Haitink. London 411616-2 [CD].

Completed only two years after the windy and prolix *Leningrad* Symphony, the Shostakovich Eighth is (with the single possible exception of the Tenth) the masterpiece among the composer's mature orchestral works. Beginning with one of the greatest symphonic Adagios written after Mahler, the Eighth is a dark, sprawling, grotesque, and enervating work, a combination of a stark outcry against the terrors of the Second World War and the soundtrack for some unimaginable Hollywood horror movie which, fortunately for everyone, was never made. The reactions this great and controversial work continues to provoke are perhaps more extreme than those caused by all Shostakovich's other works put together: Koussevitzky considered it the greatest orchestral piece of this century; Stalin, as well as other, infinitely more civilized listeners, considered it unpleasant, irredeemable trash.

In one of the finest performances from his admirable Shostakovich cycle, Bernard Haitink makes one of the strongest cases for the work yet. (A brilliant Angel recording by André Previn has shamefully been allowed to fall out of print.) As always, Haitink is more than content to let this powerful, often overwhelming music speak for itself. Climaxes and textures, while perfectly judged, are never pushed or overdone, and though the more grisly elements are given their full due, they are never needlessly emphasized. At the conclusion of the performance—the acid test of any interpretation of the Shostakovich Eighth—you do feel very much as though you'd been run over by a freight train, which was the effect the composer intended.

A live 1982 recording of a performance by Yevgeny Mravinsky, the Symphony's dedicatee, and the Leningrad Philharmonic is certainly worth owning, as a souvenir not only of a great musician but also of what was once an incomparable interpretation. Though the sound of this Philips recording (422442-2 [CD]) is the best the conductor ever got, most of his earlier, hideously recorded versions are preferable. In short, this is an Eighth to complement, but by no means displace, Haitink's.

Of available tapes, Solti's is the preferred version (RCA 60145-4-RC).

Symphony No. 10 in E minor

London Philharmonic, Haitink. London 421353-2 [CD].

If we are to believe Shostakovich in his posthumously published *Testimony,* the Tenth Symphony was his rueful, bitter, sardonic reflection on the Stalin years. In fact, the composer even goes so far as to tell us that the diabolical Scherzo of the work was a portrait of that murderous psychopath himself. Whatever the immediate source of the Tenth's inspiration, it is one of the greatest symphonies of the twentieth century and one of the most compelling works a Russian composer has so far produced.

In the late 1960s, Herbert von Karajan, in one of his last palatable recordings, left a staggeringly brilliant account of the Tenth, since superseded by one of his typical smooth-shod monstrosities, which is to be avoided at all costs. On the other hand, Bernard Haitink's sober, sobering, yet ultimately triumphant London recording shows what an ego of human proportions coupled with an immense talent can do. The performance has a sense of dogged decency about it, as if the conductor feels the need to keep the work as far removed as possible from the obscenity that inspired it. It also has moments of snarling rage and dizzy excitement, and is exceedingly well played.

Neeme Järvi's recording for Chandos (ABTD-1319) won't exactly sweep you off your feet, but it is the best of the available tapes.

Symphony No. 15 in A; *From Jewish Folk Poetry,* for Soprano, Contralto, Tenor, and Piano (orchestrated 1964)

> Söderström, soprano; Wenkel, contralto; Karczykowski, tenor; Concertgebouw Orchestra of Amsterdam, Haitink. London 417581-2 [CD].

Even for those of us who consider Shostakovich the most important symphonist of the twentieth century, the Thirteenth and Fourteenth Symphonies are difficult pills to swallow. As great as they clearly are, they are also unspeakably depressing. *Babi Yar,* a setting of Yevtushenko's powerful poem on the subject of an infamous Nazi atrocity, and its haunted successor, which is less a symphony than a cycle of orchestral songs on the subject of death, are too painful to be heard more than once or twice in a lifetime.

For those who are inclined to approach them more frequently, Bernard Haitink's London recordings are unlikely to be superseded. The performance of *Babi Yar* bristles with anger and savage indignation (417261-2 [CD]), and the exhausting interpretation of the Fourteenth (417514-2 [CD]) is marked by the unusual but highly effective novelty of presenting each of the poems by García

Lorca, Apollinaire, Rilke, and the rest in their original languages instead of the run-of-the-mill Russian translations that were sung in earlier recordings. If the purpose was to make this death-obsessed work even more universal, it was achieved admirably.

If with its peculiar quotations of the *William Tell* Overture and a motif from Wagner's *Götterdämmerung* the Fifteenth Symphony would seem to be a far less serious work, it was Haitink's recording which finally demonstrated that the quirks and clowning were only skin-deep. Although some of the material still sounds rather thin for a valedictory, Haitink was the first, and to date is the *only*, conductor to prove conclusively that Shostakovich's cryptic final symphony was not some sort of elaborate practical joke. The orchestral version of *From Jewish Folk Poetry*, one of the most engaging song cycles by a Russian composer since the death of Mussorgsky, rounds out this generous and important release.

Trio No. 2 in E minor for Piano, Violin, and Cello

Palsson-Tellefsen-Helmerson. Bis CD-26 [CD].

The E minor Piano Trio might just be Shostakovich's chamber masterpiece; at very least, it is one of his most powerful and deeply personal works. Written in memory of the composer's closest friend, the brilliant musicologist Ivan Sollertinsky, who somehow survived both the Stalinist purges of the 1930s and the Nazis only to drink himself to death in 1944, the Trio is an exercise in hilarious anguish, or anguished hilarity, depending on which paradoxical designation you prefer. Its most excruciating moment is the finale, a *danse macabre* that breaks the bonds of conventional gallows humor to enter a previously unexplored realm of darkness.

After more than twenty years, this remains one of the greatest of all Shostakovich recordings. The three young Swedish musicians expose the bitter heart of the Trio more fearlessly than any ensemble ever has. They bring a special insight and finish to each of these problematical movements, but it is their performance of the grotesque final dance that will chill you to the bone. In spite of its age, the recorded sound is still a model of warmth and intimacy.

Sibelius, Jean (1865–1957)

Concerto in D minor for Violin and Orchestra

Perlman, violin; Pittsburgh Symphony, Previn. Angel CDC-
47167 [CD], 4AM-34769 [T].

In many respects, Jean Sibelius remains the most mysterious
composer of modern times. A national hero in his native Finland
while still quite a young man, and a composer who, during his lifetime, enjoyed as much critical and popular adulation as any composer ever has, Sibelius simply closed up his musical shop in the
mid-1920s, writing nothing of significance for the next thirty years.
(Rumors of a completed Eighth Symphony circulated for more than
three decades, although no such work was found in his papers at
the time of his death.)

The popular Violin Concerto dates from 1903, the period of
some of his finest theatrical music (*Pelléas et Mélisande*), the tone
poem *Pohjola's Daughter,* and the Second Symphony. Beginning
with a famous early electrical recording by Jascha Heifetz and Sir
Thomas Beecham, the Concerto has always been brilliantly represented on records, from an unforgettable performance in the late
1940s by the French violinist Ginette Neveu to the more recent—
and finer—of Itzhak Perlman's two versions. Compared to his earlier outing with Erich Leinsdorf and the Boston Symphony, the new
recording with André Previn and the Pittsburgh Symphony is at
once more dramatic and more relaxed. While tempos, especially in
the first two movements, tend to be on the leisurely side, there is
nothing in the performance that could be considered even remotely
lethargic or slack. The interpretation has a wonderful feeling of expansiveness to it, a performance cast and executed on the grandest
possible scale. The support Perlman receives from Previn and his
forces is, as usual, exemplary, and the recorded sound is absolutely
first-rate.

Finlandia; En Saga; The Swan of Tuonela; Night Ride and Sunrise; Pohjola's Daughter

L'Orchestre de la Suisse Romande, Stein. London 417697-2
[CD].

Except for the *Karelia Suite* and *Tapiola,* which are now being brilliantly served on another London recording by the Philharmonia Orchestra led by Vladimir Ashkenazy (417762-2 [CD]), this reissue of material originally recorded in the early 1970s includes the most significant of Sibelius's shorter works now being offered on compact disc.

On the basis of this and a handful of other recordings made two decades ago, many (myself included) predicted that Horst Stein, a German conductor known primarily for his work in the opera house, was on the brink of a major international career. (God knows, with plum posts like the Concertgebouw Orchestra of Amsterdam and now the New York Philharmonic going to either rank incompetents or plodding kapellmeisters, the conductor shortage has become dangerously acute.)

Be that as it may, these versions of some of Sibelius's most popular tone poems are among the best on the market, with *Night Ride and Sunrise* and *Pohjola's Daughter* being especially well-played and thrilling. Those who grew up on L'Orchestre de la Suisse Romande during the long and memorable Ansermet era will hardly recognize the ensemble. The solo woodwinds manage to lose that pinched quality which suggested the players weren't being adequately fed, and the brass bring off feats that recall the exploits of their colleagues in Vienna and Berlin.

Songs for Male Choir (complete)

Helsinki University Chorus. Finlandia FACD-205-S [CD].

Since almost all of Sibelius's vocal music remains terra incognita (how many people know he actually wrote an opera called *The Maiden in the Tower,* a pair of cantatas with the irresistible titles *Oma maa* and *Maan virsi,* and more than a hundred songs?), here is an unusually alluring invitation to wander down this unbeaten path. In addition to a stunning vocal setting of the hymn from *Finlandia* that will snap the goose pimples to attention, the Helsinki University Chorus offers elegant, virile performances of twenty-four other a cappella works whose quality ranges from the merely splendid to the nearly sublime.

Symphonies (7)

Boston Symphony, Davis. Philips 416600-2 [CD].

There was a time, not so terribly long ago, when some of these seven extraordinary works were heard as often as the nine symphonies of Beethoven. In fact, during the 1930s and '40s they were probably the most frequently performed orchestral works written during the preceding hundred years. Much of the credit for Sibelius's popularity, aside from the power and originality of the music itself, was due to a group of gifted and tireless champions, including Sir Thomas Beecham, Leopold Stokowski, and Serge Koussevitzky, men whose compelling, highly individual interpretations made the Finnish symphonist's name a household word throughout the musical world.

From Koussevitzky's time to the present, the Boston Symphony has remained one of the world's great Sibelius orchestras. And while several individual interpretations might be marginally preferable—George Szell's immaculate yet blazing performance of the Second with the Concertgebouw Orchestra of Amsterdam has now appeared on a Philips compact disc (420771-2), and Simon Rattle's dazzling Angel recording of the Fifth (CDM-64122 [CD]) deserves all the lavish critical praise it has received—the BSO's complete set of the Symphonies under Sir Colin Davis is one of the best imaginable introductions to the music, either for the novice or the most jaded of collectors. As a Sibelius conductor, Davis represents a golden mean between the audacity of his predecessors and the somewhat cooler approach of the modern school. All the strength and cragginess of the music remain intact, though Sir Colin is also meticulous with textures and details. In short, these are performances which, while they remove some of the bark, leave the trees healthy and intact.

The Boston Symphony plays this music like no other orchestra in the world, and Philips's recorded sound, after more than a decade, remains a model of clarity and warmth. As a bonus, the generously packed discs include superlative performances of the ever-popular *Finlandia, Swan of Tuonela,* and *Tapiola.* All in all, one of the few authentic bargains on the market today.

Smetana, Bedřich (1824–1884)

The Bartered Bride

Běnáčková-Capová, Dvořsky, Novák, Czech Philharmonic
Orchestra and Chorus, Košler. Supraphon 10-3511-2
[CD].

Three Dances from The Bartered Bride

Cleveland Orchestra, Szell. CBS MYK-36716 [CD],
MYT-36716 [T].

As immensely and eternally entertaining as *The Bartered Bride*
certainly is, its historical importance in the development of Czech
music is all but impossible to calculate. Prior to *Prodaná Nevěsta*,
Bohemia had been widely known as the conservatory of Europe, a
tiny province of the sprawling Austro-Hungarian empire that had
always supplied the courts of Europe with some of their finest musicians. Yet Czech composers, before Smetana, were indistinguishable from their German and Austrian counterparts; many, in fact,
in order to secure important positions Germanized their names.

The Bartered Bride was Bohemia's musical Declaration of Independence. A work that not only was based on decidedly Czech
themes but also captured the essential spirit of Czech folk music and
dance, *Prodaná Nevěsta* made its difficult, irascible composer a national hero. (The only Czech opera that has entered the standard
repertoire of every major opera house, it is revered as a national
monument in Czechoslovakia.) Without it, the masterworks of
Smetana's maturity are virtually unthinkable, and had it never been
written, composers like Dvořák and Janáček might never have
evolved as they did.

A number of fine recorded performances of the opera have
been available through the years, but none can begin to approach
this brilliant Supraphon release, which will undoubtedly set the
standard for *Bartered Brides* for decades to come. In the title role,
Gabriela Běnáčkova-Capová—the reigning queen of Prague's National Theater and one of the finest dramatic sopranos in the world
today—will probably not be bettered for the remainder of this cen-

tury. She sings with an ease, warmth, femininity, and freshness that only Elisabeth Schwarzkopf, in a few tantalizing German-language excerpts from the late 1950s, could begin to match. Peter Dvořsky is equally outstanding as the wily hero Jenik, and the rest of the cast—especially the marriage broker of Richard Novák—could not have been surpassed either on records or off.

Although Zdeněk Košler's interpretation is as zestful and refreshing as any the opera has ever received, the principal selling point in a recording loaded with selling points is the playing of the great Czech Philharmonic. They perform this music as no other orchestra possibly could, and the lusty, brilliantly trained chorus is as rowdy, rousing, and tender as anyone could wish.

For those poor misguided souls who think they can do without a complete recording of *The Bartered Bride* (then, too, there are probably people who can live without sunshine, root beer popsicles, and sex), George Szell's classic recording of the three popular dances (the Polka, Furiant, and Dance of the Comedians) is the greatest single performance ever given of the opera's most frequently heard orchestral excerpts. Actually, this is one of the most valuable recordings of Czech music ever made, including, as it does, what may easily be the definitive versions of Smetana's popular *Moldau,* and the *Carnival Overture* of Dvořák.

Má Vlast (My Fatherland)

Vienna Philharmonic, Levine. Deutsche Grammophon 419768-2 [CD].

Smetana began work on what would prove to be his only major contribution to symphonic thought in the same week of 1874 that he resigned his post as principal conductor of Prague's Provisional Theater. At the age of fifty, the composer of *The Bartered Bride* was totally deaf. What had at first been diagnosed as a minor ear infection proved to be a symptom of the syphilis that would also claim his sanity and, ultimately, his life.

Má Vlast, his magnificent, uneven, terribly moving collection of six symphonic poems, is perhaps the greatest musical love letter a composer ever wrote to his native country. *The Moldau* from it has become justly famous, and the entire cycle contains much of the best that the father of Czech music had to give to nineteenth-century music. It is one of the cornerstones of Romantic art, and one of the purest expressions of the nationalistic spirit ever heard in Western music.

As a performance of the cycle, no modern recording has ever managed to efface the memory of those two versions the great Václav Talich made in the mid-1930s and late 1940s. (A third version, from 1941, is one of the rarest recordings any major conductor has ever made.) Although James Levine might not have the same instinctive grasp as the man who was probably the greatest Czech conductor of all time, his recent version of the cycle is the most impressive to have appeared in years. The Vienna Philharmonic play with tremendous bite and conviction, and while Levine is at his best in the more dramatic, declamatory passages, he also infuses the performance with considerable sensitivity and finesse. *From Bohemia's Meadows and Woods* has rarely sounded more delicately shaded, and the moonlit passages of *The Moldau* have magic that only a handful of other recordings (Szell's in particular) can equal.

Levine's compact disc is now an easy first choice among all recorded versions of the cycle; however, when some enterprising little label reissues the final Talich recording on CD (*The Moldau* and *From Bohemia's Meadows and Woods* are now available as filler for Talich's Supraphon CD of the Dvořák Eighth [11-0627-2]), the situation will change completely.

String Quartet No. 1 in E minor, *From My Life*

Smetana Quartet. Denon C37-7339 [CD].

Emerson Quartet. Book-of-the-Month Club Records 21-7526 [CD], 11-7525 [T].

There is no more poignant chamber work in music than this autobiographical string quartet Smetana completed shortly after he was engulfed by the deafness that would stay with him throughout the remaining ten years of his life. While the final movement, which contains the famous high-pitched E in the first violin (representative of the initial symptom of his hearing loss), is one of the most shattering moments in nineteenth-century music, the Quartet is in fact a predominantly buoyant and cheerful work. It looks backward to the composer's youth with a charming and gentle nostalgia, and even manages to look forward to the troubled future with great dignity and courage.

The recording by the Emerson Quartet, available only as part of their hugely successful "Great Romantic Quartets" series, is the most technically accomplished since the Juilliard's famous CBS recording, now withdrawn. The clarity of texture and articulation is truly exceptional, as is their grasp of the essentially tragic nature of the piece. In no other version is the fateful note made to sound quite so terrifying, and the closing bars have just the right feeling of resigned exhaustion.

The Smetana Quartet also does handsomely by its eponym, with playing that is a hint more lush and idiomatic. As a bonus, the recording offers the rare opportunity to examine the composer's seldom heard but utterly worthy Second String Quartet.

A choice between the two is such a coin toss that the more extravagant collector will want to have both.

Sousa, John Philip (1854–1932)

Marches

> Philip Jones Brass Ensemble, Howarth. London 410290-2 [CD], 410290-4 [T].
>
> Eastman Wind Ensemble, Fennell. Mercury 416147-2 [CD].

What, I hear you ask, is an entry on John Philip Sousa doing in a book dealing with Official Classical Music? Has the author no standards? Is nothing sacred? The answer to the last two questions is "No."

If, like me, you find the music of the March King irresistible, by all means snatch up two of the four greatest Sousa march collections ever released. (The others were a collection led by Henry Mancini, an ace piccolo player and a top-notch bandsman in his day, and an old Capitol album called *The Military Band,* presided over by the hugely gifted Felix Slatkin.) The playing on the London recording is as clean as the most demanding drum major could wish.

Rhythms are crisp, the ensemble is razor-sharp, and this British group can certainly teach us a thing or two.

The first of what I hope will be innumerable CD reissues of Frederick Fennell's storied Mercury recordings from the early 1960s is unusually welcome, not only because of the impeccable performances but also for the unusual repertoire. The half dozen "greatest hits" are here, and so are *Bullets and Bayonets, National Game, Riders for the Flag, The Pride of the Wolverines,* and other worthy rarities.

In short: Fellow Sousa cuckoos, rejoice.

Still, William Grant

(1895–1978)

Instrumental Works

Kaufman, violin; et al. Bay Cities BCD-1033 [CD].

Revered for decades as the dean of Afro-American composers, William Grant Still was one of the first musicians to incorporate elements of his African heritage into the symphonic mainstream of European music. His extraordinary and shamefully neglected *Afro-American Symphony* of 1931 was a milestone in the history of American music, and not simpy because it was the first modern symphony by an American composer of African descent. In its best pages, it ranks with the finest symphonic works written by *any* American and deserves a first-rate modern recording.

Still never had a more tireless or eloquent champion than the wonderful American violinist Louis Kaufman, whose pioneering recordings are now finding their way onto compact disc. While the recorded sound of these performances, many of them taken from radio airchecks, is understandably variable, the interpretations themselves are marvels of fire, color, and finesse, especially those involving Kaufman's gifted wife, Annette.

Another recent CD from Music and Arts (CD-638) features later, though equally incomparable, versions of two of the *Danzas de Panama* and the splendid *Ennanga* for String Quartet, Harp, and Piano from 1956. Either as music by an important American composer or souvenirs of a great American violinist, both issues are indispensable.

Strauss, Johann II (1825–1899)

Die Fledermaus

> Gueden, Köth, Resnik, Zampieri, Wächter, Kmentt, Berry, Kunz, Vienna State Opera Chorus, Vienna Philharmonic, Karajan. London 421046-2 [CD].

> Varady, Popp, Kollo, Prey, Rebroff, Bavarian State Opera Chorus and Orchestra, C. Kleiber. Deutsche Grammophon 415646-2 [CD], 415646-4 [T].

More than 125 years since the first production of *Die Fledermaus*, it is difficult to imagine how Vienna could have been so cool to the greatest operetta ever written—that is, of course, unless you know the Viennese. Their overwhelming indifference to the original production in 1874 places *Die Fledermaus* in some very good company. The city was also unqualified in its scorn of Mozart's *Don Giovanni*, Beethoven's *Fidelio,* and countless other new works, proving that although it was at one time the musical capital of the world, Vienna in the 1870s was as reactionary as its brutally despotic emperor, Franz Josef.

Die Fledermaus has never had a more effervescent recording than London's "Gala" production of the late 1950s. In addition to memorable star turns from many of the finest singers of the day in the Act II party scene (Leontyne Price's version of Gershwin's "Summertime" is especially haunting), the rest of the production is an unqualified triumph. As in her earlier London recording from the late 1940s, the scrumptious Hilde Gueden was and remains the ideal Rosalinde—wise, wily, sexy—and captured here in wonderful voice. The supporting cast, led by Regina Resnik as the marvelously dissolute Prince Orlovsky and the ageless Erich Kunz as the drunken, irrepressible Frosch, is one of the best ever mustered in a recording studio. The Vienna Philharmonic play *Fledermaus* as only they can play *Fledermaus,* and Herbert von Karajan, in one of his last successful recordings, conducts with tremendous joy, delicacy, and verve.

As a tape alternative, the performance led by Carlos Kleiber is only slightly less engaging than London's classic release. The choice of the Russian bass Ivan Rebroff as Prince Orlovsky, generally a mezzo-soprano role, had a particularly daffy inspiration to it, and Kleiber, as always, finds many new and interesting things to say.

The Gypsy Baron

Schwarzkopf, Köth, Gedda, Kunz, Prey, Philharmonia Orchestra and Chorus, Ackermann. Angel CDH-69526 [CD].

Written eleven years after *Die Fledermaus, Der Zigeunerbaron* was the last of the Strauss operettas that Strauss himself actually composed, and as such marked a kind of formal conclusion to the Viennese operetta's Golden Age. *The Gypsy Baron* has never attained but certainly deserves the worldwide popularity of *The Bat.* The plot and characterization are just as ingenious, and the piece overflows with instantly memorable tunes, from the hero's "Als flotter Geist," with its immortal waltz refrain, to "Ja, das Schreiben und das Lesen," a dialect number sung by the pig farmer Zsupan, which, in the right hands, can be the most uproarious moment in all of Strauss.

The Gypsy Baron was in some *very* good hands for this recording from the mid-1950s; in fact, the very best. Produced by Walter Legge, it was one in a series of bubbling versions of all the Strauss operettas that had as their common denominators the inspired conducting of Otto Ackermann (replaced by Karajan for *Die Fledermaus*) and casts headed by Legge's wife, soprano Elisabeth Schwarzkopf.

This *Zigeunerbaron* is by far the finest ever recorded, and not necessarily because of Schwarzkopf's singing, although she is incomparable as the gypsy girl, Saffi. The real treasures here are the young Nicolai Gedda in the title role, and the great Viennese baritone Erich Kunz, who turns Zsupan into one of operetta's greatest comic creations.

The other recordings in the series are just as good; the versions of *Eine Nacht in Venedig* (CDH-69530 [CD]) and *Wiener Blut* (CDH-69529 [CD]), the ersatz-Strauss operetta patched together in 1899 from previously existing material, might even be slightly better. In *A Night in Venice*, the charm of Kunz and Gedda is once again scarcely to be believed, and the way Schwarzkopf and the tenor sing the title duet from *Vienna Blood* will cause all but the most self-possessed to lunge at the nearest object of desire.

Waltzes, Polkas, etc.

Vienna Philharmonic, Boskovsky. London 425425/9-2 [CD].

Vienna Strauss Orchestra, Boskovsky. Angel CDC-47052 [CD].

Chicago Symphony, Reiner. RCA 60177-2-RG [CD], 60177-4-RG [T].

The next time you hear a serious-music snob say something demeaning about the waltzes and polkas of Johann Strauss, tell him or her that he or she is full of it. Or even better, haul off and kick the person in the shin. Johann Strauss II was admired by Brahms, Wagner, and almost every other important musician of his time. His waltzes are every bit as important as, and even more memorable and entertaining than, those of Chopin, and to dismiss them as "light music" or mere pops-concert fare is to miss the point entirely. Almost all of them are brilliantly made, ingeniously crafted little tone poems that will undoubtedly survive long after most of the serious music of that era is forgotten.

The recordings listed above have much to offer both the beginning and experienced collector. All of the many recordings made by the longtime concertmaster of the Vienna Philharmonic, Willi Boskovsky, are graceful, stunningly played, and close to the last word in idiomatic grace. The generous RCA compact disc of recordings made by Fritz Reiner and the Chicago Symphony in the late 1950s is a bargain no Strauss lover can afford to resist. The interpretations are full of Viennese lilt and schmaltz, and the performances are more zestful and precise than any others I know.

Strauss, Richard (1864–1949)

Eine Alpensinfonie

Bavarian Radio Orchestra, Solti. London 414676-2 [CD].

Probably the best thing that can be said about *An Alpine Symphony* is that it is not quite as embarrassing as the *Symphonia domestica,* written eleven years before. Unlike the epically vulgar and, in its bedroom sequence, blatantly pornographic *Domestic Symphony,* this loud and aimless hike through the Alps is merely overblown, overwritten, and dumb. For all practical purposes, there is only one viable theme, a rising, slightly menacing fanfare, which the composer beats to death.

Pervert that I am, I have collected almost every recording of this magnificent trash ever made, beginning with an amazing performance led by the half-mad Oskar Fried that was crammed onto a set of acoustical 78s. Among versions in which you can hear something more than the trumpet and an occasional violin, Sir Georg Solti's outing with the Bavarian Radio Orchestra is pretty thrilling, especially in the richly ferocious playing he draws from the brass.

Along with the fabulous execution and recorded sound, the recording has one more thing in its favor. Since Solti's tempos tend to be brisker than usual, he gets it over with quicker than almost anybody else.

Also sprach Zarathustra

Chicago Symphony, Reiner. RCA 5721-2-RC [CD], 6722-4-RG6 [T].

Since Stanley Kubrick's *2001* made it a popular hit, Strauss's tone poem after Nietzsche, *Also sprach Zarathustra,* has had dozens of recordings, most of them with some outer-space scene cleverly placed on the record jacket. (Say what you will about them, recording companies are no dolts when it comes to marketing.)

In spite of the flood of new *Zarathustras*, the one that continues to speak most eloquently is Fritz Reiner's phenomenal 1954 recording with the Chicago Symphony. It was one of RCA's very first stereo efforts, and one of the first recordings Reiner made with his new orchestra; no one could have expected quite so great a result. The playing remains a wonder of alertness, fire, and whiplash attacks, while the recording, old though it may be, is as warm, detailed, and sensual as many made in the 1970s. Incidentally, Reiner was one of Strauss's favorite conductors. This classic recording will show you why.

The CD comes with what remains that most sparkling of all versions of the *Bourgeois Gentilhomme* Suite and Reiner's own arrangement of the *Rosenkavalier* Waltzes. The tape offers the conductor's 1962 remake of *Zarathustra*, which was not quite as superhuman as the 1954 effort, nor, strangely, as brilliantly recorded. This *Zarathustra* (also available on CD as 6722-2-RG) is accompanied by Leontyne Price's languorous version of the *Four Last Songs* and a stunning account of the Empress's Awakening Scene from *Die Frau ohne Schatten*.

Arabella

Donath, Varady, Fischer-Dieskau, Schmidt, Berry, Bavarian State Opera Chorus and Orchestra, Sawallisch. Orfeo 169882 [CD].

For the last of his operas on a text by his greatest collaborator, Hugo von Hofmannsthal, Strauss returned to the scene of his greatest triumph, the Vienna of *Der Rosenkavalier*. If *Arabella* does not begin to match the earlier opera's sustained inspiration, it has much of the same scintillating atmosphere, to say nothing of a superb libretto and many inspired touches. A fine performance can persuade you that it is the greatest of the composer's later operas; a performance as good as this one might almost have you believing it's something even more.

Julia Varady has much of the shrewd intelligence and innate musicality that characterized the work of Vienna's first Arabella, the great Lotte Lehmann. Varady's singing is rich, warm, and irresistibly feminine, and she is offered able support by her real-life husband, Dietrich Fischer-Dieskau, as Mandryka. The conducting of Wolfgang Sawallisch represents his finest work in the studio, and the recorded sound is superb. in short, this is the one *Arabella* that seems like anything but a cut-rate *Rosenkavalier*.

Ariadne auf Naxos

Schwarzkopf, Seefried, Schock, Streich, Donch, Cuénod,
Philharmonia Orchestra, Karajan. Angel CDMB-69296
[CD].

No less a Strauss authority than Sir Thomas Beecham insisted in his book *A Mingled Chime* (1944) that in the original version of *Ariadne auf Naxos*, "the musical accomplishment of Strauss attained its highest reach, yielding a greater spontaneity and variety of invention, together with a subtler and riper style, than anything that his pen has yet given to the stage . . ."

While *Ariadne* has always skirted the edges of the concert repertoire, it has enjoyed a charmed life in the recording studio, beginning with this miraculous version taped in London in 1954. Even those who fail to respond to either the chamber dimensions (the orchestra is limited to thirty-nine players) or the studied artificiality of the play within the play cannot help being bowled over by the singing of Rita Streich, Elisabeth Schwarzkopf, and the amazing Irmgard Seefried at the height of their powers, or the deft, imaginative conducting of Herbert von Karajan, who very nearly equals the achievement of his historic *Rosenkavalier* (see below).

Concertos (2) for Horn and Orchestra

Brain, horn; Philharmonia Orchestra, Sawallisch. Angel
CDC-47834 [CD].

When Dennis Brain died in a car crash September 1, 1957, while rushing back to London from the Edinburgh Festival, the world lost not only the preeminent French horn player of the century but one of its greatest musicians. In the years since his death, players of comparable technical prowess have arisen, but none have managed to combine a flawless technique with such an audacious yet aristocratic musical personality. He was, to use a hackneyed phrase, a one-of-a-kind phenomenon, and it would seem extremely unlikely that we will see his equal again.

With his famous recordings of the Mozart concertos, these versions of the two concertos of Richard Strauss constitute Dennis Brain's most lasting memorial. The actual playing, of course, is breathtaking, but so is the unerring rightness of the interpretations, from the youthful ardor he projects in the early concerto to the mellow wisdom he finds in its successor.

The highest praise that can be bestowed on Wolfgang Sawallisch's accompaniments is to say that they are completely worthy of the soloist. The definitive recording of the Horn Concerto Paul Hindemith wrote for Brain, with the Philharmonia conducted by the composer, fills out the disc.

The composer's overly ripe, phenomenally difficult Oboe Concerto has finally been recorded by the man whose chance remark inspired it. As a GI serving in Germany after the war, John de Lancie, later the principal oboist of the Philadelphia Orchestra, happened to ask the aging composer why he had never written a concerto for the instrument. The Concerto for Oboe and Small Orchestra was the result. Though one could only wish that de Lancie had recorded the work in his prime, his 1987 version (RCA 7989-2-RG [CD], 7989-4-RG [T]) is a brilliant one and a significant historical document.

Strauss's impossibly difficult de facto piano concerto, *Burlesk,* is currently best served on another RCA recording featuring the phenomenal, albeit tightly wound, Byron Janis with the Chicago Symphony led by Fritz Reiner (5734-2-RC [CD]).

*D*aphne

> Gueden, Little, King, Wunderlich, Schoeffler, Vienna State Opera Chorus, Vienna Symphony, Böhm. Deutsche Grammophon 423579-2 [CD].

In many respects, *Daphne* is a perfect living room opera: not much happens in this stately pastoral romp, and its central event — the transformation of the heroine from a flesh-and-blood fisherman's daughter into a warbling tree — is best left to the listener's imagination. Yet of all the late Strauss operas, *Daphne* is also, paradoxically, the least artificial and possibly the most charming. The level of musical invention, while certainly not that of *Der Rosen-kavalier*, rises well above decadent, stillborn efforts like *Die Liebe der Danaë* and *Friedenstag*, and the central character—in the proper hands—can be one of the most enchanting of Strauss's creations. The incomparable Hilde Gueden gives a gleaming performance in this live 1964 recording led by the man to whom the opera was dedicated. The rest of the cast is an unusually strong one, and Karl Böhm's suave, incisive conducting makes even the least inspired pages come alive.

*D*eath and Transfiguration; Don Juan; Till Eulenspiegel's Merry Pranks

Cleveland Orchestra, Szell. CBS MYK-36721 [CD], MYT-36721 [T].

The young Richard Strauss initially made his reputation with this trio of early tone poems, which remain the most popular and frequently performed of his orchestral works. Although there may have been finer individual recordings of each (a live Salzburg Festival recording of *Death and Transfiguration* led by Victor de Sabata is so white-hot in its intensity that it might melt the plastic elements in your speaker system), no collection of all three has ever been more successful than this one.

The Cleveland Orchestra is honed to a fine state of perfection by George Szell, who leads it through a *Till Eulenspiegel* of enormous wit and character, a *Death and Transfiguration* of great power and grandeur, and a *Don Juan* that is a model of swagger and romance. Given the 1960s vintage, the sound is surprisingly good, although the compact disc remastering, like most of CBS's efforts with recordings from this period, tends to be on the hissy side. This is a minor drawback, though, to one of the great Strauss recordings of modern times.

*D*on Quixote

Harrell, cello; Cleveland Orchestra, Ashkenazy. London 417184-2 [CD].

Not counting the shamelessly self-indulgent *Ein Heldenleben* (A Hero's Life), *Don Quixote* is easily the greatest of the mature Strauss tone poems. The structure—a set of variations "on a theme of knightly character"—is beautifully worked out, the orchestration a wonder of subtle ingenuity, and the dramatic content (who can forget the final, sliding note in the cello as old Don dies?) among the most powerful and moving of all Strauss's works.

While I continue to have great affection for Fritz Reiner's Chicago Symphony recording, now available on an RCA compact disc (5734-2-RC), this recent version by Vladimir Ashkenazy is not only a breathtaking example of state-of-the-art recording technology, but also a genuinely wonderful performance. The orchestra seem to take tremendous delight in playing for the fine Russian pianist-turned-conductor. At almost every turn, they uncover some felicitous detail we've never heard before, and in general play with the wit, precision, and fire that characterized their work during the height of the golden Szell days. Cellist Lynn Harrell acquits himself magnificently in the "title role," and the recorded sound is among the most natural I have heard yet from a compact disc.

Elektra

Nilsson, Collier, Resnik, Stolze, Krause, Vienna
Philharmonic, Solti. London 417345-2 [CD].

In many ways, *Elektra* is the most successful and satisfying of all the Strauss operas. For one thing, it is loaded with all those ingredients that make an opera great (cruelty, horror, bloodshed, and revenge), and for another, it is *not* twenty minutes too long (a charge that has been leveled at every other Strauss opera, with the exception of the equally compressed and gory *Salome*).

There is only one completely acceptable recording of the opera currently available, and a very great one it is. In the title role, Birgit Nilsson gives one of her most absorbed and shattering recorded performances, from the savage confrontations with her mother, Klytemnestra, sung to chilling effect by Regina Resnik, to one of the most beautiful and moving versions of the thrilling Recognition Scene. The rest of the cast is splendid. Sir Georg Solti's conducting is vividly dramatic and intense, and the recorded sound in the compact disc format—the only one currently available—will rattle the rafters of the best built house.

RCA has recently issued on compact disc some generous selections from the opera, together with excerpts from *Salome,* in the classic recordings made by Inge Borkh (my favorite Elektra of all time) and the Chicago Symphony conducted by Fritz Reiner (60874-2). As much as I tend to dislike operas chopped up into what George Bernard Shaw used to call "bleeding chunks of meat," this recording is a very special one and shouldn't be passed up.

Four Last Songs

Schwarzkopf, soprano; Berlin Radio Symphony, Szell.
Angel CDC-47276 [CD].

Written when Strauss was in his early eighties, the ravishing *Four Last Songs* are the work of a man who, if he was not anxious to die, was certainly more than ready for death. There is a case to be made that Strauss was artistically dead long before his actual demise in 1949. He was a nineteenth-century revolutionary who lived to see himself become a twentieth-century reactionary; his music from the 1920s onward became increasingly repetitive and uninspired until he was finally reduced to such drivel as *The Happy Workshop* and the pleasant but featherweight Oboe Concerto. With the *Four Last Songs* Strauss dug deep into himself and the past and became, for the final time, the great composer he had once been: the Strauss of *Der Rosenkavalier* and *Death and Transfiguration,* one of whose themes is quoted so movingly in the last of the songs.

Among all the superb interpretations of Strauss's final masterpiece, by Lucia Popp, Arleen Auger, Jessye Norman, and Leontyne Price (to say nothing of the recording of the world premiere with Kirsten Flagstad and Wilhelm Furtwängler that has been slipping in and out of print for forty years), no performance has ever captured more of the serenity or melancholy intensity of the music than this one Elisabeth Schwarzkopf taped in the mid-1960s with the Berlin Radio Symphony and George Szell. Both these superlative musicians respond to every musical nuance in the score, and the soprano brings a depth of understanding to the words that demonstrates why she was the greatest German singer since Lotte Lehmann.

A generous selection of the composer's orchestral songs rounds out what may be the finest Strauss recording available today.

Die Frau ohne Schatten

Nilsson, Rysanek, Hesse, King, Berry, Vienna State Opera Orchestra and Chorus, Böhm. Deutsche Grammophon 415472-2 [CD].

Many consider this heavily symbolic Wagnerian fairy tale the high point of Richard Strauss's collaboration with the doomed, brilliantly accomplished Viennese poet and playwright Hugo von Hofmannsthal, which is to say an even greater work than *Elektra*, *Ariadne auf Naxos*, or *Der Rosenkavalier*. There are also those who believe that the composer always got the better end of the bargain, including Hofmannsthal himself, who is alleged to have confessed to a friend, "How nice it would be if (Franz) Lehár had composed the music for *Rosenkavalier* instead of Strauss." (Apropos of absolutely nothing, *Die Frau* served as the basis for one of the most arcane musical bumper stickers I have ever seen. Unlike the amusing though rather obvious "*Carmen* made Mérimée Prosper," "O Milhaud My," and "The Sugar Plum Fairy made the Nutcracker Suite," this one read "Die Frau ohne Schatten once a day." Think about it.)

Although history has not been especially kind to this most demanding and far-reaching of Strauss's creations, *The Woman without a Shadow* has had a small but fanatically loyal following from the very beginning; it can be an extremely difficult nut to crack, but it will more than repay any amount of time the listener is willing to invest.

This live 1977 performance led by the composer's old crony Karl Böhm makes the most persuasive case for *Die Frau* of any recording so far. The cast is an extremely strong one, headed by the ageless Leonie Rysanek as the Empress and Birgit Nilsson as the Dyer's Wife. Still, for all the fine, frequently superlative singing, it is Böhm's warm, effortlessly dramatic, infinitely resourceful conducting that best convinces us that *Die Frau*'s admirers could be right. For a live performance, the recording is exceptionally clear and detailed, with both the foot-shuffling onstage and noises from the usually rude Viennese audience kept to a bare minimum.

Ein Heldenleben

Chicago Symphony, Reiner. RCA RCD1-5408 [CD].

Richard Strauss was not, by any stretch of the imagination, a lovable, or even particularly likable, man. He collaborated openly with the Nazis from the late 1930s onward, was shamelessly mercenary throughout his life, and was probably the only composer in history whose ego could be compared with Richard Wagner's. The great German conductor Hans Knappertsbusch may have summed it up best when he said, "I knew him very well. We played cards every week for forty years and he was a pig."

In spite of the fact that it is one of the most self-indulgent pieces in the history of art, *Ein Heldenleben* is a very great work. The "Hero's Life" that the tone poem celebrates is, of course, Strauss's own. And though we blush for the sheer audacity of the man, he does blow his own horn (in fact, all eight of them) magnificently.

In a heroically crowded field of superb recordings, the one by Fritz Reiner should now be regarded as the very best. Perhaps more than any of his other Strauss recordings, the Reiner *Heldenleben* is a study in disciplined lunacy: the battle music erupts with a horrible yet carefully studied violence, and the love music is infused with an overt yet almost gentlemanly eroticism. Like all of RCA's Reiner recordings, this one wears its age with exceptional grace.

Der Rosenkavalier

Schwarzkopf, Ludwig, Stich-Randall, Edelmann,
Philharmonia Orchestra and Chorus, Karajan. Angel
CDCC-49354 [CD], 3CDX-3970 [T].

Shortly after his last and dreadful Deutsche Grammophon recording of the loveliest of the Strauss operas was released, Herbert von Karajan, tactful gentleman that he always was, said something to the effect that he was *so* happy to have finally made a recording of *Der Rosenkavalier* with "an adequate cast." Taking nothing away from Anna Tomowa-Sintow, just what did the maestro think he had in Elisabeth Schwarzkopf thirty years ago? Chopped liver?

This first Karajan *Rosenkavalier* has all the tenderness, charm, impetuosity, and dramatic tension that his newer recording lacks.

And with Madame Schwarzkopf, he clearly has the finest Marschallin since Lotte Lehmann was singing the role in the 1930s. From either the compact disc or the tapes, the recording emerges as what it has clearly been since it was first released: one of the great opera recordings of the century.

Salome

Nilsson, Hoffman, Stolze, Kmentt, Wächter, Vienna
Philharmonic, Solti. London 414414-2 [CD].

Salome, that tasteful, wholesome entertainment whose first Berlin performance Kaiser Wilhelm II personally banned, has served as the vehicle for some of the most startling operatic creations of recent years. Montserrat Caballé, whom one would not immediately think of as the nubile heroine, made a dazzling recording for RCA a number of years ago that has finally resurfaced on compact disc (6644-2-RG). Vocally and visually, Maria Ewing's recent performances with the Los Angeles Music Center Opera proved a revelation. In addition to a Dance of the Seven Veils in which this disturbingly beautiful soprano did not stop, as is the custom, with veil number six (in the original production she wore a G-string under protest; in the revival, she eschewed it, arguing that Salome herself would never have given in to something so ridiculously modest), the final scene was a musical and dramatic tour de force. If someone doesn't record it soon, it will only prove what I have long assumed—to wit, that the recording industry is nuts.

As Strauss's terrifying, oversexed adolescent, Birgit Nilsson gives one of the most powerful performances of her long and brilliant career. The closing twenty minutes, when she has that grisly "duet" with the head of John the Baptist, are among the most chilling ever captured in a recording studio. Sir Georg Solti, here as elsewhere, lends the kind of sympathetic, though never sycophantic, support of which most singers only dream. The rest of the cast, especially Gerhard Stolze as King Herod, is overwhelming, and the remastered sound will take your breath away.

Symphonia domestica

Chicago Symphony, Reiner. RCA 60388-2-RG [CD],
60388-4-RG [T].

Say what you will about the *Domestic Symphony,* it is one of the most shamelessly vulgar musical works ever written by the man who once claimed he could set anything to music. It traces, in gruesome detail, the singularly banal events transpiring in the Strauss household during an average day, including the composer's young son being given his bath and the composer and his wife fulfilling their conjugal obligations. Many of Strauss's closest musical friends pleaded with him not to publish the Symphony's program; he did, and ever since, the work has remained his most justly maligned.

Fritz Reiner's classic recording from 1956 is so completely spellbinding that you can almost overlook the yawning vapidity of the piece itself and simply revel in the phenomenal execution. Even the closing pages, which can seem so overwritten and overblown, have a magnificent inevitability about them, together with a brassy grandeur that will silence all criticism. The recorded sound, like the Chicago Symphony's playing, remains a marvel.

Stravinsky, Igor (1882–1971)

*A*pollo; Orpheus

> Orchestra of St. John's of Smith Square, Lubbock.
> Nonesuch H4-71401 [T].
> City of Birmingham Symphony, Rattle. Angel CDC-49636 [CD].

From the early 1920s, when the Russian "primitive" was busy transforming himself into a Parisian gentleman, to the mid-1950s, when his discovery of the music of Anton Webern lured him, belatedly, into the serialism and twelve-tone procedures of the Schoenberg camp (many of his closest musical friends never forgave him for the "defection"), the longest and most productive creative phase of Igor Stravinsky's career—the so-called neoclassical phase—yielded many of the finest works that great chameleon of twentieth-century music would produce.

The 1928 ballet *Apollon Musagète* (Apollo, Leader of the Muses) is one of the purest expressions of Stravinsky's fascination with the musical procedures and disciplines of the past. The music not only projects a cool, detached tranquillity that is perfectly attuned to its subject matter, it manifests a sweet and unmistakable sentimentality of which this tough-minded realist was very rarely accused.

John Lubbock and the strings of the Orchestra of St. John's are alternately tender and incandescent in this magnificent music, and also do very handsomely by the strangely neglected *Orpheus* of 1947, which is an only slightly less inspired score. The more amiable and easygoing performance led by Simon Rattle is the best of the currently available CDs.

Concerto in E-flat, *Dumbarton Oaks;* Eight Instrumental Miniatures for Fifteen Players; *Pulcinella* Suite

Orpheus Chamber Orchestra. Deutsche Grammophon 419628-2 [CD].

Stravinsky once said with disarming honesty, "I love Mozart so much, I steal his music." And so, with *The Rake's Progress*, the twentieth century's great recycler produced a complete eighteenth-century number opera modeled on *Don Giovanni*. Rossini, Tchaikovsky, American jazz, Russian folk song, Webern, and the fourteenth-century Frenchman Guillaume de Machaut were all grist for Stravinsky's incredible refracting mill, as were his two favorite Baroque composers, Bach and Giovanni Battista Pergolesi. It was music attributed to the startlingly ugly, sadly short-lived Pergolesi that he arranged into *Pulcinella*, the first of his great neoclassical ballets, and the spirit, to say nothing of the actual letter, of Bach's *Brandenburg* Concertos that he lifted for the *Dumbarton Oaks* Concerto of 1938.

The Orpheus Chamber Orchestra give predictably polished and enthusiastic performances of the Concerto and the *Pulcinella* Suite, as well as the equally marvelous Eight Instrumental Miniatures. This is prime middle-period Stravinsky, affectionately played and handsomely recorded.

For anyone interested in the complete *Pulcinella* (and it's such a hospitable, thoroughly outgoing work, everyone *should* be interested in it), Claudio Abbado's recording with the London Symphony and a trio of excellent soloists headed by the exquisite Teresa Berganza shouldn't be passed up, especially since it is generously packaged with a superb version of the "Ballet in Three Deals," *Jeu de cartes* (Deutsche Grammophon 423889-2 [CD]).

The Fairy's Kiss

Scottish National Orchestra, Järvi. Chandos CHAN-8360 [CD].

With the possible exception of *Perséphone* (the 1934 ballet with recitation and chorus which eventually led to a bitter mud-slinging match between the composer and his collaborator, André Gide), *The Fairy's Kiss* is probably the most physically beautiful score Stravinsky ever wrote. Taking Tchaikovsky's music as its point of departure—Stravinsky always claimed that about half the melodies in the ballet were by his great predecessor, half were his own—*Le Baiser de la fée* is a fetching amalgam of instantly lovable tunes (the final apotheosis on "None But the Lonely Heart" makes every audience melt), inspired instrumentation (a graduate seminar in orchestration could be devoted solely to the composer's use of the horns), and that quirky, increasingly sophisticated rhythmic thinking that characterized Stravinsky's work throughout the 1920s.

Neeme Järvi's recording of the complete ballet, which features more than twice the music of the far more familiar Divertimento, is a delightful one. If it's not *quite* as good as the composer's own version (and I must admit my fondness for that recording may have something to do with the fact that it revives memories of a performance I once heard with Stravinsky himself and the Chicago Symphony), it's close enough, and besides, it's the only one available. As they habitually do for Chandos, the Scottish National Orchestra sound like a world-class ensemble in both the ballet and the fascinating "freeze-dried" arrangement Stravinsky made of the Bluebird pas de deux from Tchaikovsky's *Sleeping Beauty*.

The Firebird (complete ballet)

Concertgebouw Orchestra of Amsterdam, Davis. Philips 400074-2 [CD].

At a fashionable party, Igor Stravinsky was once thanked by an effusive grande dame for writing her favorite work, *Scheher-*

azade. "But Madame, I did not write *Scheherazade,*" he tried to explain. To which she allegedly replied, "Oh, all you composers are so modest."

In Stravinsky's first great popular success, *The Firebird,* it's easy to hear why the poor woman was so confused. In its opulence, drama, and brilliant orchestration, *The Firebird* is a direct descendant of Stravinsky's teacher's masterwork. Only in the closing bars, with its majestic apotheosis in 7/4 time, does this early ballet give any clue to the rhythmic experimentation that eventually would change the course of twentieth-century music.

Although many great *Firebird* recordings have come and gone over the years (including another Philips recording by the London Philharmonic and Bernard Haitink that desperately needs to be returned to print), this stunning version by Sir Colin Davis and the Concertgebouw Orchestra is as fine as any. Davis's approach is extremely colorful and dramatic. The Scherzo barely rises above a whisper, and some of the more aggressive moments suggest that this was, indeed, a work by the future composer of *The Rite of Spring.* The orchestra is virtually unbelievable in its ease and power of execution, and the recorded sound is top-drawer.

On tape, the precise yet immensely sensual version by Charles Dutoit and the Montreal Symphony (London 414409-4) is far and away the pick of the crop. In fact, many might even prefer the Dutoit CD (414409-2) to the Davis. (And to tell the truth, there is little to choose between them.)

L'Histoire du soldat (complete)

Lee, speaker; Scottish Chamber Orchestra, Friend. Nimbus NIM-5063 [CD].

The composer's old friend Lukas Foss has always insisted that *L'Histoire du soldat* was Stravinsky's most utterly original work. And as was so often the case in Stravinsky's career, the mother of originality was necessity.

Sitting out the First World War in Switzerland, cut off not only from his native roots but also from the immense orchestra of Sergei Diaghilev's Ballets Russes, the composer gradually abandoned both the Russian themes and opulent scoring of his early ballets. Convinced that the impoverishment of the postwar world would require a new economy in musical settings, he produced *The Soldier's Tale,* music for an ensemble of only seven musicians to accompany a sparse, sinister morality play by the Swiss novelist C. F. Ramuz.

For the producers of this recording to choose Count Dracula to perform all the speaking parts was both surprising and exceptionally canny. Christopher Lee's close association with things that go bump in the night lends an added dimension of eeriness to the supernatural tale; he is also a gifted and versatile actor who turns in a major theatrical tour de force. Lionel Friend and the members of the Scottish Chamber Orchestra prove to be worthy minions for the Count, and the recorded sound is excellent.

The best available recording of the popular Suite is the composer's own, made in the early 1960s, which comes with his rather spartan but intriguing version of *The Firebird* (CBS MK-42432 [CD]).

"The Igor Stravinsky Edition"

Various soloists, choruses, orchestras, ensembles, Stravinsky. Sony Classical SX22K-46290 [CD].

Here, on twenty-two tightly packed compact discs, is one of the unique achievements in the history of the gramophone: the bulk of the music of one of the two major composers of the twentieth century in performances led by the composer himself.

Sony's "Igor Stravinsky Edition" is essentially a CD remastering of the thirty-one-LP set originally issued in 1982. Predictably, the sound has been substantially improved, and the performances retain the special energy and insight the ageless composer brought to his music toward the end of his life.

Aside from the obvious convenience and the handsome packaging, the principal reason to invest in this lavish collection is to acquire the recordings that are not yet available separately. For instance, the composer's own version of his only full-length opera, *The Rake's Progress,* has never been surpassed, nor are more refreshing, idiomatic versions of *The Fairy's Kiss, Les Noces* (whose pianists were Aaron Copland, Samuel Barber, Lukas Foss, and Roger Sessions), and *Perséphone* ever likely to be made. Moreover, worthy oddities like the television ballet *The Flood* and Stravinsky's last major score, the *Requiem Canticles*, simply can't be found in any other form.

Needless to say, the investment is substantial. But so too is the amount of history and enjoyment this invaluable document provides.

Les Noces; Mass

Soloists, English Bach Festival Orchestra and Chorus, Bernstein. Deutsche Grammophon 423251-2 [CD].

Written as long ago as 1917, *Les Noces,* the "Four Choreographic Scenes" for vocal soloists, mixed chorus, four pianists, and a percussion ensemble of seventeen instruments, has remained one of the most paradoxical and underappreciated of all Stravinsky's works. An apparently guileless celebration of a Russian peasant wedding, the ballet is in fact one of the century's most audacious rhythmic experiments. It is also an unprecedented study in monochromatic orchestral color. (In addition to the "orchestra" of pianos, bells, mallet instruments, and drums, the voices, with all their barking and chanting, are treated almost as components of an extended percussion section.)

Similarly, the Mass is a major sacred work that manages to complement without repeating the achievement of the *Symphony of Psalms,* written eighteen years before. (It was the austere yet moving Mass that marked the beginning of the end of Stravinsky's association with his old friend, the conductor Ernest Ansermet. Ansermet, who led the world premiere in 1948, was tactless enough to wonder aloud how someone who pretended to be a lifelong nonbeliever—as the composer was doing at the time—could write such deeply spiritual music.)

Leonard Bernstein leads the most expressive and dramatic recorded performances either work ever received. *Les Noces* has a driven intensity that serves the choppy, primitive rhythms extremely well, while the passionate simplicity he reserves for the Mass makes it seem like one of the key sacred works of modern times.

Petrouchka (complete ballet)

London Symphony, Abbado. Deutsche Grammophon 423901-2 [CD].

Given its first performance the year after *The Firebird* made Stravinsky an international sensation, *Petrouchka* not only confirmed the young Igor Stravinsky's remarkable gift but also proved he was neither a flash in the pan nor a composer who was willing to simply go on repeating himself for the rest of his life. Harmonically, structurally, and, most important, rhythmically, *Petrouchka* marked a significant leap ahead of *The Firebird,* and was one of his earliest works that the elderly Stravinsky professed to like. (He often said that aside from some of the orchestration, he found *The Firebird* utterly uninteresting.)

At least a dozen superlative recordings of the ballet are available today; the most thoroughly satisfying of them is the one by Claudio Abbado and the London Symphony on Deutsche Grammophon. No nuance of texture, no quirky rhythm, no elegant phrase or ingratiating tune escapes Abbado's attention. And unlike the composer's own celebrated recording (CBS MK-42433 [CD]), a "revisionist" interpretation that tried to prove the ballet was a little drier, more acerbic, and more "modern" than it actually was, Abbado refuses to deny *Petrouchka*'s Romantic roots, and thus does a great service to both the listener and the work itself.

As with available versions of *The Firebird,* Charles Dutoit's recording with the Montreal Symphony is not only the first choice among tapes (London 417619-4), but also has a fair claim to being the best of the current CDs (417619-2). The playing and recording are predictably sensational, and coupled with a version of *The Song of the Nightingale* that is as witty as it is sexy, it is a bargain few collectors should be able to pass up.

The Rite of Spring

Columbia Symphony, Stravinsky. CBS MK-42433 [CD], MGT-39015 [T].

Philadelphia Orchestra, Muti. Angel CDC-47408 [CD]. Mobile Fidelity MFSLI-519 [T].

Le Sacre du printemps and Schoenberg's *Pierrot Lunaire* (premiered only a few weeks apart) are the two seminal works that began modern music. While *Pierrot* remains under a cloud of polite neglect, *The Rite of Spring* has nearly become a pops-concert staple. (As early as 1940, a mauled and emasculated edition of the ballet was used as part of the soundtrack of that tedious Disney classic *Fantasia.*)

For one of the clearest and most provocatively objective of all the ballet's many recordings, the composer's own is irreplaceable. As in so many recordings of his own music, Stravinsky the conductor sought to tone down the overtly barbarous moments in the music in favor of greater clarity and restraint (though by this time, much of the nuts-and-bolts rehearsal work was being done by his protégé and amanuensis, Robert Craft). In short, Stravinsky seemed intent on proving, late in life, that stylistically there wasn't all that much separating his music from that of Rossini, Mozart, or Bach.

The approach, needless to say, casts some fascinating light on this great twentieth-century watershed. But for those who want a vicious, untamed, and yet to be housebroken version of the ballet, Riccardo Muti's Angel recording is a bracing tonic to the composer's own. The Philadelphia Orchestra plays as though possessed, and the recorded sound will rid you of any loose putty on the living room windows, and possibly even the family cat.

Symphony in Three Movements; Symphony in C

Israel Philharmonic, Bernstein. Deutsche Grammophon
415128-2 [CD].

Stravinsky said a few indiscreet things about Leonard Bernstein, both behind his back and in print. Yet on balance, the mercurial conductor was always one of Stravinsky's finest interpreters, as these gleaming performances of the neoclassical Symphony in C and Symphony in Three Movements clearly prove.

While keeping a very firm rein on the proceedings—the Adagio of the Symphony in C is especially moving in its compassion and restraint—Bernstein never loses the opportunity to make the dramatic best of this music. The finale of the wartime Symphony in Three Movements is as unbridled in its joyousness as any performance of any Stravinsky work yet recorded. The Israel Philharmonic responds with great precision given the live-performance conditions, and the recorded sound has tremendous clarity, warmth, and depth.

Symphony of Psalms

CBC Symphony, Toronto Festival Singers, Stravinsky. CBS
MK-42434 [CD].

If *The Rite of Spring* was not Stravinsky's masterpiece, then this proud, aloof, deeply stirring sacred work probably was. Written "To the Glory of God and Dedicated to the Boston Symphony Orchestra" (Serge Koussevitzky never forgave Stravinsky for giving his orchestra second billing), the *Symphony* is one of the half dozen great sacred works of modern music. In fact, with a small handful of companion pieces—Poulenc's *Gloria*, Schoenberg's *Moses und Aron*, Vaughan Williams's *Hodie*—it is one of the few works of this century that have kept the divine spirit in music alive and well.

Stravinsky's own performance from 1963 has been issued on a generous CBS compact disc that also features the composer's somewhat spartan but always revealing performances of the Symphony in Three Movements and Symphony in C. Here, for once, the composer's predilection for a drier sound in his music than most conductors favored serves this particular masterpiece extremely well. The *Symphony of Psalms* emerges with all its pride, devotion, and admiration (as opposed to adoration) of the Supreme Being blissfully intact.

Suk, Josef (1874–1935)

Serenade for Strings in E-flat

London Chamber Orchestra, Warren-Green. Virgin Classics VC-7-91165-2 [CD].

Josef Suk composed his most celebrated work while still a student at the Prague Conservatory. Impressed by the young man's talent but concerned that both his musical and personal outlook were far too serious, Suk's teacher, Antonín Dvořák, suggested that his grim young pupil lighten up with something a bit less earnest than the sternly academic music he was writing at the time. The result was the luscious Serenade for Strings.

Although written when its composer was only eighteen and modeled quite consciously on Dvořák's famous E Major String Serenade, Suk's piece, rather incredibly, is the superior work. Although it owes much to Dvořák—the lilting Waltz, particularly, has an unmistakably Dvořákian flavor—the Serenade is also the work of a precocious master, who is melodically and rhythmically far more subtle than his teacher was when his own Serenade was written, and who projects a melancholy tenderness that is already very much his own.

If no recording will ever surpass the magical one made by the composer's friend Václav Talich, whose 1938 version is now available on a Koch CD (3-7060-2), the recent effort by Christopher Warren-Green's brilliant London Chamber Orchestra is the best modern alternative. Not only is the Suk given a graceful, if somewhat overly animated performance, it comes with delectable versions of the Dvořák and Tchaikovsky serenades, therefore making it an irresistible bargain.

For the adventurous, a far more important release is the newest version of Suk's masterpiece, the *Asrael* Symphony. Begun shortly after Dvořák's death in 1904, the Symphony was already well under way when Suk's wife, Dvořák's favorite daughter Otilie, died in the following year. The result is a powerful, crippling eruption of grief equal to the greatest Requiems in music. Until Talich's pioneering recording is reissued, the stunning new version by Libor Pesek and the Royal Liverpool Philharmonic (Virgin Classics VC-7-91221-2 [CD], VC-7-01221-4 [T]) will serve to introduce many to a neglected but authentic late-Romantic masterwork.

Sullivan, Sir Arthur

(1842–1900)

(Also see Gilbert and Sullivan)

Pineapple Poll

Royal Philharmonic, Mackerras. Arabesque Z-8016 [CD], A-9016 [T].

The life of that Eminent Victorian Arthur Seymour Sullivan is a mournful study in the seemingly endless human capacity for self-delusion. To the end, Sullivan remained unshakably convinced that he was an important composer who only wrote those flippant entertainments with W. S. Gilbert to maintain himself in a style to which few composers of *any* sort ever become accustomed. Even a passing acquaintance with Sullivan's "serious" music—the turgidly pious oratorio *The Light of the World* and his positively lethal opera after Sir Walter Scott's *Ivanhoe* (the mere titles of cantatas like *The Martyr of Antioch* speak for themselves)—proves conclusively that had Sullivan never met Gilbert, he would be best remembered today for his bellicose, imperialistic, loot-the-world-for-Queen-and-Christ hymn, "Onward, Christian Soldiers," and that wilted hot-house flower, "The Lost Chord."

For those who, for inexplicable (I am almost tempted to say *demented*) reasons of their own, can't seem to abide Sullivan *with* Gilbert, Sir Charles Mackerras's arrangement of Sullivan's frothy pastiche ballet *Pineapple Poll* is one of the best ways of absorbing these immortal melodies without their equally immortal lyrics. Sir Charles's EMI recording from the early 1960s, available now on Arabesque, is marginally preferable to the more recent version from London: the playing of the Royal Philharmonic is as precise and polished as it is wantonly giddy, and the interpretation—needless to say—is definitive.

Another fine album of Sullivan going solo is Alexander Faris's recording with the Scottish Chamber Orchestra of the overtures (Nimbus NI-5066 [CD]).

Suppé, Franz von (1819–1895)

Overtures

Montreal Symphony, Dutoit. London 414408-2 [CD].

In some quarters, an enthusiasm for Suppé overtures (the operas and operettas they served to introduce have long since disappeared) is looked on very quizzically. It is as though the person who professes the enthusiasm also admits a fondness for cheap detective movies of the 1940s, spy novels, and long summer afternoons in front of the television, watching baseball and drinking beer.

I admit that, like millions of others, I am thoroughly addicted to these cornball classics. And listening to these crisp, no-nonsense, and, most important, uncondescending performances by Charles Dutoit and the Montreal Symphony may even make a believer of you. Dutoit and his forces play these familiar classics as though they were crammed to the gunnels with zest, unforgettable melody, and brilliant craftsmanship. In short, they only show us why these imperishable warhorses deserve to be just that.

Suppé lovers, rejoice. Suppé haters, in your ear.

Szymanowski, Karol

(1882–1937)

During the last years of his unhappy life, Karol Szymanowski lamented the fact that he ever became a composer. One can hardly blame him. Even now, more than half a century after his death, his music remains an unknown commodity to most people, in spite of the fact that he was the only incontestably great Polish composer after Chopin and one of the giants of twentieth-century music.

To some extent, the recording industry must bear the responsibility for the shabby treatment Szymanowski has received. Compared to his compatriots Witold Lutoslawski, whose inspiration has grown increasingly threadbare with the passage of time, and Krzysztof Penderecki, one of the founding fathers of the grunt-and-groan school of modern music, Szymanowski has been recorded far less frequently over the years, even though he could outcompose both of them standing on his head with one hand tied behind his back while lighting a cigarette.

King Roger, one of the most beautiful of all modern operas, is finally back in circulation on a set of Koch compact discs (CD-314014-K2). The performance by the Warsaw Opera is polished and idiomatic, and the recorded sound, while less than ideal, is perfectly acceptable.

The adventurous Marco Polo company has so far issued two invaluable Szymanowski CDs. The first (8.223292) contains the wonderful ballets *Mandragora* and *Harnasie*—the latter sounding like an impossibly profound and civilized *Carmina Burana*—and the second (8.223293) is devoted to the choral music, including a setting of the *Stabat Mater* that ranks with the great sacred works of Western music.

On a Muza compact disc (PNCD-064), Wanda Wilkomirska gives commanding performances of the two ravishing Violin Concertos, and the Olympia recording of the two String Quartets (OCD-328 [CD]) is unusually desirable and revealing. Not only are the performances by the Varsovia Quartet top of the line, but also the opportunity to compare them to the Lutoslawski and Penderecki quartets that fill out the album is fascinating: Hamlet's disparaging crack about "a hyperion to a satyr" immediately comes to mind.

The breathtaking *Myths* for violin and piano is the centerpiece of a beautiful Szymanowski recital on Chandos (CHAN-8747 [CD], ABTD-1386 [T]) featuring the bewitching violinist Lydia Mordkovitch. Carol Rosenberger's lovely Delos recording of some of the piano music (DE-1002 [CD]) only serves to underscore Szymanowski's position as Chopin's heir, and the RCA recording of the *Symphonie concertante* with Artur Rubinstein (60046-2-RG [CD], 60046-4-RG [T]), while not the greatest performance of one of the composer's weaker pieces, is more than worth the investment.

Finally, one of the most exciting Szymanowski reissues features Antal Dorati's matchless recordings of the Symphony No. 2 in B-flat and the Symphony No. 3, called *Song of the Night*. While the earlier work is an intriguing, if somewhat derivative, piece that clearly shows an interesting, ambitious young composer on the verge of becoming a major one, the *Song of the Night* is one of the undoubted masterworks of twentieth-century orchestral music: strange, exotic, wholly original, and, once heard, never to be forgotten.

Tallis, Thomas (c. 1505–1585)

Church Music

The Tallis Scholars, Phillips. Gimell CDGIM-006 [CD].

After rudely dismissing the music of his contemporary Ralph Vaughan Williams, as was his wont—following a BBC broadcast of the *Pastoral* Symphony, the conductor could be heard to say, quite audibly, "A city life for me!"—Sir Thomas Beecham was reprimanded by a friend, who said: "But surely you wouldn't write off that wonderful *Fantasia on a Theme by Thomas Tallis?*" "No," Beecham said. "But Vaughan Williams made the cardinal error of not including in all his compositions a theme by Tallis."

If the modern revival of interest in this colossus of Tudor music began with Vaughan Williams's haunting masterpiece of 1910, its continuation has depended on the extraordinary quality of Tallis's music itself, including one of the most complex of all polyphonic studies, the celebrated *Spem in alium non habui*, a "Song of Forty Parts" for eight five-part choirs. In addition to the famous motet, the Tallis Scholars under Peter Phillips offer some ethereally beautiful performances of their eponym's other sacred hits, including a perfectly betwitching setting of *Sancte Deus* which may be even more eloquent.

As Tallis was one of the first composers to write sacred music on English texts for Henry VIII's newly founded Church of England, his English anthems are of special historic interest and can be heard on a superlative companion album (Gimell CDGIM-007 [CD], 1585T-07 [T]) in which the singing of the Tallis Scholars is equally inspired.

Taylor, Deems (1885–1966)

Through the Looking-Glass

Seattle Symphony, Schwarz. Delos DE-3099 [CD].

Although best known as a commentator and critic—for seven years he hosted the intermission broadcasts of the New York Philharmonic, and who could forget his introduction to Disney's *Fantasia* or his fascinating explanation of how the cannons and bells were recorded in Antal Dorati's early stereo version of the *1812 Overture?*—Deems Taylor was also a composer of considerable accomplishment. His operas *The King's Henchmen* (on a text by Edna St. Vincent Millay) and *Peter Ibbetson* were both mounted by the Metropolitan Opera, and his five pictures from Lewis Carroll, *Through the Looking-Glass,* is among the most endearing orchestral scores ever written by an American. From the tender Introduction with its heart-dissolving principal theme, through the witty "Jabberwocky," to the soaring romance of "The White Knight," *Through the Looking-Glass* is one of those magical, instantly memorable works that most listeners find impossible to forget.

Gerard Schwarz and his fine orchestra miss none of the work's color, vitality, or charm, making this a worthy successor to Howard Hanson's celebrated 1953 recording. The playing has a wonderful (albeit paradoxical) sense of relaxed intensity, with first-rate solo contributions from the orchestra's principals; the conductor has never led a more sensitive, completely understanding performance. With equally evocative versions of four marvelous works by the hugely underrated Charles Tomlinson Griffes, including his masterpieces, *The Pleasure-Dome of Kubla Khan* and *The White Peacock,* this cannot possibly be missed.

Tchaikovsky, Piotr Ilyich

(1840–1893)

Capriccio italien; Marche slave; Nutcracker Suite; *1812 Overture*

Montreal Symphony, Dutoit. London 417300-2 [CD], 417300-4 [T].

Although an enormous percentage of music lovers first made their way into Serious Music via the works of Tchaikovsky, many seem strangely loath to admit it. As our tastes mature and we become ever more knowledgeable and sophisticated, we tend to abandon—or perhaps even become ashamed of—our youthful enthusiasms. (Who was it who said, "Don't let the young confide to you their dreams, for when they drop them, they'll drop you"?)

Although he can be extremely obvious, bellicose, cheap, and vulgar, Tchaikovsky more than earns his position as one of the three or four most popular composers. He never cheats his listeners, giving them huge doses of overwhelming (and often surprisingly complex) emotions, a keen sense of orchestral color, and one of the greatest melodic gifts any composer possessed. In short, if you love Tchaikovsky, don't be ashamed. And don't think you're alone. Uncounted millions of us can't *all* be wrong.

This superb and unusually generous London collection brings together four of the composer's most popular works in performances as civilized as they are exciting, as brash and brazen as they are thoughtful and refined. Although the *1812 Overture* could be a bit noisier for my taste (remember the great old Mercury recording with Antal Dorati and the Minneapolis Symphony, and Deems Taylor explaining how they got the bells and cannon blasts?), these are the performances I turn to whenever the mood strikes.

Concerto for Piano and Orchestra No. 1 in B-flat minor

Cliburn, piano; RCA Victor Orchestra, Kondrashin. RCA 5912-2-RC [CD], RK-1002 [T].

It's no accident that this is one of the best-selling classical recordings of all time. Naturally, much of it had to do with the ballyhoo that attended Van Cliburn's winning of the Tchaikovsky Competition in Moscow during one of the chilliest moments of the Cold War. (Yes, the Russians had a definite jump in the space race — remember all those films of our rockets blowing up on the pad? — but we had this long, lanky Texan who beat them, and beat them decisively, at their own game.)

Three decades later, in the midst of the *glasnost* thaw, it's time we started judging this recording on its own merits, and not its historical context. I have, and simply stated, in *any* context, this is one hell of an exciting performance. Cliburn's mixture of elfin delicacy and animal ferocity has remained intact since the recording was first released. It is a poetic, explosive, lyrical, and deeply humane interpretation that no recording of the last thirty years begins to match.

Concertos for Piano: No. 2 in G; No. 3 in E-flat

Donohoe, piano; Bournemouth Symphony, Barshai. Angel CDC-49940 [CD].

The long overdue rehabilitation of Tchaikovsky's "other" piano concertos would be hastened if performances of them were as committed and electrifying as these. Using the composer's uncut original version, Peter Donohoe transforms the Second Concerto into something as engrossing — and very nearly as exciting — as the First: with substantial contributions from the concertmaster and principal cellist, the slow movement emerges as one of Tchaikovsky's most original inspirations, and the finale erupts in a blaze of Vesuvian fireworks that outshines even the startling version Gary Graffman recorded a generation ago. Though it is a much lesser piece, the Third Concerto also responds brilliantly to Donohoe's poetry and panache, and the equally poetic and impassioned accompaniments supplied by the canny Rudolf Barshai are close to ideal.

Concerto in D for Violin and Orchestra

Heifetz, violin; Chicago Symphony, Reiner. RCA 5933-2-RC [CD].

Oistrakh, violin; Philadelphia Orchestra, Ormandy. Sony
Classical SBK-46339 [CD], SBT-46339 [T].

From a purely technical point of view, there has never been
a recording of this work to match Jascha Heifetz's famous version
with Fritz Reiner and the Chicago Symphony. Although the violinist
was placed uncomfortably close to the microphone, which accounts
for the unaccustomed rasp in his famous tone, the playing is genuinely spellbinding. Listen especially to the first-movement cadenza,
in which the soloist uses one of his own devising that makes Tchaikovsky's original seem like child's play.

On the other hand, if you're after the warmth, color, and abiding romance of the Tchaikovsky Concerto, then David Oistrakh's
meltingly lovely recording with Eugene Ormandy and the Philadelphia Orchestra is clearly the one to own.

Eugene Onegin

Kubiak, Hamari, Burrows, Sénéchal, Weikl, Ghiaurov,
Orchestra and Chorus of the Royal Opera House,
Covent Garden, Solti. London 417413-2 [CD].

Of the ten Tchaikovsky operas that survive, only *Eugene Onegin* and *The Queen of Spades*, both based on works by Pushkin,
have made any inroads into the standard repertoire. (For any Slavic
opera to do so has been next to impossible, given the language barrier. To this day, Smetana's masterpiece is usually heard as *Die
Verkaufte Braut* or *The Bartered Bride*, as opposed to *Prodaná
Nevěsta*, and even *Boris Godunov* didn't begin making the international rounds until the title role was taken over by a lunatic
named Chaliapin.) Although *Onegin* can often seem to lack sus-
tainable dramatic interest or clearly delineated characters (part of
the problem lay in the fact that the composer adored Pushkin's heroine and regarded his hero as "a cold, heartless coxcomb"), it is full
of unforgettable set pieces like Tatiana's Letter Scene, the Waltz and
Polonaise, and the exquisite aria in which the doomed Lensky recalls his youth. (Like his tenor, Pushkin himself was killed in a duel,
only six years after completing *Onegin*, defending the "honor" of
his not entirely honorable wife.)

Besides being the best *Onegin* ever recorded, Sir Georg Solti's
version of the opera is one of the finest recordings that much-
honored conductor has so far made. In addition to coaxing some

exceptionally subtle and elegant playing from the Covent Garden orchestra, he holds the loose threads of the opera together more effectively than anyone ever has; for once, *Onegin* emerges as a coherent, cohesive dramatic structure, instead of what it can sometimes seem: a lengthy prelude and interminable epilogue to Tatiana's big moment of self-revelation.

Vocally and dramatically, Teresa Kubiak is a splendid Tatiana. The Letter Scene is done superbly, of course, but she is even more convincing in the closing pages of the opera, where the once flighty innocent is transformed into a figure of genuinely heroic stature. If Bernd Weikl is only adequate as Onegin—and perhaps it *is* an impossible role—Stuart Burrows's Lensky is a striking amalgam of ardor, manliness, and finesse. In short, for anyone who is persuaded that Russian opera begins and ends with *Boris* (as indeed it might), this *Onegin* might make all of us think again.

The Nutcracker

> L'Orchestre de la Suisse Romande, Ansermet. London 417055-4 [T].
>
> Berlin Philharmonic, Bychkov. Philips 420237-2 [CD].

If ever a recording deserved the designation "Imperishable," it is Ernest Ansermet's triumphant early stereo version of *The Nutcracker,* which has more sheer interpretative magic than you can shake a sugarplum at. Although the sound has definitely begun to show its age, the performance never will. Ansermet's conception brings out every ounce of charm and color that this often hackneyed work offers, and does it with a touch so light and sure, we're reminded once again of what we all owe this great pioneer of the stereo age.

While the Philips compact disc recording by Semyon Bychkov and the Berlin Philharmonic can't quite match the winsomeness and delicacy of the Ansermet, it still has much to recommend it. In addition to some razor-sharp playing from one of the world's great orchestras, this compact disc will introduce many to a stupendously gifted young conductor.

*R*omeo and Juliet (Fantasy Overture)

> Royal Philharmonic, Ashkenazy. London 421715-2 [CD], 421715-4 [T].

London Symphony, Simon. Chandos CHAN-8310/11 [CD].

Vladimir Ashkenazy's Royal Philharmonic recording offers an excellent, old-fashioned *Romeo*. While it lacks the dash and drama of Leonard Bernstein's Deutsche Grammophon recording with the Israel Philharmonic, it does feature superior playing and recorded sound. With stellar performances of *Francesca da Rimini, Capriccio italien*, and the *Elegy for Strings* tossed in as a bonus, it makes for an easy first recommendation.

Geoffrey Simon's Chandos recording is an entirely different matter. In this fascinating and, for Tchaikovsky aficionados, can't-live-another-day-without-it release, Simon unearths the original 1869 version of the work that put the composer on the musical map of Europe in the early 1880s. This is not simply an early version of *Romeo and Juliet*, but a virtually unrecognizable piece: less finished and professional than the *Romeo* we're used to, yet one whose unvarnished enthusiasm and power are hard to resist. In addition to this proto-*Romeo*, the Simon collection offers a version of *Hamlet* that features both the overture and the incidental music, including a mad scene for Ophelia and a lively (if that's really the right word) "Gravedigger's Song," together with some bona fide off-the-wall discoveries such as the *Festival Overture on the Danish National Anthem* and, as I have now come to think of it, the absolutely indispensable *Serenade for Nikolai Rubinstein's Saint's Day*.

Serenade in C for String Orchestra

Australian Chamber Orchestra, Pini. Omega OCD-1010 [CD].

Academy of St. Martin-in-the-Fields, Marriner. London 417736-2 [CD].

With so many first-rate recordings of the popular Serenade for Strings floating around, the final choice for many people might depend on how the piece is packaged. For those who want the traditional pairing with the Dvořák Serenade, Sir Neville Marriner's London recording isn't going to be bettered, at least until Angel bestirs itself and issues those spellbinding Barenboim–English Chamber Orchestra performances on a medium-priced CD.

For a less predictable yet far more logical coupling, the brilliant Australian Chamber Orchestra and Carl Pini offer one of the most alert and amiable performances on the market with an arresting version of the composer's own favorite piece, the *Souvenir of Florence.*

Suites (4) for Orchestra

> USSR Academic Symphony, Svetlanov. Melodiya MCD-109
> (Suites No. 1 and 4); MCD-153 (Suite No. 2, Symphony
> No. 2); SUCD-10-00104 (Suite No. 3) [CDs].

Their small but devoted circle of admirers have always realized how much wonderful music is to be found in Tchaikovsky's four Orchestral Suites; now, thanks to what have to be counted as the most inspired of Evgeny Svetlanov's recordings thus far, everyone else will, too. In these miraculous performances, a new insight, a fresh inspiration, an astonishing gee-why-didn't-anyone-ever-think-of-doing-it-that-way-before? solution seems to leap out at every turn. Under Svetlanov's firm but infinitely flexible guidance, the USSR Academic Symphony performs the music with such effortless grace and joy that you're very nearly persuaded they must be making it up as they go along.

The only serious snag in what is otherwise one of the finest Tchaikovsky recordings now available is the idiotic layout. Instead of two CDs with two Suites apiece, the Second Suite is packaged with Vladimir Fedoseyev's unremarkable recording of the *Little Russian* Symphony. Which means that the disc containing the Third Suite also offers the Fourth Suite, which is *exactly* the same performance you already have if you've bought the Suite No. 1. Granted, the recordings came out in the midst of the collapse of the Soviet Union, but is that any excuse?

Swan Lake (complete ballet)

> Philharmonia Orchestra, Lanchbery. Angel CDCB-49171
> [CD].

To his everlasting credit, Tchaikovsky never gave up on the two forms he most wanted to master but whose perplexing secrets always just eluded him. And it is his masterpiece, *Swan Lake,* that best explains why he never became the great opera composer and symphonist he so earnestly wanted to be. For the glory of Tchaikovsky's art was neither its intellectual depth nor grasp of structure, but its ability to make melody and emotion indistinguishable from one another. In no other composer's work is melody the *meaning* of the music to the extent that it is in Tchaikovsky, and nowhere else is his melodic genius more finely tuned than in *Swan Lake*. In none of his major works, except perhaps for *The Sleeping Beauty*, do we have the sense of such concentration and economy, even in spite of its formidable length; the sense that every tune is not only memorable but absolutely necessary, and that not a note or gesture is wasted. It is a unique achievement which by itself would refute the nonsensical suggestion that Tchaikovsky was not a great composer.

If it doesn't have all the character of some fine recordings of the recent past—Gennadi Rozhdestvensky's Moscow Radio, as opposed to his BBC, performance, and André Previn's senselessly deleted London Symphony recording—John Lanchbery's is an enthusiastic and completely professional job and is easily the best *Swan Lake* left on the map. The playing of the Philharmonia Orchestra is fairly stupendous, though it might not be *quite* as impressive as that of the Amsterdam Concertgebouw Orchestra in their version of *The Sleeping Beauty* under Antal Dorati (Philips 420792-2 [CD]).

For those who might not need the entire ballet(s), Riccardo Muti and the Philadelphia Orchestra offer colorful, spectacularly well-played versions of excerpts from *Swan Lake* and *Sleeping Beauty* (Angel CDC-47075 [CD], 4DS-38117 [T]).

Symphonies: No. 1 in G minor, *Winter Dreams;* No. 2 in C minor, *Little Russian;* No. 3 in D, *Polish*

> Oslo Philharmonic, Jansons. Chandos CHAN-8042 [CD], ABTD-1139 [T] (Symphony No. 1); CHAN-8460 [CD], ABTD-1173 [T] (Symphony No. 2); CHAN-8463 [CD], ABTD-1179 [T] (Symphony No. 3).

My own introduction to the Tchaikovsky symphonies came via an RCA Victor Camden recording of the Fifth with the Oslo Philharmonic led by its longtime (1931–61) conductor, Odd Grüner-Hegge. I remember that exciting interpretation virtually note for note, not only because it was so exceptionally good but also because, forever after, no other performance of the piece has ever sounded quite right. Grüner-Hegge, who studied conducting with Felix Weingartner, observed the whopping cuts his old teacher made in the score, including the whole of the last movement's development section. This still heads my list of must-be-reissued Tchaikovsky Fifth recordings, followed closely by the zany Paul van Kempen version made with the Concertgebouw Orchestra of Amsterdam at about the same time, which includes, among *its* enthralling perversities, a pair of cymbal crashes just before the final stretto and an additional horn note that creates an unresolved seventh chord at that great pause before the march—undoubtedly a holdover of one of the many tricks conductors have tried in an attempt to head off the applause that customarily breaks out at that inopportune moment. (Stokowski tried to cure this premature congratulation by simply having the timpani keep rolling through the break, but the only time I heard him do it, with the Chicago Symphony, the unwashed and unsanctified fell in where they always do, earning a withering Stokie glare.)

But I digress.

The current conductor of the Oslo Philharmonic, Mariss Jansons, has built a considerable reputation as a Tchaikovsky conductor thanks to his Chandos recordings, and while all of them—even his game go-round with the hopeless *Manfred* Symphony (CHAN-8535 [CD], ABTD-1245 [T])—are among the finest currently available, his versions of the three early symphonies will probably remain the standard recordings for years. The interpretations are both disciplined and spontaneous, with wonderful playing from an orchestra that sounds, for much of the time, like a junior edition of the Berlin Philharmonic. Although none of the available alternatives can begin to match them, two classic recordings should be returned to print to provide at least *some* choice: Carlo Maria Giulini's whirlwind version of the *Little Russian* for Angel, and one of the most electric Tchaikovsky recordings ever made, the Deutsche Grammophon *Winter Dreams* with the Boston Symphony conducted by Michael Tilson Thomas.

Symphonies: No. 4 in F minor; No. 5 in E minor; No. 6 in B minor, *Pathétique*

> Leningrad Philharmonic, Mravinsky. Deutsche Grammophon 419745-2 [CD].

This series of recordings, made in London when the Leningrad Philharmonic was on tour in the early 1960s, is one of the few stu-

dio recordings by one of the most important and enigmatic conductors of the twentieth century, Yevgeny Mravinsky. A friend of
Shostakovich and one who led many premieres of the composer's
symphonies, Mravinsky, over a period of nearly a half century, galvanized the Leningrad Philharmonic into the Soviet Union's greatest
orchestra.

These performances of the last three Tchaikovsky symphonies
are among the most exciting, pulverizing, uplifting, and wacky ever
made. For instance, Mravinsky sets a pace for the finale of the
Fourth that no orchestra could possibly play, and yet there it is —
playing of such superhuman virtuosity that it takes at least a dozen
hearings to believe it. The interpretations are larger than life; the
orchestral execution a wonder of unanimity, courage, and bravado,
and the recorded sound remarkably detailed and clear.

For those who prefer to acquire the symphonies singly, a few
reasonable alternatives exist. Leonard Bernstein's early CBS recording of the Fourth (MYK-37766 [CD], MYT-37766 [T]) still packs
plenty of wallop and highly individual pizzazz. Claudio Abbado's
brooding yet exhilarating performance of the Fifth ranks with the
finest of his Chicago Symphony recordings (CBS MK-42094 [CD],
IMT-42094 [T]). And among recent versions of the *Pathétique,*
Mariss Jansons's thrilling, lacerating performance for Chandos
(CHAN-8446 [CD], ABTD-1158 [T]) brings his superlative Tchaikovsky series to a most satisfying conclusion.

Variations on a Rococo Theme for Cello and Orchestra

**Rostropovich, cello; Berlin Philharmonic, Karajan. Deutsche
Grammophon 413819-2 [CD].**

By common consent, Mstislav Rostropovich has all but owned
Tchaikovsky's de facto cello concerto for a generation, and this
most eloquently argued of his several recordings demonstrates why.
The cellist refuses to treat the piece as merely an engaging ball of
cuddly virtuoso fluff, but approaches it as a major work that requires major concentration. Which is not to say he misses any of
the charm or fun of the piece. Quite the contrary. His impish enthusiasm even infects his usually grim-lipped conductor, who here
delivers one of the most uncharacteristically witty and humane of
his later performances.

A good though by no means exceptional performance of the Dvořák Concerto rounds out the CD, and on cassette Rostropovich's earlier Deutsche Grammophon recording with Gennadi Rozhdestvensky and the Leningrad Philharmonic is an equally obvious first choice (413161-4).

Telemann, Georg Philipp
(1681–1767)

During his lifetime, Georg Philipp Telemann completely overshadowed his near-contemporary, an obscure German organist and composer named Johann Sebastian Bach. Later centuries slowly realized that what had made Telemann so fashionable during his lifetime—the clear, uncomplicated structures, the easy-to-follow contents of a music that had nothing profound to say—ultimately gave him next to no staying power, especially in comparison with the *real* Baroque giants, Handel and Bach.

While I can make no specific recommendations for recordings of the man's music (it all sounds more or less the same to me), I will offer a few general hints for the Telemann shopper: (1) Avoid any recording with a reproduction of an eighteenth-century landscape painting on the cover. (2) Avoid any concerto for more than one instrument (anything that complicated seems only to have confused him). (3) Avoid any recording featuring Nikolaus Harnoncourt, his wife Alice, or their friend Gustav Leonhardt. If you see them in the cutout or used-record bins, and I mean *anything* produced by the Telemann Society, shun them as though your life depended on it. (Several people have laughed themselves to death listening to their well-intentioned but hopelessly feeble efforts.) (4) If the temptation to buy a Telemann recording proves irresistible, make certain your cupboard is well stocked with strong, and I do mean *strong,* coffee.

Thompson, Randall

(1899–1984)

Symphony No. 2; Symphony No. 3

New Zealand Symphony, Schenck. Koch International
Classics 3-7074-2 [CD].

One of the most urbane and gentlemanly of American composers, Randall Thompson was primarily known for vocal works
like the elegant *Alleluia* of 1940 and the stirring *Testament of Freedom* on a text by Jefferson. He was also the composer of two of the
finest of all American symphonies, both of which are memorably
served on this Koch recording.

Although the Third Symphony of 1949 is a spirited, beautifully made work that never wears out its welcome or wastes a single
gesture, the Second Symphony of 1931 is a masterpiece: virile, tuneful, seamlessly argued, and completely satisfying.

The New Zealand Symphony under the late Andrew Schenck
makes a virtually airtight case for both works. The young orchestra
plays with polish and enthusiasm; only the occasional thinness in
the upper strings reveals that it is not quite a world-class ensemble.
The recording, if slightly distant, is excellent.

Thomson, Virgil (1896–1989)

The Plow That Broke the Plains (orchestral suite); *The River* (orchestral suite); *Autumn* (Concertino for Harp, Strings, and Percussion)

> Los Angeles Chamber Orchestra, Marriner. Angel CDC-47715 [CD].

Even if it's still too soon to get a clear picture of Virgil Thomson's stature as a composer, his position as one of America's most perceptive, courageous, and bitchy music critics is assured. During his enlightened reign of terror (1940–54) at the *New York Herald-Tribune,* Thomson enraged and delighted readers with countless inflammatory observations, including the then-heretical suggestions that Arturo Toscanini was *not* the risen Christ, and that the Second Symphony of Jean Sibelius, at the height of his popularity at the time, was "vulgar, self-indulgent, and provincial beyond all description."

After *Four Saints in Three Acts,* the transcendentally daffy opera he wrote with Gertrude Stein—which can be heard on a superbly successful Nonesuch recording (79035-2 [CD], 79035-4 [T])—Thomson the composer is probably best represented on record these days by the music he wrote for Pare Lorentz's WPA documentary films, *The Plow That Broke the Plains* and *The River.*

Like his *Symphony on a Hymn Tune,* an ingenuous portrait of the nineteenth-century American Midwest painted by a citified Parisian in the 1920s, recently returned to print in Howard Hanson's classic Mercury recording (434310-2 [CD]), these are folksy, openhearted, sophisticated works that immediately enfold the listener in a bear-hug embrace. The performances by Sir Neville Marriner and the Los Angeles Chamber Orchestra are even more affectionate and evocative than Leopold Stokowski's famous Symphony of the Air recordings, and the twenty-year-old recorded sound remains fertile and uneroded.

434

Tippett, Sir Michael (1905–)

A Child of Our Time

Armstrong, Palmer, Langridge, Shirley-Quirk, Brighton
Festival Chorus, Royal Philharmonic, Previn. MCA
MCAD-6202 [CD].

Sir Michael Tippett, England's greatest living composer, has
spent most of his career in the tremendous shadow cast by his far
more famous contemporary, Benjamin Britten. In many ways, Tippett is the more interesting composer (and this from someone who
has always adored Britten's music). Unlike Britten, Tippett has ven-
tured down several important modern roads in his later years. His
idiom has become increasingly harsh and dissonant, while his expression has grown ever more concentrated and precise. Late Tippett (from, say, the early 1970s onward) can be a very thorny,
though immensely rewarding, row to hoe.

A Child of Our Time, completed in 1941, is not only one of
Tippett's most accessible pieces, it is one of the most shattering yet
heartbreakingly lovely choral works of the last hundred years. Pat-
terned consciously after the Passions of Bach, Tippett's oratorio presents black spirituals in place of the familiar chorales at key
moments in the drama. Their effect, especially in a recording like
this one, is overwhelmingly moving and beautiful.

The oratorio has been recorded twice before, in handsome
performances led by John Pritchard and Sir Colin Davis, but this
new version by André Previn is one of the conductor's finest recordings to date, and the greatest recorded performance A Child of
Our Time is ever likely to receive. The complex textures of the work
are untangled with a pristine clarity, and the soloists are inspired
to do some of the finest work of their careers. And the way Previn
has the often gigantic forces swing their way through the spirituals
is enough to raise the hair on the back of your neck, particularly
in "Steal Away." In short, this is an indispensable performance of
a great modern classic that belongs in every recording library.

For Tippett admirers (and the man certainly deserves millions
more than he has so far attracted), two other important recordings
can also be recommended without reservation. The first is Sir Neville Marriner's collection of three of the composer's most accessible

and beautifully made early works, the Concerto for Double String Orchestra, the *Little Music* for String Orchestra, and the pivotal *Fantasia Concertante on a Theme of Corelli*, all superbly performed and recorded (London 421389-2 [CD]). The second, also from London (425646-2 [CD]), features all four of the symphonies Sir Michael has written to date, packaged with the slender but enchanting *Suite for the Birthday of Prince Charles*, in the virtually definitive performances by led by Sir Colin Davis (1–3) and Sir Georg Solti (4, *Suite*).

Philips and London have temporarily withdrawn all their recordings of the Tippett operas, except for the generally spare and thankless *King Priam*. In the case of the extremely knotty *Knot Garden*, such bad manners can be overlooked, if not excused. But for Philips to deep-six the mysterious, exuberant *Midsummer Marriage*—which has a fair claim to being (with all due apologies to Benjamin Britten) the greatest modern English opera—is an act of wanton barbarism that can be expiated *only* by immediate reissue on compact disc.

Tubin, Eduard (1905–1982)

Symphonies: No. 4, *Sinfonia lirica;* No. 9, *Sinfonia semplice*

> Bergen Philharmonic Society Orchestra; Gothenburg Symphony, Järvi. Bis CD-227 [CD].

Unlike sex, politics, and television, music is always full of surprises. Until quite recently, the surprising music of Eduard Tubin was a carefully guarded secret outside his native Estonia and adopted Sweden; now, thanks largely to the Estonian conductor Neeme Järvi and the enterprising Swedish label Bis, Tubin has at last begun to take his rightful place among the most substantial and original of mid-twentieth-century symphonists.

Each of the ten completed symphonies that Tubin composed over a fifty-year period (an eleventh was left unfinished at the time of his death) manages to say something fresh and individual. Although the spirits of near-contemporaries like Sibelius, Prokofiev, and Shostakovich might flit in and out of the music from time to time, Tubin is very much his own man: a rational yet emotionally intricate personality whose superbly crafted, immediately engaging music says what it has to say—which is often an earful—without wasting a moment of our time, or its.

The pairing of the Fourth Symphony of 1943 and the Ninth of 1969 is an ideal introduction to Tubin's bracing, lucid, mysterious universe, and Järvi's interpretations reveal a deep and obvious affection for his countryman's music. The only serious drawback is that the recording may prove addictive, forcing you to snap up the other symphonies as quickly as possible.

Varèse, Edgar (1883–1965)

Amériques; Arcana; Density 21.5; Intégrales; Ionisation; Octandre; Offrandes

> Ensemble InterContemporain, New York Philharmonic, Boulez. Sony Classical SK-45844 [CD].

Following a brief bout of unlikely popularity in the 1960s— due in part to the *Poème électronique*, which, when performed over 400 speakers at the Philips Pavilion, became an unexpected hit at the 1958 Brussels World's Fair, and thanks, too, to the spirited advocacy of Frank Zappa, another unruly genius who immediately knew a kindred spirit when he heard one—Edgar (née Edgard) Varèse slipped back into the not-so-benign neglect in which he languished for most of his career.

In his entry on Varèse in *Baker's Biographical Dictionary of Musicians*, Nicolas Slonimsky drops the usual one- or two-word preparatory appraisal ("Distinguished conductor"; "Famous Bulgarian heckelphone virtuoso") in favor of this: "One of the most remarkable composers of his century, who introduced a totally original principle of organizing the materials and forms of sound, profoundly influencing the direction of new music." That just about says it.

Pierre Boulez's recordings are by far the most valuable yet made of this composer's music, and with seven major works crammed onto a single medium-priced CD, this is a bargain no one interested in twentieth-century music should be able to resist. Predictably, the French conductor is most impressive whenever Varèse is at his thorniest: the dense, barbaric fabric of *Arcana*, for instance, is untangled to an astonishing degree, and *Offrandes* emerges with a Mozart-like clarity coupled with a sensuousness that will remind many listeners of Debussy.

All in all, the major step to date in the rehabilitation of a modern giant.

Vaughan Williams, Ralph
(1872–1958)

English Folk Songs

London Madrigal Singers, Bishop. Seraphim 4XG-60249 [T].

Put as clearly and simply as possible, these Vaughan Williams settings for unaccompanied chorus are far and away the most beautiful arrangements of English folk songs ever made, and these are far and away their most beautiful recorded performances. If you don't own a cassette deck, by all means buy one. It's impossible to say when, if ever, the CD version of this gorgeous tape will ever appear, and believe me, you simply *cannot* live without it. Be warned, though: Some of the items, like the version of "Greensleeves" with its unforgettable solo from tenor Ian Partridge, will open your heart as easily as one peels a ripe banana.

In short, be prepared to be dissolved.

Fantasia on a Theme by Thomas Tallis; Symphony No. 2, *A London Symphony*

London Philharmonic, Boult. Angel CDM-64017 [CD].

For those who have yet to acquire the gentle addiction of Ralph Vaughan Williams's music, this superb Angel recording should do the trick. On it are two of his finest and most characteristic pieces, the ravishing *Fantasia on a Theme by Thomas Tallis* and that greatest of modern English musical travelogues, *A London Symphony.*

Although both works have had marginally finer, but currently unavailable, performances (Sir John Barbirolli's version of the Symphony ranks with the great orchestral recordings of modern times), these performances by Sir Adrian Boult are excellent in every way. A close friend of the composer, Boult has unimpeachable credentials as a Vaughan Williams conductor, which shine through every bar of these works. The *Fantasia* has enormous dignity, as well as sensual beauty; the performance of the Symphony, if not quite as colorful a tour as Barbirolli's, is unforgettable. The London Philharmonic is at the top of its form in both performances, and the remastered sound of the compact disc is extremely impressive.

Five Mystical Songs; *Dona nobis pacem*

Wiens, soprano; Rayner-Cook, baritone; London Philharmonic Orchestra and Choir, Thompson. Chandos CHAN-8590 [CD], ABTD-1297 [T].

As his Chandos cycle of the Vaughan Williams symphonies clearly proves, in the decade prior to his untimely death the gifted Bryden Thomson was just beginning to come into his own as a conductor. With a few exceptions (such as his rather too literal version of the highly atmospheric *Sinfonia Antartica,* a considerable disappointment), the Thomson recordings are in most respects competitive with the far more celebrated ones of Sir Adrian Boult and André Previn.

The early Five Mystical Songs and *Dona nobis pacem* are two of the most serious and gravely beautiful of all Vaughan Williams's vocal works, and both are given sumptuous performances under

Thomson's direction. The soloists acquit themselves admirably, as do the chorus, the orchestra, and Chandos's highly skilled engineers.

Job (A Masque for Dancing)

London Philharmonic, Handley. Angel CDM-62016 [CD].

Here, as in his admirable Elgar, Delius, and Walton recordings, Vernon Handley continues to prove that he is one of the most gifted and comprehensive conductors of English music now before the public. His enthusiasm for Vaughan Williams is more than understandable: he studied these scores with the composer's old friend Sir Adrian Boult.

In the oddly neglected ballet *Job,* one of Vaughan Williams's supreme creations, Handley's only competition comes from his teacher on another Angel recording; Boult no doubt would have been proud (if not necessarily pleased) to have been bested so handily by his former pupil. From its subtlest shadings to its most booming climaxes, this is the first and only recording to date that seems to release the full scope and drama of this spectacular score. Even with the generous bonus of the Partita for Double String Orchestra, the Boult version simply cannot compete.

Serenade to Music

London Philharmonic, Boult. Angel CDM-64022 [CD].

Written to a text from Shakespeare's *Merchant of Venice,* the *Serenade to Music* may be the most bewitchingly beautiful work Vaughan Williams ever wrote. And to say that of the man who wrote *The Lark Ascending,* the *Fantasia on a Theme by Thomas Tallis, Flos Campi,* and the folk opera *Sir John in Love* is to say a very great deal indeed.

Although it is usually performed with a full chorus, Sir Adrian Boult gives a gleaming performance of the work as it was originally written. Composed for Sir Henry Wood's Golden Jubilee, the *Serenade* included solo parts for sixteen singers with whom Sir Henry had been especially close. That historic interpretation, recorded by

Sir Henry and company in 1938 only a week after the *Serenade*'s premiere, is now out on a Pearl compact disc (GEMM CD-9342). While obviously for specialists, it is a lovely performance and a recording of considerable historic importance.

For those who can do without history—especially the late-'30s recorded sound (which isn't all that bad, by the way)—the Boult interpretation remains a modern classic. Packaged with equally charming and authoritative versions of *In the Fen Country*, *The Lark Ascending*, the *English Folk Song Suite*, the *Norfolk Rhapsody*, and the *Fantasia on "Greensleeves,"* this is probably the most desirable Vaughan Williams recording now available.

Symphonies: No. 4 in F minor; No. 6 in E minor

New Philharmonia Orchestra, Boult. Angel CDM-64019 [CD].

A number of years ago at the first San Francisco Symphony performance of Vaughan Williams's Sixth Symphony, the conductor—a very fine one, who will remain nameless—decided that since the piece was bound to be unfamiliar to most of the audience, he should probably say a few words about it. He began his impromptu talk with the unfortunate sentence, "The Vaughan Williams Sixth is basically a very depressing piece . . ." Before uttering another syllable, he was abruptly cut off by a shy, retiring friend of mine (a full professor of Vaughan Williams), who pointed an accusing finger at the luckless musician and said, "But that *simply* isn't true!" Stunned and speechless, the conductor broke off his comments and began the piece without further ado.

The most bleakly pessimistic of the composer's symphonies it most certainly is; yet it is no more "depressing" than Robert Lowell's poetry, Max Beckmann's paintings, or some of Ingmar Bergman's films. Begun in the midst of World War Two and completed two years after the war ended, the Sixth is an appropriately dark vision of life from the middle of the darkest century in recorded history.

Sir Adrian Boult's powerful recording is one of the best from his historic Vaughan Williams cycle. The performance is honest and unblinkingly courageous, with a final movement that rises to tragic heights reminiscent of the greatest Mahler Adagios. Coupled with the explosive, dissonant Fourth Symphony in an equally unnerving performance, this is *not* a recording for fans of the *"Greensleeves"* *Fantasia* who are looking for more of the same.

Symphony No. 5 in D

London Symphony, Previn. RCA 60586-2 [CD], 60587-4 [T].

The Fifth is not only the most beautiful of the nine Vaughan Williams symphonies, it is also one of the most completely characteristic. In it, we hear an impeccable craftsman with a complex yet thoroughly humane mind—an utterly modern man who was content with stirring us deeply, and left probing the depths or shaking the heavens to others.

There are many who feel that André Previn is the most persuasive of all living Vaughan Williams conductors, and I agree. This Fifth, part of Previn's cycle of all nine symphonies for RCA, remains one of the best recordings the conductor has made so far. In general, Previn brings more life and freshness to this great work than any conductor ever has. The themes of the first movement unfold with an ease and naturalness that not even Sir Adrian Boult can match. For a very different view of the work, and one packaged with something more substantial than the admittedly delightful Tuba Concerto and *Three Portraits,* Boult's Angel recording comes with perhaps the finest version of the *Pastoral* Symphony (No. 3) (CDM-64018 [CD]).

While space, alas, does not permit a complete discussion of all nine Vaughan Williams symphonies, the other Angel recordings by Boult and those by Previn on RCA can be recommended enthusiastically. The Boult interpretations have the advantage of the conductor's long friendship with the composer and his fifty-year immersion in the music. Previn, on the other hand, brings an engaging spontaneity to the music and a youthful interpretative insight that make his recordings no less valuable. The wise collector will want them all, especially since all have been reissued on compact disc.

The Wasps (incidental music, after Aristophanes); *Five Variants of "Dives and Lazarus"; The Lark Ascending*

London Philharmonic, Handley. Angel CDM-62018 [CD].

In addition to its cracking good overture, which features, among its many glories, the most wonderfully annoying insect sounds since *The Flight of the Bumblebee*, the Aristophanic suite *The Wasps* contains some of Vaughan Williams's wittiest music. Vernon Handley and company give it a stylish, energetic performance and are equally persuasive in the gentler companion pieces. The Boult recording of *The Lark Ascending* may be a bit more sinuously poetic, but there is no finer version of the folksy *Five Variants of "Dives and Lazarus"* in the catalog. Given the superb recorded sound and the reasonable price, this is one of the most desirable VW anthologies currently available.

Verdi, Giuseppe (1813–1901)

Aida

> Milanov, Barbieri, Björling, Warren, Christoff, Orchestra and Chorus of the Rome Opera House, Perlea. Victrola 6652-2-RG [CD], ALK3-5380 [T].

> Price, Bumbry, Domingo, Milnes, London Symphony, Leinsdorf. RCA 6198-2-RC [CD], ARK3-2541 [T].

Verdi is unique among the great composers in that his posthumous fame is of virtually the same magnitude as that which he enjoyed during his lifetime. In 1842, the year of *Nabucco,* Verdi became a national hero in his own country, and in the next few years he was lionized throughout the opera world. Although there were occasional setbacks (the famous initial failure of *La Traviata,* for instance), he experienced more than half a century of increasing honors, and died, at the age of eighty-seven, steeped in wealth and adulation.

Aida, which was to have been his final opera, is a good indication of why Verdi, now as then, is the very heart of Italian opera. Amid all its pomp and spectacle, *Aida* is essentially a work about human conflict—the conflicting emotions of its central characters, both with each other and within themselves. Given an even halfway decent production, *Aida* easily demonstrates why its power is virtually indestructible, and why it remains one of the three or four most popular works of the operatic stage.

As a performance, no recording has yet to supersede the brilliant version made in Rome in the mid-1950s, which featured what was, and remains, an ideal cast. Beginning with Zinka Milanov, who is as poignant as she is powerful in the title role, all the parts are covered by superb choices, from the glorious Rhadames of Jussi Björling to the menacing, ink-black Ramfis of the young Boris Christoff. The conducting of the vastly underrated Jonel Perlea is full of fire and poetry, and the recorded sound is much better than you'd expect from that era.

For the best modern version of the score, Leontyne Price's RCA recording easily sweeps the field. Although not quite so intense and probing as in her London recording with Sir Georg Solti, the singing clearly shows why Price, after Rosa Ponselle, was the greatest Verdi singer America has so far produced.

Un ballo in maschera

M. Price, Pavarotti, Ludwig, Battle, Bruson, National Philharmonic, Solti. London 410210-2 [CD], 410210-4 [T].

At first glance, this didn't look at all promising. (Actually, it did, but I hate to tell you exactly *what* it seemed to promise.) At the time, Luciano Pavarotti was obviously in serious vocal trouble, Margaret Price was merely getting louder and louder, and Sir Georg Solti hadn't made an opera recording with any genuine passion in it for nearly a dozen years.

The surprising result is a milestone in recent operatic history. This *Masked Ball* takes off like a shot, and refuses to let up until the very end. The cast could not have been better (Pavarotti sounds like the Pavarotti of old), and there is no praise too high for Solti's alert, incisive conducting. In short, this is a *Ballo* for you.

Don Carlo

Caballé, Domingo, Verrett, Milnes, Raimondi, Orchestra and Chorus of the Royal Opera House, Covent Garden, Giulini. Angel CDCC-47701 [CD].

The universal acceptance of *Don Carlo* as one of the greatest of Verdi's operas is a fairly recent phenomenon that was helped along by two historic productions: the 1950 revival with which Sir Rudolf Bing began his controversial but always lively tenure at the Metropolitan Opera, and Luchino Visconti's Covent Garden production eight years later, which introduced many to a brilliant new Italian conductor named Carlo Maria Giulini.

Taped in London thirteen years later, Giulini's Angel recording of the 1886 five-act Italian version is not only the best *Don Carlo* we are likely to hear this century, but also one of the great Verdi recordings yet made. While the cast is one of the strongest assembled during the 1970s—Placido Domingo as the feckless hero and Ruggero Raimondi as the King are especially engrossing—it is Giulini's subtle intensity that makes the recording click. Even the problematic Auto-da-fé Scene explodes with an uncommon point and veracity; many listeners, no doubt, will be tempted to break out the weenies and marshmallows. As with most of Angel's CD restorations, the recording sounds as though it had been made last week.

Ernani

L. Price, Bergonzi, Sereni, Flagello, RCA Italiana Opera Chorus and Orchestra, Schippers. RCA 6503-2-RG [CD].

One of *Ernani*'s harshest early critics was Victor Hugo, who considered Verdi's adaptation of his play *Hernani* a complete travesty. A century and a half later, it is this "travesty" alone which keeps the memory of that once-popular play alive.

For his fifth opera, Verdi produced a score bursting with vigor, rousing tunes, and good old-fashioned moustache-twirling melodrama. By the standards of the masterworks of the 1850s, much of this can seem fairly naive and obvious stuff; yet in the right hands, the opera can pack a tremendous vocal and emotional wallop, as it does in this powerful recording from 1967.

If Leontyne Price was not at her absolute dramatic peak as Elvira, it is still her usual vocal tour de force. With suave and powerful support from the always wonderful Carlo Bergonzi and the magnetic conducting of Thomas Schippers, this is the *Ernani* for you.

Falstaff

Schwarzkopf, Moffo, Merriman, Barbieri, Alva, Gobbi,
Philharmonia Orchestra and Chorus, Karajan. Angel
CDCB-49668 [CD].

Ligabue, Freni, Simionato, Krause, Evans, RCA Italiana
Opera Orchestra and Chorus, Solti. London 417168-2
[CD], 417168-4 [T].

More than in his two recordings of Strauss's *Rosenkavalier*,
the Jekyll-Hyde nature of the old and new Herbert von Karajan is
obvious here. This Angel recording from the early 1960s is one of
the most nearly perfect opera recordings of the stereo era. Each
member of the cast is coaxed into an imperishable performance by
a conductor who obviously cares as much for his singers as he does
for the score. (In his later Philips catastrophe, it is equally apparent
that all Karajan cared about at that point was Karajan himself.) In
its transfer to compact disc, this early performance sounds even
more brilliant and endearing than ever. The opera rushes by, as it
should, like quicksilver, and the lyrical moments are given more
than their due.

Among available tapes, the performance led by Sir Georg Solti
is nearly as exciting. Apart from a tendency to throttle some of the
swifter passages, the interpretation is excellent and features Sir
Geraint Evans as the only Falstaff who begins to compete with Tito
Gobbi in the Karajan recording.

La forza del destino

Price, Cossotto, Domingo, Milnes, Bacquier, John Alldis
Choir, London Symphony, Levine. RCA RCD3-1864
[CD].

Of all the great middle-period Verdi operas (from *Rigoletto* of
1851 through *Aida,* 1871), *La forza del destino* is easily the most
incredible. And I mean incredible in the literal sense, something that
strains belief. The plot of the opera is hopelessly twisted and complicated, the irony so extreme it would have made Charles Dickens
blush. And yet, in spite of the unintentional silliness of its goofy and
frequently embarrassing story line, *Forza* is one of the greatest of

Verdi's operas. And despite its considerable length, it is one of the most compressed. In its musical concentration and dramatic power, *Forza* is the one early Verdi work that clearly points the way to *Aida* and, ultimately, *Otello*.

After Rosa Ponselle, Leontyne Price was probably the finest Leonora of the century. The power of her middle register, the incomparable beauty of her high notes, and the enormous strength and dignity of her characterization turn this performance into the stuff of legend. While it is clearly Price's show, the rest of the cast is splendid. Placido Domingo and Sherrill Milnes are almost as fine as they are in their superb *Otello* (see page 449), and James Levine offers here some of his most assured and sympathetic conducting on records. Without question, this is one of the best opera recordings of the last three decades and, quite clearly, the one *Forza* to own.

On tape, Riccardo Muti's La Scala performance with Mirella Freni and Domingo (Angel 4DSC-3995) is completely acceptable, though I wouldn't recommend listening to *any* recording of *Forza* during rush hour in your car.

*L*uisa Miller

> Ricciarelli, Obraztsova, Domingo, Bruson, Orchestra and
> Chorus of the Royal Opera House, Covent Garden,
> Maazel. Deutsche Grammophon 423144-2 [CD].

Finished just before *Rigoletto* launched the composer's incomparably rich middle period—that canon on which every opera company of the world depends for its very existence—*Luisa Miller* is very nearly a great opera. There are many who insist that it actually is one, including Placido Domingo, who maintains that the tenor's big moment is his favorite single aria. (He facetiously claims it is such because "Quando le sere al placido" contains his name, but it *is* an extravagantly beautiful moment, one of the finest Verdi ever wrote.)

Domingo and almost everyone else perform magnificently in this first-rate Covent Garden production. The only exception is Elena Obraztsova, who again does her best to shatter flowerpots with her guttural braying. Lorin Maazel has rarely sounded more confident and relaxed in the recording studio, and the physical sound is superb.

Macbeth

Cappuccilli, Verrett, Ghiaurov, Domingo, Orchestra and
Chorus of La Scala, Abbado. Deutsche Grammophon
415688-2 [CD].

In many ways *Macbeth* was Verdi's *Fidelio,* the work that cost
him more time and anguish than any other in his career. A comparative failure at its Florence premiere in 1847, it was revised substantially for an 1865 production in Paris, where it proved to be an
even bigger flop. In spite of its lack of success, it remained one of
Verdi's own favorite operas for reasons that aren't difficult to explain. For along with being the finest opera of the 1840s (the decade
Verdi called his "years as a galley slave"), *Macbeth* is also the first
in which we hear the unmistakable voice of the composer Verdi
would eventually become. For here, dramatic values become as significant as musical ones, and the revelation of character, which
Verdi sought all his life to perfect, had its first great success in the
figure of Lady Macbeth, one of the most important female roles he
would ever conceive.

If Shirley Verrett's voice isn't really suited to the part, that has
not prevented her from becoming the great Lady Macbeth of our
time. In fact, the characterization is so menacing, eerie, and vivid
(the Sleepwalking Scene would chill a Sicilian's blood) that it nearly
overwhelms the fine performance of Piero Cappuccilli in the title
role. Claudio Abbado's sharply dramatic conducting ranks with his
best on records, and the rest of the cast is excellent, as is the recorded sound.

Nabucco

Suliotis, Prevedi, Gobbi, Cava, Vienna State Opera
Orchestra and Chorus, Gardelli. London 417407-2
[CD].

Nabucco, Verdi's first great success, is the only one of his
operas—unless one counts that anvil thing in *Trovatore*—that is
best known for a chorus: the celebrated lamentation "Va, pensiero," which immediately became the unofficial anthem of the Italian
independence movement and, sixty years later, would be sung spon-
taneously by Milan's heartbroken masses at Verdi's funeral. While
certainly not a great opera, *Nabucco* can be an entertaining and

intermittently enthralling experience, especially in a performance such as the one London recorded in Vienna in the mid-1960s.

The principal attractions of this fine recording—which, in spite of its age, is to be preferred to Giuseppe Sinopoli's mannered and finicky outing for Deutsche Grammophon—are the Nabucco of Tito Gobbi, who here demonstrates why he was the most accomplished dramatic baritone of his generation, and the spirited, sensitive conducting of Lamberto Gardelli, one of the major Verdi specialists of the last half century.

For those who are interested only in "Va, pensiero," it can be heard to supreme tear-jerking effect (along with other favorite Verdi choruses) on Claudio Abbado's stylish Deutsche Grammophon compact disc (413448-2).

Otello

**Domingo, Scotto, Milnes, National Philharmonic, Levine.
RCA RCD2-2951 [CD], CRK3-2951 [T].**

The choice of a recorded Otello inevitably becomes a choice between the two great Otellos of modern times, Jon Vickers and Placido Domingo. On balance, I tend to favor the Domingo version, but only by a hairsbreadth. The Domingo Otello is a large, powerful, beautifully sung, and ultimately withering experience. While the Vickers is no less enthralling, both his recorded versions have drawbacks: a spotty cast and strangely inert support from Tullio Serafin in the RCA recording, and Herbert von Karajan's heavy hand in the more recent version for Angel.

The Domingo Otello, however, is not without its flaws. It features the often shrill Desdemona of Renata Scotto, and conducting from James Levine that is occasionally so enthusiastic some very important singing is lost. (In the opening "Esultate," for instance, Domingo is practically drowned out.) Nevertheless, with the splendid Iago of Sherrill Milnes, this Otello is an outstanding performance, and we are not likely to hear a finer one any time soon.

Requiem

**Schwarzkopf, Ludwig, Gedda, Ghiaurov, Philharmonia
Orchestra and Chorus, Giulini. Angel CDCB-47257
[CD].**

This is the recording of the Verdi Requiem—that magnificent opera disguised as a sacred work—to make even the most unregenerate sinner *believe*. (If the Day of Judgment isn't as overwhelming as Verdi and Giulini make it sound, I, for one, will be extremely disappointed.) In the quarter century since its release, this version of the Requiem has dominated the catalog in a way no other recording has. In its compact disc format, the performance is even more thrilling than ever, and if this one doesn't spur you on to buying a compact disc player, nothing will.

If any recording on tape came within an inch of this one's instep, I'd be the first to recommend it. To date, no such recording exists. Packaged with Giulini's incomparable version of the *Four Sacred Pieces,* this is now a bargain that no Verdi lover—no music lover, for that matter—can possibly resist.

*R*igoletto

> Callas, di Stefano, Gobbi, Zaccaria, La Scala Orchestra and Chorus, Serafin. Angel CDCB-47469 [CD].

The ultimate test of any performance of *Rigoletto* is your reaction to the final scene. Are tears rolling down your cheeks or are you laughing so hard you're afraid of committing an indiscretion on your seat? *Both* reactions, by the way, are perfectly plausible. Consider the bare bones of the scene itself. A hunchback jester opens a gunnysack, thinking it contains the corpse of the heartless rogue who deflowered his daughter. Much to his surprise, he discovers his daughter herself, who, while bleeding to death, sings one of the most demanding duets in all of opera. (If you think *singing* on your side isn't a tough trick, just try drinking a glass of beer that way.)

Whenever I hear that final duet in this historic version of Verdi's early masterpiece, I am *never* tempted to laugh. One of the most enduring of the many great recorded collaborations of Maria Callas and Tito Gobbi, this *Rigoletto* virtually defines the term "grand opera." To Callas and Gobbi, add the slightly edgy but still magnificent Giuseppe di Stefano as the Duke, and the firm yet flexible conducting of Tullio Serafin, and you have something close to a *Rigoletto* for the ages. The mid-1950s recorded sound is more than adequate, and in the compact disc transfer, its bite and clarity are amazing.

Simon Boccanegra

Cappuccilli, Freni, Carreras, Ghiaurov, Van Dam, Fioani,
Orchestra and Chorus of La Scala, Abbado. Deutsche
Grammophon 415692-2 [CD].

Except for the overly long and generally uninspired *I vespri
siciliani* (even the composer himself complained about the excessive
length of his made-to-order French grand opera), *Simon Boccanegra* is the only one of Verdi's works composed after *Rigoletto* that
has failed to become a staple of the standard repertoire. Part of the
reason this masterpiece has been so long in catching on—and a masterpiece it most certainly is—has to do with the casting of the title
role.

Whenever a production is blessed with a magnetic star-caliber
baritone—Victor Maurel for the premiere of the 1881 revision,
Lawrence Tibbett at the Metropolitan in 1932, Leonard Warren,
Tito Gobbi, and Sherrill Milnes in more recent years—the opera
usually proves to be an overwhelming success. Claudio Abbado's
sensational 1977 recording with the bright, musical, though hardly
heart-stopping Piero Cappuccilli proves that *Simon* is *not* a one-
man show, and that it can stand on its own with any middle-period
Verdi opera.

Most of the credit for one of the most exciting and nearly
perfect of all modern Verdi recordings must go to Abbado, who has
never been more impressive in the recording studio or out; the conducting is noble, poetic, subtle, and intense, with a sense of life and
on-the-spot creativity rarely encountered in a commercial recording. The soloists, chorus, and orchestra all catch fire under Abbado's incandescent direction, and DG's engineers come through with
their very best recorded sound.

If for you *Simon Boccanegra* is still a question mark, this is
the recording that will turn it into an exclamation point.

La Traviata

Sutherland, Pavarotti, Manuguerra, London Opera Chorus,
National Philharmonic, Bonynge. London 430491-2
[CD].

This fair but generally uninspired run-through of Verdi's popular opera is now the preferred recording of *La Traviata*, although

only by default. Everyone, especially Joan Sutherland, sings well enough, yet the performance simply will not grab you by the throat. Sadly, none of the other versions of this usually foolproof opera come any closer. Until something better turns up, this perfectly serviceable release will have to do.

Il Trovatore

Milanov, Björling, Barbieri, Warren, RCA Victor Orchestra and Chorus, Cellini. RCA 6643-2-RG [CD], Victrola CLK2-5377 [T].

This (to use a phrase without which every sportscaster in America would be unable to do his job) really *is* what it's all about. Add a Leonora made of 50 percent volcano and 50 percent pathos, a gleaming, heroic Manrico (his high C in "Di quella pira" will shake you down to your socks), and a sinister, brooding, old-fashioned Azucena "whose very urine" (to use Philip Wylie's immortal phrase) "would probably etch glass," and you have one of the most electric operatic recordings ever made. The combination of Zinka Milanov, Jussi Björling, Fedora Barbieri, and Leonard Warren, the same team responsible for that greatest of all recorded *Aidas*, is all but unstoppable here. Even the occasionally phlegmatic Renato Cellini catches fire, and turns in what is undoubtedly the performance of his career.

For those who are bothered by the monophonic, mid-1950s recorded sound (and if you're listening to sound instead of music, you might want to make sure you have the right hobby), another fine RCA release (6194-2-RC [CD]) with Price, Cossotto, Domingo, Milnes, and Mehta at the top of *their* forms is the best recent alternative.

Victoria, Tomás Luis de

(c. 1548–1611)

*M*issa *"Ave maris stella"; "O quam gloriosum est regnum"* (motet); Missa *"O quam gloriosum"*

Westminster Cathedral Choir, Hill. Hyperion CDA-64114 [CD].

King Philip II was correct in his famous assertion that "the destiny of Spain cannot await upon the fitness of time." Alas, it *did* have to await upon the whims of that arrogant, boneheaded monarch who in a single, ill-advised stroke managed to throw away one of the greatest empires since the fall of Rome. When the Armada went down in the unforgiving waters of the English Channel in 1588, it not only marked the end of the Spanish domination of both the Old and New Worlds, but also the beginning of the end of the golden age of Spanish art, as epitomized by the paintings of El Greco, the fiction of Cervantes, the drama and poetry of Lope de Vega, and the music of composers like Tomás Luis de Victoria.

Nearly four centuries after his death, Victoria's music retains the ardor and spiritual daring that made it one of the purest Renaissance manifestations of Spanish mysticism, an intense, ecstatic, transcendent beauty that is projected to absolute perfection in this lovely Hyperion recording. The committed, emotionally high-powered interpretations that David Hill draws from the Westminster Choir are far removed from the typical dry-as-dust approach to early sacred music, and the warm, enfolding acoustic of Hyperion's recording proves an ideal setting for the spirit of a very great composer and his glittering age.

Villa-Lobos, Heitor

(1887–1959)

Bachianas brasileiras Nos. 1, 5, and 7

Hendricks, soprano; Royal Philharmonic, Bátiz. Angel CDC-47433 [CD], 4DS-38334 [T].

Almost everyone who discovers the music of South America's foremost composer, the Brazilian Heitor Villa-Lobos, does so through the wordless aria from the hauntingly beautiful *Bachiana brasileira* No. 5. An imaginative transplanting of the spirit of Bach in the soil of Brazil, the *Bachianas* are major contributions to the music of the twentieth century, as is the work of Villa-Lobos in general.

Not since the Brazilian soprano Bidú Sayão made her famous recording with the composer in the 1940s has there been a more heart-stopping version of the work than this gleaming Angel recording by Barbara Hendricks, who certainly has the talent, the drive, and the looks to become one of the dominant singers of the waning years of the twentieth century. This stunning recording is one of her best to date. The singing has a lush yet otherworldly quality that suggests an oversexed seraph, and the accompaniment she receives from Enrique Bátiz is a model of sympathetic support. For something slightly off the beaten track, i.e., as a gift for the collector who seems to have *almost* everything, you can't go wrong with this lovely recording, even if you simply give it as a gift to yourself.

Etudes (12) for Guitar; Preludes (5) for Guitar

Fernández, guitar. London 414616-2 [CD].

This splendid recital by the Uruguayan guitarist Eduard Fernández offers not only spirited, idiomatic performances of the most popular guitar music of the artfully disheveled and always poetic-looking Heitor Villa-Lobos, but also a major work by his brilliant Argentine colleague, Alberto Ginastera, described by one close friend as having "all the rakish personal charm of a bank teller."

While most listeners will probably be drawn to the recording by the colorful, moody, refined, and explosive Etudes and Preludes of Villa-Lobos, Ginastera's 1976 Guitar Sonata is an equally important and appealing work: folksy, intelligent, beautifully turned out, and immediately accessible.

On the basis of this recording, Fernández would seem to have joined the very front rank of the world's finest guitarists, and even those who consider the guitar itself something of a noninstrument (I speak from decades of experience) cannot fail to be impressed.

Vivaldi, Antonio (c. 1678–1741)

I'm the first to admit that I have a blind spot when it comes to this composer. Everyone loves Vivaldi, right? At very least, he is the perfect yuppie composer, a man whose tuneful, relentlessly good-natured, cleverly made music turns up more frequently at brunch than that of anyone else. And the music *is* inventive, distinctive, and exceedingly well made. Yet apart from the surface details (what instrument is playing, what key the work is in, and so forth), most of his music seems exactly the same to me. Stravinsky certainly had a point when he said that Vivaldi wrote the same concerto several hundred times. This explains why there are only two entries devoted to this composer. Vivaldi lovers, forgive me. Besides, isn't your BMW double-parked?

The Four Seasons

> Loveday, violin; Academy of St. Martin-in-the-Fields, Marriner. Argo 414486-2 [CD], 414486-4 [T].
>
> Standage, violin; English Concert, Pinnock. Deutsche Grammophon 400045-2 [CD], 400045-4 [T].

With the possible exception of Pachelbel's *Kanon*, nothing makes me want to start throwing things more than a half dozen bars of *The Seasons*. I hate it with the same irrational intensity I reserve for peanut butter, for reasons that remain as difficult to explain. Like all his other concertos, these four are exceedingly inoffensive and exceptionally graceful. In me, alas, they stimulate nothing but violence, and if allowed to go on too long, reverse peristalsis.

The recording I have found least offensive over the years is the Argo version by Alan Loveday and Sir Neville Marriner. The playing is as exciting as it is tidy, and communicates a deep and abiding sense of enjoyment. Among period-instrument recordings, the interpretation by Simon Standage and Trevor Pinnock's superb English Concert is undoubtedly the best.

Gloria in D

> Nelson, Kirkby, Watkinson, Elliott, Thomas, Christ Church Cathedral Choir, Academy of Ancient Music, Preston. Oiseau-Lyre 414678-2 [CD], 414678-4 [T].

This is the sort of recording that almost makes one believe in miracles, for, miraculously, I managed to remain conscious to the very end.

Wagner, Richard (1813–1883)

The Flying Dutchman

> Bailey, Martin, Kollo, Talvela, Chicago Symphony Orchestra and Chorus, Solti. London 414551-2 [CD].

It was with this, the first of his operas destined to occupy a place in the standard repertoire, that the musical world encountered the man who, after Beethoven, would become the most influential composer history has so far known. Although much of *Der fliegende Holländer* places it in the company of traditional nineteenth-century opera (the discrete arias, choruses, and other set pieces), there is much to indicate that as early as 1843, Wagner the arch-revolutionary was beginning to evolve. For one thing, *The Flying Dutchman,* in its original version, was cast in a single, continuous act. (Two and a half hours without a break was an outrageous demand to make on mid-nineteenth-century derrières.) Also we can hear the composer flirting with odd harmonies and dissonances, and an embryonic version of the leitmotif technique which would eventually lead to those vast music dramas that changed not only opera but the course of Western music.

With a very strong cast led by Norman Bailey, the finest Dutchman of the last twenty years, Sir Georg Solti leads a performance as incisive as it is atmospheric, as brilliantly played as it is wonderfully sung. Unfortunately, the performance is now available only on compact disc, and there is no tape version that warrants a serious recommendation.

*L*ohengrin

> Domingo, Norman, Randová, Nimsgern, Fischer-Dieskau,
> Vienna State Opera Chorus, Vienna Philharmonic, Solti.
> London 421053-2 [CD].

Never expect to hear a *Lohengrin* like this at your neighborhood opera house. For one thing, your local opera company couldn't afford to mount one with singers of this caliber. For another, it's not every day that you hear the likes of the great Vienna Philharmonic in the pit. The reasons why this is the finest recording of Wagner's early opera have as much to do with the conducting as with the choice of the tenor for the title role. Given the wonderful idea of casting Placido Domingo as Walther in *Die Meistersinger* a number of years ago, it's a bit surprising that no one ever thought of doing it again until now. No, Domingo is obviously *not* a Wagnerian in the grand tradition: his command of the language is questionable, and his sense of the character is at times rather sketchy. Yet what a pleasure it is to hear a world-class voice *singing* the part, instead of the usual grunting, howling, and groaning that passes for Wagnerian singing today.

For the remainder of the cast, London put together a formidable ensemble, and Sir Georg Solti's conducting is precisely what it needs to be—neither overly measured nor uncomfortably rushed. The Vienna Philharmonic has not sounded this impressive since their epoch-making recording (also with Solti) of Wagner's complete *Ring*, and the recorded sound will send shivers down your spine.

*D*ie Meistersinger von Nürnberg

Bode, Hamari, Kollo, Bailey, Weikl, Moll, Vienna State Opera Chorus, Vienna Philharmonic, Solti. London 417497-2 [CD].

Ligendza, Ludwig, Domingo, Fischer-Dieskau, Orchestra and Chorus of the German Opera, Berlin, Jochum. Deutsche Grammophon 415278-2 [CD].

While *Tristan und Isolde* is probably his masterpiece, and the *Ring*, taken as a whole, his most significant achievement, *Die Meistersinger* finally showed the world the human side of Richard Wagner. Given the nature of the beast that Wagner was, his human side proved to be shockingly warm, generous, and complete. In the only operatic comedy worthy of comparison with Verdi's *Falstaff* and Mozart's *Figaro*, Wagner succeeds in showing us not only what is finest and best in the German people, but also by inference what is finest and best in ourselves. For this one Wagner opera cast on a completely human scale is about friendship and trust, young love and mature wisdom, tradition and rebellion—in short, the human condition itself.

Among available recordings of the opera, the difficult choice is between the versions conducted by Sir Georg Solti and Eugen Jochum. Each has its particular strengths and weaknesses. The Jochum recording suffers from the disappointing Hans Sachs of Dietrich Fischer-Dieskau, which is as badly overacted as it is oversung. On the other hand, Placido Domingo, as Walther, is a vocal revelation. As in the recent recording of *Lohengrin*, it's a pleasure to hear a voice of this stature in the part.

The Solti recording, which features the marvelous Hans Sachs of Norman Bailey, has to contend with a very wobbly Walther (René Kollo). The conducting from Solti is only marginally less graceful and stately than what we hear from Jochum. For my money, neither can begin to match that virtually flawless, but now out of print, mid-1950s Angel recording conducted by Rudolf Kempe. But if a choice must be made, then it's Solti by a nose.

Overtures, Preludes, and Excerpts

For those who accept the old saw that Wagner wrote some of the most inspired minutes and some of the most tedious hours in the history of music—or for people who simply prefer to do without all that singing—the recorded selection of overtures, preludes, and the rest of what Shaw called "the bleeding chunks of meat" has always been varied and impressive, all the more so since the introduction of the compact disc.

Fritz Reiner's Chicago Symphony recording for RCA (RCD1-4738 [CD]) of thrillingly played excerpts from *Meistersinger* and *Götterdämmerung* is an absolute necessity, as is George Szell's lean and athletic CBS recording of the best-known orchestral excerpts—including an especially rousing "Ride of the Valkyries"—from *The Ring* (MYK-36715 [CD], MYT-36715 [T]). Solti (London 410137-2 [CD]), Stokowski (London 411772-4 [T]), and Tennstedt (Angel CDC-47007 [CD], 4DS-37808 [T]) also lead highly successful anthologies of *Ring* excerpts that are as individual as they are exciting.

The loveliest version of Wagner's most gently human work, the *Siegfried Idyll,* is still Bernard Haitink's exquisite one for Philips. Unfortunately, the superb medium-priced Wagner collection on which it was found has now been withdrawn, which means that it can only be had as a filler for Haitink's admittedly masterly recording of Bruckner's Eighth Symphony (412465-2 [CD]).

Bruno Walter is handsomely represented on CBS (MPK-45701 [CD]) by that extraordinary version of the overture and Venusburg Music from *Tannhäuser,* together with typically warm and avuncular interpretations of the *Lohengrin, Flying Dutchman,* and *Meistersinger* preludes. Walter's old friend Otto Klemperer, whose Wagner is neither as heavy nor as lethargic as those who have never heard his recordings suggest, utters the last word on the *Parsifal* prelude, together with some fascinating comments on *Ring* and *Meistersinger* excerpts for Angel (CDM-63618 [CD], 4AE-34407 [T]).

Finally, if the absence of demonstration-quality recorded sound is not the end of the world for you, four of the most individual of all Wagnerians are still on hand to instruct, amaze, and delight. Hans Knappertsbusch's famous Munich recordings—including the slowest performance of the *Rienzi* Overture ever attempted—are out on a pair of MCA compact discs (MCAD2-

9811); a representative collection by perhaps the greatest Wagner conductor of all, Wilhelm Furtwängler, is available from Deutsche Grammophon (427406-2 [CD]); the work of the deeply misanthropic, profoundly spiritual Karl Muck may be sampled on a pair of InSync tapes (C-4133, C-4136).

Parsifal

Dalis, Thomas, London, Hotter, Neidlinger, Bayreuth
Festival Orchestra and Chorus, Knappertsbusch. Philips
416390-2 [CD].

There used to be an ancient Metropolitan Opera curse that one still hears from old-timers: "May you be trapped in a performance of *Parsifal* without a sandwich." And truly, nothing can be more thoroughly numbing than an indifferently prepared production of the opera, which does tend to go on and on, just as nothing can be more genuinely stirring when all the parties involved are giving the opera all it demands, which is to say, *everything*.

Recorded live at the 1962 Bayreuth Festival, this performance proves more conclusively than any other that *Parsifal* was in fact a fitting conclusion to Wagner's career, containing as it does many of the most inspired pages the composer ever wrote. With a cast that includes George London, Jess Thomas, and the great Hans Hotter among others, the recording features some of the finest Wagner singing heard on records. *Parsifal* was always a great house specialty of Hans Knappertsbusch, and he leads a performance of unparalleled dignity, depth, and majesty. Although the recording is of an actual performance, the foot-shuffling, coughing, and vocal drop-outs are kept to a bare minimum, and besides, the thrill of hearing those incomparable Bayreuth acoustics more than compensates for the occasional glitch.

Rienzi

Wennberg, Martin, Kollo, Schreier, Adam, Dresden State
Orchestra and Chorus, Hollreiser. Angel CDMB-63980
[CD].

Rienzi, The Last of the Tribunes was Wagner's *Nabucco*. Introduced in October of 1842, only seven months after Verdi's third opera made him an overnight success, Wagner's third effort also proved to be a charm: it soon became the most popular work in the Dresden Opera's repertoire and made the twenty-nine-year-old composer's name known throughout Germany for the first time. Although long and frequently derivative—the shadow of Giacomo Meyerbeer hangs heavily over the proceedings—*Rienzi* has many wonderful moments, and the ardent Wagnerian will certainly want to give this recording a try. Unfortunately, the performance is one to admire rather than cherish. Heinrich Hollreiser's able conducting and René Kollo's sturdy interpretation of the title role are the best things in the set; the less said about the women, the better. Still, the passion and youthful enthusiasm of the music carry most of the day.

Der Ring des Nibelungen (Das Rheingold, Die Walküre, Siegfried, Götterdämmerung)

Nilsson, Flagstad, Crespin, Watson, Ludwig, Madeira, Windgassen, Svanholm, King, Stolze, London, Fischer-Dieskau, Hotter, Frick, Neidlinger, Vienna Philharmonic, Solti. London 414100-2 [CD].

It is only fitting that one of the most titanic outbursts of the human imagination inspired one of the genuine cornerstones of recording history: the now legendary English Decca/London version of Wagner's *Ring*. In spite of its obvious flaws, and there are several, this will undoubtedly be our once and future *Ring:* an enterprise so massively ambitious, audacious, and successful that it boggles the mind.

True, this is not the ideal performance of Wagner's sprawling fifteen-hour tetralogy. Then again, much evidence suggests Wagner himself at last concluded that an ideal *Ring* existed only in his mind. The major flaws in the recording include a Siegfried who is barely adequate (although Wolfgang Windgassen was the best the world had to offer at the time) and the rather wobbly Wotan of the once great Hans Hotter.

In spite of these important drawbacks, the great moments far outnumber the uncomfortable ones. Here is Kirsten Flagstad, singing the *Rheingold* Fricka, a role she learned especially for this recording. Here, too, are those extravagant bits of casting, including Christa Ludwig as Waltraute, and Joan Sutherland as the Forest

Bird. Through it all, one still feels the spirit of John Culshaw (the most imaginative recording producer of his generation), who here, with Sir Georg Solti in the pit and the finest cast that could then be assembled, puts together not only his greatest achievement but also that of many who were involved.

Tannhäuser

> Dernesch, Ludwig, Kollo, Braun, Sotin, Vienna State Opera Chorus, Vienna Philharmonic, Solti. London 414581-2 [CD].

Sir Georg Solti has now recorded every Wagner opera from *The Flying Dutchman* to *Parsifal,* and none of those recordings is finer than this stupendous version of the Paris edition of *Tannhäuser.* In Helga Dernesch and Christa Ludwig he has a pair of ladies for whom any conductor would give what remains of his hair. And René Kollo, who has had serious vocal problems over the years, here sounds freer and fresher than he ever has on recordings. But it is Solti's conducting, as languorous and limpid as it is ferocious and exultant, that makes this one of the great Wagner recordings of the last twenty years.

As is now so frequently the case, there is no recording of the opera available on cassette.

Tristan und Isolde

> Flagstad, Thebom, Suthaus, Fischer-Dieskau, Greindl, Royal Opera Chorus, Philharmonia Orchestra, Furtwängler. Angel CDC-47321 [CD].

> Behrens, Minton, Hofmann, Weikl, Sotin, Bavarian Radio Orchestra and Chorus, Bernstein. Philips 410447-2 [CD], 410447-4 [T].

The famous 1952 Furtwängler recording of *Tristan und Isolde,* most collectors concede, is the greatest single Wagner recording yet made. In spite of a frequently negligible Tristan and an Isolde who was crowding sixty at the time, no other version of this passionate masterwork has captured as much black magic or animal intensity as this one. In her finest studio recording, the legendary

Kirsten Flagstad beguiles and terrifies with equal ease, and this Isolde is more convincingly and beautifully sung than any we are ever likely to hear.

Wilhelm Furtwängler's conducting is similarly inspired, and more than confirms his reputation as the greatest Wagner conductor of his time. The dynamic contrasts range from the merest whisper to the most shattering climaxes. Phrases are stretched out to unimaginable lengths, and in general, the performance creates a feeling no Wagner opera ever does—that it is far too short.

The most amazing thing about Leonard Bernstein's amazing Philips recording is how favorably it compares to what has been for years an incomparable recording. Although his Isolde, Hildegard Behrens, is no match for Flagstad, the Tristan of Peter Hofmann is virile, exciting, and exceptionally musical, and the rest of the cast is extremely strong. Nevertheless, the conducting is so obviously the center of attention that the voices seem to disappear. Rarely has anyone taken so many chances with what is already a very chancy work (some of the tempos are so slow that Furtwängler's seem brisk in comparison), and rarely have such chances paid off as handsomely as here. In another thirty years, posterity will probably view this *Tristan* with the same hushed reverence we now reserve for the Flagstad-Furtwängler recording. Wise collectors will acquire them both.

Die Walküre, Act I

Lehmann, Melchior, List, Vienna Philharmonic, Walter.
Angel CDH-61020 [CD].

So much has been said and written about this legendary 1935 recording—including the frequently repeated suggestion that it was, is, and will always be (with the possible exception of the Furtwängler *Tristan*) the greatest Wagner recording of all time—that all that really needs to be said is the CD transfer is even better than anyone could have hoped. The voices, especially Lotte Lehmann's, have never sounded more realistic, and the orchestral detail (which was always rather phenomenal for 1935) is clearer and cleaner than ever.

That other desert-island Wagner recording, the 1929 version of the *Tristan* love duet with an even younger Lauritz Melchior, that most warm and feminine of the great Isoldes, Frida Leider, and the astonishing Albert Coates, whose conducting manages to maintain the tension and animal excitement of the scene in spite of the fact that it was recorded in two separate cities (Berlin and London), several months apart, can now be found with other historic versions of excerpts from the opera on a pair of Legato Classics compact discs (LCD-146-2).

*W*esendonck Lieder

**Flagstad, soprano; Vienna Philharmonic, Knappertsbusch.
London 414624-2 [CD].**

Cut from the same cloth as *Tristan und Isolde,* these ravishing songs were settings of the rather feeble poetry of Mathilde Wesendonck, the pretentious wife of one of Wagner's most generous patrons and the composer's real-life model for Isolde. Characteristically, once *Tristan* was finished, Wagner completely lost interest in the woman who inspired it, leaving her to return to her understanding husband.

Although the great Kirsten Flagstad was nearly past sixty when she recorded the songs in 1956, the voice was still in magnificent shape. Supple, commanding, rich, and phenomenally voluminous, it allowed Flagstad to explore the full range of expression inherent in these wondrous lieder as no singer has before or since. Hans Knappertsbusch's accompaniments are as ardent as they are sensitive, and the recorded sound barely shows its age.

Walton, Sir William

(1902–1983)

Belshazzar's Feast

Luxon, baritone; Royal Philharmonic Orchestra and
Chorus, Previn. MCA MCAD-6187 [CD], MCAC-6187
[T].

The only disappointing thing about André Previn's newest and
finest recording of the most lurid, prurient, suggestive, and rousing
of all twentieth-century sacred works is the album cover photo.
While perfectly acceptable, it is certainly no match for the dazzling
image that adorned his early Angel recording, which, alas, is no
longer in print. In every other respect, however, this exhilarating
version of Walton's colorful oratorio is easily the most impressive
yet made. The chorus and the huge orchestral forces are managed
with the ease of a Haydn symphony, and over the years the interpretation has become both more thoughtful and more rambunctious. The unbridled joy that Previn coaxes out of the final cry of
"Alleluia" is as exciting as anything you've heard in years.

And if there remains any doubt that Previn is now the world's
foremost exponent of Walton's music, two other recordings will
more than convince you. The first, an Angel version of the Viola and
Violin Concertos with the brilliant Nigel Kennedy (CDC-49628
[CD]), contains the most admirable and adult interpretation either
work has yet received. And in his latest version of the great Symphony No. 1 in B-flat minor (Telarc CD-80125 [CD]), Previn releases all the beauty, vitality, and majesty of one of the major
symphonies of the twentieth century.

Façade

Pears, Sitwell, speakers; English Opera Group Ensemble,
Collins. London 425661-2 [CD].

Listening to the voice of Dame Edith Sitwell, one is strangely
reminded of W. H. Auden's description of his own face late in life

as "a wedding cake left out in the rain." Among the major modern poets, only Dylan Thomas has a comparably individual instrument. But it is not merely Dame Edith's indescribable voice—to say nothing of her overwhelming authority (she wrote the poems the piece is based on)—that makes this so far and away the greatest recording this daffy entertainment has ever received. In the faster poems, the superhuman diction of Sir Peter Pears must be heard to be believed, and Anthony Collins's conducting is a model of crack-brained panache.

Partita for Orchestra; Symphony No. 2; *Variations on a Theme by Hindemith*

> Cleveland Orchestra, Szell. Sony Classical Masterworks MPK-46732 [CD].

This is probably the single most valuable Walton recording now available. Not only does it offer George Szell's incomparably polished and exciting versions of two masterpieces, the Second Symphony and the absurdly underperformed *Variations on a Theme by Hindemith,* it also returns to circulation the recording of the delightful Partita for Orchestra made by the man who commissioned it.

Sir William was an ardent admirer of Szell's interpretations of his music, and from these classic recordings it isn't difficult to hear why. In addition to the usual mechanical perfection (which somehow never *sounds* mechanical or machinelike), there is a buoyancy and an indefatigable love of life in the playing that match the zest of the music itself. Rarely, if ever, were Szell's dramatic flair and sense of humor given a more attractive outlet, and in all the performances—though especially in that of the *Variations*—the Cleveland Orchestra has never been more impressive.

Warlock, Peter (1894–1930)

Capriol Suite

Ulster Orchestra, Handley. Chandos CHAN-8808 [CD], ABRD-1436 [T].

On the night of December 17, 1930, a brilliant, erratic English composer fulfilled the secret fantasy of every composer who has ever lived by actually murdering a music critic. Tragically, the composer Peter Warlock and his victim, the critic Philip Heseltine, were one and the same person.

At thirty-six, Warlock was already one of the most distinctive English voices of his generation. His charming, gemlike miniatures reflected the two great passions of his life: the gentle impressionism of his friend Frederick Delius and the forms of the great English music of the Renaissance.

His most popular work, the *Capriol Suite,* which is based on Elizabethan dances and gives them an unmistakably modern yet at times surprisingly sentimental spin, is superbly represented by Vernon Handley's colorful recording with the Ulster Orchestra. Other than the undoubted quality of the performance itself, the principal advantage of the recording is that it presents the composer's rarely heard version for full orchestra (instead of the more usual string band), and also offers Warlock's marvelous Serenade for String Orchestra as a bonus. The Serenade in G and Nocturne—unqualified winners both—by Warlock's contemporary E. J. Moeran round out this unusually desirable collection.

Warlock's dangerously addictive songs are elegantly served by Benjamin Luxon, who with pianist David Willison has recorded thirty-two of them for Chandos (CHAN-8643 [CD]). The incomparable English tenor Ian Partridge, accompanied by his sister Jennifer, can be heard in a dozen of them on Etcetera (KTC-1078 [CD]); sadly, his version—with the Music Group of London—of Warlock's masterpiece, the song cycle *The Curlew,* ranks with the great vocal recordings made since the war, has been temporarily withdrawn. A very fine Pearl recording (SHECD-9510 [CD]) featuring tenor James Griffett will certainly do until it reappears.

Weber, Carl Maria von

(1786–1826)

Concertos for Clarinet and Orchestra: No. 1 in F minor; No. 2 in E-flat; Concertino in E-Flat for Clarinet and Orchestra

> Pay, clarinet; Orchestra of the Age of Enlightenment. Virgin Classics VC-7-90720-2 [CD], VC-7-90720-4 [T].

Midway between the Old Testament (the Concerto, Quintet, and Trio of Mozart) and the New (the late masterpieces of Brahms) fall those several appealing works that the third undisputed master of the instrument, Carl Maria von Weber, composed for the clarinet. Written for his friend the suave Bavarian clarinetist and lady-killer Heinrich Bärmann, Weber's concertos and chamber works not only represent one of the high-water marks of early Romantic wind writing but also display the composer's talent at its freshest and most inventive.

In his period-instrument recording with the Orchestra of the Age of Enlightenment, the English clarinetist Anthony Pay strikes the perfect balance between swagger and sensitivity in his approach to the music; the playing has both bite and delicacy, as does the finely drilled (but by whom?) contribution of the conductorless orchestra. Again, the Virgin Classics engineers prove that they are among the best in the business with impeccably clear and detailed recorded sound.

Der Freischütz

> Janowitz, Mathis, Schreier, Weikl, Adam, Dresden State Opera Orchestra and Chorus, C. Kleiber. Deutsche Grammophon 415432-2 [CD].

The next time you're trapped in a game of musical trivia and need a question that will stump everyone, ask "What is the second most frequently performed opera in Germany today?" The totally unexpected answer is Albert Lortzing's *Zar und Zimmermann*. In fact, the work that occupies the number one spot will also come as a surprise to most people, simply because it isn't performed very often outside the German-speaking world. The reasons for the phenomenal popularity of *that* opera, Weber's *Freischütz,* are as obvious now as they were when it was new. Along with its wonderfully dark atmosphere (Germans love anything set in a forest), *Der Freischütz* boasts a succession of unforgettable arias, choruses, and other set pieces. Also, with *Der Freischütz* Carl Maria von Weber brought Romanticism into the opera house, and thus composers as diverse as Meyerbeer, Berlioz, Wagner, and Strauss owe Weber an incalculable debt.

This splendid Deutsche Grammophon release marked Carlos Kleiber's recording debut as an opera conductor, and what an auspicious debut it proved to be. Kleiber leads the superb cast and the always impeccable Dresden State Opera forces with tremendous energy, enthusiasm, and imagination. Only in the most darkly brooding moments of the second act do hints of Weber's poetry escape him. Still, this is a bracing introduction to a wonderful opera. Unfortunately, a tape is not available.

Overtures (6) and *Invitation to the Dance*

Hanover Band, Goodman. Nimbus NI-5154 [CD].

There was a pressing need for a good modern recording of the six Weber overtures and the Berlioz orchestration of *Aufforderung zum Tanze;* alas, Hermann Scherchen's zestful yet scrappy interpretations (now out on an Adès compact disc) have almost outlived their usefulness, while the more recent releases by Herbert von Karajan and Wolfgang Sawallisch are, respectively, perverse and inert.

The Hanover Band under Roy Goodman captures both the sweep and wit of these captivating pieces, and to do so on period instruments is no mean feat. The whirlwind performances of *Peter Schmoll* and *Abu Hassan* are especially marvelous, but so are the others, including an *Invitation to the Dance* that few will be able to refuse.

Webern, Anton (1883–1945)

Passacaglia for Orchestra; Five Movements for String Quartet; Six Pieces for Orchestra; Symphony for Chamber Orchestra

Berlin Philharmonic, Karajan. Deutsche Grammophon 423254-2 [CD].

Anton Webern was the most tragic member of the so-called Second Viennese School, whose other members were his teacher, Arnold Schoenberg, and his fellow pupil, Alban Berg. Webern was accidentally shot by an American soldier during the postwar occupation of Austria, but his tragedy had in fact begun years earlier. Both his daughters were married to high-ranking Nazi officials, and he himself seems to have been extremely sympathetic to the cause, not because he was evil, but because he was incredibly naive. On the day the Nazis marched into Vienna, Webern allegedly said, "Well, now at least we will be able to hear Mahler!"

Until quite recently, this pathetic, lonely figure was one of the most influential composers of the twentieth century. In fact, "Post-Webern" became a designation that was once used as frequently as "neoclassicism" or "New Romanticism."

Perhaps it is the inherent aloofness of the music, or perhaps it was the natural sympathy he felt for a kindred political spirit, but Herbert von Karajan's performances of these four astounding works were among the finest of the conductor's later recordings. It is not only the disturbing precision of the Berlin Philharmonic, but also the curious sense of nonterrestrial detachment in the conducting that serve the music so effectively.

Those with a more serious interest in Webern's rarefied art will find the bulk of it collected on three medium-priced Sony CDs (SM3K-45845), in those meticulous performances from the 1960s under the general supervision of Pierre Boulez. As always, the conductor's sense of reverent enthusiasm is matched only by the depth of his understanding. The orchestral performances are unfailingly refined and beautiful, and the Juilliard String Quartet and others work comparable wonders with the chamber music. It isn't often that one can encounter virtually the whole of a major composer's output in such a compact and attractively priced container.

Weill, Kurt (1900–1950)

The Threepenny Opera

Lenya, Litz, Gunter, Mund, Markworth, Murch, Southwest
German Radio Orchestra and Chorus, Brückner-
Rüggeberg. CBS MK-42637 [CD].

When the gruff, foul-mouthed Marxist playwright was first
introduced to the shy young composer after a performance of one
of the latter's symphonies, he got right to the point: "My name is
Bert Brecht," he announced, "and if you want to work with me
you're going to have to stop writing that shit stuff and come up with
some *tunes*." And so began the collaboration that would culminate
in *The Threepenny Opera* of 1928, the apotheosis of the spirit of
Berlin in the '20s, and one of German art's last great creative gasps
before the Nazi deluge.

With Kurt Weill's widow, Lotte Lenya, singing Jenny—a role
she created and made world-famous—this *Dreigroschenoper* from
the mid-1950s will never be superseded. With the help of an excellent supporting cast and a very canny conductor, Lenya conjures
up the darkness, danger, and sense of all-pervasive corruption that
hung over the Weimar Republic like a sickeningly sweet poison gas,
a decadent miasma that makes a sanitized entertainment like *Cab-
aret* seem like innocent child's play.

Lenya's sour, world-weary voice can also be heard to beautifully cynical and vulnerable effect in a collection of her husband's
German and English songs on an irreplaceable Mastersound recording (DFCD1-110 [CD]), while the best version of the *Threepenny
Opera* Suite is David Atherton's snide and bubbly quickstep with
the London Sinfonietta, which comes with winning performances of
the *Mahagonny-Songspiel* and the Violin Concerto (Deutsche
Grammophon 423255-2 [CD]).

Weinberger, Jaromir
(1896–1967)

Schwanda the Bagpiper

Prey, Popp, Jerusalem, Killebrew, Malta, Nimsgern,
Bavarian Radio Chorus, Munich Radio Orchestra,
Wallberg. CBS M3K-36926 [CD].

One of the most frequently performed of all twentieth-century
operas (within five years of its Prague premiere it would be heard
in literally thousands of performances in dozens of productions
around the world), *Schwanda the Bagpiper* was given an unaccountably cool reception at the Metropolitan Opera in 1931, and
two years later, with the advent of Hitler, its fate in Europe was
sealed.

As this first commercial recording demonstrated a few years
ago, *Schwanda*'s once-phenomenal popularity was obviously no
fluke. In fact, it is such a tuneful, vibrant, utterly disarming work
that one can only wonder why more companies don't take a chance
on it today. It has fantasy, spectacle, romance, and an abundance
of unforgettable set pieces: in addition to the well-known Polka and
Fugue (the last is in truth a triumphal chorus), the first-act aria "Ich
bin der Schwanda" is one of those arias which, once heard, can't
be forgotten, no matter how hard you try.

This recording, produced by George Korngold, should be
mandatory listening for every director of every opera company in
the civilized world, especially those who are now planning their
seasons and can't face the prospect of yet another *Bohème*. Surefire
winners don't come along all that often, and a surefire, iron-
clad, gold-plated, hock-your-grandmother-and-bet-the-bundle winner *Schwanda* most certainly is. With Hermann Prey in the title role,
the luscious Lucia Popp as his wife, the young Siegfried Jerusalem
as the robber Babinsky, a first-rate supporting cast, and superlative
conducting from Heinz Wallberg, this is one of the most thoroughly
enjoyable opera recordings ever made.

I strongly recommend doing what I did: Buy a half dozen extra
copies to use as *very* special gifts.

Widor, Charles Marie
(1844–1937)

Symphonies for Organ: No. 5 in F minor; No. 10, *Romaine*

Chorzempa, organ. Philips 410054-2 [CD].

Like his immensely prolific near-contemporary Henry Charles Litolff, Charles Marie Widor is one of history's mercifully few examples of a Part-of-a-Work Composer. For just as poor Litolff is remembered only for the mercurial Scherzo from his *Concerto Symphonique* No. 4 (most ably represented these days on a Philips anthology, 411123-2 [CD], featuring Misha Dichter and the Philharmonia Orchestra conducted by Sir Neville Marriner), Widor survives almost entirely on the strength of the Toccata from the Organ Symphony No. 5.

Although it can be found in any number of recorded grab bags of organ favorites, the best way to hear the remorselessly buoyant piece is in the context of the Symphony—actually, an extended suite—in which it originally appeared. The American organist Daniel Chorzempa gives a crashingly fine performance of the work on his Philips compact disc, and almost—*almost*—makes one wonder why the entire Symphony isn't heard more often. The recorded sound is exceptional, the sort that might melt the fillings in the unwary listener's teeth.

Wirén, Dag (1905–1986)

Serenade for Strings

**Academy of St. Martin-in-the-Fields, Marriner. Argo
417132-2 [CD].**

Dag Wirén was a Swedish composer of enormously agreeable
music who remains best known outside his native country for a
single work, the enchanting Serenade for Strings of 1937. It is an
infectiously tuneful, immediately appealing piece that bears more
than favorable comparison with Grieg's *Holberg Suite* and Nielsen's *Little Suite for Strings,* the other major pieces on this irresistible anthology of Scandinavian music. Marriner and company
give it an ideally fresh and enthusiastic performance, while Argo's
engineers bathe it in the richest, most beautifully detailed sound.

By the way, this is a perfect recording with which to catch a
reluctant object of your affections off guard. (It's worked for me;
it will work for you.)

Wolf, Hugo (1860–1903)

Songs

After Schubert, there were only three incontestably great composers of German lieder: Schumann, Brahms, and Hugo Wolf. And
if Schubert practically invented the form, then it was Wolf who
presided over its final, bittersweet flowering. In the work of no other
composer are words and music so intimately connected, and in no
other German songs do we encounter so much effortless perfection.

Among the available recordings of Wolf songs, and there are
shamefully few, the Nonesuch recording (N2-78014 [T]) of the *Italian Song Book* is exceptionally appealing. Elly Ameling sings flaw-

lessly, and Tom Krause gives one of his best performances in years. Similarly, the classic Deutsche Grammophon recording (423934-2 [CD]) of the *Spanish Song Book* with Elisabeth Schwarzkopf and Dietrich Fischer-Dieskau is among the most nearly perfect lieder recordings ever made. And finally, although certainly not perfect from a technical point of view, Schwarzkopf's famous recording of a Wolf recital given at the 1953 Salzburg Festival is currently available on a Fonit-Cetra compact disc (CDC-21). The young Schwarzkopf was never more enchanting than in these twenty-two songs, and the accompaniments are highly unusual and individual: the pianist was Wilhelm Furtwängler.

Zelenka, Jan Dismas

(1679–1745)

Orchestral Works

Camerata Bern. Deutsche Grammophon 423703-2 [CD].

Among the odd fish washed up on the wave of the great Baroque Revival of the 1960s, none was odder or more interesting than that Bohemian recluse Jan Dismas Zelenka. Little is known about the man's life other than the fact that Bach was one of his most passionate admirers. He may or may not have been mystic, a visionary, or simply a short-tempered hypochondriac (two of his works are called *The Angry Man* and *Hipocondria*); the lack of an authenticated portrait has fueled the legend that he was either severely deformed or hideously disfigured.

Whatever it was that combined to create this strange and mysterious figure, he was one of the most startlingly original composers of his period, a kind of nonvocal, Central European equivalent of the batty Carlo Gesualdo, whose experiments in form, harmony, and expression were as radically daring a century before.

The recordings by Camerata Bern, highlighted by some truly phenomenal contributions by oboist Heinz Holliger and horn player Barry Tuckwell, are the perfect introduction to Zelenka's peculiar and beautiful world. While some of the music is so advanced that Zelenka might sometimes seem a contemporary of Chopin and Schumann rather than of Handel and Bach, he remains, for all his apparent flirtations with Romanticism, a figure of the Baroque era, and possibly a major one at that.

Zemlinsky, Alexander von
(1871–1942)

Die Seejungfrau; Psalm XIII

Berlin Radio Orchestra and Chorus, Chailly. London 417450-2 [CD].

Until quite recently, the name of Alexander von Zemlinsky came up only in relation to his onetime pupil and brother-in-law, Arnold Schoenberg. Actually, he was one of the most respected teachers and conductors of his era and, as we're beginning to discover only now, one of its most interesting and original composers. For the collector who has everything, or for anyone who is simply interested in making the acquaintance of a fabulously beautiful work, this recent London recording of *Die Seejungfrau* (The Mermaid) cannot be recommended too highly. The piece itself is a startling amalgam of Mahler, Strauss, and Zemlinsky's own elusive originality. The performance, led by Riccardo Chailly, could not have been more poised or luxuriant, and the version of Zemlinsky's *Psalm XIII* is similarly enthralling. Those who find either or both works to their taste might want to explore the LaSalle Quartet's brilliant recording of the four Zemlinsky quartets (Deutsche Grammophon 427421-2 [CD]), or the wonderful recording of the large and fascinating *Lyric Symphony* by Lorin Maazel and the Berlin Philharmonic, also from Deutsche Grammophon (419261-2 [CD]).

Zwilich, Ellen Taaffe

(1939–)

Concerto Grosso 1985 (after Handel); Concerto for Trumpet and Five Players; Double Quartet for Strings; *Symbolon*

Smith, trumpet; New York Philharmonic, Mehta, Zwilich. New World NW-372-2 [CD].

Born in Miami in 1939, Ellen Taaffe Zwilich is a member of that talented generation of musicians who have finally been able to shake off the designation "female composer." There was always something condescending and faintly preposterous in that usage; how often, for instance, does one hear the phrase "the celebrated male composer, Beethoven"?

As these recordings of four of her works from 1984 to 1988 clearly show, Zwilich is an intelligent, important composer whose music more than deserves the celebrity it has begun to receive. While the *Concerto Grosso 1985,* written for the tercentenary of Handel's birth, is the most immediately accessible piece in the collection, the others are also challenging and enjoyable, proving, if nothing else, that music is neither a "male" nor a "female" but a wholly human art.

Index

479

The Record Shelf Guide Makes a Great Gift
for Other Music Lovers!

Yes, I'd like to order another copy/copies of Jim Svejda's *The Record Shelf Guide to the Classical Repertoire* at $16.95 each plus $3.50 shipping and handling. California residents please add sales tax.

_____ Check enclosed for $_____, payable to Prima Publishing

Charge my _____ Mastercard   _____ Visa
Account No. _____

Signature _____

Your Name _____
Address _____
City / State / Zip _____
Daytime Telephone _____

GUARANTEE
YOU MUST BE SATISFIED!
You get a 30-day, 100% money-back guarantee on all books.

Thank you for your order.